新时代北外文库

语言与文化之间

Between Languages and Cultures

王克非 著

人民出版社

作者简介
ABOUT THE AUTHOR

王克非　北京外国语大学讲席教授，《外语教学与研究》主编，中国外语与教育研究中心资深研究员。

兼任国务院学位委员会外语学科评议组成员，国家社科基金学科评审组专家，教育部长江学者通讯及会议评审专家，教育部人文社科项目评审专家，教育部高等学校优秀科研成果奖评审专家，教育部新世纪优秀人才会议评审专家，中组部青年拔尖人才支持计划评审专家。

主要研究领域为语言学和翻译学，在双语平行语料库和翻译文化史等研究领域卓有建树，分别担任全国语料库翻译学研究会会长和翻译文化研究会会长。在国内外学术期刊发表论文190多篇。著有《中日近代对西方政治哲学思想的摄取》、《翻译文化史论》、《语料库翻译学探索》、《国外外语教育研究》、《世界语言生活报告》等十多部著作。主持国家社科基金重大项目等十四个重要科研项目。三十多次应邀赴国外大学从事合作研究和教学。两次获得教育部优秀成果奖，两次获得北京市哲学社会科学优秀成果奖，并获评全国百篇优秀博士论文指导教师、北京市优秀博士论文指导教师、首都劳动奖章，享受国务院颁发政府特殊津贴。

内容提要

EXECUTIVE SUMMARY

本书为作者数十年学术研究的部分结晶。全书分上下两编，上编是语料库研究，下编是关于语言与翻译的论述，合为作者在语言与文化之间的思考。

作者开展双语语料库研究逾二十年，一直紧盯国际双语语料库研究前沿。在上编里，作者分析语料库研究范式的兴起和进展，论述双语平行语料库的开发、设计、研制和加工，并在英汉平行语料库基础上开展了一系列语言与翻译问题的研究，以及超大型语料库检索平台和应用问题的探讨。作者从宏观和微观考察了汉译语言特征，并与英译语言特征加以对比。作者还通过文本信息特征统计分析了双语文本的基本形式特征，通过赋码语料处理双语文本的深层句法信息，并运用潜语义分析方法计算出语句意义间的相似度。

在翻译与研究方面，作者的新视点是，察言可以观世。作者近十年持续关注和考察世界语言生活状况，既试图了解和掌握各国语言生活的变化及其与政治、经济、文化等的关系，又注意我国语言在世界发展格局中的地位和变化，即观察语言变化是观察世界动态的重要而且及时的窗口。在翻译研究上，作者认为翻译涉及语言和文化两个层面，与国际上多元系统论、“文化转向”和翻译研究学派观点有同也有异，其重要特征在于从两方面分析翻译的中介性，即不仅注重文化对译介的影响，也探究翻译对目标语文化的作用，故而提出从文化的深度和广度重新认识和阐释翻译现象的翻译文化史观。

《新时代北外文库》编委会

出版说明

2021年是中国共产党成立100周年，也是北京外国语大学建校80周年。作为中国共产党创办的第一所外国语高等学校，北外紧密结合国家战略发展需要，秉承“外、特、精、通”的办学理念和“兼容并蓄、博学笃行”的校训精神，培养了一大批外交、翻译、教育、经贸、新闻、法律、金融等涉外高素质人才，也涌现了一批学术名家与精品力作。王佐良、许国璋、纳忠等学术大师，为学人所熟知，奠定了北外的学术传统。他们的经典作品被收录到2011年北外70年校庆期间出版的《北外学者选集》，代表了北外自建校以来在外国语言文学研究领域的杰出成果。

进入21世纪尤其是新时代以来，北外主动响应国家号召，加大非通用语建设力度，现获批开设101种外国语言，致力复合型人才培养，优化学科布局，逐步形成了以外国语言文学学科为主体，多学科协调发展的格局。植根在外国语言文学的肥沃土地上，徜徉在开放多元的学术氛围里，一大批北外学者追随先辈脚步，着眼中外比较，潜心学术研究，在国家语言政策、经济社会发展、中华文化传播、国别区域研究等领域颇有建树。这些思想观点往往以论文散见于期刊，而汇编为文集，整理成文库，更能相得益彰，蔚为大观，既便于研读查考，又利于学术传承。“新时代北外文库”之编纂，其意正在于此，冀切磋琢磨，交锋碰撞，助力培育北外学派，形成新时代北外发展的新气象。

“新时代北外文库”共收录32本，每本选编一位北外教授的论文，均系进入21世纪以来在重要刊物上发表的高质量学术论文。既展现北外学者在外国文学、外国语言学及应用语言学、翻译学、比较文学与跨文化研究、国别与区域研究等外国语言文学研究最新进展，也涵盖北外学者在政治学、经济学、教育学、新闻传播学、法学、哲学等领域发挥外语优势，开展比较研究的创新成果。希望能为校内外、国内外的同行和师生提供学术借鉴。

北京外国语大学将以此次文库出版为新的起点，进一步贯彻落实习近平新时代中国特色社会主义思想和党中央关于教育的重要部署，秉承传统，追求卓越，精益求精，促进学校平稳较快发展，致力于培养国家急需，富有社会责任感、创新精神和实践能力，具有中国情怀、国际视野、思辨能力和跨文化能力的复合型、复语型、高层次国际化人才，加快中国特色、世界一流外国语大学的建设步伐。

谨以此书，

献给中国共产党成立100周年。

献给北京外国语大学建校80周年。

文库编委会

庚子年秋于北外

目　录

上编　语料库研究

下编　语言与翻译研究

自　序

语言学家说，语言是一种符号；文学家说，语言是一种力量；哲学家说，语言是人类的精神家园；但大家都承认，语言是思想文化的载体。语言最重要的功能和价值，一是作为交流工具，沟通人类情感，二是作为思维工具，认知自身和世界，三是作为承载工具，存储文化信息。这一记载、传承功能，使人类的经验得以超越时代、跨越地域——知识得以累积，社会得以进步。

可见，无论何种语言，的确是一种特殊的符号，特别的力量，特有的家园。

我在"文革"后期开始点滴自学英语。由英语学着翻译，学着语言学，进而走入翻译学和语言学的大门，走入广阔的外部世界。也因为外语和翻译，开始了跨文化的比较，饶有兴致地将跨语言的翻译同中外文化关联起来考察。现代科学技术的进步带动计算机和网络技术的发展，于是我从语言的研究、翻译的研究，再迈入将二者同语料库挂钩的研究。一切都不是预设好的，只是摸着石头过河一般地向前。也许这是一条蜿蜒的小路、多岔的小路，所幸我向来享受探索的乐趣和知识增进的过程。于是有了本书兼有语料库、语言学、翻译学，以及教育和文化的拼盘。不过其间的关联还是清晰的。

语料库研究是我近二十年来学术上的主要领域。主要开展的是双语语料库研究，特别是英汉双语平行语料库和双语类比语料库。2000 年正式开启这一研究时，我清醒地认识到，双语语料库的研究，天然地落在外语学人的肩上，这是外语界的机遇。因为单语的语料库，当时已经开展三十多年，英语或其他外语的单语语料库建设与研究，主要是英语国家或其他外语国家的学者的领地，汉语语料库是中国汉语界学者的领地。我们外语界做什么？那就是利用所学英语（及其他外语），加上自己的汉语母语，研制和应用双语语料库来开展相应的研究。说 2000 年正式开启双语语料库研究,是当年获得教育部人文社科重点研究基地重大项目的支持,创建大型双语平行语料库,而此前只是在学习和思考中。率先开启并研制大型双语语料库,是自己学术上一项重要成就。

我在语料库研究领域另一项重要建树是边建库、边研究,利用双语语料库开展语言对比研究、翻译研究、教学研究、双语词典研编四大方面的学术探讨与人才培养。其中,在语料库翻译学学科构建、相关学术概念确立、英汉语的特点等方面,特别是历时复合语料库的构念及相关研究的开启,具有独到之处。书中各文不是我语料库研究的全部,但从语料库范式、语料库构建、语料库研究、语料库应用这四个方面的论述可以看出我双语语料库研究的概貌。

翻译文化史研究是自己多年学术研究的另一主要领域,也是最早开始的一个领域。我的翻译文化史观点是,从翻译的定义看,翻译是一项语言转换活动,语言同文化密不可分,转换同浸润在文化中的译者密切相关,所以翻译活动说到底是一项人为的文化活动,翻译史就必然同文化史特别是跨文化的沟通、融合相关联。翻译受到异域文化和本族文化的管轨,又会反过来影响目标语文化。这类研究在本书仅有若干篇,笔者在高教出版社出版的另一文集《翻译:文化的传通》里,有更多的阐发。

书中还收有语言、文化、翻译和外语教育方面的论述,不是非常精彩。可作圈点的大概是"察言观世"类的世界语言生活研究,在社会经济发展的背景下看待外语教育政策的演变,以及透视翻译中的显化和隐化等问题。有些研究,历经岁月而日显其价值,也有些文章,会暴露出幼稚和局限,我不做评价。如同鲁迅先生将其早年文字集于《坟》中,以为纪念吧。毕竟都是自己的 baby。在北京外国语大学,这个人们一提及就会想到许国璋、王佐良等大师的独一无二的大学,我们与中国语言文化圈里的学者们看待语言和文化是有所不同的。我们发现不同的语言符号之美,体验不同的语言力量之美,感受不同的精神家园之美。在各国语言和文化间穿行,捡拾各色小花,端详、欣赏、比较、撷取,乐在其中。惟如此,方可略领鲁迅之训:首在审己,亦必知人。比较既周,爰生自觉。若得之一二,亦自足矣。

谨以小作,献于敬爱的导师许国璋先生!献于八十华诞的母校——北京外国语大学!

上编　语料库研究

中国英汉平行语料库的设计与研制

本文论述超大型双语平行语料库的设计与研制问题。在综合述介国内外双语语料库建设情况之后，作者着重论述了中国英汉平行语料库这一超大型双语平行语料库的设计特点（主要有分类架构、历时处理、语料平衡以及通用的和各种专门语料的采集）和研制方法（主要讲述语料的加工标注、检索平台以及各个专门语料库、历时语料库和口译语料库的构建）。其设计与研制对于其他大型语料库的建设具有借鉴意义。

一、中国英汉平行语料库的研制意义

在全球化、信息化的当今世界，翻译已成为解全球信息、扩大对外交流、获取国际资源的重要手段。同计算机技术结合而兴起的双语平行语料库建设，则为语言研究、翻译研究、外语教学、词典编纂和跨语言信息检索等提供了最好的平台，同时还可用来考察和验证基于单语语料库或者基于直觉提出的假设，具有广阔的应用前景。

平行语料库承载着相互对应的两种语言，与语言对比研究有着天然的联系，成为语言对比研究中的默认数据源；平行语料库中的两种语言互为对应，记载着两种语言中的对应词和对应单位，成为词典编纂者最可靠的数据来源；平行语料库中的源语言和目标语言互为对应，在翻译教学和外语学习中的用途更是不言而喻。

除此之外，平行语料库对机器翻译和自然语言处理也极为重要。对齐的平行语料能为基于例句和统计的机器翻译系统提供实证模型，同时也可以为基于规则的机器翻译提供验证，为机助翻译提供大量翻译记忆。正如欧赫（Och，2002）所言，“只要给我足够的双语对应数据，几个小时内我可以给你一个机器翻译系统”。然而现有的英汉平行语料库规模有限，且大多是利用现有同质翻译资源建立的，并非平衡语料库，常常不能较好地代表广泛含义上的源语—译语关系，依此生成的语言模型常常不能够有效地解释翻译语言，这极大地阻碍了翻译和词典编纂等学科研究的深入，已成为提高机器翻译译文质量的瓶颈。

鉴于此，我们提出设计和研制更大规模、更多功能的超大型平行语料库，即一亿词以上的“中国英汉平行语料库”，以满足各方面研究的需求和语料库事业的发展。

中国英汉平行语料库的研制意义可从以下两方面体现出来。

第一，理论价值。

（1）大型双语平行语料库规模超大、采样严格，能够较好地代表源语—译语关系，因此能为翻译研究、语言对比研究、语言演化研究、口笔译比较研究等提供可靠的翻译实例和量化数据，从而提高上述研究的可信度。

（2）在超大型双语平行语料库建设的基础上，我们还将展开多项具有理论意义的语言和翻译研究。这些研究主要包括历时研究和类比动态描写。研究的时间跨度大，涉及层面多。

第二，应用价值。

（1）在研究方法上，我们将据此探索基于语料库的翻译语言动态类比和描述，为语言的共时与历时比较研究提供有效的、可操作性强的分析模式和研究平台。

（2）在大型双语平行语料库的采样和加工方面，将提出更有借鉴价值的模板和方法。

总之，“中国英汉平行语料库”这一超大规模的英汉/汉英平衡语料库，为今后其他语对的双语平行语料库或多语平行语料库的研制、双语对比与研究、英汉语言接触与现代汉语历时变化研究等，提供共同的大型的实证研究基础，为中国的语料库研究走向世界前沿作出贡献。

二、国内外双语平行语料库研制现状

平行语料库的研制历史并不长，从世界上第一个初步的平行语料库 The Canadian Hansard Corpus（包括英法语版本的加拿大议会辩论语料）建成到目前仅 20 年左右。但由于平行语料库对于语言对比研究、翻译研究、翻译教学、翻译技术开发（如机器翻译系统、机辅翻译工具）、双语词典编纂等语言学和自然语言处理研究具有巨大的潜在应用价值，平行语料库的建设在世界上得到迅速发展（参见王克非等 2004；McEnery & Xiao 2007）。目前，平行语料库研究大多集中在欧洲，涉及语言也主要与欧洲语言有关，特别是欧共体/欧盟等机构的文件。

如兰卡斯特大学早期创建的 ITU/Crater 平行库包含欧洲委员会有关电信的英法双语文件各 100 万词，句级对齐。

欧洲委员会联合研究中心的 JRC-ACQUIS 多语种平行语料库包括成员国的 22 种欧洲语言，目前的 3.0 版包括 20 世纪 50 年代至 2006 年的欧洲法律文件 463792 个，共计 10 亿词。

欧洲人类语言技术研究网络（ELSNET）1994 年发布的欧洲语料库规范多语种语料库 1 期（ECI/MCI）包括 27 种语言（主要是欧洲语言，也包括汉语、日语和马来语），以官方文件为主，但也包括少量的报纸、小说、技术报告、词典和词表；该库共 48 个部分，共计 9800 万词，其中 12 个部分包含有平行语料。

MULTEXT 语料库是由欧洲语言资源协会资助的项目，其目的是开发多语种工具和语料库；该语料库包括采样于欧洲委员会官方杂志（JOC）的 5 种语言各 40 个文档，句级对齐，其中 10 个文档还做了词性标注。

PAROLE 语料库包括欧洲 14 种语言，采样年代为 1997—1998 年，文本来源包括书籍（20%）、报纸（65%）、杂志（5%）以及杂类文本（10%），共计 2000 万词，每个子库中 25 万词按照统一标准做了词性标注。

多语种语料库合作（MLCC）项目建立了一个多语种平行语料库，包括 9 种欧洲语言，语料来源为上述提到的欧洲委员会官方杂志 1992—1994 年的文本。

爱丁堡大学的 Europarl Parallel Corpus 收集了 1996—2009 年间欧洲议会会议记录，涉及 11 种语言，以双语平行的形式发布，句级对齐，丹麦语、德语、希腊语、西班牙语、芬兰语、法语、意大利语、荷兰语、葡萄牙语、瑞典语分别与英语对应，共约 5000 万词（以英语计）（Koehn 2005）。

上述这些语料库基本上都是文本来源单一、标注也简单的欧洲语言专用语料库，主要用于语言识别、文档级对齐、术语提取等自然语言处理研究，而非从语言学角度研究语言（参见 Xiao 2008）。

除此之外，也有少数几个精心设计的平行语料库，如由挪威奥斯陆大学研制的最早的英语—挪威语平行语料库，包含英语和挪威语各 100 个 1 万—1.5 万词的英—挪对应母语文本及其挪—英翻译文本，共 260 万词，语料采样考虑到平衡性而非局限于少数几个语域或语体，涉及小说（儿童小说、侦探小说、一般小说）和非小说（宗教、社会科学、法律、自然科学、医学、艺术、历史地理）。该语料库不仅在句子层面对齐，而且对英—挪语料均做了词性标注和词形还原（lemmatisation）处理。

英语—瑞典语平行语料库则是采用英语—挪威语平行语料库的建库标准、由隆德大学（Lund University）和哥特堡大学联合研制的平衡语料库，包括 64 个英语原文文本及其瑞典语译文和 72 个瑞典语原文文本及其英语译文，共计 280 万词。

在这两个语料库的基础上，近年来奥斯陆大学又以同样标准开发了奥斯陆多语种语料库（OMC），除了英语、挪威语、瑞典语外还涉及德语、法语、荷兰语、芬兰语和葡萄牙语。这些精心设计的平行语料库适合于翻译与跨语言对比等研究，但局限于欧洲语言。

欧洲语言之外的平行语料库，包括汉语在内，还不多见，精心设计的大型平衡语料库则更少。主要有兰卡斯特大学研制的英国少数民族语料库 EMILLE，包含了 15 种南亚语言口语及书面语料近 1 亿词，其中平行语料库部分包含 20 万词的英语文本及印地语、孟加拉语、旁遮普语、古吉拉特语及乌尔都语平行对应文本。语言数据联盟（LDC）于 2004 年发行了香港平行文本库（Hong Kong Parallel Text），包括 590 万词的英语文本和 980 万字的汉语文本，英汉文本句级对齐;该库由 2000 年所发行的 3 个英汉平行语料库组成:香港法律辩论语料库、香港法律语料库、香港新闻语料库。英国兰卡斯特大学创建的 Babel 英汉平行语料库由从《英语世界》等刊物采样的 327 篇英汉双语时文构成,采样年代为 2000—2001 年,共计 54 万词;该库实现句级对齐,并对英汉语文本都进行了分词和词性标注。台湾辅仁大学初步建立了范本财经英日汉平行语料库,收集语料约 10 万句对。最近,香港理工大学和北京外国语大学的学者联合研制了英汉旅游文本语料库,约 100 万字词(参见李德超、王克非 2010)。

在我国内地,双语平行语料库的建设近 10 年来也取得了重大进展,已有多个英汉及日汉等双语平行语料库建成。如北京大学计算语言学研究所的汉英平行语料库(5 万多句对)及其所承担的 863 项目所建的英汉平行语料库(20 万句对)、哈尔滨工业大学的英汉双语语料库(40 万—50 万句对)。不过这些语料库有一个共同之处,即建库目的主要是自然语言处理而非语言学研究,因此所谓的句对通常是脱离上下文、打乱次序的孤立的句子,英译汉与汉译英语料夹杂,用户不易识别翻译方向。另外,国内近年来也建成了一些专门用途语料库,如上海交通大学的莎士比亚戏剧英汉平行语料库、燕山大学的《红楼梦》译本平行语料库、绍兴文理学院的鲁迅小说汉英平行语料库等。这些语料库因为是专门性的,语料来源单一,规模比较小,适合专门研究而不适合通用语言研究。

国内学界平行语料库研制方面最值得一提的是,2002 年以来,北京外国语大学中国外语教育研究中心先后在教育部人文社科重点研究基地重大项目基金和国家社科基金的支持下,建成了规模约 3000 万字词的大型通用汉英平行语料库,是目前最大规模的平行语料库,包括英译汉和汉译英双向翻译语料,而且采样均衡,语体、语域及采样年代覆盖面广,全库实现句级对齐及词性标注。其中部分语料(200 余万字词)已提供在线检索,为全社会服务。在该语料库基础上开展了一系列课题研究,如语料库研制方面的研究(王克非等 2004;常宝宝 2004)、基于语料库的翻译学研究(秦洪武、王克非 2004;王克非、黄立波 2006,2008;王克非、胡显耀 2008,2010)、基于语料库的对比语言研究(秦洪武 2009;王克非、秦洪武 2009;何文忠、王克非 2009;秦洪武、王克非

2010)。总之,该语料库为超大型的中国英汉平行语料库的建设提供了重要的语料库基础和相关研究基础,积累了研制大型平行语料库的经验。

上面对国内外研究现状的简述表明,平行语料库研究目前主要涉及欧洲语言,而且欧盟机构和欧洲国家的研究基金愿意在该领域投入大量研究经费。现有涉及英语和汉语的双语语料资源现状与这一"大语种"语对的地位还不相称,与研究的需要也不相适应,亟须一个大型、平衡的英汉双向平行语料库,使之成为既适用于自然语言处理与语言工程,又能应用于英汉语言对比研究(包括共时与历时对比)和翻译研究、翻译教学与实践、双语词典编纂的共同研究平台,以便从不同角度展开的研究能真正揭示语言的本质,避免由于不同研究使用不同数据而造成的差异。我们希望通过研制这个中国英汉平行语料库,并在此基础上开展上述各项研究,使中国的双语平行语料库研制与加工走在世界前列。

三、中国英汉平行语料库设计架构

我们在 10 年前创建汉英对应语料库的基础上(参见王克非 2004),开始研制超大型英汉平行语料库——中国英汉平行语料库,包括历时性的平行语料库和若干专门语料库以及口译语料库。在此基础上我们将进一步开展(1)平行语料库深加工与标注研究、对齐检索等工具研究,(2)英汉语言对比、英汉互译、语言接触与汉语历时发展等方面的研究,(3)专门语料库和口译语料库的建库类型与特点研究,(4)建库过程中的语料采样标准、数据源标示等标准类研究。

1. 总体框架

本项目设计的超大型英汉平行语料库是研制与加工并重、语言研究与翻译研究并重的语料库,是兼顾笔译和口译文本、兼顾文本共时和历时研究的语料库,力求设计科学,分类合理,加工到位。注重以下特点和要点:超大规模、深度加工、多项检索、软件兼容、语料平衡、双语双向、共时历时、通用专门、笔译口译。

2. 主要内容

(1)提出科学的语料采集方法,使双语语料的采集既符合随机、真实的原则,又比较对应、完整和具有一定代表性,便于今后语言、翻译、教学等研究工作的开展。

(2)进一步优化双语语料的对齐、标注问题,研制过程中开发和改进相关软件,探讨适合汉语词语切分和标注的理论与方法,尝试英汉专门语料和英汉口译语料等特殊语料的标注和检索,为有深度的语料检索打好基础。

(3)探讨优化双语平行语料库的分类和架构,拟分文学、新闻、政论、科技、应用文5大类和若干子类,使之更适合建成后的语言与翻译研究。

(4)研制适用基于语料库的语言与翻译历时研究的检索平台,充分发掘双语语料库的研究潜力。

(5)合理架构英汉/汉英双向语料,大致按英汉2/3、汉英1/3的原则收集。

(6)注意语料的时代标志,拟将整个20世纪的对应语料的一部分做历时处理,在收集整理和标注加工方面,注意每20年为一阶段,重点收集各阶段后5年或某5年的相关语料,以便开展历时的语言变化研究及语言与翻译的关系研究。

就待建语料库的架构设计而言,为了兼顾语言研究和自然语言处理等语言工程的不同需要,并考虑到对一般语言和专门用途语言的研究需要,该库将由通用型的平衡语料库和专用型的特定语域的专门语料库构成,两者大致各占一半。其中通用平衡库约5000万字词,兼顾共时与历时及翻译方向的平衡性。

语料的共时平衡是指从语言实际应用的角度,按一定比例包括尽可能多的语体和语域。中国英汉平行语料库拟采用国际语料库语言学界研制Lancaster-Olso-Bergen(LOB)等经典语料库的方法,按文本类别采样后整合。但考虑到那些经典英语语料库在实际应用过程中常常将建库时分类过细的语体按大类合并检索分析,我们将直接按5大类体裁采样:文学、新闻、政论、科技、应用文。各大类采样时再兼顾小类的均衡性,如文学类中的小说、戏剧等,新闻中的报道、综述等,科技类的书籍与期刊等介质以及文理工农医等特定语域等。

语料的历时平衡是指从现代汉语发展的实际情况出发，分段采样以便所建语料库能反映出现代汉语的发展轨迹，并在英汉平行语料库的基础上探究英汉语语言接触及英语通过翻译对汉语发展产生的影响。我们将克服英国国家语料库（BNC）由于历时连续采样而造成的各阶段差异模糊的缺陷，拟将20世纪的平衡语料的一部分，大致分5个阶段，重点收集各阶段某5年的语料，各100万至300万字词，计1000万字词以上，总的平行语料库为5000万字词以上。

就翻译方向而言，考虑到我国翻译界的实际情况是英译汉多于汉译英，并且前者质量高于后者，中国英汉平行语料库将包括三分之二的英译汉语料和三分之一的汉译英语料。英汉对比部分主要指在所建平衡语料库的基础上研究英语和汉语这两个不同语系的国际大语种之间在总体上的相同和相异之处，同时考虑两种语言在不同语体之间的异同；语言对比的另一个方面是比较对应的汉（英）语母语文本和汉（英）语译文文本，以检验目前国际上翻译共性研究领域基于小型对应语料库所做出的假设，在理论上做出新的探索。

四、中国英汉平行语料库的研制

研制工作主要涉及语料库设计、语料收集、语料加工、语料库检索工具的设计、基于语料库的研究、语料库在线检索6个部分。

1. 研制上的简要描述

语料库设计

语库规模：1亿字/词以上。

语库架构：（1）通用英汉平行语料库5000万字词；（2）专门英汉平行语料库5000多万字词，分交通英汉平行语料库、时政新闻英汉平行语料库、财经英汉平行语料库和口译语料库。

语库性质：双语库、平行库；通用和专门、共时和历时、笔译和口译。

语料类型：书面语料为主，口译语料为辅。

语料分类：分文学、新闻、政论、科技、应用文 5 大类体裁。

翻译语向：英汉（2/3）和汉英（1/3）双语双向。

语料收集

语料收集的原则：按照年代收集，跨度为一个世纪的英汉双语语料，并注意各阶段语料在数量和质量上的大体均等。

语料的体裁：通用语料库考虑平衡性，借鉴国外平衡语料库的建构方法，按照前述 5 大体裁分类收集语料。

语料加工

元信息的设计：按照语料的来源、年代、语域、题材等设计多维元信息标签，包括语料库中英文名称、所采集样本的发生年代、语体、翻译方向、原始数据篇名、作者、译者、责任方（数据采样人等信息）。

对齐方式：句对齐。

标注：实施词性标注，根据研究需要尝试对部分语料实施中英文句法标注；视研究条件尝试翻译技巧信息的人工识别和标注；人工识别翻译对等语块。

存贮方式：采用 tmx 格式的 xml 标记语言，统一码 UTF-8 编码，以便于存储与交换；便于读入数据库，也便于检索和机器翻译系统的直接利用。

语料库检索工具的设计

检索工具拟综合利用 Perl 和 C 等语言的优势，充分利用元信息，针对不同用户，提供简单检索、复杂检索和有条件检索，包括实施较精确的词汇、语块检索，实现搭配信息的呈现。

基于语料库的研究

主要包括：（1）基于语料库的英汉语对比研究；（2）基于语料库的历时翻译研究；（3）基于语料库的翻译共性研究；（4）基于语料库的汉语历时变化研究；（5）基于平行语料库的词典研编问题。

语料库在线检索

在线平台实现单机平台相似的功能，同时实现语料库的翻译辅助功能：系统可将析出语料保存为 tmx 等格式，为现有的翻译辅助软件如 Trados、Dejavu 或者雅信等软件所用。

2. 具体研制思路

2.1 关于语料库的加工标注和语料检索

(1)对语料库中的各类文本进行合理的元信息标注,以便按照用户设定的条件,从语料库中抽取不同类型的双语对齐文本。拟将元信息与文本分别独立保存,即元信息脱离文本本身,便于对文本内语言信息的快速检索。

(2)对语料库中的语言信息进行标注,以方便从语料库中抽取用户所需的多种语言信息。语言信息的标注主要包括词性标注和部分文本的句法标注。

(3)建立大规模机器翻译记忆库。研究中拟采用兼容性较好的通用标记语言存储文本,建立大规模机器翻译记忆库(translation memory),使语料库可以为机器翻译系统所直接使用。

(4)研制功能强大的配套软件系统。软件系统主要包括:a.元信息检索系统,用于根据用户设定从语料库中抽取文本;b.标注文本还原系统,用于析出便于用户阅读的检索词及语境;c.翻译记忆交换文件(tmx)生成和解析系统,用于自动生成和解析翻译记忆交换文件;d.单机和基于网络的平行语料库检索系统,用于准确、高效地对语料库进行检索。

2.2 专门英汉平行语料库的研制

根据经济社会发展的现实需求,研制多个专门用途平行语料库。

(1)专门英汉平行语料库的研制:分别建立时政新闻英汉平行语料库(2000 万字/词)、交通英汉平行语料库(1500 万字/词)、财经英汉平行语料库(1500 万字/词)、英汉口译语料库(>100 万字/词)。分别收集处理各专门语料库,制定此类语料库文本的选取和抽样细则,并设计和研制适合此类文本标注和检索的应用平台。

(2)专门英汉平行语料库的应用研究。课题组拟应用专门英汉平行语料库,深入分析汉英语言词汇之间的对应关系和转换规律,研究当代英汉翻译规范、汉语文本英译语言特征和英语文本汉译语言特征,克服目前语料库翻译学研究过多依赖于文学语料的缺陷,从而提高语料库翻译学研究的可信度和说服力。

(3)基于语料库的汉英口译研究。课题组拟应用汉英口译语料库,分析汉英口译语言的具体特征、口译过程中的语言转换规律以及口译策略和方法等，研究口译认知过程的本质及口译活动的制衡因素，为构建实证、科学的口译理论框架提供重要的物质基础。

2.3 平衡语料的收集整理与历时语言/翻译研究

在语料库创建阶段，按照子课题 1 制定的平衡语料收集和抽样原则将选取的语料处理成机读语料，完成语料处理的前期工作，主要包括双语语料的校对、段对齐和片头元数据标注，为后期的语料处理打好基础。

除了前面说过的历时语料处理外，在语料库建设后期，我们将使用该语料库开展汉语的历时语言演化研究，重点研究翻译在现代汉语发展过程中的作用；开展基于大型语料库的语言与翻译研究，探讨翻译共性、翻译技巧的历时变化、汉语翻译语言的特性、不同语域翻译文本的特征等。

在处理历时研究和共时研究的关系时，我们采用历时研究方法对翻译规范和目的语语言规范的发展变化进行类比研究，将共时研究渗透于各微观研究层面，将静态的整体性描述和动态的连续性分析有机结合起来。

在处理定性研究和定量研究的关系时，拟将定性分析与定量分析相结合。定量分析描述语言成分的使用频率、语言特征的相关性和语言变化的趋势；定性分析用于归纳、推理和解释，即运用合适的理论来阐释语言变异。

（本文原载《中国外语》2012 年第 6 期）

参考文献

G.Anderman, & M.Rogers, *Incorporating Corpora: The Linguist and the Translator*, Clevedon: Multilingual Matters Ltd., 2007.

P.Koehn, *Europarl: A Parallel Corpus for Statistical Machine Translation*, MT Summit, 2005.

A.Lüdeling, & M.Kytö, *Corpus Linguistics: An International Handbook*, New York: Walter de Gruyter, 2008.

T.McEnery, & Xiao.Z, "Parallel and Comparable Corpora: What is Happening", M.Rogers & G.Anderman (eds.), *Incorporating Corpora: The Linguist and the Translator*, Clevedon:

Multilingual Matters, 2007, pp.18-31.

Z.Xiao, "Well-known and Influential Corpora", A.Lüdeling & M.Kytö (eds.), *Corpus Linguistics: An International Handbook*, Berlin: Mouton de Gruyter, 2008, Vol 1, pp.383-457.

常宝宝:《英汉对应词的自动提取》,载王克非等:《双语对应语料库:研制与应用》,外语教学与研究出版社 2004 年版,第 80—96 页。

冯志伟:《统计机器翻译》序,载[德]P.Koehn:《统计机器翻译》(*Statistical Machine Translation*),宗成庆、张霄军译,电子工业出版社 2012 年版。

何文忠、王克非:《英语中动结构修饰语的语料库研究》,《外语教学与研究》2009 年第 4 期。

李德超、王克非:《新型双语旅游语料库的研制和运用》,《现代外语》2010 年第 1 期。

秦洪武、王克非:《基于语料的翻译语言考察》,《现代外语》2004 第 1 期。

秦洪武、王克非:《基于对应语料库的英译汉语言特征分析》,《外语教学与研究》2009 年第 2 期。

秦洪武、王克非:《论元实现的词汇化解释:英汉语中的位移动词》,《当代语言学》2010 年第 2 期。

王克非:《新型双语语料库的设计与构建》,《中国翻译》2004 年第 6 期。

王克非、胡显耀:《基于语料库的翻译汉语词汇特征研究》,《中国翻译》2008 年第 6 期。

王克非、胡显耀:《汉译文学作品中人称代词的显化和变异》,《中国外语》2010 年第 4 期。

王克非、黄立波:《关于翻译共性研究》,《外语教学与研究》2006 年第 5 期。

王克非、秦洪武:《英译汉语言特征探讨——基于对应语料库的宏观分析》,《外语学刊》2009 年第 1 期。

王克非等:《双语对应语料库:研制与应用》,外语教学与研究出版社 2004 年版。

汉英对应语料库的检索及应用

英汉双语对应语料在经过对齐标注校对入库之后，便转化为可管理的数据库系统。为使这一宝贵的语言资源能够更好地服务于翻译教学，我们制作了一个前端用户访问后台数据库的服务接口，通过较好的人机交互界面，提供了一个对双语语言事实进行更多复合条件查询的检索系统。本文简要介绍这一系统的设计开发思路及其应用。

为统计机器翻译系统建造一个较好的语言模型和翻译模型，技术界已经搜集整理并加工了一批多语言语料；语料库越建越大，加工越来越精细（Koehn 2005）。更有一些专门研究探索利用网络爬虫等技术手段从互联网上获取更多翻译语料来丰富语料库的建设（叶妮莎等 2008）。为服务于对比语言学和翻译教学与研究等目的，语言学家和翻译学者也创建了大型双语对应语料库（徐一平等 2002；王克非 2004）。建库是为了用库，一些方便快捷的语料库检索工具也被开发问世了。由于版权限制及网络速度等原因，目前能够在互联网上运行的双语语料库检索系统并不多见。即使有部分能够运行，检索界面也通常比较简单，只提供简单的中英文字词级别的语言形式查找，甚至没有基本的词形还原功能。由于检索词和语料分词不一致造成的漏检经常发生。多数检索系统还不提供翻译文本属性过滤、限制条件检索等功能，例如，翻译方向究竟是汉译英、还是英译汉；文本语体究竟是书面语还是口语。对于为研究者和学习者发现语言现象、总结翻译规律服务的语料库应用项目来说，这无疑是不够的。

北京外国语大学中国外语教育研究中心近期建成了当前世界上经过专业人员校对、属性较完备的、规模最大的汉英平衡对应语料库（王克非、熊文新

2009)。本着切实服务语言对比和翻译研究的目的,我们分别设计完成了一个网络在线和桌面应用的检索系统①,希望能够通过简单的人机交互接口,使更多用户方便地利用这一宝贵的语言资源。

一、语料库的数据库设计

语料库作为海量语言材料的集合,采用通常的文件处理系统难以管理,譬如,我们完成的汉英对应语料库总字数就以千万计。搜集双语对应语料本身不是目的,更重要的是后续的对齐加工以及利用。对语料的检索则可自行设计数据结构或用专门软件处理。

为简化开发时间,我们在汉英对应语料库平台项目中,采用关系型数据库来保存、管理、检索语料。因为关系型数据库系统具有良好的数据存储及管理与维护功能,方便后续语料库的不断追加;此外数据库还提供较好的检索二次开发的接口设计,开发者能够在此基础上方便快捷地定制特定的查询处理。在本项目中,双语对应语料库实际上设计为数据库中的一个表(table)。该表是由一个个汉英对应的句对(sentence pair)以及其他与该句对相关的文本属性共同构成的记录(record)组成。每条记录都包含有如表 1 所示字段(field,属性)的信息内容。

表 1　汉英对应语料库的数据库结构设计

字段名	类型	备注
英文句	字符型(5000)	一个英文句子不超过 5000 个字母
中文句	字符型(2000)	一个中文句子不超过 2000 个汉字
源语言	字符型(1)	当前句对摘自文本的源语言(英语或汉语)
作者	字符型(50)	当前句对摘自文本的作者名

① 网络在线检索系统,名为"中英双语在线 Chinese-English Online"可以登录网址 http://www.fleric.org.cn/ceo,注册成为用户后使用汉英对应语料库中 100 万字词的语料。限于计算机和网络原因,检索结果只提供前 100 条。

续表

字段名	类型	备注
篇名	字符型(50)	当前句对摘自文本的篇名
类型	字符型(1)	当前句对摘自文本所属类型(取规定值之一)
文体	字符型(1)	当前句对摘自文本所属文体(取规定值之一)
语体	字符型(1)	当前句对摘自文本所属语体(取规定值之一)
时代	字符型(1)	当前句对摘自文本所属时代(取规定值之一)
段落 1I D	数值型	当前句对英语句子所在段落相对全文的偏移量
句子 1ID	数值型	当前句对英语句子相对段落的偏移量
段落 2ID	数值型	当前句对汉语句子所在段落相对全文的偏移量
句子 2ID	数值型	当前句对汉语句子相对段落的偏移量
文件名	字符型(50)	当前句子所在文件名

在以上数据库字段的规划中,最主要的是“英文句”和“中文句”,分别存入互有对应关系的完整英语和汉语表述单位(以句子作为基本单位,也存在非 1∶1 的句子对齐关系)。英汉两种语言句子都分别进行了词类赋码操作。在数据库中实际存放的是带有赋码标记的字符串。其他字段记录的是当前句对所出自的语篇文本属性(源语言、文体)或其他依附属性(如作者名、篇名)。譬如从该句源语言的属性可以推知究竟是“英译汉”还是“汉译英”等不同的翻译方向;从文体属性可以推知是文学体还是非文学体等。在对语料库检索时,可以根据这些字段属性的取值不同,实施不同检索限制条件的综合检索。

二、检索系统设计

对原始双语语料搜集整理和对齐是创建双语对应语料库的基础,标注是对其加工的深入,校对能够保证其质量,入库使得语料库成为可便捷管理的数据库系统。检索系统是终端用户与数据库之间的接口,通过这一界面,用户能够简捷、方便、有效地获取对语料库不同需求的访问。

1. 检索问题

对数据库的管理维护操作可以借助数据库系统的结构化查询语言(Structured Query Language,SQL)完成。虽然 SQL 对数据库管理员等专业人士来说并不困难;但不能对从事翻译教学与研究的用户 IT 技能要求太高,为此检索系统配备了一个图形化用户界面(Graphic User Interface,GUI)的查询处理。通过这个界面,用户可以直接键入待查询的内容,选择不同属性的限制条件;系统接受用户输入后,在后台自动生成并执行转换后的 SQL 指令语句。这些转换后的指令既可以是对翻译语言现象本身的简单查询,也可以是结合更多翻译文本属性限制条件的复合查询。

所谓检索就是把满足用户指定限制条件的某些特定记录从数据库中找出来。从上文介绍的数据库结构设计中可以看出:所有翻译文本外在属性(文体、语体、写作时间及类型等)的字段取值都来自固定集合,并且取值是唯一的。譬如,对任意一个汉英翻译句对出处的写作时间必定是“20 世纪前”“20 世纪上半叶”“20 世纪下半叶”这三个值中的某一个。在数据库结构设计时,字段“时代”的赋值编码是{1,2,3}之一①。因此只要熟悉编码规则,或借助帮助文件,就能简单直接地利用这些属性取值作为限定条件。

针对翻译语言现象本身检索的难度要复杂得多。至少包含以下几类:

- 查询的语言不一,可能是中文或是英文,抑或是两者混合;
- 查询长度不一,可能只有一个词语,也可能是词语数量不定的短语;
- 查询对象不同,可能是词语,也可能是词码,或是词语加词码的组合;
- 查询性质不同,可能是需要在目标句对中出现的词语,也有可能是不需要在目标句对中出现的过滤词。

词类赋码有一个相对封闭的标记集,这些标记能够悉数枚举,检索起来并不困难。但有可能用户输入的查询词与实际在语料库中出现的词由于词形不一致而造成漏检或误检。有鉴于此,我们在本系统中分别采用模糊检索和词形还原来解决此类问题。

---

① 可以事先约定编码中的 1 表示“20 世纪前”,2 表示“20 世纪上半叶”,3 表示“20 世纪下半叶”。编码与实际情况的对应可以自行规定,譬如 1 也可用来表示“20 世纪下半叶”,只要在检索时知道某一特定编码表示什么意思即可。

(1)解决汉语分词不一致的模糊检索

为满足不同用户对词码的检索,数据库中存储的中文句子都是已经过分词和词类赋码的文本。汉语词之间都已经添加了空格,并且每个词语后面都缀上了与之对应的词码。这就有可能出现这样一种情况:语料库中分词系统切分出来的词语与用户输入的词语不一致。例如,假定用户输入字符串"中国人民解放军",认定这是一个词,没有加空格。而在语料库中,字符串"中国人民解放军"有可能切分成"中国_np 人民_n 解放军_n"等三个"词语 + 词码"的字符串拼接(concatenation)形式。由于形式匹配不一样,将检索不到用户希望得到的句对。由于用户和分词系统对词的认识不一致,采用字符形式严格匹配的方法容易造成漏检。

我们的解决策略是,首先将输入的查询字符串拆解,汉语以单字、英语以单词为基本单位;在每个基本单位后采用正则表达式拼接 0 或 1 个词类编码形式,构成新的基本单位;然后再拼接各基本单位构成新的查询表达式,这样就能够检索得到与原查询串基本单位序列相同并且字形一致但可能被打散或整合的汉语句子,防止对分词理解不同造成的漏检。应该注意的是,这种处理有可能误检出基本单位字形相同并且排列相同但实际并非用户希望检出的句子。如假定要检索"华人",将该查询串拆解为字后,语料库中"中华人民共和国"将会被检出。因此,模糊检索是保证检出率(recall rate)的一种选择,它适合希望获得全部可能结果,不要有任何遗漏的情况,在计算机检出的相对较小的语言集合中逐一筛查,以获得最终"全而准"的处理结果。

(2)解决英语词语匹配不一致的词形还原

作为一种形态相对丰富的语言,英语的词形变化有可能会导致字符串形式匹配的困难。譬如,可数名词有单复数的曲折变化,动词也会有现在分词、过去分词及过去式等各种规则或不规则的形式变化。针对用户输入的英语查询串,假定输入的是词典词的原型形式,还应检索出实际文本中出现的该词的其他屈折变化形式。例如,输入待查询的原型动词是"go",则还应将实际例句中可能出现的 going/went/gone 等变体形式也检索出来。如果输入串的英文词本身就已经是屈折形式,则不作扩展。像作为检索串的"be asked",新形成的子串有 be 及其变体 am/is/are/was/were/been/being 等以及 asked 词语本身。

为此,我们编制了一个包含4万词语及其相应不规则形式的词表。词表格式为词典词的原型及其与之相关的名词单复数、动词各类时态或形容词比较级及最高级等屈折变化形式。实际查询时,采用查(look up)词表的方式对输入查询串中的英语词进行扩展。新扩展的词语与查询串中的原型词之间保留逻辑上的“或(or)”关系,即在语料库的句子中只要找到原词形式或其扩展词形式的任何一个,都将视作对满足查询条件。

2. Web和桌面应用程序设计

目前我们分别实现了两种检索系统雏形。一是网络查询,一是桌面查询。前者通过Web浏览器联网注册成为用户后,登录指定网站,根据界面指导可以完成查询工作;后者采用光盘介质将检索系统和相关数据安装在用户的计算机桌面使用,可以通过用户图形界面检索。

网络检索系统在后台选用开源数据库MySQL作为语料库的管理查询工具,前端采用脚本语言php制作用户交互的Web查询界面,如图1所示。文本框用来接受用户的输入查询,文本下拉框用来指定特定的过滤属性。用户

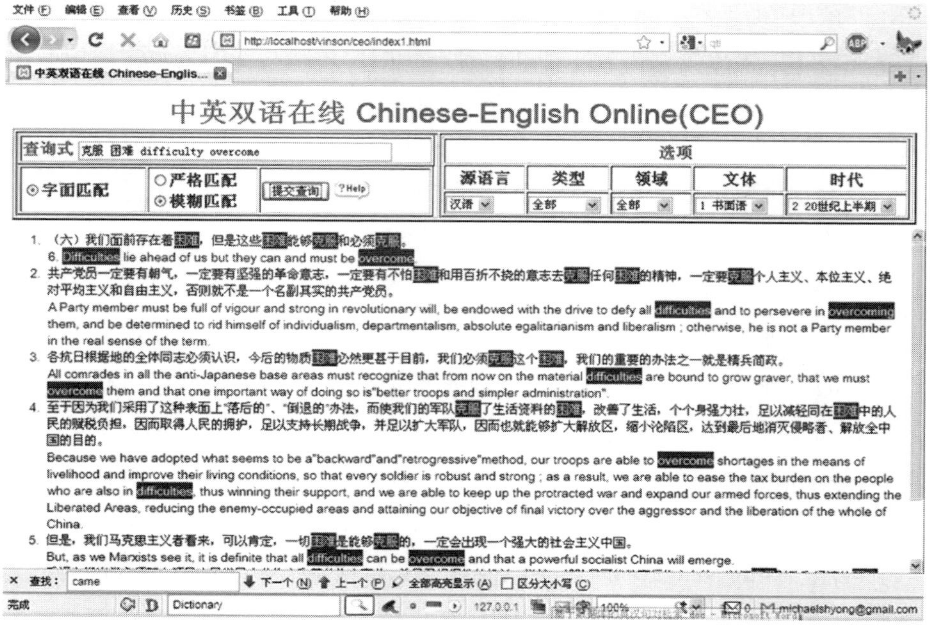

图1 Web方式的检索系统

在相应区域键入相关内容,点击“提交查询”按钮之后,即可生成并执行一个可直接对数据库操作的查询语句,并将执行结果输出到用户的浏览器页面。用户在文本框中键入的查询词语将会以高亮形式凸显。这是典型的“瘦客户端”工作方式。用户的计算机无需安装特别的程序,只要浏览器能够联网就能访问并利用已经创建好的双语对应语料库系统。缺陷是服务器的负担较重,如果在某一时段的并发访问过多有可能造成服务器宕机。另外,对用户的网络连接速度要求也较高,否则有可能因访问超时导致浏览器停止工作。

至于单机版检索系统,考虑到我国用户大多数使用 Windows 操作系统,项目组采用 C#和嵌入式数据库 Sqlite 在微软 DotNetFramework 平台下完成了一个集语料校对、数据入库等内部处理和查询检索等外部工作为一体的开发平台。查询界面与 Web 方式相同,通过文本框和下拉框实现用户输入查询串和选择过滤属性,再经由程序将用户输入内容翻译为等价的 SQL 命令语句,最后将结果高亮呈现在 webBrowser 浏览器控件中,如图 2 所示。

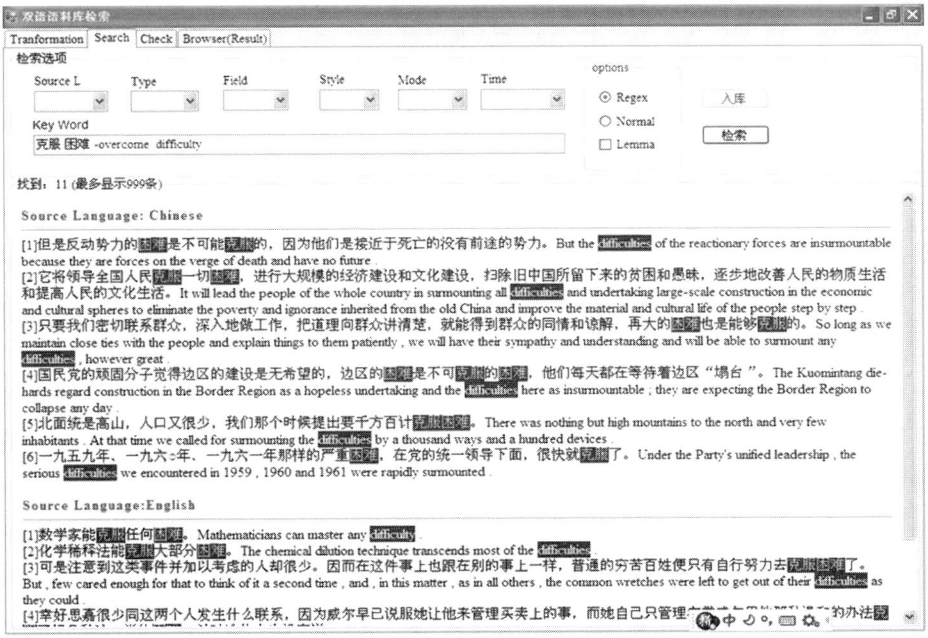

图 2　桌面版检索系统

图 1 和图 2 分别显示 Web 和桌面应用环境下的查询实例。Web 方式显示的是用户查询“克服困难 overcome difficulty”的情形。系统设计查询串的所有原子项之间缺省为逻辑“并(and)”关系,因此所有中文句子包含“克服”“困难”并且与之对应的英文句子带有“overcome”“difficulty”及其变体词形的句子实例都将作为结果输出,同时这些被查询的词语也将高亮显示。桌面应用程序显示的是用户查询“克服困难-overcome difficulty”。根据系统设计,前加“-”的查询词语被当作排除词,包含该词的句子将被过滤,因此针对该例,所有中文句中包含“克服困难”而英文句子带有“difficulty”,但不包含“overcome”的句对将会被检索出来。采用这种限制出现的方式,能够检索汉语“克服困难”在当“困难”翻译成“difficulty”时,“克服”不用 overcome 翻译的各类情形。这意味着能够找到英语中与 difficulty 搭配表示“克服困难”义的所有其他动词。

三、汉英对应语料库检索的应用

将句子层面对齐的双语语料库转换为数据库后,借助用户图形界面,人们就能方便地使用 SQL 语言进行各种组合条件的查询。属性限制条件通常是由某个确定值或多个确定值的组合。确定值通常是二选一或多选一,比如通过看字段“源语言”的取值是英语还是汉语,判断翻译方向是英译汉还是汉译英。通过看字段“时代”的取值决定选取哪个年代的文本。由于对应语料库在句子层面实施了对齐,因此有可能从某种语言的字词出发,找到包含该字词的句子,再输出与该句子对应的另一种语言的句子,从而完成从一种语言检索另一种语言的检索任务。

以下我们从汉语出发,介绍如何利用检索工具来检索动宾关系的“克服困难”在英语中是如何体现的。假定对文体、时代等其他属性不做限制。语料规模为英汉汉英对应语料库中的 200 万中英文字词语料。

如表 2 所示,用“克服 困难”作为查询串检索,能够检索出中文语句中包含“克服困难”的双语句对。如果想要知道“克服 困难”中的“困难”翻译

成“difficulty”的实例，可以采用形如 A1 的检索串。想要知道“克服 困难”中的“困难”不翻译为“difficulty”的例子，可以采用形如 A2 的检索串。针对 A1 检索串，如果再细化，要检索中文串包含“克服 困难”，同时相对应的英文词分别翻译为“overcome difficulty”的实例，可以选用 A11 串；检索“克服 困难”中与“克服”对应的英语词为非“overcome”的其他词的实例，选用 A12 串。检出的实例数参见频数栏。频数关系满足|A| = |A1| + |A2|；|A1| = |A11| + |A12|。

表 2　利用不同检索字符串确定翻译对应

	检索串	频数	汉→英：英→汉
A	克服 困难	98	82 : 16
Al	克服 困难 difficulty	86	76 : 10
A11	克服 困难 overcome difficulty	70	68 : 2
A12	克服 困难-overcome difficulty	16	8 : 8
A2	克服 困难-difficulty	12	6 : 6

使用 A 式检索，在本文实验所用的语料中实际得到 100 条记录。由于汉英句子都只经过词类赋码处理，而没有句法分析；返回的检索结果只是在一定范围内同时包含“克服”“困难”这两个词语的句子，这就不可避免地带来垃圾。譬如句子“克服投降，战胜困难”中的“克服”“困难”就处在语料库检索的跨距(span)中，但却不是用户希望的表示动宾关系的“克服困难”。经过人工排查过滤，最终满足要求的结果数为 98 例。

从表 2 中可见，检索中文句子包含“克服 困难”的句对，绝大多数是汉译英文本，占 83.67%，少部分是英译汉文本，只占 16.33%。浏览检索结果，至少能够发现如下现象。

1. 汉英翻译的英文句大多中规中矩

这些翻译句对的文本多数是政论文体。如表 3 所示，在将“克服”翻译成英语时，除了有 1 例意译(to do so)，主要有两种译法：分别是“overcome”(70 例，占 85.36%)和“surmount”(11 例，占 13.41%，包含 4 例“不可克服”译作“insurmountable”的句子)。经过查询汉英词典取证，“克服”在汉译英时基本上是取其高频的英译词而成①。“困难”的翻译也基本如此:直译为“difficulty”有 76 例,占总数的 92.68%;在剩余 6 例非 difficulty 译法的实例中,有 3 例是采用代词“them”,或“to do so”,在返回的英语句子中找不到相应的“困难”译词,存在着承前省略现象。另有 2 例翻译作“obstacle”,如“克服暂时的困难/surmount the temporary obstacles”“克服自己道路上的各种困难/surmount all the obstacles in their path”,形成 surmount 和 obstacle 的搭配。

表 3 英语译词的选择

类型	“克服”			“困难”
	词数	翻译实例分布	词数	翻译实例分布
汉英	4	overcome(70), surmount/insurmountable(7/4), to do so(1)	4	difficulty(76), they/them(3), obstacles(3), to do so(1)
英汉	10	overcome(4), Ø(4), transcend(1), fought(1), contend with(1), struggle with(1), get out of(1), master(1), straighten out(1), vanquish(1)	4	difficulty(10), Ø(3), hardship(2), obstacles(1)

利用“Google 翻译”来验证“克服困难”的英译,其“翻译:中文→英语”栏目结果显示为“to overcome difficulties”②;而在“字典:”栏目显示的也是“surmount difficulties”。使用“雅虎翻译”③来翻译“克服困难”,结果依然是“overcomes difficulties”。这与我们从汉译英语料中观察到的结果相一致。

按汉语动宾关系的实现模式,根据词典释义词或词表对译词直接套用生成英语译文,是忠实原文的表现;同时也间接反映出作为外语,中国译者的语言表达的丰富性还是比较欠缺(Xiong 2010)。有证据表明,无论是对何种水平的中国英语学习者来说,采用词语替换的直译方式都比较常见(赵秀花 2011)。

① “克服”根据《远东汉英大辞典》(张芳杰主编,新华出版社、远东图书公司 1994 年版)第一个义项为 to overcome(difficulties, etc.);《现代汉英词典》(外语教学与研究出版社 1988 年版)第一个义项为(战胜)surmount; overcome; conquer。

② http://translate.google.cn/translate_t? q = 克服困难 zh-CN |en|克服困难。

③ http://fanyi.cn.yahoo.com/translate_txt.

2. 英译汉的实例较少,但却用例丰富

实例较少与英译汉时有更多的汉语可选择词有关。从英语翻译成汉语,可理解为有两个连续的过程:其一是根据英语形式理解其意思,这是个从语言形式到意义的英语分析(analysis)过程;其二是将该意思用汉语表述出来,这是个从意义到语言形式的汉语生成(generation)过程。由于有不同句式及不同词语的表述方式,在反映"用坚强的意志和力量战胜(困难)"这一意义时,在汉语中可选用"战胜""克服""跨越"等词形不同的多个同义或近义词语替代。由于汉语中有更多的可选译词竞争,因此能够完全匹配"克服困难"这四个字的汉语译文自然就相对较少。

在检出的 82 个汉译英包含"克服"的实例中,只有 3 个不同的英语词(surmount 与 insurmountable 视作同类)。而只有 16 个英译汉实例却有 10 个不同的英语用词。英译汉实例中的用词比较发散,而且有相当数量的短语形式,如 contend with,get out of,struggle with,straighten out 等。与汉译英时严格按照词典释义用词"overcome"和"surmount"相比,英译汉的英语表述更加自然地道,因而需要特别学习。

3. 英译汉有增译现象

"克服 困难"在汉译英文本中基本没有发现漏译的情况。这可能与政论文体有关。相比较而言,政论文体翻译较为正式。语料库中的政论文本多数采自我国的一些重要决议和领导人著述。这些都是经过反复推敲琢磨的文本,为保证译文的准确达意,对这些文本的翻译通常都不会增减。而在英译汉文本中"克服困难"发现有 4 处增译,它们都不是政论文本。实例如下。

(1) Greater things than the Doctor had at that time to contend with, would have yielded before his persevering purpose.即使当时医生要克服的困难比现在还要大得多,在他那坚持不懈的努力之下困难也是会退让的。

(2) If she could only win to Ellen! 要是她能够克服这一切困难到达爱伦身边,那就好了!

(3) ...tried so hard that it was only kept under with great and painful difficulty;这种努力非常顽强,大家全力以赴,痛苦不堪地克服困难,才把它压了下去。

(4) It was with the greatest difficulty that the boy gathered bodily force to speak; But, his spirit spoke with a dreadful emphasis.那少年是克服了最大的困难才集中了全身的力量说出话来的,但是他的神色却起着可怕的强调作用。

其中,例(1)英语原文是"things(事情)",译成汉语时,根据与其构成动宾关系的动词短语 contend with 具有"对付困难或不愉快事情"①的意义,而将"事情"具体化汉译为带有不好意味的"困难"。例(2)是完全增译,原文只是一句简短的表示虚拟语气的感叹句,经过翻译使"赢得爱伦"需要花费很大精力才能完成,这种艰辛变得更为凸显。例(3)和例(4)增译了"克服",原文中并没有突出"克服",只是强调了"把它压下去"和"说出话来"具有一定的难度,间接表明要完成这些事情需要有一些特别的处理,因而汉译中加入了对困难的处理——"克服"这一原本没有的词语。

四、结语

在确定研究对象和目标后,我们搜集、整理、加工、标注好语料,建起了较大规模的汉英对应语料库。我们将语料库以关系型数据库方式存储,以便能够更方便地使用数据库管理系统实现数据的存储、管理和检索。考虑到广大翻译用户的计算机技术实际,提供了一个简单方便的访问手段。通过良好的用户交互界面,能够生成合适的数据库查询语句,这使翻译研究和学习者无需掌握复杂的计算机指令和更多的计算机操作技能,就能及时方便地利用经过语言学家和翻译学家精心整理加工的双语对应语料库。

当前对应语料库的检索系统实现了语言学特定词、词类及其两者的混合查询;能够从某一语言出发实现双向翻译单位的检出;能够根据翻译文本的外在属性的不同实现限定检索;还能够完成限制某词出现的过滤检索等。输出结果为 HTML 形式,查询词语高亮显示,方便对返回结果集进行二次检索以

① 根据朗文当代英语词典对 contend with 的解释为 to have to deal with something difficult or unpleasant。

及对结果的显豁观察。对当前的检索系统善加利用,是能够从翻译文本中找到一些有趣的、值得深思的现象的。

限于现有语料的加工处理深度,当前我们采用检索词语以句间共现作为例句检出的依据。在保证检出率的情况下,准确率将受到一定影响。虽然为人工翻译研究与教学服务的检索系统由于有人工的参与,将召回率作为第一优先的考虑,但可以考虑适当引入浅层语法分析,以增加准确率的选项(Lin 2003)。另外系统当前还是采用查询词语出现与不出现的布尔查询模式,今后可以借鉴信息检索向量空间检索模式,实现近似句的查找。

(本文原载《外语电化教学》2011 年第 6 期)

参考文献

P.Koehn, *Europarl: A Parallel Corpus for Statistical Machine Translation*, MT Summit, 2005.

D.Lin, "Dependency-based Evaluation of MINIPAR", A. Abeille. (ed.), *Treebanks: Building and Using Parsed Corpora*, Netherlands: Kluwer, 2005, pp.317-329.

W.Xiong, "Collocations Studies from Chinese English Learner's Perspective", *Proceedings of International Conference on Intelligent Computing and Cognitive Informatics*, IEEE Computer Society, 2010.

王克非:《双语对应语料库:研制与应用》,外语教学与研究出版社 2004 年版。

王克非、熊文新:《用于翻译教学与研究的英汉对应语料库的加工处理》,《外语电化教学》2009 年第 6 期。

徐一平、曹大峰:《中日对译语料库的研制与应用研究论文集》,外语教学与研究出版社 2002 年版。

叶妮莎、吕雅娟、黄赟、刘群:《基于 Web 的双语平行句对自动获取》,《中文信息学报》2008 年第 5 期。

赵秀花:《一项基于语料库和双语对应词表的特异组合发现方法——以"动词 + 名词"组合为例》,北京外国语大学 2011 年硕士学位论文。

构建新型的历时复合语料库

20 世纪语言学研究，从索绪尔开始，获得极大的进展。其中在方法和工具层面的进步，以语料库的研制与应用最具标志性意义。随着现代计算机技术的发展，单语语料库研制从 20 世纪中叶起步，至今已助力语言学研究取得不少新成果。双语语料库虽然迟至 20 世纪 90 年代上路，但势头很强，带动了双语对比、翻译及双语词典研编等一系列研究。

一、语料库研制存在的问题

目前国际上双语语料库研制的主要问题：第一，语料库大多文本来源单一、标注比较简单，且多为欧洲语言，其他双语语料库甚少，主要用于语言识别、文档级对齐、术语提取等自然语言处理研究，而非从语言学和翻译学角度研究语言与翻译问题。第二，少数双语语料库开展了相应的语言与翻译研究，但双语语料库在质和量上都有待提升。第三，语言是发展变化的，在外语和翻译的作用下，语言之间的各种接触可能导致语言发生另样的变化，原生语言和翻译语言也存在种种的相似和相异。国际上现有的双语语料库或是缺乏历时语料，或是语料库库容有限，上述研究课题也就悬而未探。第四，现有的无论单语还是双语语料库，很少做合成架构，即要么是单语或双语的，要么是平行或类比的，少见组合，不利于语言和翻译发展变化的考察和比较。

针对上述问题，尤其是第四个问题，有必要思考如何突破语料库研制的局限性。构建新型的历时复合语料库，就是我们最新的尝试。

历时语料库可提供各时期语言的相互比较,发现语言运用的变化及其过程,为语言变化考察、翻译研究以及翻译语言与目标语之间的互动,提供客观的描写和可分析的数据。在中外历史上都有不少翻译与目标语演化关系密切的案例。已往研究的语料来源不够丰富,考察范围有限,研究的深度和广度大受制约,对原生汉语同翻译汉语间的互动关系也缺乏了解,而这些都有望通过历时语料数据的获得和分析取得新的突破。

由此可见,研究语言及其变化不仅需要设计合理、规模较大的语料库,还需要平衡的历时语言素材。国际上,应对这一需求的历时语料库近些年开始构建。第一个历时语料库 AVIATOR 在 1990 年由伯明翰大学研制成功,另一个历时语料库 ACRONYM 于 1994 年建成。这两个语料库都使用连续出版的报刊为语料。代表性更强、跨度长达 300 多年的平行英语语料库(ARCHER)、4 亿字词的美国英语历史语料库(COHA)也陆续建成。但是,单语的历时语料库还不能解决双语的和翻译的问题。例如,现代汉语(包括翻译的汉语)的发展变化,单从历时语料库还不能很好地考察,应加入更多的比较成分,如英语源语的因素、汉语译文的变化和汉语原文的变化,三者之间形成全方位的比较研究,才有可能更充分地描写和分析。因此,不仅要构建历时的语料库,还应设计复合的历时语料库。

二、历时—复合:语料库研制的一大突破

新型历时复合语料库的构建是语料库研制的一项重要突破,国际上在这方面刚刚起步。德国学者尤莉安娜·豪斯项目组近年构建了一个小型历时复合型语料库,共 550 篇文本、80 万词。但因语料库容量小,语料不够平衡,时间节点不清,目前仅开展了初步的德英/英德翻译研究和语言接触研究。大规模英汉平行语料库——英汉双语的历时复合语料库,可以有效地解决上述语料库简单、语料库质量以及语料库的历时考察和复合对比研究等问题,为翻译与目标语之间的互动建立比较完整的描写和分析框架,使多层面、系统性的翻译和语言变化历时研究成为可能。

历时语料不是随意将各时期语料收集即可，需要平衡和分期。就汉语来说，语料的历时平衡要通盘考虑现代汉语发展的实际情况，分期采样，以便所建语料库能反映出现代汉语的发展轨迹，并在英汉平行语料库的基础上探究英汉语言接触及英语通过翻译对汉语发展产生的影响。在语料、库容、架构、历时、复合等方面必须突出自己的建库特点，突破国际上一般双语语料库的语料选取和语库架构等方面的局限，还要避免英国国家语料库（BNC）由于历时连续采样而造成的各阶段差异模糊的缺陷。

我们的设计思路是，在库容上达到1亿字词，含百万字词的口译语料，并进行深度加工标注。除了语料平衡和库容巨大这两点外，历时复合是创新亮点，复合即平行语料、类比语料、参照语料三结合，而非单一的平行语料。我们从汉语和翻译发展的动态研究出发架构历时和复合的语料库：将20世纪100年间的汉语语料分成三个阶段，约30年为一个阶段，重点采集各阶段某10年的语料，各阶段收集：（1）英汉平行文学语料400万字词。（2）汉语原生文学语料200万字词。（3）再辅以19世纪末受现代翻译影响的原生态汉语文学语料200万字词，以及不谙外语的单语作家语料100万字词，合计近2000多万字词。

历时复合语料库的构建除了注重时间段的划分，还需在语料取样上考虑双语文本和翻译研究的特定，即不同于一般的单、双语语料库，并需要考虑汉语早期白话文语料（包括翻译文本）有限，本研究在语料取样时做了适当变通，扩大了采样数量。英汉历时翻译语料库样本结构参照Brown语料库，样本大小参照挪威语/英语平行语料库（The English-Norwegian Parallel Corpus，ENPC），大多数样本为15000英语词和对应的25000汉字，汉语译文取样最多不超过30000字，一般从正文起始部分开始连续选取。

构建新型语料库时，还需要相应的语料库技术支撑，需要综合型的便捷检索平台。例如充分调用篇头（Header）标注中的文本属性信息，让这些元信息作为检索条件出现在检索平台界面上，提升复合检索水平；像类别、风格、体裁、作者、时间、出版社、时代等都可以用作检索条件，保证语料检索定向准确、针对性强。目前，以xml格式存储的语料可以在专门设计的平台上使用。

三、历时复合语料库的应用

语言发展变化的因素有些属于语言自身运动，有些是语言间的相互接触影响所致，特别是翻译在两种语言间所起的作用，如近代以来的翻译就对现代汉语白话文的发展起了重要推动作用。同时，汉语规范始终在隐性地规约翻译语言变化的范围。语言的发展变化会在词素、词语、搭配、短语、句式、句长、语篇等层面上反映出来。借助于历时复合语料库这个平台，就可以充分比较和分析这些语言层面的历时变化过程，并建立翻译语言与现代汉语白话文间相互影响的动态模式；还可以通过和汉语原创参照库对比，分析发现汉语历时变化与翻译之间的关系。研究内容包括宏观和微观两大方面。宏观语言特征：重视使用语料库驱动研究方法，侧重考察句长、句段长、POS 频率、类符型符比，以及某些特定语言项目的历时分布特征。微观语言特征：语料库驱动研究与基于语料库的研究二者并用。前者通过 WordSmith 或 AntConc 的关键词对比分析（keyness）词汇和词丛使用上的历时差异，发现有价值的语言点，继之归类、分析；后者重视现有研究成果的有效运用，基于现有的研究提出理论假设，找到细化了的语言项目，或者通过细读翻译文本，观察可分析的语言使用特征，在此基础上基于历时语料进行描述、分析和解释。

总之，历时复合语料库是研制设计上的一大创新，其应用研究前景极为广阔。

参考文献

Juliane House, "Using Translation and Parallel Text Corpora to Investigate the Influence of Global English on Textual Norms in Other Languages", in Alet, Kuger, Kim Wallmach & Jeremy Munday (eds.), *Corpus-Based Translation Studies: Research and Applications*, London: Continuum International Publishing Group, 2011: pp.187-208.

A.Renouf, "Corpus development 25 years on: from Super-corpus to Cyber-corpus", in C. Mair et al. (eds.), *Language and Computers: Studies in Practical Linguistics*, Amsterdam/New York:Rodopi.2007.

P.Studer, *Histroical Corpus Stylistics*, London:Continuum.2008.

秦洪武、王克非,《历时语料库:类型、研制与应用》,《外语与外语教学》2004 年第 4 期。

王克非:《中国英汉平行语料库的设计与研制》,《中国外语》2012 年第 6 期。

王克非、秦洪武,《英汉翻译与汉语原创历时语料库的研制》,《外语教学与研究》2012 年第 6 期。

(本文原载《中国社会科学报》2016 年 9 月 13 日,后为国家社科基金网"最新成果集萃"转发)

Introducing the Chinese-English/English-Chinese Parallel Corpus

This paper introduces the design and compilation of the Chinese-English/English-Chinese Parallel Corpus (CE/ECPC), the largest one of its kind in the world at the National Research Center for Foreign Language Education of Beijing Foreign Studies University. The discussion is to cover its design scheme, distinctive features, composition and procedure of data processing.

1. INTRODUCTION

Since the 1990s, Corpus-based Translation Studies have achieved much, especially in studies of translation universals and translator's style. A corpus-based translation studies paradigm came into being as a result. At the beginning, monolingual comparable corpora became the major source of data. Later, some influential parallel corpus projects such as English-Norwegian Parallel Corpus (ENPC), German-English Parallel Corpus of Literary Texts (GEPCOLT), the English-Italian Translational Corpus (CEXI), the Portuguese-English parallel corpus (Compara) etc. demonstrate their strengths in translation studies as well as contrastive analysis. However, until very recently, most of the parallel corpora in the world are confined to the Indo-European languages. The aim of this paper is to introduce the Chinese-English/English-Chinese Parallel Corpus (CE/ECPC) designed and compiled by the National Research Centre for Foreign Language Education, Beijing

Foreign Studies University.The discussion is to cover its design scheme,distinctive features,composition and procedure of data processing.This corpus is parallel and bidirectional in nature with Chinese and English original texts and their translated texts respectively.The alignment between the two languages is at the sentence level.

2. OVERALL SCHEME

The overall design of a corpus is of great significance to its application in later studies.The selection and organization of textual material to be included are more likely to decide almost every achievement based on it(Sinclair 1991:13).One of weaknesses of the present monolingual comparable corpus paradigm is the denial of source texts in translation studies in that translation,fundamentally speaking,is a transferring activity between source texts and target texts.In that sense,the parallel corpus helps to reintroduce source texts into translation studies(Kenny 2005).On a whole,the design of a Chinese-English Parallel Corpus is out of the following considerations:

1) Goals:the CE/ECPC is to be applied to language studies,translation studies,language teaching studies and bilingual dictionary-making etc.

2) Capacity:the multi-purpose has decided that CE/ECPC should be built with a large capacity,which means tens of millions of English words and Chinese characters will be included.

3) Scope:the goals mentioned above require that the texts contained should be encyclopedic in nature to fully represent the language.

4) Representativeness and comparability:textual materials in the corpus are to be categorized into fiction and non-fiction.The former can be further divided into novel,prose and drama etc.while the latter into humanities,social sciences,and science and technology.All the sub-categories can be further narrowed down.Meanwhile,the ratio of each category should be taken into account.

5) Proportion between two languages: the corpus contains four types of texts, namely, Chinese original texts and their English translations, English original texts and their Chinese translation. Much attention is paid to their comparability and balance. There is a slighttendency of more English-Chinese translation than vice versa.

6) Synchronicity/diachronicity: on a whole, the texts are collected synchronically and mostly belong to the twentieth century. The English parts contain some texts of eighteenth and nineteenth century while the Chinese parts mainly belong to the twentieth century excluding texts in traditional classical Chinese. All the texts are tagged with time markers so as to show the diachronic features.

7) Types of language: at the first stage, only texts in written language are collected.

8) Quality of the texts: original texts of high quality are selected and special attention is given to the quality of translated texts. Over-or under-translations are avoided to the best.

9) Strategies for sampling: sampling and full texts collecting are both involved. The former is intended to be of help for language and lexicography studies while the latter for translation and teaching studies. Texts of one-original-with-many-translations are also included to a certain extent. Texts of less than ten thousand words or characters are wholly included and those of more than ten thousand words of characters are selected by random sampling.

10) Tagging and processing: first of all, alignment at the sentence level is ensured in order to facilitate concordance for various studies; secondly, preliminary word partition and tagging are guaranteed. Rooms are preserved for future tagging at high levels such as syntax and grammar.

All the procedures mentioned above are accomplished step by step. The whole corpus can be further divided into four sub-corpora, namely, encyclopedic, specialized, translational and parallel sentential translation corpora, which can be used collectively as well as separately.

3. DISTINCTIVE FEATURES OF THE CE/ECPC

The fundamental notion of building the CE/ECPC is that firstly, the corpus can be applied to both language studies and translation studies in future research, and secondly, both encyclopedic and specialized textual materials are included. This is the most conspicuous characteristic which differentiate the CE/ECPC for the other corpora home and abroad. Altogether the distinctive features can be summarized as the following:

1) The notion that the corpus be applied to both language studies and translation studies is run through the designing and building scheme;

2) Great attention is paid to balance and representativeness of the texts selected;

3) Chinese and English texts are aligned at the sentence level automatically (with an accuracy of 80%-90%);

4) Concordance can be made at the aligned sentence level automatically.

5) Concordance can also be made in basic grammatical tagging and words, frequency, phrases, sentence patterns and collocations etc.;

6) All the texts are tagged with parameter markers such as type, field, style, mode, time, author/translator and size etc.;

7) Chinese-English and English-Chinese texts are stored in separate files. It is the same with the fiction and non-fiction materials. Consequently, the corpus can be used as a whole and separately as well.

More importantly, the treatment of alignment between Chinese and English is different from that of the other bilingual corpora (including translational corpus). The practical value of a bilingual corpus is usually determined by the alignment of linguistic units in the corpus. Since Chinese and English belong to different language families, they differ largely form each other in word order, sentence structure and expression of logical meaning etc. So it is hardly possible to achieve one-to-one correspondence at the word level and it is also difficult for alignment at the sentence level. The solution to those problems in CE/ECPC is to achieve correspondence at the paragraph level and then to the sentence level. More specifically, problems such as 1) one original sentence to several translated sentences, 2) several original sentences to one translated sentence, 3) surplus of the original text to several sentences in the translated texts, and 4) the disagreement in sentence order between the original and translated texts are to be solved. The exploration into such-problems is helpful not only to the alignment of parallel texts but also to discussions about such theoretical issues as linguistic unit and translation unit.

4. COMPOSITION OF THE CORPUS

Out of considerations mentioned above, the Chinese-English Parallel Corpus built at Beijing Foreign Studies University is to develop into a corpus of 30 million characters or words. It contains four sub-corpora with a structure as Table-1 shows:

Table-1 Structure of the general Chinese-English Parallel Corpus (of about 30 million characters or words)

Four sub-corpora	content	Size(: million characters / words)
Translational texts corpus	Full texts including one original text with many translations are contained. Most of the texts are literary in nature.	20
Encyclopedic texts corpus	The texts are selected in a balanced manner (with 3 million taken from the translational texts corpus).	10
Specialized texts corpus	One to two subjects are to be selected from arts and science respectively as examples for future studies in the field of MT.	(Vacant for the time being)
Sentence-to-sentence translations corpus	One-to-one translations of phrases, sentences taken from various readings, textbooks and reference books etc.	8

The main contents of the four sub-corpora are shown as Table-2:

Table-2 A demonstration of the structure of translational texts corpus

Sub-corpus	C-E /E-C	Fiction /Non-fiction	content	Size (million)	% of the total
Transla-tional texts corpus	C-E	Fiction (55%)	*Ziye* (Midnight), *Chuncan* (Spring Silkworms), *Luotuoxiangzi* (The Camel of Xiangzi), *Jia* (Family), Weicheng (Fortress Besieged) etc. and various short stories and proses	About 8	40%
		Non-fiction (45%)	*Mao Zedong Xuanji* (Selected Works of Mao Zedong), *Deng Xiaoping Wenxuan* (Selected Works of Deng Xiaoping), *Zhonghua Renmin Gongheguo Xianfa* (The Constitution of PRC), various legal documents and different White Papers		
	E-C	Fiction (60%)	*Pride and Prejudice*, *A Tale of Two Cities*, *Tess of the D' Urbervilles*, *Treasure Island*, *Sherlock Holmes*, *Sister Carrie*, *The Adventure of Tom Sawyer*, *Running for Governor*, *Love of Life*, *The Great Gatsby*, *Cop and the Anthem*, *The Godfather*, *The Old Man and the Sea*, *The Bridges of Madison County*,	About 12	60%
		Non-fiction (40%)	*Communist Manifesto*, *The Origin of the Family, Private Property and the State*, *The Glory and the Dream*, *The Protestant Ethic and the Spirit of Capitalism* and various legal works		

The specialized corpus is missing for the time being. Materials in the sentence-to-sentence translations corpus are mainly taken from various translation textbooks, exercises, bilingual readings and reference books etc.

Profiles for all the sub-corpora are identified taking the encyclopedic corpus as an example (as Table-3 shows):

Table-3 A demonstration of the structure of the encyclopedic corpus

Sub-corpus	Size (:million)	field	content
Encyclopedic corpus	10	Literature(30%)	Novels, prose and drama etc.
		Humanities(25%)	Philosophy, culture & education, arts, life and biography etc.
		Social science(30%)	Current affairs, laws, finance and others
		Science & technology(15%)	Industry and communications, agriculture and forestry, medicine and health and others

5. PROCESSING AND ARRANGEMENT OF THE DATA

In processing and arrangement of the data, we refer to the *Manual of Data Collection, Processing and Arrangement for Bilingual Corpus* (by Chang Baobao et. al) by the Computational Linguistics Research Center of Peking University and the relevant norms abroad. Since every step will be critical for the result of the next step, spelling out the concepts, norms and procedures is very important.

5.1 Major Concepts

1) Raw material: textual materials collected through all channels, such as internet, manual typing and electronic scanning are selected according to certain principles to ensure matching between the two languages, namely, the source and target texts;

2) Bilingual parallel corpus: it consists of texts aligned at the sentence, paragraph and text levels. Original texts and theirs translations are guaranteed.

3) Alignment at the textual level: one aligned unit at the text level consists of anumber of aligned paragraphs including original texts and their translations. The source texts and the target texts are put into two folders with the same file name but

different suffixes(the Chinese and English texts are indicated by cn respectively) ;

4) Aligned units at the paragraph level: one aligned paragraph unit consists of a number of aligned sentences including original texts and their translations;

5) Aligned units at the sentence level: one aligned sentence unit consists two parts, namely one or several natural Chinese/English sentences. Both original sentences and their translations are included;

6) Source language: source language here refers to the language employed by the original text aligned at the textual level. In the CE/ECPC, the source language can be Chinese or English;

7) Relationships between languages: The CE/ECPC consists of four types of languages: original Chinese and its English translations, original English and its Chinese translations, which can be applied to a) language studies or contrastive studies, b) Chinese - English or English - Chinese translation studies, c) the comparative studies between target language and the original language in the target language, for instance, comparisons between original English and translated English or between original Chinese and translated Chinese, and d) the studies of translated languages, for instance, compassion between translated English and translated Chinese.

Table-4 Profile of the encyclopedic corpus

Category / Language			File names		Text type		Field				Style							Mode		Time			Publishing information		size	
language	Serial number	nature	Text name	File name	Imaginative 1	Narrative 2	1	2	3	4	1	2	3	4	5	6	7	1	2	1	2	3	Author	Publishing company	1	2
English		Source (%)																								
		Target (%)																								
Chinese		Source (%)																								
		Target (%)																								

Text type: 1. imaginative, 2. descriptive;

Field: 1. literature; 2. humanities(2.1 culture and Education; 2.2 arts; 2.3 life; 2.4 biography; 2.5 philosophy); 3. social science(3.1 current affairs; 3.2 laws; 3.3 finance; 3.4 others); 4. science & technology(4.1 industry & communications; 4.2

agriculture & forestry;4.3 medicine & health;4.4 others);

Style:1.literature(1.1 novels;1.2 prose;1.3 drama);2.narrative;3.argument;4.practical writing;5.news;

Mode:1.written;2.spoken;

Time:1.before the 20th c.;2.the 1st half of the 20th c.;3.the 2nd half of the 20th c.;

Size:1.number of characters/words,2.bytes.

5.2 Processing Procedure

1)The raw materials including Chinese-English and English-Chinese texts collected form the above mentioned channels is sorted out systematically.Redundant and useless information is eliminated.All the texts are stored in the same format;

2)Alignment is established between texts.The aligned texts are stored properly to facilitate later use.Meanwhile,repeating texts and the ones of poor quality are removed;

3)The texts are further sorted out and marked with headers which include text title,author/translator,style,field,mode,time,publisher and size etc.as Table-5:

Table-5 the Header in the CE/ECPC

Content marker	markers
Header	<TEXT_HEAD>...</TEXT_HEAD>
Chinese title	<CH_TITLE>...</CH_TITLE>
English title	<EN_TITLE>...</EN_TITLE>
Author's name	<AUTHOR>...</AUTHOR>
Translator's name	<TRANSLATOR>...</TRANSLATOR>
Style	<STYLE>...</STYLE>
Field	<FIELD>...</FIELD>
Mode	<MODE>...</MODE>
Time	<TIME>...</TIME>
Publisher	<PUBLISHER>...</PUBLISHER>
Size	<SIZE>...</SIZE>

As for the design of the header, some corpora abroad, for instance, the German - English Parallel Corpus of Literary Texts (GEPCOLT) designed by Dorothy Kenny is more meticulous(Kenny 2001:215-216) ;

4)The aligned texts at the sentence level are processed in XML,that is,words partition,part of speech tagging and bilingual linkage for concordance of different kinds.

6. FURTHER DEVELOPMENT IN THE FUTURE

The CE/ECPC is now preliminary established.The task in the near future is the further processing of the data.It means that the texts are to be tagged with syntactical and semantic markers.Proper software for tagging and concordance are to be developed to facilitate future studies in linguistic correspondence at word,phrase and sentence levels,and grammatical features in sets of words and structures.In addition,part of the data in the corpus is to be processed further and made into a disk for CD-ROM which will be helpful for relavent language and translation studies.

During the building process of the CE/ECPC, studies based on the corpus have already begun.For instance,the CE/ECPC-based studies on sentence parallelism in English - Chinese/ Chinese - English, features of the translated Chinese and transferring of Chinese sentence patterns in translation(Wang Kefei 2003) are all first of their kind in China.However,studies in a number of areas,such as studies on English - Chinese/Japanese - Chinese sentence structure comparison and translation, the data preparation for automatic translation and similarity of sentences,directions of translation,features of translated language,quantitative investigation of style of translation,and the"sanitization","simplification","explicitation" or "normalization" in translation, need further discussions based on the parallel corpus of a larger scale.

（本文曾发表于2008年10月下旬美国波特兰州立大学一次国际研讨会）

References

Mona Baker, "Corpus Linguistics and Translation Studies: Implications and Applications", Mona Baker, Gill Francis and Elena Tognini-Bonelli (eds.), *Text and Technology: In Honour of John Sinclair*, Philadelphia & Amsterdam: John Benjamins Publishing Company, 1993, pp.233-250.

Mona Baker, "The Role of Corpora in Investigating the Linguistic Behaviour of Professional Translators?" *International Journal of Corpus Linguistics*, 1999 Vol 4, No.2, pp.281-298.

Dorothy Kenny, *Lexis and Creativity in Translation: A Corpus-based Study*, Manchester: St.Jerome, 2001.

John Sinclair, *Corpus, Concordance, Collocation*, Oxford: Oxford University Press, 1991.

John Sinclair, *Council of Europe Multilingual Lexicography Project*, Report submitted to the Council of Europe under Contract No.57/89, 1991.

Kefei, "Bilingual Parallel Corpora: A New Way to Translation Studies", *Foreign Languages and Their Teaching*, 2002, No.9, pp.35-39.

Kefei Wang, "To Observe Translation through Corpora", *Foreign Languages and Translation* 2003, No.4, pp.15-18.

Dorothy Kenny, "Parallel Corpora and Translation Studies: Old Questions, New Perspectives? Reporting *that* in Gepcolt: A Case Study", Geoff Barnbrook, Pernilla, Danielsson and Michaela Mahlberg (eds.), *Meaningful Texts: The Extraction of Semantic Information from Monolingual and Multilingual corpora*. London and New York: Continuum, 2005.

Wang Kefei, "Characteristics, Distribution and Translation of the Chinese Ba-construction", *Foreign Languages and Translation*, 2003a, No.12, pp.1-5.

Wang Kefei, "SentenceParallelism in English-Chinese/Chinese-English: A Corpus-based Investigation", *Foreign Language Teaching and Research*, 2003b, No.5, pp.410-416.

Wang Kefei et.al, *Bilingual Parallel Corpora. Compilation and Application*, Beijing: Foreign Language Teaching and Research Press, 2004.

语料库翻译学——新范式、多视角

一、翻译研究的新范式

语料库语言学是近20年发展起来的新学科，它一方面提供了新的研究手段，另一方面则反映依据语料库大量语言事实所作的关于语言的理论思考。语料库翻译学同样如此，而且更加年轻，只有十几年研究史，包括方法论或工具层面上的应用研究和关于翻译特征的抽象性的理论研究。

语料库翻译学通常都称为“基于语料库的翻译研究”。鉴于基于语料库的语言学研究通称为语料库语言学，语料库翻译学也可以成立。既然是基于语料库的研究，语料库翻译学要借鉴语料库语言学的基本方法，包括语料的整理、标注、检索、统计等，但也有它独特之处。首先是所据语料库不同。语料库语言学依据单语语料库即可，语料库翻译学一般要依靠双语语料库，主要是翻译语料库（translational corpus）、对应语料库（parallel corpus）和类比语料库（comparable corpus）。其次是标注上双语语料库更加复杂。如翻译语料库需要对翻译、译者等要素加以详细标注，对应语料库需要对两种语料作句子或某种层级上的对齐处理，类比语料库需要对文体、主题、作者、译者等要素加以信息标注。最后是研究对象有别。语料库翻译学探究的是两种语言及其转换的过程、特征和规律。

传统的翻译研究是以原语文本为参照，以忠实程度为取向，主要探讨译文与原文之间的关系或对应关系。Even-Zohar 等人提出的多元系统理论，试图不仅从语言还要从翻译外部即社会文化层面上解释翻译现象，提升了目标语文化语境对于翻译的作用;Holmes 和 Toury 等人提出的描写性翻译研究法,一是重视翻译规范(translation norms)的研究,二是试图探究翻译的普遍性特征(universal features of translation)。语料库的发展,特别是双语语料库的研制,使描写性翻译研究得以充分展开,语料库翻译学基本上就是语料库语言学加描写性翻译研究。这也可以说是一种新的研究范式。因为基于语料库的翻译研究途径在逐步从方法论发展成为连贯、综合、丰富的范式,应用于翻译理论以及翻译的描写和实践等一系列问题的探讨。新的研究方法会促进研究范式的形成和发展,新的研究范式将带来研究思路的更新和研究重点的转移。这是特别值得注意的。

由此我们可以概括地说,语料库翻译学至少有三大应用的和理论的研究课题:

(1)大范围的翻译调查,包括翻译教学、翻译文体的考察以及对应词搭配频率等统计数据的检索与分析;

(2)自动翻译研究,将开展了半个世纪的机器翻译与语料库翻译结合起来,以期取得新的实质性突破;

(3)更广泛更有效的描写性翻译研究,包括翻译规范的研究和翻译普遍特征或曰共性的研究。

Mona Baker 是最早进行语料库翻译学研究的学者之一。她在"语料库语言学和翻译研究"(1993)一文中对这两者的结合作了初步阐发。在第一大课题即大范围翻译调查方面,如翻译文体的考察,她(2000)也率先从语料库角度探讨译者的文体特征,特别是从类符/型符比、平均句长及词项使用特点等方面加以分析。

第二大课题的研究指向,主要是将基于规则的研究方法(rule-based approach)同基于语料的研究方法(corpus-based approach)相结合,为自动翻译寻找出更便利可行的途径。

值得关注的是第三大课题,即语料库基础上的描写性翻译研究,特别是有关翻译普遍性问题的探讨。Baker 在前人研究成果的基础上,提出了翻译普遍特征(universal features of translation)的假设,主要内容是翻译文本中的(1)显化(explicitation)现象;(2)消歧(disambiguation)和简化(simplification)倾向;(3)范化(normalization)特点;(4)倾向于避免重复;(5)倾向于凸显目标语语言特征;(6)某些特征呈现特定类型的分布。此外,Laviosa调查了英语翻译文本中的4种核心词汇运用模式;Kenny(1998)通过对原文、译文的语义韵比较,发现译文语言有净化(sanitisation)现象;Overas(1998)考察了英语—挪威语翻译中衔接层面上的显化现象;王克非根据大型对应语料库探讨了译本扩增情况;Laviosa讨论译文与母语在词汇使用上的不同;柯飞通过语料库考察,发现翻译过程中对原文的模仿可能使译文变得复杂化、冗长化;Xiao & McEnery发现在"体"标记的使用上,汉语译文比汉语原文多出约一倍;Ebeling比较了英语和挪威语在存现句使用上的特点;Maia以双语对应语料库观察英语和葡萄牙语在人称主语使用频率上的差异;等等。

从这些文献可以看出,语料库翻译学在研究方法上以语言学理论为指导,以概率和统计为手段,以双语真实语料为对象,对翻译进行历时或共时的研究,代表了一种新的研究范式。

二、多视角探究翻译

同时,翻译研究具有不断吸收周边领域的理论、方法为己所用的渗透能力。多视角就体现了翻译研究的综合性和多面性。当代翻译研究呈现出一种多元化的趋势,除传统的文学翻译研究方法和兴起于20世纪五六十年代的语言学研究方法外,70年代德国的功能理论和以色列的多元系统论,80年代翻译研究的文化转向和翻译研究学派的操纵论、媒介论,以及90年代以来的语料库翻译研究理论与方法,无不在向世人展示翻译研究作为一门独立的学科体系已经崭露头角。意大利Trieste大学Alessandra Riccardi教授新编一本文集:*Translation Studies Perspectives on an Emerging Discipline*(2002),其论述反映出翻译学这门"新兴"学科仍在成长之中,研究领域的边界尚未最终划定,更反映出翻译研究向来具有的一种渗透能力,即不断吸收周边领域的理论、方法为己所用。多视角其实就体现了翻译学研究的综合性和多面性,近年西方多本新出版的文集都体现了这一特点。从语料库切入翻译研究是其中引人注目的视角。

当今翻译研究主要有两大特点:其一,翻译研究的对象渐从外部转回内部即翻译本身,包括译者和翻译过程;其二,翻译的理论研究与应用研究在有机地结合,特别是利用现代语料库技术进行的各种翻译研究。

从语料库途径探究翻译的一个显著特点就是关于翻译普遍性的讨论。语料库不仅使我们可以同时观察大量的翻译文本,而且可以观察多种语言之间的翻译现象,从而有可能概括出翻译的普遍特性。

Sara Laviosa 是较早依据双语语料库开展翻译研究的学者,她提出了“基于语料库的翻译研究”(corpus-based translation studies)范式。她从 Gideon Toury 提出的“描述翻译研究”(Descriptive Translation Studies)与基于语料库的翻译研究之间的联系入手,指出了二者的共性:第一,注重从实证的角度对真实语料进行直接观察;第二,对语料库文本的选择并非基于某个固定的定义,而是建立在共识性标准和外部分类的基础上,必要时采取随机抽样的方式;第三,两种方法都坚持认为从实证性研究中得出的一般性结论只有建立在对大量文本语料研究的基础之上才能保证其有效性;第四,适用于研究对象的各种原则都是经过大量系统的研究来发现,并以概率性规则作为表述形式(见 Granger et.al.2003:45-56)。她还曾在博士论文里详尽地论述了翻译普遍性问题,包括翻译中的简化(sinplification)、显化(explicitation)、范化(normalization)等特征。总之,基于语料库的翻译研究范式是在原有研究范式的基础上孕育产生的,其最大的优势在于新颖灵活的研究方法和采用不同语言及其翻译的大量真实语料。

例如 Tiina Puurtinen 以芬兰语单语类比语料库为工具,对原创芬兰语儿童文学与译自英语的儿童文学作品中的语言进行对比。他发现,翻译文本中非限定性结构的出现频次要高于原创作品;翻译文本中所使用非限定性结构在语义、文体和语用功能上与原创作品对该结构的使用不对等。他由此得出结论(见 Granger et.al.,2003:141-156):非限定性结构是芬兰翻译儿童文学中翻译语言的一大特征。然而,这一特征与通常的翻译普遍性假设——简化、显化、范化相违背,因为非限定性结构的使用会降低译文的明晰度,增大词汇密度和信息负载,而且大量的非限定性结构背离了原创儿童文学的语言规范。

尽管基于语料库的研究方法的优势不言而喻,但这一研究却为我们提出了一些新问题:第一,印欧语系内部基于语料库的研究的结果是否具有更广泛的普遍性呢?如果有,那么这一普遍性存在的基础是什么呢?如何将这样的共性特征应用于翻译实践中?第二,基于语料库的翻译研究方法的有效性到底有多大?对此有效性的衡量应以何为标准?这些问题的探究将有利于基于语料库的研究方法的进一步完善。

Juliane House 则探讨"翻译中的普遍性与文化特性"(Universality versus cultural specificity in translation, in Riccardi 2002:92-110)。她回顾了翻译研究中语言学范式和文化范式的历史,尤其是对语言—文化相对论与翻译理论及实践之间的关系。她主张采用以语言学为主导、兼顾语用与跨文化的研究范式,并确认了两个基础性的翻译类型/范畴:"显形翻译"(overt translation)与"隐形翻译"(covert translation)。前者是指在译文中保留原作特色,使其明显不具有译语文化中原创文本的特征;后者是指在译作中掩盖原作的特色,使之完全迎合译语读者的口味,看不出其与译语文化中原创文本的差异。她进而提出"文化过滤器"(cultural filter)的概念,用来指译者在翻译中对文化特性进行补偿的手段。通过纯语言学研究范式与纯文化研究范式的有机结合,House 的观点填补了两者之间的鸿沟。她还指出,英语作为全球通用语在文化过滤中的角色所导致的结果就是"文化普遍主义"(cultural universalism)的出现。

三、结语

当代翻译研究的特点是多视角多层面并存的状态。其中,从语料库的角度对翻译开展的研究尤为值得注意,带有新的研究范式的倾向。

描述翻译研究从 20 世纪五六十年代在西方开始出现,而语料库翻译研究是 90 年代涌现,二者呈现出一定的共同点,即注重从实证的角度细致观察真实语料,从大量的语料考察基础上建立实证研究的一般性结论,这些结论或原则阐述是以概率性作为其表述形式。总之,语料库的发展和语料库视角切入翻译研究，给翻译学科带来新的发展契机。

（原文发表于《中国外语》2006 年 2 期，此处结合另文做了修补）

参考文献

G.Anderman, and M.Rogers, *Translation Today: Trends and Perspectives*, Clevedon: Multilingual Matters Ltd., 2003.

Mona Baker, "CorpusLinguistics and Translation Studies: Implications & Applications", Mona Baker, Gill Francis & Elena Tognini-Bonelli(eds), *Text and Technology: In Honour of John Sinclair*, Philadelphia & Amsterdam: John Benjamins Publishing Company, 1993.

Mona Baker, "Towards a Methodology for Investigating the Style of a Literary Translator?" *Target*, 2000, Vol.12, No.12, pp.241-266.

S.Granger, J.Lerot and S.Petch-Tyson, *Corpus-based Approaches to Contrastive Linguistics and Translation Studies*, Amsterdam: Rodopi, 2003.

Maeve Olohan, *Introducing Corpora in Translation Studies*, London and New York: Routledge, 2004.

Alessandra Riccardi, *Translation Studies: Perspectives on an Emerging Discipline*, Cambridge: Cambridge University Press, 2002.

Lawrence Venuti, *The Translator's Invisibility, A History of Translation*, London: Routledge, 1995.

王克非：《双语对应语料库：研制与应用》，外语教学与研究出版社 2004 年版。

Corpora and Translation in the Chinese Context

INTRODUCTION

In 1993, Mona Baker's paper "Corpus Linguistics and Translation Studies—Implications and Application" signals the beginning of a new era in Translation Studies. Baker proposes the "corpus-based investigation" in Translation Studies, which develops later from a methodology into "a new paradigm" (Laviosa 1998a)—Corpus-based Translation Studies (CTS). Based on various corpora composed of large-scale authentic machine-readable translation-related texts, the new branch, which is descriptive in nature, aims at explorations into translation performance involved in all types of translation, including how translators make use of the target language in their translations and what kind of linguistic regularity or probability is demonstrated in the bilingual transfer between different languages. For more than twenty years, CTS has already explored a series of research topics such as (universal) features of translated language or translation universals, translator's style, translational norms, diachronic changes of target language, etc. The new paradigm has been developing both methodologically and technologically. This chapter offers an overview of CTS in the Chinese context in the past decades, which can be divided into four major stages, namely introducing period, corpora building and related researches, hypotheses testing in the Chinese-English context, further development and prospect.

INTRODUCING PERIOD

In China, machine-readable corpora appeared in 1979, when the Corpus of Modern Chinese Literary Texts with a size of 5.27 million Chinese characters was built at Wuhan University. From then on, a series of representative Chinese corpora had been established in the following two decades with the focus on the Chinese language of various registers or genres. Explorations in the field of mono-lingual corpus research provided substantial experience for the later development of CTS in China.

Application of corpora to machine translation

Studies of application of corpora to translation studies started with discussions of how the corpus technology might support machine translation (MT) in the 1990s. The parallel corpora compiled for translation studies or practice did not come into being until the last decade of the 20th century, when a number of English-Chinese parallel corpora were being built or completed. For instance, the Chinese-English parallel corpus designed by the Institution of Computational Linguistics at Peking University, the HKUST English-Chinese Parallel Bilingual Corpus, the Sinorama Chinese-English parallel corpus, the Chinese-English parallel corpus designed by Harbin Institute of Technology, etc. Those translation-oriented corpora were built mainly for the studies that serve MT from the perspective of corpus linguistics or computational linguistics. They are more mathematical linguistics oriented and technologically dependent on statistical analysis.

Commencement of corpus-based translation studies

Corpus-based Translation Studies (CTS), in its own right, was first introduced into China at the beginning of the new century. Both Liao (2000) and Ding (2001) introduced the latest development of CTS in the west, especially Mona Baker's ideas about the application of various translation-related corpora to translation studies, the Translational English Corpus (TEC) designed by University of Manchester Institute of Science and Technology (UMIST), and some preliminary studies based on it. By that time, few researchers in China had the knowledge of what CTS was about. Nevertheless, the 6th Symposium of Translation and Interpreting Teaching held at Chang Jung Christian University (CJCU), Taiwan in 2002 brought about an abrupt change in the field of CTS in China. Some preliminary thinking and findings about translation and interpreting based on corpus investigations are presented at the symposium (e.g. Gao 2002; Ke 2002; etc.). Scholars began to make the map of CTS in China step by step through theoretical and empirical researches based on various corpora.

According to Baker, since translations differ from the naturally produced comparable texts within the same language, the regular differences can be detected with the help of corpus technologies through identifying the "universal features of translation, that is features which typically occur in translated texts", including "explicitation", "disambiguation and simplification", "preference for conventional 'grammaticality'", "tendency to avoid repetitions", and "tendency to exaggerate features of the target language" (Baker 1993: 243-244). Explicitation (the tendency of translations to be more explicit in comparison with the sources texts or the non-translated target language texts) and simplification (the tendency of simplifying the language or message in translations, consciously or subconsciously), together with normalisation/conservatism (tendency in translated language to conform to and even exaggerate the typical patterns or practices of the target language), leveling off ("the tendency of translated text to gravitate around the centre of any continuum rather than move towards the fringes") (Baker 1996: 176-177), and other distinctive features of translated language or texts, are later developed into the so-called translation universals. Besides, Baker also holds corpora can be employed to investigate the "textual exponents of translational norms", "the intermediate stages of translation", "the size and nature of the unit of translation", and "the type of equivalence" in translating practice, etc (Baker 1993: 246–248). By the end of the 20th century, those topics had been widely investigated in the west. The special issue "The Corpus-based Approach" of *Meta* (43/3) in 1998 is a demonstration of the achievements made by then.

Those research topics including translation universals, translator's style, and translational norms, etc. were introduced to China at the beginning of the new century (see Wang et.al.2004). Chinese scholars, a decade after the birth of CTS, started their own explorations in this field in a non-Indo-European language context. By 2004, a bidirectional Chinese-English parallel corpus (CEPC) had been established by the National Research Centre for Foreign Language Education, Beijing Foreign Studies University. As a landmark of CTS development in China, it is the first of its kind in the world with a size of 30 million Chinese characters and English words. In 2007, The Conference and Workshop on Corpora and Translation Studies was held at Shanghai Jiaotong University. It was the first of its kind specialising in CTS. The topics cover almost everything within the scope of CTS then. The conference serves as another landmark in the development of CTS in China. It is indicated that CTS preliminarily declared its commencement in China by then.

Major research topics explained

Translation universals refer to the distinctive features of translated language (or texts). The features identified in comparison with the corresponding source language (or texts) are, in Chesterman's words, the S-universals (S stands for source), which are the "universal differences between translations and their source texts, i.e. characteristics of the way in which translators process the source texts" (Chesterman 2004: 39). Those recognized in comparison with the naturally produced non-translated language (or texts) within the same language are called T-universals (T stands for target), which are the "universal differences between translations and comparable non-translated texts, i.e. characteristics of the way translators use the target language" (Ibid). The former, investigated through the use of parallel corpus, is also called the interlingual contrastive universals while the latter, identified with the help of comparable corpus, is labeled as intralingual comparable universals. Among all the features proposed, explicitation, simplification and normalisation are the mostly investigated topics. All the translation universals fall into two categories: S-type and T-type. The parameters employed to identify those features include standardised type/token ration (STTR, which is the ratio of different words to the overall number of words in a text), average (or mean) sentence length (ASL or MSL), use of high-frequency words, lexical density, etc. For instance, when two groups of texts are compared with each other, the STTR can be used to decide the lexical variety of them respectively. The lower the value of STTR is, the higher the lexical variety in the text. Those statistical figures can be obtained directly or indirectly with the help of software such as WordSmith Tools, ParaConc, AntConc, etc.

Translator's style, a topic proposed by Baker (2000), refers to the distinctive way of translating manifested in all translated works of a specific translator. Two translators are selected and their translations, collected in an exhaustive way, are made into two corpora respectively. One translator is the object of study while the other is used as a reference. The two corpora are comparable with each other in size, time, mode, etc. Then the two corpora are compared with each other in terms of specific testing parameters, such as STTR, ASL or MSL, etc. so as to find out the differences between them. Baker suggests the stress, in identifying a translator's style, be put on the "patterning" or "preferred or recurring patterns of linguistic behaviour" in all translations by the same translator regardless of the corresponding source texts. This comparable mode of comparison is target text-oriented. Apart from the comparable model, another way of discussing translator's style is based on the parallel corpora consisting of one source text and its several translations by different translators. For instance, Bosseaux (2007) discusses the free indirect speech in Virginia Woolf's *The Waves* and *To the Lighthouse* and in their French translations. Her investigation is particularly concerned with the potential problems involved in the translation of linguistic features that constitute the notion of point of view, such as deixis, modality and transitivity and free indirect discourse, and seeks to find out whether and how the translators' choices affect the transfer of narratological structures differently.

Translation universals and translator's style are the two major research topics much discussed in recent years. The other topics such as translational norms, changes in target language brought about by translations, etc. are relatively less explored due to lack of large-scale diachronic corpora or effective automatic annotating tools.

CORPORA BUILDING AND RELATED RESEARCHES

The beginning decade of the 21st century witnesses an upsurge of translation-oriented corpora building in accordance with specific purposes of different CTS research projects in China. The comparative model of CTS, just as it has developed in the west, falls into two major categories, namely the parallel model and the comparable model. Studies based on the parallel model focus on regularity in language use in the interlingual transfer, that is, translator's regular treatment of the source language (or text) in the target language (or text). Those based on the comparable model pay more attention to the linguistic features of translated language in contrast with the non-translated language within the same language, i.e. the target language. Accordingly, various parallel or comparable corpora have been constructed in accordance with specific research aims. Related researches have been carried out.

The parallel model

The most influential parallel corpora built during the first decade of the new century include the Babel Chinese-English Parallel Corpus designed at Peking University, the Chinese-English Parallel Corpus (CEPC) designed by the National Research Centre for Foreign Language Education, Beijing Foreign Studies University, the English-Chinese Parallel Corpus of Shakespeare's Plays designed by Shanghai Jiaotong University, the Chinese-English Parallel Corpus of *Hóng Lóu Mèng* (《红楼梦》*The Dream of the Red Mansion*) constructed at Yanshan University, the Pool of Bilingual Parallel Corpora of Chinese Classics built by Shaoxing University, the Bilingual Corpora of Tourism Texts developed in the Hong Kong Polytechnic University, to name but a few.

As one of the early representative parallel corpora, the CEPC is bidirectional with both Chinese and English original texts and their corresponding translated texts respectively. The otherdistinctive features can be summarized as follows:

(1) The Chinese and English texts are aligned at the sentence level automatically;

(2) Concordance can be made at the aligned sentence level automatically by POS tags, specific words, phrases, sentence patterns and collocations etc.;

(3) All the texts are headed with information such as type, field, style, mode, time, author/translator and size etc.;

(4) Chinese-English and English-Chinese texts are stored in separate files and the corpus, therefore, can be used as a whole and separately as well. (see Wang 2004)

The CEPC is a corpus for general purpose and can be applied to both language studies and translation studies. Besides, both encyclopedic and specialised textual materials are included. A series of research topics have been explored with the help of the CEPC, including translation unit, features of translated language/translation universals, translator's style, language and translation teaching, and so on and so forth. Based on the CEPC, Wang and Hu (2008) identify the salient lexical features of translated Chinese, including lower lexical variety, lower lexical density, greater explicitation of functional words and pronoun usage, and a higher incidence of common words. Through an investigation of the general features of translated Chinese, Wang and Qin (2009) find that translated Chinese demonstrates higher type-token ratio, longer sentence segment and a strong tendency to expand some constructions' load capacity, which means it tends to cram into a construction more words than it normally contains. The construction of "*prep.* + NP + word for space" (e.g. "在……里", which means "in..." in English), for instance, in Chinese is a closed structure which can only accommodate very limited number of NPs between the *prep.* and the word for space. In English-Chinese translation, however, more NPs than usual could be added in the translated Chinese versions. Another example is the construction of "personal *pron.* + *de*1 (的, used as the marker of possessive case) + *de*2 (used as the marker of an adjective) + n." Between the two *de*s, only limited number of adjectives can appear. But in translated Chinese, more adjectives could be added. The findings show that those features specific to translated Chinese, which are more translationese like, do not fully support the hypothesis of translation universals because of the interference of the source language.

The English-Chinese Parallel Corpus of Shakespeare's Plays and the Chinese-English Parallel Corpus of *Hong Lou Meng* are two specialised corpora of translations of classics.

The corpus of Shakespeare's plays is made up of the English original dramatic texts and their three representative Chinese versions. With the help of the parallel corpus, the translators' distinctive translating styles are investigated. The use of some unique Chinese linguistic items, such as the *bǎ*-construction (把-'a structure indicating "dispose" something'), *bèi*-construction (被 'a structure indicating passive voice'), and *shǐ*-construction (使 'a structure indicating "to be made to do"') are investigated. Translation universals, such as explicitation and implicitation manifested in translations are explored. The corpus are also employed to investigate many a linguistic phenomena in the translated texts, including discourse markers, modal particles, delexical verbs, grammatical metaphors of modality, etc. Those researches reveal various translation phenomena to which otherwise we could not have access without the help of corpus so as to facilitate an"elucidation of the nature of translated text as a mediated communicative event"(Baker 1993:243).

The Chinese-English Parallel Corpus of*Hóng Lóu Mèng* is another representative corpus specialising in translation of classic works. The corpus is composed of the Chinese original text and three of its English versions. One peculiarity of the corpus is that, apart from the POS tagging automatically, sentences in the texts are tagged manually in terms of type, register, and voice, rhetorical devices, idioms or sayings with the Multi-modal Annotation in XML(Liu 2010:39-43). The in-depth annotation facilitates the retrieval of a variety of data. It has been applied to investigations of translator's style and features of the translated texts in terms of the regular use or linguistic patterns of narrative markers, idiom translation, translation of cultural terms, translation of forms of address, etc.

Another representative specialised corpus is the Bilingual Corpora of Tourism Texts established by the Department of Chinese and Bilingual Studies, the Hong Kong Polytechnic University, which aims at both teaching and research of tourism translation(see Li and Wang 2010, 2011). Compared with the other general or specialised corpora which focus more on literary textual materials, the corpus of tourism texts is a collection of vocative texts which demand a different translation strategy in bilingual transfer. It is made up of two sub-corpora: one parallel(i.e. Chinese-English) and the other comparable(i.e. translated English vs. original English). Theoretically, the corpus can also be used to study the language use in various tourism texts and the bilingual transfer between different cultures. As far as English for Specific Purposes(ESP)-oriented corpus is concerned, the Bilingual Corpora of Tourism Texts methodologically set a model for similar researches.

Apart from the research based on large-scale corpora built by some academic institutions, there are a lot of other parallel corpora designed by individual scholars in carrying out their own researches and fulfilling their research objectives. The focus is mainly on the linguistic or cultural features demonstrated in translations of specific classic works, such as *Ulysses*, *Hóng Lóu Mèng* (《红楼梦》*The Dream of the Red Mansion*), *Shuǐ Hǔ Zhuàn*(《水浒传》*Outlaws of the Marsh*), *Wéi Chéng* (《围城》*Fortress Besieged*), etc. synchronically or diachronically. Translator's style is investigated and interpreted from the perspective of ideology contained in the translations. Some specialised corpora are also employed to test the hypothesis of translation universals.

The comparable model

Apart from the parallel corpus-based research, comparable corpora are also built and employed to decipher the features of "the third code" or "translationese" against the background of the non-translated language within the target language in terms of lexical use, collocation and syntactic structure, etc. As previously mentioned, the CEPC is a bilingual parallel corpus with four types of texts in both directions, namely Chinese original texts, their English translations, English original texts and their Chinese translated texts. It has also been used in comparable studies to find out more about the features of translated language or translation universal (e.g. Wang and Qin 2009; Wang and Hu 2008, 2010; etc.). For instance, the frequency of personal pronoun subjects in translated Chinese texts, both fiction and nonfiction, is higher than that of the comparable non-translated Chinese texts.

Designed as a monolingual corpus of translated Chinese, the Zhejiang Corpus of Translated Chinese (ZCTC) is combined with the Lancaster Corpus of Mandarin Chinese (LCMC) so as to form a comparable Chinese corpus made up of translated and non-translated Chinese texts. Texts in either of the two corpora are classified into 15 genres consisting of 500 written texts with 2,000 Chinese characters for each (see Xiao 2012:42-47). Features of the translated language are analyzed against the norms demonstrated by the non-translated text. The comparable corpus are mainly employed to study the translation universals proposed by Baker (1993), more precisely, the T-universals in general. With the integration between the comparable corpus and a parallel corpus, the phenomenon of "Source Language (SL) Shining through" proposed by Teich (2003:145), is investigated (see Dai 2013). It is demonstrated some of the features of the source language have been carried over to the translations.The collocates for the node word being investigated in translated Chinese texts are more diversified than those in the non-translated Chinese.The investigations, in essence, are from the perspective of the source language interference, one of the two laws proposed by Toury(1995).The research findings show source language interference is one of the major reasons for those translation universals.Translation, here, is taken as one form of language contact which may elicit changes within the target language.Diachronically, corpora may be of great help in depicting the changes taking place in a specific language.

The Contemporary Chinese Translated Fiction Corpus(CCTFC) is another corpus consistingof only Chinese texts translated from many other different languages (Hu 2008).Combined also with the LCMC, it aims to find out systematically the features of translated fictional Chinese, translation universals, translation norms and cognitive models of translation. Based on the methodology proposed by Laviosa (1998b) in finding out the core patterns of lexical use in a comparable corpus of English narrative prose, Hu(2007) makes an investigation of the lexical patterns in the translated Chinese fiction and draws the conclusion that translated Chinese fictions demonstrate the features of simplification and normalisation.More specifically, translated Chinese fictions tend to use less different words or less lexical words and more high-frequency words than the comparable non-translated Chinese fictions do.The corpus is also employed to explore the overall stylistic features of the translated fiction, explicitation, syntactical structures of attributives, *bèi*-contruction, *bǎ*-construction in order to find out more about the nature of the translated language.In analysing the features of translated language based on the comparable corpora, the method of multi-dimensional analysis proposed by Biber(1988) is employed and proves to be effective in differentiating translated Chinese from non-translated one.The application of multi-dimensional analysis goes beyond the available statistical methods, such as type-token ratio(TTR), average word length (AWL), average sentence length(ASL), etc.in exploring translation universals.

Corpus-based translation teaching

One of the applications of CTS is in the area of teaching, that is, translator or interpreter training. It is generally agreed that "because corpora can be used to raise awareness about language in general, they are extremely useful in training translators and in pointing up potential problems for translation" (Hunston 2002: 123). Trainers are exposed to a large number of parallel or comparable texts. It is, therefore, easy for them to actively observe various types of equivalence between different languages and consciously make use of information provided by corpora, which cannot be obtained in dictionaries, in their own practice. A lot of efforts have been made in exploring the application of corpora in translation or interpreting teaching (e.g. Ke 2002a, 2002b; Wang and Qin 2015; etc.). Since parallel or comparable corpus is useful in creating an autonomous learning environment, it is suggested that, in a proper application of the approach, precedence be given to observation over generalisation, to presentation over explanation, and to self-directed learning over the teacher's instruction (Qin and Wang 2007). Learners can induce or generalize translation techniques by themselves and reflect on their own translation behaviours through data presentation. Research findings show that descriptions of distribution of POS, the length of sentence segments, the load capacity of constructions are helpful in improving translation assessment.

Apart from theoretical discussion of feasibility and methods of applying corpora in translator education, some online teaching platforms are established and put into practice. For instance, the Chinese-English Online (CEO) based on part of the data of the CEPC, the Pool of Bilingual Parallel Corpora of Chinese Classics at Shaoxing University, the Online Chinese-English Translation Retrieval System designed at National Taiwan University, the CityU On-line Teaching Platform at the City University of Hong Kong, the bilingual search engine of the BLCU Chinese Corpus (BCC) designed by Research Centre of International Education Technology, Beijing Language and Culture University which contains 16 language pairs, etc.

Most of the above platforms can be accessed on-line and equivalent translational sentence or paragraph pairs can be retrieved easily. As one of the representative teaching platforms, the CityU On-line Teaching Platform is characterized by textual accountability-driven mode (focusing on textual analysis), in-depth annotation (containing nine categories of tag-words covering translation techniques, rhetorical information, information structure, cultural backgrounds, etc.), variety of genres (including 6 major topics and 30 sub-topics), user-friendliness (though detailed explanatory notes and exercises), etc. (see Wang and Zhu 2012; Zhu and Mu 2013; Wang 2015; etc.). Much of the information shown on the platform is tagged into the texts manually. It demonstrates that apart from automatic annotation, a certain amount of manual interference is essential in building a corpus-based teaching platform. Besides, the web as corpora and translation memory (TM) systems supported by corpora are also applied to teaching translation.

Corpus-based Interpreting Studies (CIS)

Studies of interpreting based on authentic corpora date back to the 1960s in Europe, whileCorpus-Based Interpreting Studies (CIS) did not become a technical term in the field of Translation Studies until 1990s. In China, CIS started even later. At the end of the first decade of the 21st century, some MA theses began to focus their attention on conference interpreting studies or courtroom interpreting studies. In the following years, some corpora for interpreting studies are built. Among the representatives are the Parallel Corpus of Chinese EFL Learners - Spoken (PACCEL-S) set up at Beijing Foreign Studies University, the Chinese-English Conference Interpreting Corpus (CECIC) built at Shanghai Jiaotong University, the Corpus of Chinese-English Interpreting for Premier Press Conference (CEIPPC) constructed at Guangdong University of Foreign Studies, to name but a few. Some are still in progress, for instance the Chinese Interpreting Learners Corpus (CILC) designed at Beijing Language and Culture University for instance.

CIS develops very rapidly later. Relevant researches fall into five categories:

(1) discussions on the construction of corpora for interpreting studies; (2) literature review of CIS; (3) technological issues involved in building corpora for interpreting studies; (4) corpus-based empirical interpreting studies and research methodologies; (5) corpus-based interpreting teaching. Although CIS in China had lagged behind its development in the west, it has achieved rapid growth within a short period of time. As far as the research topics are concerned, CIS focus more on the features of the interpreting texts, translation strategies, and translation norms. Most of the investigations are carried out in the manner of parallel model and abide by the methodology on which CTS depends. Conference interpreting studies has been given more attention than other forms of interpreting.

HYPOTHESES TESTING IN THE CHINESE-ENGLISH CONTEXT

Corpus-based Translation Studies (CTS), in essence, involves hypotheses testing mainly in a top-down manner. Among the most explored topics, (universal) features of translated language, translation universals and translator's style have attracted much more attention in China as in other parts of the world. The research findings, however, do not always conform to the available hypotheses. Some support them while others disagree with findings of similar research designs in the Indo-European context. This has led to a re-examination of the established methodology from the perspective of Chinese-English translation.

Translation universals

Testing of the same hypothesis in different contexts of language pairs produces different results. According to the hypothesis of normalisation, translations tend to exaggerate the typical linguistic patterns of the target language. Based on the Corpus of Translated Finnish (CTF), Tirkkonen-Condit put forward the "unique items hypothesis" by which she means translated texts would manifest lower frequencies of linguistic elements that lack linguistic counterparts in the source languages (Tirkkonen-Condit 2002:209). Since those unique items are frequently and typically used in the non-translated language, the lower frequency of them in translated texts shows that the hypothesis is against the so-called universal feature of normalisation. Similar investigation has been made in the English-Chinese context. In Mandarin Chinese, *bǎ*-construction is a frequently used syntactic construction indicating "dispose" something. According to Ke's (2003) investigation, the frequency of *bǎ*-construction in translated Chinese is much higher than that in non-translated Chinese and there is also more use of it in fictional texts than in non-fictional texts. Since the *bǎ*-construction is often employed to express some complicated meanings in an unambiguous manner, the frequency of *bǎ*-construction in translated Chinese shows the tendency of explicitation of the translated text. The researches done by both Tirkkonen-Condit and Ke are about the use of target language (TL) unique items in translations but the results differ a great deal from each other. Ke (2005) makes the conclusion that explicitation and implicitation usually co-occur in translation and they are subject to many constraints such as degree of formalisation of language, direction of translation, personal preference of translator, social and cultural factors, etc. That, to a certain extent, explains the disagreement between the local studies of translation universals.

Translator's style

As far as translator's style is concerned, Baker (2000) proposes a methodology which focuses on corpus statistics, such as the standardised type-token ratio (STTR), mean sentence length (MSL) and reporting structures exemplified by the frequencies of the reporting verb SAY in all its forms, to explore into the distinctive ways of translating of two literary translators. The methodology proves to be effective. Nevertheless, Huang and Chu (2014) replicate the methodology in their examination of the translator's style of Howard Goldblatt, a research professor and translator who has translated many modern and contemporary Chinese novels into English. They select 17 works by different writers translated by Goldblatt independently as the corpus for investigating his translating style. Since the translator's style should be the "way of translating" which "distinguishes the translator's work from that of others" (Saldanha 2011: 31), the translated works by Gladys Yang, another renowned translator who had translated many contemporary Chinese novels, are used as a comparable corpus. The textual characteristics of translations by Goldblatt and Yang are shown in Table 1:

Table-1 A comparison between Goldblatt and Yang in terms of corpus statistics

Translator	STTR	M.sentence length
Goldblatt	44. 99	15. 17
Yang	46. 01	11. 92
Discrepancy	1. 12	3. 25

It may be noticed in Table-1 that the discrepancy between STTR for Goldblatt (44. 99) and Yang (46. 01) is 1.12, and that between Mean sentence lengths of the two translators is only 3.25. These differences between the two groups of statistics are not significant enough to decide Goldblatt and Yang differ in their translating styles in terms of lexical diversity or sentential complexity. The research findings show that, as far as translation of Chinese novels is concerned, statistics provided by computer software cannot always effectively tell one translator from another. It is proposed by Huang and Chu (2014) that translator's style, in accordance with the binary classification of translation universals, namely S-universals and T-universals, be categorized into two sub-types: S-type (source text type) and T-type (target text type). The former refers to the regularities manifested in the distinctive strategies adopted by a translator in coping with specific source language phenomena in all his or her translations, while the latter focuses on the habitual linguistic behaviour of individual translators. The S-type is "a way of responding to the source text" (Saldanha 2011:27) regularly. Compared with the T-type translator's style, the S-type, which shows consistently in all the translated works by the same translator, can differentiate one translator from another regardless of the source texts and is of more significance in terms of translation studies. Huang (2014) makes a further investigation into the S-type of translator's style by analysing the treatment of discourse presentations in three English translations of *Luotuo Xiangzi* (《骆驼祥子》*Camel Xiangzi*), a classic work in Chinese literary history by Lao She. In translating the ambiguous forms of discourse presentations in the Chinese novel, it is for the translator to decide on the person and the tense in the target text which may result in target texts with quite different effects on the readers. The investigations show that, in terms of corpus statistics, the three translations of the same source texts show similar features in STTR, MSL, and the frequency of optional reporting *that*. The translator's style based on Baker's (2000) methodology are more similar to translational style or the style/feature of the translational language, which is the object of study in the research of translation universals. In contrast, the translator's style detected in this way is the patterned linguistic features resulting from the translator's subconscious choices and belongs to what we term as the T-type translator's style. Since the source text is given, it is the translator's choice that makes a difference in the effect on the target language readers. The results to some extent confirm the dual nature of translator's style.

In less than a decade, CTS in China had experienced the introducing period and a rapid development and have achieved much progress. Within the non-Indo-European context, some of the previously advocated hypotheses or methodologies are challenged, polished or reformulated. Relevant investigations in China have provided some distinctive perspectives for the research paradigm. Some of the new topics are attempted and further probed into. The above mentioned researches on translation universals or translator's style indicate that although statistics provided by corpus tools are effective in revealing some of the phenomena which we cannot notice otherwise, they are still far from enough to sustain CTS as a methodology or paradigm. More efforts have to be paid to the corpus-based textual or linguistic analysis itself and the interpretation of it afterwards.

FURTHER DEVELOPMENT AND PROSPECT

In recent years, there are many CTS projects which have won support of the National Social Science Fund or the Humanities and Social Science Fund of the Ministry of Education in China. "The China English-Chinese Parallel Corpus (CECPC): Construction and Application" designed by the National Research Centre for Foreign Language Education, Beijing Foreign Studies University, for instance, is a project that gained support from the Major Program of the National Social Science Fund (see Wang 2012; Huang and Qin 2015). Research topics, such as corpus-based studies of collocation, diachronic language changes, translational norms, construction of multimodal corpus for interpreting studies, etc. are being further explored. A large number of monographs and papers on CTS have been published at home and abroad. For instance, the "CTS Library" is a series of monographs on CTS published by the Shanghai Jiaotong University Press that demonstrate the latest development of CTS in China; *Corpus Linguistics and Linguistic Theory* produced a special issue of "Translation and contrastive linguistic studies at the interface of English and Chinese" in 2014.

Development of new topics

The phenomenon of language changes brought by translation has always been a focus of attention in language as well as translation studies. Diachronic corpora are more contributive in locating the changes of different periods of time. In her keynote speech, Laviosa makes a summary of the achievements attained by CTS previously at the International Conference and Workshop on Corpora and Translation Studies held in Shanghai in 2007. Translation universals are still a major topic by then but the methodology for investigation has been greatly improved. New topics have gone beyond translated texts themselves and extended to language changes brought about by translations. As a super-large-scale bilingual parallel corpus, the CECPC is diachronically designed with a target size of 100 million words (including 50 million for general purpose and 50 million for specialised purpose). Representativeness of texts, balance between different types and segmentation of time span are taken into account in advance in the design. The collection of textual materials covers a century from 1910 to 2010 with every 20 years as a sub-corpus. The corpus includes five major genres, namely literary, journalistic, political, scientific and practical. The specialised section contains a series of parallel sub-corpora in the field of current affairs, transportation, financial, interpreting, etc. An on-line data retrieval platform is being built. The project aims at providing substantial data for translation studies, contrastive linguistic studies, language contact, diachronic Chinese change, interpreting studies, ESP researches, etc.

A part of the CECPC has been used for preliminary investigations into interactions between translated Chinese and original Chinese, and the diachronic changes of the Chinese language brought by translation at different historical periods (e.g. Zhao and Wang 2013, 2014; Zhao 2014). Based on corpus materials of the period of 1915-1949, Zhao and Wang (2013) makes the hypothesis that, diachronically speaking, Chinese-English translations would show differentfeatures when they are variously positioned (i.e. either in the center or at a peripheral position of the whole literary system) and changes in the features of translations might take place diachronically, closely relating to the position of translations within the whole Chinese literary system. For instance, as far as literary texts are concerned, translated Chinese texts differ conspicuously from their counterparts in terms of standardised type-token ration, average sentence length and average clause length in different historical periods including the time spans of 1905-1910, 1915-1920, 1925-1930, 1935-1940 and 1945-1949.

Exploration in the multimodal interpreting corpora

One of the recent trends in CIS worldwide is the construction of multimodal interpreting corpora. Liu and Hu (2015) introduces the annotation scheme of a multimodal corpus for interpreting studies at Shanghai Jiaotong University, in terms of collection of audio and visual materials, segment and transcription, multi-tier annotation model including annotation of verbal and nonverbal signs, paralinguistic features, alignment of source text and target text in line with the time axis, assessment of annotation reliability, etc. The multimodal corpus can be applied to interpreting studies and machine translations.

Corpus tools development

Since the Chinese language differ from the alphabetising English morphologically, the Indo-European language-based design of some software often has difficulty in processing the Chinese texts. For instance, a English text is made up of individual words while a Chinese text is composed by Chinese characters which can be combined into one-character, two-character, three-character or four-character words. As a result, a Chinese text has to be segmented into words before it is further processed. Moreover, the tagging system for it is quite different from that for the alphabetical languages. Besides, the complexity of sentence in Chinese and some alphabetical language cannot be calculated by the same way of measurement. All of those peculiarities of the Chinese language contribute to the incompatibility of western developed tools.

Consequently, Chinese scholars have already developed their own corpus tools. For instance, Liang and Xiong (2008) introduce the PatCount, a type of text processing software, which is designed by themselves and can be used to count the frequency of lexical, syntactic and discoursal features, that is, both explicit and implicit features contained in texts. Liang and Xu (2012) present the design of a software system which can greatly facilitate metadata creation, paragraph-level alignment as well as sentence level alignment and can be of great help in building parallel corpora. Xu and Jia (2013) designed the R-gram Based Corpus Analysis Tool "PowerConc" which can fulfill major functionalities of concordancing, wordlist generation and keyword analysis more effectively. What underlies the whole design of PowerConc, according to Xu and Jia (2013), is the inventive synergy of regular expressions and N-gram. All of those technological innovation offer substantial support to the development of CTS in China.

Corpora of various language pairs

Besides, corpora beyond the English-Chinese language pair are also being built in China for specific theoretical or practical purposes. For instance, the Japanese-Chinese Parallel Corpus, the Japanese-Chinese Interpreting Parallel Corpus, the parallel Russian-Chinese corpus of academic texts. Those corpora are employed to explore similar research topics such as features of translated language, or translation universals, translator's style, etc. in different contexts. The findings are supplementary to the investigation in the Chinese-English context.

In around one and a half decade, Corpus-based Translation (Interpreting) Studies (CTS/CIS) in China has made its contributions to the evolution of the new research paradigm theoretically and methodologically. Its development presents some characteristics. To begin with, the focus is shifted from the translation proper to the context of translation, that is, from translated texts to factors that constrain the translation text production and to the changes taking place in the target language; secondly, there is a shift from description to explanation with an increase in empiricism and multi-disciplinariness; thirdly, the single comparable or parallel research model, or an integrated one of both has been replaced by the multiple-complex model in relation to researchneeds; fourthly, in terms of research model, there is a tendency toward process and causality.

New trends

The efforts to be made in future include the following respects: (1) further exploration of the nature of translated language as a linguistic variety and the diachronic changes brought to the target language, explicitly or implicitly; (2) more focus on the cognitive or psychological process of translation or interpreting, with the help of modern technology, eye-tracking system for instance; (3) establishment of independent CIS methodology for interpreting studies; (4) building of multi-modal corpora of various types which can be more widely used both theoretically and practically; (5) building of translation oriented corpora of language for specific purposes (LSP) and application of them in corresponding areas.

Related topics within this volume:

Computer-aided Translation

Computational linguistics and Translation Study

Corpus Methods for Empirical Translation Studies

(本文原载 Shie & Gao (eds), *The Routledge Handbook of Chinese Translation*, London: Routledge, 2017.作者为王克非、黄立波)

REFERENCES

Mona Baker, "Corpus Linguistics and Translation Studies: Implications and Applications", Mona Baker, Gill Francis and Elena Tognini-Bonelli (eds.), *Text and Technology: In Honour of John Sinclair*. Amsterdam: John Benjamins, 1993, pp.233–250.

Mona Baker, "Corpus-based Translation Studies: The Challenges that Lie Ahead", Somers Harold (eds.), *Terminology, LSP and Translation: Studies in Language Engineering in Honour of Juan C. Sager*. Amsterdam: John Benjamins, 1996, pp.175–186.

Mona Baker,"Towards a Methodology for Investigating the Style of a Literary Translator",*Target*,2000,Vol.12,No.2,pp.241-266.

Charlotte Bosseaux,*How Does it Feel? Point of View in Translation:The Case of Virginia Woolf into French*.Amsterdam:Rodopi,2007.

Andrew Chesterman,"Beyond the Particular",Anna Mauranen and Kujamäki Pekka (eds.),*Translation Universals:Do They Exist?* Amsterdam:John Benjamins,2004,pp.33-49.

戴光荣:《译文源语透过效应研究》,上海交通大学出版社 2013 年版。

丁树德:《浅谈西方翻译语料库研究》,《外国语》2001 年第 5 期。

Zhao-Ming Gao,"The Design of a Searching System of Chinese-English Translational Equivalent Sentence Pairs",*Proceedings of the 6th Symposium of Translation and Interpreting Teaching*,Taipei,Jan 19,2002.

胡显耀:《基于语料库的汉语翻译小说词语特征研究》,《外语教学与研究》2007 年第 39 卷第 3 期。

胡显耀:《现代汉语语料库翻译研究》,外语出版社 2008 年版。

Libo Huang,and Chiyu Chu,"Translator's Style or Translational Style? A corpus-based Study of Style in Translated Chinese Novels",*Asia Pacific Translation and Intercultural Studies*,2014,Vol.1,No.2,pp.122-141.

黄立波:《〈骆驼祥子〉三个英译本中叙述话语的翻译——译者风格的语料库考察》,《解放军外国语学院学报》2014 年第 1 期。

黄万丽、秦洪武:《英汉平行历时语料库的创建与语料检索》,《当代外语研究》2015 年第 3 期。

Susan Hunston *Corpora in Applied Linguistics*, Cambridge: Cambridge University Press,2002.

柯飞:《语料,网路与口笔译教学》,《外语教学与研究》2002 年第 34 卷第 3 期。

柯飞:《汉语"把"字句特点,分布及英译》,《外语与外语教学》2003 年第 12 期。

柯飞:《翻译中的隐和显》,《外语教学与研究》2005 年第 37 卷第 4 期。

Sara Laviosa,"The Corpus-based Approach:A New Paradigm in Translation Studies",*Meta*,1998a,Vol.43,No.4,pp.474-479.

Sara Laviosa,"Core Patterns of Lexical Use in a Comparable Corpus of English Narrative Prose",*Meta*,1998b,Vol.43,No.4,pp.557-570.

李德超、王克非:《新型双语旅游语料库的研制和应用》,《现代外语》2010 年 33 卷第 1 期。

李德超、王克非:《基于双语旅游语料库的 DDL 翻译教学》,《外语电化教学》2001 年第 1 期。

梁茂成、熊文新:《文本分析工具 PatCount 在外语教学与研究中的应用》,《外语电化教学》2008 年第 5 期。

梁茂成、许家金:《双语语料库建设中元信息的添加和段落与句子的两级对齐》,《中国外语》2012 年 9 卷第 6 期。

廖七一:《语料库与翻译研究》,《外语教学与研究》2000 年第 32 卷第 5 期。

刘剑、胡开宝:《多模态口译语料库的建设与应用研究》,《中国外语》2015 年第 12 卷第 5 期。

刘泽权:《〈红楼梦〉中英文语料库的创建及应用研究》,光明日报出版社 2010 年版。

秦洪武、王克非:《对应语料库在翻译教学中的应用:理论依据和实施原则》,《中国翻译》2007 年第 28 卷第 5 期。

Gabriela Saldanha, "Translator Style: Methodological Considerations", *Translator*, 2011, Vol 17, No.1, pp.25-50.

Erich Teich, *Cross-linguistic Variation in System and Text: A Methodology for the Investigation of Translations and Comparable Texts*, Berlin: Mouton de Gruyter, 2003.

Sonja Tirkkonen-Condit, "Translationese—A Myth or an Empirical Fact: A Study into the Linguistic Identifiablity of Translated Language", *Target*, 2002, Vol. 14, No. 2, pp. 207-220.

Gideon Toury, *Descriptive Translation Studies and Beyond*. Amsterdam: John Benjamins, 1995.

王惠:《"精加工"平行语料库在翻译教学中的应用》,《中国翻译》2005 年第 36 卷第 1 期。

王惠、朱纯深:《翻译教学语料库的标注及应用:英文财经报道中文翻译及注释语料库》,《外语教学与研究》2012 年第 44 卷第 2 期。

王克非:《新型双语对应语料库的设计与构建》,《中国翻译》2004 年第 25 卷第 6 期,第 73—75 页。

王克非等:《双语对应语料库:研制与应用》,外语教学与研究出版社 2004 年版。

王克非、胡显耀:《基于语料库的翻译汉语词汇特征研究》,《中国翻译》2008 年第

29 卷第 6 期。

王克非、胡显耀:《汉语文学翻译中人称代词的显化和变异》,《中国外语》2010 年第 7 卷第 4 期。

王克非、秦洪武:《英译汉语言特征探讨——基于对应语料库的宏观分析》,《外语学刊》2009 年第 1 期。

王克非、秦洪武:《论平行语料库在翻译教学中的应用》,《外语教学与研究》2015 年第 47 卷第 5 期。

王克非:《中国英汉平行语料库的设计与研制》,《中国外语》2012 年第 9 卷第 6 期。

肖忠华:《英汉翻译中的汉语译文语料库研究》,上海交通大学出版社 2012 年版。

许家金、贾云龙:《基于 R-gram 的语料库分析软件 PowerConc 的设计与开发》,《外语电化教学》2013 年第 1 期。

赵秋荣:《翻译与现代汉语中数量词的使用:基于历时语料库的分析》,《外文研究》2014 年第 2 卷第 4 期。

赵秋荣、王克非:《现代汉语话语重述标记的语料库考察》,《中国翻译》2014 年第 35 卷第 5 期。

赵秋荣、王克非:《英译汉翻译语言的阶段性特点:基于历时类比语料库的考察》,《中国翻译》2013 年第 34 卷第 3 期。

朱纯深、慕媛媛:《以文本解释力为导向的语料库翻译教学:香港城大翻译与双语写作在线教学/自学平台的设计与试用分析》,《中国翻译》2013 年第 34 卷第 2 期。

FURTHER READING:

Kaibao Hu, *Introducing Corpus-based Translation Studies*. Berlin: Springer, 2016. (The book has provided not only an outline of what has been and will be done in corpus-based translation studies but also guidance on how to carry out corpus-based translation studies and interpreting studies. Some major topics of corpus-based translation studies have been introduced.)

胡开宝 Kaibao Hu,《基于语料库的莎士比亚戏剧汉译研究》(*A Corpus-based Study of the Chinese Translations of Shakespeare's Plays*), Shanghai: Shanghai Jiaotong University Press, 2015. (The study in this book is based on a specialised bilingual parallel literary corpus of Shakespeare's plays covering topics such as translation universals, features of translated language, translation strategies, etc.)

Libo Huang, *Style in Translation: A corpus-based perspective*, Berlin: Springer, 2015. (The book attempts to explore styles involved in literary translation with a corpus-based approach. The style in translation is approached from perspectives of the author/the source text, the translated texts and the translator.)

王克非 Kefei Wang,《语料库翻译学探索》(*An Exploration into Corpus-based Translation Studies*), Shanghai: Shanghai Jiaotong University Press, 2012. (The book has provided a comprehensive overview of the Corpus-based Translation Studies. The achievements made by Chinese scholars in the field are introduced in detail with various case studies.)

Richard Xiao and Xianyao Hu, *Corpus-based Studies of Translational Chinese in English-Chinese Translation*, Berlin: Springer, 2015. (Based on the comparable corpus consisting of the Zhejiang Corpus of Translated Chinese (ZCTC) and the Lancaster Corpus of Mandarin Chinese (LCMC), the book presents the studies of translational Chinese from both the macro- and the micro-perspectives.)

英汉/汉英语句对应的语料库考察

本文应用自行研制的英汉双语平行语料库考察英汉、汉英语句对应现象。研究发现,在各种语料中,1∶1的对应语句都占多数;从文学汉译英、非文学汉译英、文学英译汉到非文学英译汉,在这四种语料中1∶1语句对应呈递增曲线。从语句对应扩展到语篇考察,发现无论英译汉或汉译英,都呈现目标语文本扩增特点,不同类型的文本在扩增程度上有差别。

一、平行语料库与语言考察

语料库语言学是近三十年发展起来的分支学科。它的主要任务和目标是,以电脑储存足量的真实语料,对这些语料做各种带有研究目的的标注,利用研制的检索工具对标注语料作方便快捷地搜寻和分析,试图发现以往因条件所限而未能发现或未注意的语言事实和特征。当然,要做到上述每一步都不容易,都需要艰苦的努力。单语语料库如此,双语平行语料库更是如此。双语平行对应,就是两种语言经过翻译后的对应;有单向(uni-directional)的对译,如从英语译成汉语,英语是原语,汉语是译语;有双向(bi-directional)的对译,如从英语译成汉语,和从汉语译成英语,英语与汉语的语料里均既有原语又有译语。创建双语语料库比单语语料库困难之处在于:1)双语对应的语料不及单语的丰富;2)要寻找合适的对译文本,不能收翻译得过于僵硬的译本,也不能收翻译得过于随意的译本;3)语料选材要考虑代表性,即不可全是文学经典或全非文学经典(all-or-none classical texts),并确保可比性(参看 Halverson 1998);4)双语是否对应(尤其是在句子层级的对应),需要花费更多的力量做检查、校对。但它特有的价值却是单语语料库所不具备的,因为它可供两种或两种以上语言作对比研究,可以为翻译研究者提供素材,可以为双语词典的编纂提供更多可挑选的语料。简言之,双语平行语料库为相关研究者展现了一个令人兴致勃勃的研究领域,也使语言研究者和翻译研究者有更多合作的空间(参看 Baker 1993;Malmkjær 1998;王克非 2002)。

鉴于语料库在基础研究中的重要性,我们近两年自行研制了一个 3000 万字词的大型英汉双语平行语料库。在创建之初,我们充分考虑到将来开展语言与翻译多重研究的需要,并考察了国外语料库研制情况,将本库设计为既有英译汉,又有汉译英,既有文学文本,又有非文学文本(非文学部分另分人文、社会科学、自然科学三大类、十二小类,文学部分另分小说、散文、剧本三类),既有百科抽样语料,又有翻译全本语料的综合性双语平行语料库(参看王克非 2001)。目前本库已收录 3000 多万字词的英汉/汉英双语对应语料,其中含 2000 万字词以上的句级对齐语料,近 1000 万字词已初步标注的可检索语料。

关于双语语料库的库容计算单位,国内外尚未见有研究论及(目前世界上的双语语料库,包括翻译和可比语料库,多是印欧语系各语言的,以词为单位,因其语词之间有间隔,不像汉语语词之间无间隔);本库对中、英文分别采用字、词为单位,即中文部分以字为单位(用词为单位最理想,但很难统计),英文部分以词为单位,这样可以准确快捷地反映语料库的大小,也方便我们讨论双语语句语篇在量上的对应。

英语与汉语语句对应的问题,在双方都是原语的情况下很难找到作比较的材料,只能通过双语对译来观察。这也是双语平行语料库的重要研究功用。例如国际上有人做过英语和葡萄牙语、英语和挪威语以及其他语言之间的语料对比研究(分别见 Maia 1998;Ebeling 1998;Øverås 1998)。本文以英汉平行语料库为资源,探讨以下语句对应问题:

1)英汉对译在语句层面的对应比例,这涉及翻译的单位;

2)不同类型的文本或不同翻译方向的文本其对应比例有无特点?

3)英汉互译后的文本在文字量上有何变化?

这些问题以前均未见有探讨，我们希望借助平行语料库对此作出一个初步的回答。

二、英汉、汉英语句对应问题

一部英文书翻译成中文，或一部中文书翻译成英文，其中数以百计以至数以万计的句子是如何对应的？几乎可以肯定不会逐句一一对应，因这两种语言在各层面上有较大的差异，但并未见到相关的调查和数据。这个问题不是通过一两本译作的考察就可以得出结论的，应有大量的数据支撑。我们现在利用1000万字词的英汉平行语料库对此作一初步探讨。

我们设想汉译英与英译汉这两个方向的翻译应有各自的特点，文学文本与非文学文本在文体、遣词、修辞、句式等方面也多有区别，故将这1000万字词的平行对应语料分为汉译英文学语料、汉译英非文学语料、英译汉文学语料和英译汉非文学语料四个部分，亦即四个子库；其中汉译英约占40%，英译汉约占60%，文学与非文学文本分别占55%和45%左右。英文语料主要取自19—20世纪的文本，中文语料则取自20世纪的白话文本；较古旧的语言和诗歌语言均不收录。

我们在北京大学计算语言学研究所的支持下，用新研制的汉英自动对齐软件将收集、整理后的双语语料作句级对齐处理，对齐有效率平均达85%以上（视文本质量而有所不同），并经过仔细的人工校对、调整，达到全部句级对齐。识别为句子的标准是句号、分号、问号以及经过判断的感叹号和冒号等（因感叹号和冒号不总是标志一个句子）。对齐处理过的语料，程序会自动标注句对比例，即中英文对应语句是1∶1或1∶2、2∶1、1∶3、3∶1、2∶2等句对比例（本文设定比号前为中文句数，比号后为英文句数，即1∶2表示1句中文对应2句英文，2∶1表示2句中文对应1句英文，其余类推）。用检索软件作随机抽样检索。表1和表2分别是汉英/英汉抽样语句对应比例。

从表1和表2的数据可以做出以下分析。

1）1∶1的语句对应比例在汉英、英汉对译文本中都呈现出高频特点，从大约 60%的比例到 90%以上的比例不等,并与汉英、英汉翻译方向和文学、非文学文本类型有很大关系。在汉译英文学语料中,1 ∶ 1 对应比例为 54%—82%,平均 63.3%;汉译英非文学语料中,1 ∶ 1 对应比例为 64%—91%,平均 80.2%;英译汉文学语料中,1 ∶ 1 对应比例为 70%—97%,平均 81.9%;英译汉非文学语料中,1 ∶ 1 对应比例为 71%—94%,平均 84.7%。可以看出在这四类语料中,对应比例呈递增曲线。从翻译方向看,英译汉时语句一一对应的比例高于汉译英。从文本类型看,非文学文本的英、汉语句一一对应比例高于文学文本。

表 1　汉英语句对应比例

译本种类		句对总数	1∶1 句对数及其百分比		1∶2 句对数及其百分比		2∶1 句对数及其百分比		1∶3 句对数及其百分比		其他比例数
汉译英（文学）	散文 1	55	41	74%	9	16%	2	0.36%			
	散文 2	50	27	54%	5	10%	11	22%			
	散文 3	43	27	63%	11	25%	3	0.7%			
	散文 4	57	35	61%	10	17%	8	14%			
	散文 5	159	104	65%	18	11%	17	10.7%	20	4.1%	
	小说 1	481	282	58%	121	25%	16	3.3%	65	7%	15(2∶2)
	小说 2	934	543	58%	245	26%	25	2.7%	32	7%	
	小说 3	456	280	61%	118	25.8%	6	1.3%	115	9.4%	
	小说 4	1217	654	54%	362	29.7%	22	1.8%	72	10%	
	小说 5	722	426	59%	173	27%	10	1.4%	20	4.1%	
	小说 6	223	135	60%	50	22.4%	9	4.0%			
	小说 7	712	478	67%	186	26%	33	4.6%	33	4.6%	
	小说 8	475	335	70%	81	17%	15	3.1%			
	小说 9	216	177	82%	16	7.4%	14	6.5%			
	（平均）		63.3%		19.7%		5.5%				
汉译英（非文学）	文本 1	429	392	91%	25	5.8%	7	1.6%			
	文本 2	711	603	84%	75	10.5%	6	0.8%	22	3.1%	
	文本 3	188	148	78%	15	7.9%	17	9%			
	文本 4	261	195	74%	48	18.3%	6	2.2%			
	文本 5	195	143	73%	32	16.4%	10	5.1%			

续表

译本种类		句对总数	1∶1句对数及其百分比		1∶2句对数及其百分比		2∶1句对数及其百分比		1∶3句对数及其百分比		其他比例数
汉译英（非文学）	文本6	196	159	81%	25	12.7%	3	1.5%			
	文本7	379	317	83%	41	10.8%	7	1.8%			
	文本8	197	143	72%	32	16.2%	10	5.1%			
	文本9	735	671	91%	13	1.7%	1	0.1%	1		
	文本10	56	49	87%	41	7.1%	1	1.7%	1		
	文本11	48	75	64%	5	31.2%	7	14.5%	3	6%	
	文本12	170	153	90%	15	8.8%	1	0.6%			
	文本13	76	53	70%	12	15.7%	3	3.9%			
	文本14	80	61	76%	15	18.7%	2	0.3%			
	文本15	54	48	89%	4	7.4 %	1	1.9%			
	（平均）		80.2%		12.6%		3.4%				

表2　英汉语句对应比例

译本种类		句对总数	1∶1句对数及其百分比		1∶2句对数及其百分比		2∶1句对数及其百分比		1∶3句对数及其百分比		其他比例数
英译汉（文学）	散文1	172	158	92%	10	5.8%	2	1.2%	2		
	散文2	62	46	74%	11	17.7%	4	6.4%	0		
	散文3	223	182	82%	28	12.5%	3	1.3%	4		
	散文4	38	29	76%	1	2.6%	6	15.7%	1		
	小说1	2380	1833	77%	351	14.7%	97	4%	47	1.9%	5(3∶1)
	小说2	1910	1863	97%	26	1.3%	17	0.8%			
	小说3	2152	1608	75%	206	9.5%	255	11.8%	9	0.4%	28(3∶1),22(2∶2)
	小说4	2438	2013	86%	146	6.0%	219	9%	15	0.6%	17(3∶1),20(2∶2)
	小说5	2389	2066	86%	173	7.2%	119	5%	7	0.3%	4(3∶1),14(2∶2)
	小说6	147	119	81%	13	8.8%	10	6.8%	3	2%	
	小说7	822	697	84%	61	7.4%	47	5.7%	5	0.6%	

续表

译本种类		句对总数	1∶1 句对数及其百分比		1∶2 句对数及其百分比		2∶1 句对数及其百分比		1∶3 句对数及其百分比		其他比例数
英译汉（文学）	小说 8	1448	1331	92%	57	3.9%	43	3%	6	0.4%	
	小说 9	118	90	76%	9	7.6%	16	13.5%			
	小说 10	203	144	71%	34	16.7%	9	4.4%			
	小说 11	365	299	82%	37	10.1%	18	4.9%	3	0.8%	
	小说 12	303	251	83%	27	8.9%	18	5.9%			
	小说 13	249	209	84%	19	7.6%	15	6%			
	小说 14	547	520	95%	19	3.4%	6	1.1%			
	小说 15	121	85	70%	13	10.7%	13	10.7%			
	小说 16	100	72	72%	17	17%	7	7%			
	小说 17	144	123	85%	4	2.8%	11	7.6%			
	（平均）		81.9%		8.7%		6.3%				
英译汉（非文学）	文本 1	1266	1085	85%	41	3.2%	103	8.1%			
	文本 2	493	455	92%	14	2.8%	21	4.2%			
	文本 3	1079	966	89%	90	8.3%	13	1.2%			
	文本 4	1210	1012	83%	123	10.1%	5	0.4%			
	文本 5	479	425	88%	33	6.9%	15	3.1%			
	文本 6	130	101	78%	12	9.2%	15	11.5%			
	文本 7	62	45	72%	7	11.3%	10	16.1%			
	文本 8	127	111	87%	10	7.8%	4	3.1%			
	文本 9	55	39	71%	6	10.9%	5	0.9%			
	文本 10	61	50	82%	2	3.2%	3	4.9%			
	文本 11	41	36	88%	1	2.4%	4	9.7%			
	文本 12	67	58	86%	5	7.4%	2	3%			
	文本 13	33	27	82%	2	6%	4	12.1%			
	文本 14	3140	2750	87%	143	4.5%	181	5.7%	8	0.25%	
	文本 15	369	348	94%	13	3.5%	6	1.6%	1	0.27%	
	文本 16	1973	1786	90%	105	5.3%	51	2.6%	7	0.35%	
	文本 17	183	158	86%	9	4.9%	13	7.1%			
	（平均）		84.7%		6.3%		5.6%				

（表1表2内文本为随机取样；不足1万字词的文本基本取完本，超过此数的长文本则随机取其章节。）

2）语句对应关系间接反映翻译转换单位。翻译单位是翻译研究的一个重点问题，国内外学界对此有许多论述，涉及以词、词组、小句、句子以及句群等为翻译的单位（关于其讨论，可分别参看巴尔胡达罗夫 1985；罗选民 1992；葛校琴 1993；司显柱 2001 等）。但从本文的发现看，句子仍不失为翻译的一个主要转换单位，特别是除文学汉译英之外的另三类翻译，其 1∶1 的句对比例均达到 80%以上。即使是文学汉译英，也有近三分之二的 1∶1 句对比例。这一点在翻译教学上，特别是在自动翻译研究上，有引人重视的价值。

3）由表1和表2还可以看到，除 1∶1 句对外，比较常见的是 1∶2 和 2∶1 的句对；这两者加上 1∶1 的句对，通常占全部对应语句的 90%以上（除文学汉译英中这部分不足 90%外，其余三类均在 96%以上）。其余如 1∶3、3∶1、2∶2、2∶3、1∶4 等都只占几乎可以忽略的比例。无论汉译英或英译汉，1∶2 句对多于 2∶1，1∶3 句对多于 3∶1，表明汉语的句子长于英语的，即通常将汉语转换成英语时，一句拆译成两句的较多，反过来，英语转换成汉语时，两句合并成一句的较多。

4）中英文句子在断句、标点上的差异是影响 1∶1 对应比例以及导致中文一句对两句甚至多句英文现象多发的主要原因。英文在句法上比较严格，一句话用逗号还是句号标记，形式上有所限制，很难随意处理。中文则不同，本来就多流水句，加上断句多凭语意，甚至凭喜好，以句号断句的完整句子中就常常含有多个小句，转换成英文时只得以多句与之对应。如文学汉译英“小说4”、“小说5”出自钱锺书文笔，不仅 1∶1 语句对应比例较低，其 1∶2 和 1∶3 的比例也是最高的。这是其文本中完整句子里含小句多的缘故。请看两例：

◆〖1∶2〗

<s>你说笑话也得有个分寸，以后不许你开口——</s>

<s> Your joking can go too far.</s>

<s> From now on, you're to keep your mouth shut.</s>

◆【1：3】

<s>他抗议无用，苏小姐说什么就要什么，他只好服从她善意的独裁。</s>

<s> His protests were in vain.</s>

<s> Whatever she said must be.</s>

<s> He just had to submit to her benevolent dictatorship.</s>

5）作者的行文习惯与译者的翻译策略也是语句对应比例的影响因子。例如表2文学英译汉"小说2"的1：1语句对应比例高达97%，是因为这是海明威作品《老人与海》的翻译。作者行文简洁，少有冗长套句；译者尊重原文风格，尽可能一一对应。同样是英译汉文学作品，译者虽多按照原文转译成中文，但有时也会随手"一逗到底"，如下例：

◆【1：5】

<s>现在他住在佛罗里达，说是依阿华的一个朋友送过他一本我写的书，他看了，他妹妹卡洛琳也看了这本书，他们现在有一个故事，想必我会感兴趣。</s>

<s>He lives in Florida now.</s>

<s>A friend from Iowa has sent him one of my books.</s>

<s>Michael Johnson has read it;</s>

<s>his sister, Carolyn, has read it;</s>

<s>and they have a story in which they think 1 might be interested.</s>

这是《廊桥遗梦》英译汉中的句对。译者其实是可以照原文断句的，那样的话，句对比例就不是1：5了（不过这样的例子在此书中并不多见，基本上还是参照原文句式翻译）。这也表明，英汉1：1的语句对应比例还可能更高。

6）译文受原文影响的程度有差异。英译汉1：1的语句对应高于汉译英，主要原因是汉语译者翻译时多参照原文的句式和标点，特别是在比较严肃的文本中。而英语译者参照汉语原文较少，更多的时候是依从英语的表达习惯；当然这里面含有上述第4）条断句差异的因素。

三、英汉、汉英互译文本的文字量变化

1. 互译文本的文字量对应比例考察

两种语言互译后通常都会涉及原文文本与译文文本的文字量上的变化。一般来说，两种语言对译总有一个文字量对应比例，该比例可设为中间值，超过此比例越多，可认为是越接近过量翻译（overtranslation），低于此比例越多，则可认为是越接近欠量翻译（undertranslation）。例如，英语译成汉语时，根据经验，每1000词对译成1700—1800汉字，超过或低于此数过多，就可能是过量或欠量的翻译。这对于翻译教学或大致了解某一翻译量及其质量都有帮助。那么汉语同英语互译时的文字量对应比例是多少？双向转换时对应比例有何变化？我们从平行语料库大量的对译材料来考察。

我们抽查了550万字词的英汉、汉英语料，其中英译汉文本略多于汉译英，文学译本略多于非文学译本。表3是互译文本的文字量对应比例。

表3　英汉、汉英互译文本的文字量对应比例

译本种类	考察语料数	英、中文词、字数比例范围	常见英、中文词、字数比例范围	平均字词数比例
汉译英（文学）	150万字词	1∶0.95—1∶1.7	1∶1.25—1∶1.5	1∶1.41
汉译英（非文学）	100万字词	1∶0.85—1∶1.6	1∶1.20—1∶1.4	1∶1.33
英译汉（文学）	170万字词	1∶1.55—1∶2.1	1∶1.65—1∶1.9	1∶1.79
英译汉（非文学）	130万字词	1∶1.45—1∶1.9	1∶1.60—1∶1.8	1∶1.72

从表3可以看出，汉译英时英文与中文的词、字数比例多为1000英文词对应1200—1500汉字，即1200—1500汉字可能译成1000英文词；英译汉时英文与中文的词、字数比例多为1000英文词对应1600—1900汉字。文学与非文学类文本略有差别。进一步从平均值看，汉译英时每1000英文词对应1330—1410汉字，英译汉时每1000英文词对应1720—1790汉字；这大致是英汉语言转换时的对应比例中间值。

2. 英汉互译后呈目标语文本扩增特点

值得注意的是,英汉/汉英两个方向的翻译,其对应比例中间值有较大差异,相当于每1000英文词有350—400汉字的差距。因为从理论上讲,英译汉时每1000英文词可对译为1800汉字的话,则反过来,汉译英时每1800左右的汉字可对译为1000英文词。但实际情况却不是这样,而是我们通过语料库考察大量语料后发现的上述有差异的对应比例。

我们对这一现象的解释是,英汉语互译后发生目标语扩增。Blum-Kulka(1986)认为,译者对原文进行解译的过程,有可能使目标语文本比原文本冗长。Øverås(1998:16)做英语同挪威语翻译对应研究时也证实了这一点。她的发现是英译挪时比挪译英时文本扩增得更大。我们从英汉语翻译对应的语料考察看,应是两个方向都发生目标语扩增。若按英译汉的情况,每1000英文词对应于1750汉字,那么汉译英时1750汉字应可对应1000英文词,而实际考察结果是约1300汉字即可对译为1000英文词,1750汉字约可译成1340英文词,即汉译英时发生了目标语扩增。反过来,若按汉译英的情况,每1000英文词对应于1350汉字,则又与考察结果反映的每1000英文词对应于1750汉字相距较大,可认为是英译汉时发生了目标语扩增。取中间值为每1000英文词对应1550汉字,则可认为英汉互译均发生目标语扩增。

我们曾以汉译英的文本做了一个小实验。将英译文(不易发觉是译自汉语)交给10位英语专业硕士研究生以上学历的受试,让分别将其译为汉语(实为回译)。下面是该英译文及其汉语译文和原文。

When Uncle's family was building a house, we thought of using it to pile up a side of the house wall. This proved to be impossible, however, since the rock was of an extremely irregular shape, possessing neither sharp right angles nor any smooth, flat surfaces. We could have used a chisel to break the rock up, but no one could be bothered to expend such a great deal of effort over it; the riverbank was only a short distance away, and any old rock that we brought back from there would have been easier to use than this one. Then, when the house was nearly completed, and we were looking for something for the front steps. Uncle didn't think that the rock was even good enough for that. Another time, we had a stonemason come to grind a millstone for us. Grandmother again persuaded: "Why don't you just use this piece of rock, and save yourself the trouble of hauling another piece over from somewhere far away?" The stonemason took a good long look at the rock, and shook his head: he thought the rock's texture too fine, and unsuitable for making the mill.(195 词)

［试译文］ 伯父家盖房子时，我们曾想到用它垒一面屋墙，但最后还是没能用上，因为这块岩石外形太不规则，既没有尖利的直角，又没有光滑的平面。我们用凿子凿开它吧，可是没人愿费那么大气力。河边没多远，我们随便从那儿搬运一块石头回来都比用这块岩石省劲。后来，房子快盖好了，我们又要找石头做房前的台阶。伯父还是觉得那块岩石不太合适。还有一次，我们请了一个石匠来给我们做磨盘。奶奶又提议说："你干吗不用那块石头，省得从大老远的地方费劲另外弄一块来呀。"石匠把那石头看了好一阵，摇摇头说，那块石头材质太细，不适合做石磨。(246 字)

［贾平凹原文］ 伯父家盖房，想以它垒山墙，但苦于它极不规则，没棱角儿，也没平面儿；用錾破开吧，又懒得花那么大气力，因为河滩并不甚远，随便去掮一块回来，哪一块也比它强。房盖起来，压铺台阶，伯父也没有看上它。有一年，来了一个石匠，为我家洗一台石磨，奶奶又说：用这块丑石吧，省得从远处搬运。石匠看了看，摇着头，嫌它石质太细，也不采用。(156 字)

将汉语原文同英译文以及后来的汉语回译相比较，就可看出汉译英时已大为扩增(其英汉比例为 1∶0.8，远超出表 3 里的对应比例)。回译(选择翻译较好的一篇)尽管还不错，但其文字已比原来的汉语文字多出 90 字，增幅达 57%。

下面的两例英译汉(取自语料库)则代表性地反映汉语译者由于受原文影响而导致的目标语扩增的情况；我们在括号里给出较好的译文。

It was one of the few gestures of sentiment he was ever to make.

但那是他在感情方面所作出的很少的几次表示中的 一个例子。

(他很少表露感情，这是难得的一次。)

Can you tell me where is your cereal section?

您能告诉我你们的粮食科在哪里吗?

(请问粮食科在哪儿?)

至于英汉互译对应文本扩增的更多原因,以及其中的外显化现象,我们将另文探讨。

(本文原载《外语教学与研究》2003 年第 6 期)

参考文献

M.Baker,"Corpus Linguistics and Translation Studies:Implication and Application",M. Baker *et al.*(eds.),*Text and Technology:In Honour of John Sinclair*,Amsterdam:John Benjamins,1993,pp.233-250.

S.Blum-Kulka,"Shifts of Cohesion and Coherence in Translation",J. House & S. Blum-Kulka(eds.),*Interlingual and Intercultural Communication*,Tubingen:Narr,1986.

J.Ebeling,"Contrastive Linguistics,Translation,and Parallel Corpora",*Meta*,1998,Vol. 43,No.4,pp.602-615.

S. Halverson,"Translation Studies and Representative Corpora:Establishing Links between Translation Corpora,Theoretical/descriptive Categories and a Conception of the Object of Study",*Meta*,1998,Vol.43,No.4,pp.494-514.

B.Maia,"Word Order and the First Person Singular in Portuguese and English",*Meta*,1998,Vol.43,No.4,p.589.

K.Malmkjær,"Love Thy Neighbour:Will Parallel Corpora Endear Linguists to Translators?"*Meta*,1998,Vol.43,No.4,pp.534-541.

L.Øverås,"In Search of the Third Code:An Investigation of Norms in Literary Translation",*Meta*,1998,Vol.43,No.4,p.557.

巴尔胡达罗夫著,蔡毅等译:《语言与翻译》,中国对外翻译出版公司 1985 年版。

葛校琴:《句群——翻译的一个单位》,《中国翻译》1993 年第 1 期。

柯飞:《双语库:翻译研究新途径》,《外语与外语教学》2002 年第 9 期。

罗选民:《论翻译的转换单位》,《外语教学与研究》1992 年第 4 期。

司显柱:《翻译单位研究》,《翻译学报》2001 年四月号。

王克非:《语言与翻译研究并重的双语平行语料库》,《北京外国语大学校庆六十周年学术论文集》(上),外语教学与研究出版社 2001 年版。

基于超大型英汉平行语料库的英语被动结构汉译考察与分析

“被动”表述是语言中的普遍现象，但英汉语言的被动表达在形式、结构、语义和语用上存在很大差异，给英汉翻译转换带来困难。本文基于超大型英汉平行语料库，考察科技文本中英语被动结构在汉语中的对译形式，尝试从形式、句法、语义和文体四个维度揭示被动结构由英语到汉语的翻译转换中呈现的特征。研究发现，英语被动结构在翻译转换为汉语时仅有10%被译为被动结构，其他对译形式包括主动式、受事主语结构、动宾结构、名词化、处置式、兼语式和省略等形式，表现出英语被动结构汉译形式的灵活性和丰富性。

一、引言

语言都有表达“被动”的需要。英汉语言也如此，在形式上通常将受事置于主语位置，强调受事无法按照自己意志处理的行为（王力 2011［1943］：92）。但英汉语言在表达被动概念时采用的结构、语义和语用手段却迥然相异（参见王力 2011［1943］；Xiao *et al*.2006）。英语使用形态和句法相结合的手段，汉语则依赖词汇、语义手段，也可通过句法来实现。于是，在英汉翻译中，被动表述往往不以一种简单、固定的模式对等地译出。此外，英语中被动语态的使用频率远高于汉语，特别是在科技、新闻和公文等书面文体中。

对英语被动结构在汉语中对译形式的量化考察，有助于发现和归纳被动结构在翻译转换中的语言特征，揭示英汉语言在表述上的异同。同时，通过量化方法分析英语被动结构在汉语中的对译,可观察翻译受源语干扰的情形,进而考察汉语欧化现象。本文基于大型英汉平行语料库考察英语有标记被动结构的语言特征及其在汉语中的对译形式,探索各种形式的、充当不同句法功能、蕴含不同语义的英语被动结构在汉译转换中的特点。这一研究也有助于认识翻译过程中的显化、简化和常态化等翻译共性问题。

二、相关研究

“被动”是双语研究中英汉对比、英汉翻译和语言接触研究中广泛讨论的话题。Xiao,McEnery 和 Qian(2006)基于 FLOB、LCMC、BNC 的口语部分以及 Callhome 汉语普通话语料库,对比英汉口笔语语体中被动结构在长短形式、句法、功能、语义韵和文体上的差异。柯飞(2002:35-36)首先提出利用双语库考察汉语翻译文本中被动句的使用情况,并以此来为汉语欧化现象寻找依据,借此也可考察和认识被动句在双语文本中的翻译转换规律和特点。肖忠华和戴光荣(2010:57)基于 ZCTC 汉语译文语料库和 LCMC 原创汉语类比语料库探索翻译语言共性特征。李德超、唐芳(2015:94-95)对旅游翻译文本的考察结果也佐证了上述研究结果,发现旅游英语翻译文本中被动态使用远高于原创文本。胡显耀、曾佳(2010)和朱一凡、胡开宝(2014)分别对小说和新闻翻译文本中被动结构的语义韵在当代汉语小说翻译语料库和新闻汉译语料库进行了考察。

上述研究分别以语料库语言学、对比语言学、语言接触和语料库翻译研究作为出发点,借助语料库对被动式在英汉语中的使用情况进行量化分析,为传统语言学就被动形式的研究提供了数据佐证。但大部分研究仅统计被动发生的频率,未对被动态的形式、句法、语义和语用做全面考察。此外,绝大多数研究只关注翻译文本中被动的形式,而对被动结构的双语转换模式鲜有研究,只有 McEnery 和 Xiao(2005:24)用 65 万形符的小型英汉平行语料库进行了初步分析,发现大约只有 20%的 be-passive 被转换为汉语被动形式。

有鉴于此,本研究尝试回答以下问题:(1)英语被动结构译成汉语时主要呈现何种形式?具有何种分布特点?(2)被译为有标记被动结构的汉语是否与英语对等?呈现何种特点?

三、研究设计

1. 基本概念

英语的被动义既可使用主动形式表达,也可使用带标记的被动形式表达。前者最早可追溯到 Jespersen(1927:321-322)的"active-passive"结构,是一种不严格的被动结构。相反,英语句法被动具有严格结构,按照动词的形式分为"be + passive participle"与"get + passive participle"两种,并可选择性地通过介词"by"引出施事。其中,"be passive"被视作英语中的"标准形式(norm structure)"(Quirk *et al*.1985:160;Xiao *et al*.2006:111)。由于科技文体中"get-assive"极为罕见,因此为保证考察结果的客观性,本研究仅考察具有严格语法标记的英语被动结构及其汉语对译形式。

2. 语料来源

本研究使用北京外国语大学研制的"中国英汉平行语料库"(王克非 2012)。该语料库库容1亿字词(约5亿形符),是目前世界上规模最大、分类合理、采样规范、深度加工的超大型英汉平行语料库,因此基于该库的研究具有极高的可靠性。本研究使用该语料库的科技语料子库英译汉部分,共计8,586,397字词,英语源语文本和汉语翻译文本各584个,前者3,241,019词,后者5,435,378字,实现了语句级别的英、汉对齐,英文词语归元,汉语分词和中英文词性标注。

3. 分析工具与步骤

本研究使用王克非、刘鼎甲(2017)设计开发的"大规模英汉平行语料库检索平台v2.0"(支持正则表达式),可准确检索英语中所有被动结构,并精确提取其汉语对译文本。经验证,该检索平台可靠程度与AntConc、ParaConc一致(同上:9-10)。

第一,根据"be-passive"和"get-passive"的结构特点,使用"ProConc"语言编写检索表达式"[lem = be | get] ! [pos = v. *]{0,5} [pos = vvn]",在平台"双语检索"功能中选择科技文体,筛选英译汉方向语料,以句子为界,实施复杂检索,提取英语中所有句法被动结构及其汉语对译文本。经检索,"be-passive"结构检出 50696 个双语对译文本,"get-passive"则只检出 122 个,二者共计 50,818 个双语对译文本。

第二,由于检索结果数量庞大,为确保研究更具可操作性,且不影响研究结果的可靠性,我们用 R 对上述检索结果进行简单随机抽样,从上述 50,818 个句对中随机抽取 5,000 组共计 1 万行对译文本,并通过人工筛查,排除如例 1 所示的伪被动、表示情感的形容词性等无效形式(333 例)和零对应①(41 例)形式,剩余 4,626 例有效的语对,其中 4 例为"get-passive"结构,本文不作考察,只对 4621 例"be-passive"对译语例进行分析。

例 1:

a.For tubular members that must be sliced, *the constructor is concerned* about out-of-roundness and diameter tolerances.(text:enp_marineoffshoreconstructionsi)

b.It may be observed that*there has been limited change* during this period.(text:enp_offshoreriskassessmentsan)

c.*It was a term employed* in the same sense as the Mesopotamian encoded writings that were sealed from the eyes of the uninitiated.(text:enp_yuzhoumimal)

第三,通过手工方式对所筛查的有效对译语对进行观察和分析,分别对其中英语源语被动结构的形式、语法和语义特征及其汉语对译形式进行标注。具体标注内容如下页表 1 所示,表中的具体语法结构、形式或特征的定义及其语言学阐释在下文详述。下述标注过程经过两次核对,并通过交叉验证,以最大限度保证语料标注的准确性和客观性。

① 作者未译出源语文本或原文无对应译文。

四、被动结构的汉语对译特征分析

1. 汉语对译形式总体分布特点

上古汉语中不存在被动式,但被动义却可在保持主动形式前提下通过动词实现(王力 1989:272)。先秦至汉以后,被动用法开始显现并趋于多样化,特别是五四之后,用法变得更宽泛。翻译是语言接触活动最主要的一种形式,也是被动句最可能的主要来源(胡显耀、曾佳 2010:73)。本节利用超大型英汉平行语料库考察英语被动结构的汉语对译形式及其特征。

本文发现,科技英语被动结构的汉译有 10 种基本处置方法:受事主题结构、主动结构、虚义动宾结构、兼语式、处置式、被动式、定语短句、名词化、类虚化动宾结构和省略。此外,还有其他与翻译策略相关的一些处置方式。

第一,本研究考察的汉语对译中的被动结构只关注汉语中带标记的被动形式,如例 2a 所示。根据被动标记和词汇语义特征,又可分为:(1)经过语法化的功能词"被""叫""让""给"和较古的"为……所……"和(2)具有遭遇义的动词"遭""受""挨""蒙"这种词汇语义所实现的被动标记(王力 2011[1943]:88-92)。据统计,be-passive 中被译为被动结构的共 436 例,占总体的 9.44%。

表 1　语料标注体系

语言	标注类别	标注属性
英语原文	被动标记	be-passive、get-passive
	被动形式	长被动、短被动
	句法功能	主语、谓语、宾语、定语、状语、补语
	时态	现在、过去、将来
	体	进行、完成
	语义韵	积极、中性、消极

续表

语言	标注类别	标注属性
汉语对译	受事主题结构	一般受事主语句、……是……的、……由……
	主动结构	一般主动句、动词逻辑关系转换、受施事角色变换
	虚义动词 + VN	(对)……进行……、(对)……加以……、(对)……予/予以……、(对)……做/作……
	使役结构	……使……、……令……、……让……
	处置式	……把……、……拿……、……将……
	被动结构	句法化被动(被、叫、让、为……所……)、词汇化被动(受、遭、蒙、挨)
	定语短句	中心动词 v +“的”+ 受事名词 n 结构
	名词化	名词化
	动宾结构	得到/获/获得/……、得以……、经/经过……
	省略	报道式结构省略、语义省略
	其他	转述动词、意译、未译出

第二,受事主题结构是汉语中根据叙事焦点将受事置于“主语”位置,即受事作为整句的“话题”,凸显受事本身与施加在受事上的行为本身,构成“话题—陈述”结构(石定栩 1998;史有为 2005)。受事主题结构具有隐含的被动意义,这类意义通过语境和行为语义来确定被动关系,因而也称为“当然被动”或“意念被动”(张今、陈云清 1981:74;范剑华 1994:96;姚振武 1999:43),在本研究中,be-passive 对译形式共出现 1378 例,占总体的 29.82%,如例 2b 所示。

第三,主动式英语被动结构汉语对译中出现最多的结构,在本研究中共出现 1,671 例,占总量的 36.16%。这类对译形式中施事、动作和受事依次出现在主语、谓语和宾语位置,当源语文本中隐去施事时,则较多用无主句或采用通称或泛称(大家、有人和人们等)指明施事,如例 2c 所示。

第四,“虚化动词 + 名词”(参见刁晏斌 2004:32-38)构成的动宾结构也是英语被动句常采用的汉语对译形式,其中由名词表达源语被动结构中的行为动作部分,而虚化动词则由具备范畴性语法意义的动词来充当,这些动词包括“加以/予以/予”“进行”“从事”“做/作”“付诸”“干”“弄”“搞”等,原句中的受事则通过介词“对”引出,如例 2d 所示。本文排除了例 2e 的这种虚化动词对译形式,这一结构更符合主动式汉语对译结构。在本研究中,被译为“虚化动词 + 名词”的实例为 172 次,约占总体的 3. 72%。

第五,处置式表示施事对受事的处置,体现施事的支配行为(王力 1985:124-130),通过语法标记“将”和“把”引出受事(朱德熙 1982:185)。受事名词都必须采用有定性表达,在一定条件下可相互转换(石毓智 2006:47)。本研究发现,科技文体英语 be-passive 被动结构中,有 69 例被译为汉语处置式,占总体的 1. 49%。这一形式如例 2f 所示。

例 2:

a.原文:Both pilots *have been taken off* the roster pending inquiry and *were summoned* for questioning on Wednesday, the Directorate General of Civil Aviation said in a statement.

译文:印度民用航空总局在周三的声明中表示,两名机师已被停飞,正被传讯调查。(text:asurveybyhamburgbased)

b.原文:Research suggests that infections linger in older people because the immune *system is weakened*.

译文:研究的结果表明老年人感染长期不愈是因为免疫力功能减弱之故。(text:enp_we93-1 kangshuailaoshipin)

c.原文:Unable to find a job, he applied for a graduate fellowship at Cambridge University and *was accepted*.

译文:他找不到工作,便向剑桥大学毕业同学会求援,同学会接受了他的申请。(text:wulixuefazhanshi)

d.原文:The risk of using consultants will *be identified* and documented, and mitigating actions will be identified, subject to available resources, in the ICAO risk register.

译文:根据可用资源,对使用顾问的风险进行确认和以文件形式记录,并在国际民航组织风 险簿中确定缓解措施。(text:guojiminyonghang)

e.原文:The conversion of the amounts referred to in paragraph 2 into the national currency *is to be made* according to the law of the State concerned.

译文:将第2款所述金额折算为国家货币时,应按该国法律规定进行。(text:hamburgrules)

f.原文:The still dominant form,often called the ‘internal approach’,is concerned with the substance of science as knowledge.

译文:把科学实体作为知识来考虑,经常称之为“内部方法”,这仍然是主要的形式。(text:biyaodezhanglikexuedechuantong)

第六,英语被动结构的汉语对译形式中也出现了少量“使”“令”引导的兼语式,在本研究样本中出现23例。兼语式是汉语使役结构中较为复杂的类,本研究所关注的“兼语式”仅限于使用单纯使役动词“使”“使得”“令”“让”和“叫”等的纯兼语式(参见黄锦章2004)。如例3a所示,其中表示“施事”的成分可隐去。

第七,当原文被动结构与受事之间构成修饰或补充说明关系,即让受事充当主语或宾语,而被动结构作为定语或成分时,汉译可通过“定语短语”形式将受事置于主语位置。如例3b所示。古今明(1985:16)在研究英语被动语态翻译方法时也得出了类似结论。这一结构在本文be-passive结构的汉语对译中共出现139例。

第八,本研究对样本的考察也发现一些将被动语态中的行为动词译为名词的现象,见例3c,这类实例中汉译的名词具有动作或事件意义,译者通过强调事件本身而将事件动作置于主语或宾语位置。在带有施事时,还可被译作“施事+的+名词”结构,其中,“名词”具有行为意义,与源语被动结构的动词意义对应,如例3d所示。这类名词化现象在样本汉译中出现146次。

第九,与上述“虚化动词+名词”的形式类似,本研究也观察到81例译为“动词+行为事件名词”的实例。其中,行为事件名词表达源语被动结构中的行为动作部分,与虚化用法不同的是,这里的“动词”并不强调施事所施加的行为,而是强调受事在自身意志之外所经受到的行为,这些“动词”包括:“发生/产生”“得到/得/获得”“得以”“经/经过”和“纳入”,如例3e所示。

第十,在本研究的样本中,有272例的被动结构在其汉语对译中被省略不译,约占总体的5.23%—6.61%。据观察,这类被动结构中的动词多为

“*consider*”“*find*”“*show*”“*know*”“*describe*”和“*note*”等表达转述或者报道发现类动词;另一类省译的实例中英语行为动词采用“*made*”“*take*”“*give*”和“*do*”等形式的虚化用法;还有一些被动结构被省译,是译者根据不同语境、所述内容等采取不译的手段;译者主体性与其所采取的翻译策略有关,详细的对译形式见小节 5.2。

例 3:

a.原文:...blockers demonstrate that *cardiovascular outcomes are improved by RAS blockers*,which maintain or improve glycemic control.

译文:……阻滞剂的随机试验证实,RAS 阻滞剂可使心血管结局改善,它可维持或改善患者血糖的控制。(text:metaboliceffectscarvedilol-metoprolol)

b.原文:The number of simulations of *gas dispersion to be carried out* will therefore be quite considerable.

译文:这导致需要进行的气体散布仿真量将会非常可观。(text:off-shoreriskassessmentjiu)

c.原文:The SAMS *was designed* to be installed as a GBS.

译文:索黑北极移动式结构物设计上是作为重力基座结构物进行安装施工的。(text:marineoffshoreconstructionershisan)

d.原文:Final discharge back into the bay *is monitored by a turbidity meter*.

译文:最后进入河湾内的排放物要通过水体混浊仪的检测。(text:marineoffshoreconstructionsan)

e.原文:Several key molecular determinants of human infection with H5N1 influenza viruses *have been identified*,and the likely minimum requirements for human-to-human transmission are being defined.

译文:决定 H5N1 流感病毒感染人的一些关键分子因素已经得到了确认,而可能引发人群间传播的最低条件也正在探索中。(text:humaninfectionhighlypathogenic)

根据上述分析和表 2,be-passive 等价对译为汉语被动的实例不到 10%,

远低于我们的假设,即受英语源语的影响,其汉语对译形式较多采用被动形式。转换频率的顺序为:主动式 > 受事主题 > 被动式 > 省略 > 虚化动宾 > 名词化 > 定语短语 > 类虚化 > 处置式 > 兼语式,其中采取主动式和受事主题结构的对译形式约占总体的 66%。我们推测,产生该结果有三方面原因。首先,就英汉语言差异来说,虽然英语、现代汉语中都可用被动结构来表达被动意义,但汉语却较前者受到更为严格的形式和语义限制(参见王力 1984:128-129;吕叔湘、朱德熙 1979:87;连淑能 2010:123-126),因此难以直接将英语被动结构译为汉语形式被动结构。另有观点(古今明 1985;谢景芝 2004;连淑能 2010:126-131)认为,英语使用大量被动是出于修辞和句法的需要,而汉语语言重主体性和直觉性,无须严格遵守句法形式即可准确表达语义,且汉语使用"受事主语句""主动句(无主语或者补充泛称作为主语)""处置式""……加以/予以……"和定语短句等形式均可完整表达被动式中的行为意义,因此汉语在被动意义表达方面存在诸多选择,本文的量化考察结果验证了这一观点。其次,从翻译共性角度看,将英语被动结构大量译为"主动式""处置式""虚化动宾"等结构有助于将原被动结构隐含的受事和施事行为关系还原,并通过更加直观和明确的形式展现出来,符合汉语习惯,降低读者理解所需付出的代价,因而是显化的一种表现(王克非、黄立波 2007:101)。其中,大量将"被动"结构对译为"主动"结构是翻译中"简化"(Baker 1993:176)处理的倾向,用简单结构替代复杂结构。此外,Toury(1995)提出标准化律(law of standardization),认为译文中较多遵循目的语的语言规范,从而改变源文本结构的趋势。本文的发现亦符合上述趋势,是翻译"范化"的一个重要表现。最后,从文体角度出发,根据肖忠华、戴光荣(2010:57)的发现,原创汉语中,科技文体较之虚构文体在被动的使用上明显偏低,每 10 万词仅出现约 10 次,本文的考察结果也与这一结论不谋而合。

2. 英语被动汉语主要对译形式语言特征考察

上节讨论了英语被动结构的汉语对译在形式上的基本分类和分布特征。本节针对上述主要对译类型的具体形式、语义和语用特征进行分析和阐释。

2.1　汉译被动式特征分析

如 4.1 所述,按照所采用的被动标记词汇特征,可将汉语被动结构分为语法化程度较高的“句法被动”和语法化程度较低的“词汇被动”。按照结构中是否存在施事，又可分为长被动和短被动。本文也对译为汉语被动结构的语义韵进行了考察，结果见表 2。

表 2 汉译被动形式语言特征分析

被动形式	标记	频数	形式特征		语义特征		
			长	短	消极	积极	中性
句法被动	被	350	33	317	134	27	189
	为……所	17	17	—	5	3	9
	给	1	0	1	1	0	0
	小计	368	50	318	140	30	198
词汇被动	受	62	22	40	26	5	31
	遭	4	0	4	4	0	0
	让	2	2	—	0	0	2
	小计	68	24	44	30	5	33
总计	436	74	362	170	35	231	

表 2 显示，在全部 436 例被动式汉语对译实例中，句法被动形式出现 368 次，占 84.4%，词汇被动出现 68 例，约占 15.6%。被动标记中，“被”和“受”频数最多，“给”“让”和“叫”常在口语语体中使用（石毓智 2010:95），因而科技文体中译例甚少。通过表 2 可观察到一些显著特征：首先，“被”字句所采取的施事结构通常为短被动，带施事的长被动共 33 例，仅占 9.43%，这一结果远低于 Xiao *et al*.（2006:128）对 LCMC 语料库原创汉语长被动的考察结果（39.3%）。本研究认为，这是受科技英语中“去施事化”倾向的“源语干扰”影响。其次，由表 2 还可观察到表达消极意义的语义韵 170 例，样本中 397 例消极英语被动结构有近一半被译为汉语被动句。王力（2011［1943］:87）认为汉语被动态多表示“不如意”等消极意义。因此，受汉语语义影响，具有消极语义特征的英语被动被“自然”地对译为汉语被动结构，从而更符合汉语被动结构的语义特征，是典型的翻译“范化现象”。最后，本研究中“被”和“受”所标记的汉译被动结构在消极、积极和中性被动语义分别为 134、27、189 和 25、

5、31，分别占比38.3%、7.8%、54%和41.9%、8%、50%，较之Xiao *et al*.（2006：128）对原创汉语的考察，翻译汉语中“被”和“受”标记的被动结构消极语义占比低13%～21%，中性语义韵则高17%～40%，很明显受到英语被动结构语义特征影响，是一种源语干扰现象。

2.2　汉译主动式语言特征分析

主动式是科技文体被动结构英译汉中最频繁的对译形式，共1,670例。据观察，采用主动结构的汉语译文常常将原文被动结构中的受事、行为动作和施事还原为施事、行为动作和受事的顺序，如例4a所示，当原文中不存在施事时，可采用无主句形式来保持汉译主动形式（见例4b），也可采用通称或泛称来填充主语（见例4c）。上述形式本文称作A1型主动式。其次，本文还观察到如例4d的译例，即保留主动形式，但译文中施事和受事的行为逻辑关系发生了置换，即原受事变成动作发出者，而行为动作语义没有发生任何变化，这一现象与汉语言语思维逻辑关系有关，本文将这一主动式定义为A2型主动。此外，有一类主动式与A2型类似，原受事在译文中变成动作发出者，但与A2不同，行为动作的语义发生变化，以适应目的语的语用习惯，这一类型本文定义为A3型主动式，如例4e所示。本文对这三类主动式进行了统计，结果见表3。

例4：

a.原文：Where a longer period is specified in the notification, the denunciation shall take effect upon the expiration of such longer period after the *notification is received by the depositary*.

译文：如果通知中指明更长的时间，则在保管人收到通知后，于该更长的期间届满时起，退出生效。（text：unmtg）

b.原文：Fortunately, a *better warning system had been established* by the time, so fewer residents perished.

译文：幸运的是，那时已经建成了较为完善的洪涝报警系统，所以此次洪灾死亡人数较少。（text：tianqiwuyu）

c.原文：If the arm hangs at the side, none of the *movement is made* at the elbow.

译文：倘若手臂空悬，我们不须再用肘节的动作。（text：xiaoxue-gekexinlixue）

d.原文：To complicate matters further, if faulting occurred in the area, one block of a *rock sequence might be down-dropped* in relation to the other or thrust over another.

译文：如果这个地区存在断层，就会令问题更加复杂。一个岩石层序的块体下落后可能与另一个相接触，或是逆冲到另一个岩层之上。（text：yanshiyuteshudizhi）

e.原文：One *patient* in the no antibiotic group developed pneumonia, was admitted to the hospital, administered antibiotics, and recovered fully.

译文：不用抗生素组有 1 例病人发生肺炎，住院给予抗生素治疗后完全康复。（text：informationleafletantibioticstrategies）

表 3　汉译主动式语言特征分析

主动式类型	频数	百分比	施事结构		语义特征		
			长	短	消极	积极	中性
A1	1364	81.68%	120	1244	64	87	1213
A2	149	8.92%	2	147	12	7	128
A3	157	9.40%	14	143	15	7	135
总计	1670	100%	136	1534	91	101	1476

由表 3 可见，汉译主动式中，按原被动结构中“施事 + 行为动词 + 受事”结构保持主动形式的 A1 型主动式是用法最广的形式，占全部主动式的 81.68%，而 A2 和 A3 型用法数量相当。A2 和 A3 的译法也体现出译者为保持汉语习惯而不惜改变原文结构与行为动作逻辑关系所作的努力，符合“标准化”倾向。从另一方面也反映了汉语、英语对被动结构在语义、结构和语用上的差别，英语通过被动来强调受事意志外行为，进而表达客观性，而汉语则通过逻辑关系置换和动作语义关系变换尽力保持语句的主动性。此外，三种主动结构中不带施事的比例均高于带有施事的长被动结构，但 A2 类主动结构偏向于不带施事。值得注意的是，转换为主动式的结构偏向使用中性或积

极语义，而消极语义占比较低。

2.3 汉译受事主题结构语言特征分析

汉语的正常被动结构需指明施事（王力 1984：129），一般由标记词“被”引出（朱德熙 1980：87），这一限制使得英语中大量隐去施事的短被动结构难以转换为对等的汉语被动结构（连淑能 2010：124）。此外，汉语被动结构中多表达消极语义，而英语被动结构多表达中性语义，也造成翻译转换的困难。因此，在汉语中，受事常作为“话题”被置于句首位置，形成“主题”和“述语”结构（Chao 1968）。根据考察，汉语对译的受事主题结构主要有三类：其一，保持源语言中的受事、施事和行为顺序不变，直接转换为“受事 + 行为动词 + 施事”结构，若无施事，则直接译为“受事 + 行为动词”结构，是典型的汉语受事主语句，如 2b 所示。其二，译为汉语表示状态的静句，即“受事 + 是 + [由] + [施事] + 动词 + [的]”结构（参见李临定 2011：358），其中介词“由”用来引出施事，可省略，有时“的”也可省略。如例 5a 的对译形式所示。其三，源语存在施事时，或译文中需指明施事，则可译为“受事 + 由 + 施事 + 行为动作”句式，如例 5b 所示。下页表 5 对上述三种情况进行了统计，由于受事主题结构常被认为“意念被动”，因此，本研究也考察了源语施事结构和语义特征与三种结构间的关系。

例 5：

a.原文：The majority of HIT cases in cardiac surgery *patients mere diagnosed* postoperatively.

译文：大部分心脏外科患者发生 HIT 是在术后诊断的。

（text：incidencerecognizedheparinthrombocytopeni）

b.原文：The background of these Chi-Pin embassies has been confused, but the *elucidation* of the Greek side *has now been completed* by Tarn and others.

译文：关于这些厕宾使者的背景，曾经众说纷纭，但是希腊方面的情况，现已由塔恩及其他人完全研究清楚了。（text：diqizhang）

表 4　汉译受事主题结构语言特征分析

类型	频数	百分比	施事结构		语义特征		
			长	短	消极	积极	中性
受事主语	1180	85.57%	62	1118	78	72	1030
“是……的”	91	6.60%	26	65	10	5	76
“由……”	108	7.83%	85	23	5	5	98
小计	1379	100%	173	1206	93	82	1204

由表 4 可见,受事主题结构中,直接采用受事主语形式的汉语对译最多,占 85.57%,这类译法常常照搬英语被动事件结构,但无被动标记,是一种典型的“当然被动句”。其中,短被动被译为受事主语的实例远高于长被动结构,符合科技文体避免施事的预期,本文对语义韵的考察也发现,受事主语句多数承载了中性语义,也可承载消极和积极语义,二者数量相当,符合汉语习惯。“是……的”结构也适合无施事成分的对译,但较之受事主语,这类形式多译为中性语义。此外“由……”字结构由于需要引出施事,因此,汉语译文中长被动比例远高于短被动。这类译法也多用于表达中性语义的场合,消极和积极语义较少。

2.4　汉译动宾结构语言特征分析

1 对汉语对译的虚化和类虚化现象做了说明,这里对这类对译形式及语义韵进行考察(如表 5 所示)。不难看出,虚化动词在语义特征方面存在显著特点,即尽可能表达中性意义,避免消极义。与此不同,类虚化动宾结构中的“得到”类则超三分之一用来表达积极意义,表示某积极事件的完成状态。

为了进一步阐释虚化和类虚化动宾结构的翻译特点,本文还针对各类对译形式对源文本中所搭配的行为动词进行了统计和梳理,如表 5 所示。根据刁晏斌(2005:32),虚义动词可根据语义特征划分为“做”义类和“处置”义类。前者包括:“进行”“做”“作”“付诸”和“实施”,后者则包括“加以”“给予”和“予以/予”,本文采纳这一分类方法,对上述各类汉译形式的源文本行为动词进行了分类整理。

表 5　汉译动宾结构语言特征分析

类型	形式	频数	百分比	语义特征		
				消极	积极	中性
虚化动宾	进行	113	66.86%	2	6	105
	加以	24	14.21%	0	3	21
	予/予以/给予	14	8.28%	1	1	12
	做/作	14	8.28%	0	1	13
	付诸/实施	4	2.37%	0	0	4
	小计	169	100%	3	11	155
类虚化动宾结构	得/得到/获得/得以	73	86.91%	4	25	44
	经/经过	8	9.52%	0	1	7
	发生	3	3.57%	0	0	3
	小计	84	100%	4	26	54

此外,本文也对动宾结构的语义特征进行了分析,我们发现,虚化动词类中,表示"做"义的源语行为动词多表示持续性动作,如 *maintain*, *control*, *assess*, *study*, *inspect*, *expand*, *search*, *analyze* 等,即使源语行为动作为短暂型动词,在汉译中也被转换为相应的持续性动作;表达"处置"义的源语被动行为动词则多使用短暂或完成类行为,这一语义范畴的分界与虚化动词的语义有关(刁晏斌 2004:33)。类虚化动宾结构中也存在类似特征,即表"得到"义的动词多为瞬间完成性动词,"经过"义则多为持续性动作语义。

2.5　汉译处置式与兼语式语言特征分析

根据本文的观察,科技文体中译为处置式主要为"将""把""给",其中由于"将"字式常用于书面语和正式文体,因此频率最高,这一观察与石毓智(2010:98)一致,"把"既可用于口语语体也可用于书面体,在本研究中频率低于"将",占 27.54%。"给"多出现在口语语体中,在本研究中只出现 1 例。值得注意的是,采用处置式时,一般在"把/将/给"后引出受事。"兼语式"译例在本文中出现不多,仅 24 例,其中"令"和"让"多在口语体中出现,在本研究中仅 3 例。

表 6　汉译处置式与兼语式语言特征分析

类型	形式	频数	百分比	语义特征		
				消极	积极	中性
处置式	“将”	49	71.01%	1	0	48
	“把”	19	27.54%	1	1	17
	“给”	1	1.45%	0	0	1
	小计	69	100%	2	1	66
兼语式	“使”	21	87.50%	2	2	17
	“令”	2	8.33%	1	0	1
	“让”	1	4.17%	1	0	0
	小计	24	100%	4	2	18

从表 6 中还可看出，无论是处置式还是兼语式，其所表语义基本为中性意义，而消极和积极意义则较少或者不用。

五、结语

本文基于超大型“中国英汉平行语料库”的科技语料子库考察英语被动结构基本特征及其汉语对译形式与语言特征。研究发现，英语被动结构在转换为汉语时仅有 10%被译为被动结构，其他对译形式包括主动式、受事主语结构、动宾结构、名词化、处置式、兼语式和省略等形式，表现出英语被动结构汉译形式的灵活性和丰富性。还有一些被动结构被转译为形容词、副词、状语和汉语的情态结构，由于上述译例较少，限于篇幅，本文未详述。

造成上述特征和规律的原因，本文认为主要有三点：(1)英汉语言差异：两种语言被动结构在语法、语义和语用上存在较大差异，无法直接相互等价转换；(2)语体限制：英语正式文体趋向于较多使用被动结构达成去施事化和物称化的目的，从而使文本更为客观，而汉语则较少使用被动结构表达，即使在正式文体中，也采用主动和受事主题结构来表示文本的客观性；(3)翻译的“范化”和“标准化”趋势：译者在翻译过程中常常通过改变原文中语言、语义等形式使译文更加符合目的语的语言习惯。此外,本文考察还发现:汉语对译被动结构有近一半表达中性和积极意义,这与汉语被动的特征并不吻合,这在一定程度上是源语干扰效应的结果。王力(1957:15;1989:6,86-103)曾指出,英语等欧洲语言带标记的被动使用频率高于汉语,有可能导致汉语被动句增多,造成现代汉语中被动结构的使用更加宽泛化,是汉语欧化的重要表现之一。

(本文原载《外国语》2018 年第 6 期,作者为王克非、刘鼎甲)

参考文献

M.Baker,"Corpus Linguistics and Translation Studies:Implications and Applications", M.Baker,G.Francis & E.Tognini-Bonelli,*Text and Technology:In Honour of John Sinclair*, Philadelphia & Amsterdam:John Benjamins,1993,pp.233-250.

Y-R.Chao,*A Grammar of Spoken Chinese*,Berkeley:University of California Press, 1986.

O.Jespersen,*A Modern English Grammar on Historical Principles*(Vol 3),Heidelberg: Carl Winter,1927.

T.McEnery,& R.Xiao.Passive "Constructions in English and Chinese:A Corpus-based Contrastive Study",*Proceedings of Corpus Linguistics Conference Series* 1(1),2005,pp.1-29.

R.Quirk,J.Svartvik,G.Leech,& S.GreenBaum,*A Comprehensive Grammar of the English Language*,London:Longman,1985.

G.Toury,*Descriptive Translation Studies and Beyond*,Philadelphia & Amsterdam:John Benjamins,1995.

R. Xiao, T. McEnery, & Y. Qian, Passive Constructions in English and Chinese: A Corpus-based Contrastive Study,*Language in Contrast*,2006,Vol 6,No.1,pp.109-149.

刁晏斌:《现代汉语虚义动词研究》,辽宁师范大学出版社 2004 年版。

范剑华:《英语和汉语被动式之比较》,《华东师范大学学报(哲学社会科学版)》1994 年第 3 期。

古今明:《英汉语中被动句的对比与翻译》,《南外学报》1985 年第 1 期。

胡显耀、曾佳:《翻译小说"被"字句的频率、结构及语义韵研究》,《外国语》2010 年第3期。

黄锦章:《汉语中的使役连续统及其形式紧密度问题》,《华东师范大学学报(哲学社会科学版)》2004年第5期。

柯飞:《双语库:翻译研究新途径》,《外语与外语教学》2002年第9期。

李德超、唐芳:《基于类比语料库的英语旅游文本文体特征考察》,《中国外语》2015年第4期。

李临定:《现代汉语句型》,商务印书馆2011年版。

连淑能:《英汉对比研究》,高等教育出版社2010年版。

石毓智:《处置式产生和发展的历史条件》,《语言研究》2006年第3期。

石毓智:《汉语语法》,商务印书馆2010年版。

王克非:《中国英汉平行语料库的设计与研制》,《中国外语》2012年第6期。

王克非、黄立波:《语料库翻译学的几个术语》,《四川外语学院学报》2007年第6期。

王克非、刘鼎甲:《大规模英汉平行语料库的检索与应用:大数据视角》,《外语电化教学》2017年第6期。

王力:《汉语被动式的发展》,载《语言学论丛》(第一辑),新知识出版社1957年版。

王力:《中国语法理论》(《王力文集》第一卷),山东教育出版社1984年版。

王力:《中国现代语法》(《王力文集》第二卷),山东教育出版社1985年版。

王力:《中国现代语法》,商务印书馆1989年版。

王力:《中国现代语法》,商务印书馆2011年版。

肖忠华、戴光荣:《寻求"第三语码"——基于汉语译文语料库的翻译共性研究》,《外语教学与研究》2010年第1期。

谢景芝:《英汉被动句的对比与翻译》,《中州学刊》2004年第6期。

姚振武:《先秦汉语受事主语句系统》,《中国语文》1999年第1期。

张今、陈云清:《英语比较语法纲要》,商务印书馆1981年版。

朱德熙:《语法讲义》,商务印书馆1982年版。

朱一凡、胡开宝:《"被"字句的语义趋向与语义韵》,《外国语》2014年第1期。

汉译语言个案分析——语料库调查

翻译的一个重要标准是忠实于原文。形式上的忠实往往使译文偏离目的语，成为介乎源语和目的语之间的“语际语”。本文以英语 so...that 结构的双向翻译为研究个案，考察和分析汉语翻译语言问题，包括它的特征和偏离程度等。考察材料借助大规模双语对应语料库，结果显示非文学翻译文本比文学文本更倾向于结构上的对应；这种结构对应有借用因素，易形成异化的翻译。

一、引言

直译与意译、归化与异化是翻译界争论不已的话题。在具体翻译方法上人们见仁见智，但有一点译界看法是一致的，即译文毕竟是译文，再归化的译文也有“洋气”。为什么会出现这种偏离？Toury（1995：208）认为，原语语篇的干预是一个重要的形式来源（表现为形式上的忠实），就是这些形式明显偏离了目的语语言的一般模式。这样的译文语言通常被认为是翻译语（translationese，又称“翻译腔”），是译语文本受到源语语言对目的语施加影响造成的。但也有人认为，翻译语是两种语言的“中间地带”。这种处于中间地带的语言在翻译理论中称作“语际语”，它包含着原语的分析特征和目的语语篇的合成特征（James 1980：4）。

到目前为止，我们对翻译语的研究大都止步于直觉和感性认识上，难以深入探究翻译语言的特征和性质。为此，本文要寻找一条可行的途径尝试对翻译语言作尽可能充分的分析。我们知道，“基于语料库的翻译研究能使我们简洁、有效地进行编码，能使我们查询并获得大量的数据——没有电子技术的帮助，一个人一生再勤勉也难以收集或查询这么多的数据”(Tymoczko 1998)。本文即运用英汉语平行语料库检索并分析个案，以探究翻译语使用的状况。

二、语料库与检索方案

1. 汉英对应语料库简况

本文使用的语料出自中国外语教育研究中心的“通用汉英对应语料库”(王克非教授主持研制)。主要利用该库“翻译文本库”中的四个子库：汉英文学库、英汉文学库、汉英非文学库、英汉非文学库，分别选取语料150万字/词、170万字/词、100万字/词、130万字/词。其中，汉译英约占40%，英译汉约占60%，文学与非文学文本分别占55%和45%左右(王克非 2003)。这些语料数量适中，分布基本合理，可以反映某一语言项目运用的实际状况。

2. 关键词

James(1980:169)认为，对比分析要用一些表层结构范畴来充当比较媒介(Tertium Comparationis)。本文选择了翻译时常见的so...that结构及其汉译为比较媒介(也就是关键词)。选择该结构的原因有：1. 我们通常认为，这种结构的译文是“如此……以致”(参见吴广义 2000)。思果(2001:173)把这种句型归入“常见的一些错的句型”。2. 该结构在翻译时究竟该如何处理很少有人注意。3. 该结构在汉译时形式多样，甚至有点芜杂，需要加以分类和整理。

应注意，相同的范畴因语言不同，它的值(values)也不一样。我们选择“so...that”这一结构，是要通过语料库考察它在汉语中是否有充分对应的结构形式。我们要回答下列问题：so...that在汉语译文中是如何处理的？表面看来与“so...that”最相近的“如此……以致(至)”是不是汉语翻译时使用的典型结构呢？

3. 对比方法和统计项目说明

本文以“so...that”为参照项，在英汉和汉英语料库中均使用“so...that”为关键词，通过Concordancer软件检索英语(原文或译文)中的“so...that”结构及其汉语(译文或原文)平行对应索引。

本文在对索引进行统计时使用了以下统计项目:1. 频次:指语料库中与“so...that”结构对应的某一汉语形式的出现次数;2. 构成比例:指各对应形式在总频次中的比例;3. 频率:指某一形式在百万字/词中出现的次数。

三、So...that 结构汉英互译时的对应形式

“so...that”在英语里为非连续性搭配,有 so 和 that 两个标记词,我们假定它对应的译文最多有前后两个标记词(markers),如“如此(前)……以致(后)”。

检索时本文使用了关键词(key word)“so+20+that”,即 so 与 that 之间的跨距(span)为 20 个词形,能够检索到子库中所有相关的索引。在检索到的语料中将不属于“so...that”结构的平行语料索引剔除,其后再将剩余的索引进行分类。

1. 与 so...that 对应的汉语译文形式

从四个子库中检索到的索引显示,与 so...that 对应的汉语译文主要有五类。

a.只在前一小句用程度副词传达 so 的强调意义,that 没有对应,我们在后面表 1 中标记为“前对应”。如例(1)的译文中只用“非常”对应整个 so...that 结构;

(1)他非常想家,简直忍无可忍,泪水在眼眶里打着转儿。

He was *so* homesick *that* he could hardly endure the misery of it.The tears lay very near the surface.

b.不用程度副词传达 so 的强调意义,而是使用连词(因此)、动词(弄)和副词性连词(竟然)等表达后果或结果意义,标记为“后对应”;

(2)她一看到了那人瘦削、多皱的面孔和稍稍变形的躯体,便不由自主地再一次把婴儿紧搂在胸前,直弄得那可怜的孩子疼得哭出了声。

Again, at the first instant of perceiving that thin visage, and the slight deformity of the figure, she pressed her infant to her bosom with*so* convulsive a force *that* the poor babe uttered another cry of pain.

c.用“如此……以致”这类对等形式,标记为“前后对应”;

(3)牧师宣布了布道词引用的《圣经》章节,接着就单调乏味地进行施道,如此平淡啰嗦以至于有许多人渐渐地低下头打瞌睡——他的布道词里讲了数不清的各种各样的地狱里的刑罚,让人有种感觉,能够有资格让上帝选入天堂的真是为数极少,几乎不值得拯救了。

The minister gave out his text and droned along monotonously through an argument thatwas *so* prosy *that* many a head by and by began to nod-and yet it was an argument that dealt in limitless fire and brimstone and thinned the predestined elect down to a company so small as to be hardly worth the saving.

d.对应的汉语句中前后都没有标记,标示为“零对应”;

(4)她头上乌黑的浓发光彩夺目,在阳光下熠熠生辉。

She had dark and abundant hair,*so* glossy *that* it threw off the sunshine with a gleam.

e.使用“得”字结构;

(5)我刚挪动了一下身子,小筏子便立刻改变了原来轻盈的运动方式,径直向一个陡得令我头晕眼花的浪谷滑去,接着船头又猛地扎进了下一个浪涛的深处,溅起了一阵水花。

And I had hardly moved before the boat,giving up at once her gentle dancing movement,ran straight down a slope of water*so* steep *that* it made me giddy,and struck her nose,with a spout of spray,deep into the side of the next wave.

2. 英汉文学子库中的统计结果

表 1 英汉文学子库中 so...that 的对应结构

	频次	构成比例(%)	出现频率(次/百万字)	考察字/词(万)
前对应	66	26. 5	38. 8	170 万
后对应	67	27. 2	39. 4	
前后对应	15	6. 1	8. 8	
零对应	79	31. 7	46. 5	
“得”字结构	21	8. 5	12. 3	
合计	248	100	146	

根据我们检索到的索引，汉语译文中与英语 so...that 对应的五类结构使用了下面这些对应词。

前对应：

那样、这样、如此、大为(有)、非常、颇、十分、十足、太、异常地、很、极(尽)、实在、实在是、深深、大

后对应：

以致、致使、终于使、因此、所以、结果、以便、便、连、那么、从而、只好、不禁、真是、后来/(结果)弄得、弄(害)得、使得、使、叫、简直、根本、竟然

前后对应：

非常……于是、非常……简直、这样……致使、那样/如此……以致、实在……以致、很……所以、太……所以、十分(很)……因此、老……所以、那么……所以、很……连

"得"字结构：

V/Adj.+得

以上结构有些在汉语中是罕见的，严格讲来算不上是什么结构。根据吴竞存、侯学超(1982:255-256)，现代汉语中与上述结构相关的关联词为：

因为(因)……所以(因此　因而)/由于……所以(因此)/之所以……是因为/其所以……是因为(就因为　正因为)/唯其……所以/因为(由于)……就(便　故)/因为(由于)……才

因为……/由于……/……所以/……故/……以致/……从而/……原来/……怪不得

这些结构表达的是因果关系。我们在 150 万字/词的汉英文学语料库中进行检索，检索到"因为……所以"结构 16 个，"因为……就"结构 28 个，"因为……才"结构 7 个，均不与"so...that"结构对应。其他结构在库中未发现，从它们用法上判断，这些结构也与"so...that"无关。

同时，在汉英文学子库中，单以"因为"出现在句首的索引有 261 个，只有 2 个与"so...that"对应；单以"所以"出现的句子 236 个，但只有 2 个与"so...that"对应；其他连词没有一个与"so...that"对应或未在库中出现。

这说明，英语中的"so...that"结构只是部分与汉语表达因果关系的复句对

应。Biber *et al.*(1999:86)称:so 为表达程度的成分,它后面的 that 引导一个关联从属结构(correlative subordination),是一个表示程度的小句。由此可见,"so...that"结构更注重程度与结果之间的关系,而不是普通的因果关系,至少不是典型的因果关系。

事实上,我们从英汉文学子库中检索到的"那样/如此……以致"结构也仅出现两次,即例(3)和下面的例(6)。

(6)得奖的同学在当时显得那样的伟大,那样的光荣,以致每个在场的学生心里都产生新的野心,这种野心往往要持续一两个星期之久。

The successful pupil was*so* great and conspicuous for that day *that* on the spot every scholar's heart was fired with a fresh ambition that often lasted a couple of weeks.

"前后对应"式结构中的其他句式也最多出现两次,这些句式表面看来较"那样/如此……以致"更不正规。如:

(7)我们的人手实在太少,所以船上每个人都得出力——只有船长躺在船尾一张垫子上发号施令,因为他虽说伤势大有好转,仍需静静休养。

We were *so* short of men, *that* everyone on board had to bear a hand-only the captain lying on a mattress in the stern and giving his orders; for,though greatly recovered he was still in want of quiet.

(8)"我听得很认真,也很相信你的话,一时连他的痛苦都忘掉了",他说着摸了摸医生的椅背。

"*So* attentively,and with *so* much confidence in what you say,*that* for the moment I lose sight," touching the back of the Doctor's chair,"even of this distress."

这些结构及其出现的频次分别为:

那样/如此……以致(2)

非常……于是(2)/非常……简直(1)/这样……致使(1)/实在……以致(1)/很……所以(1)/太……所以(1)/十分(很)……因此(2)/老……所以(2)/那么……所以(1)/太……连(1)

虽然我们很难称之为结构,但它们确与"so...that"结构对应。这种临时性结构虽不如"那样/如此……以致"那么程式化,但它们出现频率之和要高于"那样/如此……以致"格式(13:2)。这说明,和我们通常的看法不同,"那样/如此……以致"并不是"so...that"的对应格式。

3. 汉英文学子库

从汉英文学子库中我们检索到与 so...that 结构对应的汉语原文有如下形式。

前对应

异常/很/那么/这么/特别/不小/极/太/因为

后对应

(连词)所以/连/

(估价副词　赵元任 1979:347)居然/

(时间副词)便/

(副词性连词　赵元任 1979:335)就/

(动词)害/使

前后对应

无

"得"字结构

V+得

Adj.+得

表 2　汉英文学子库中 so...that 的对应结构

	频次	构成比例(%)	出现频率(次/百万字)	考察字/词(万)
前对应	29	17.8	19.3	150
后对应	13	8	8.6	
前后对应	0	0	0	
零对应	45	28	30	
"得"字结构	74	46.2	49.3	
合计	161	100		
Adv./Adj./V+到	4		2.7	
连动	1		0.6	

表1和表2对比鲜明：汉英文学子库中译为“so...that”结构的没有一个是“前后对应”结构，这说明汉语文学文本罕用“如此……以致”这样的结构；更符合汉语表达习惯的是“得”字结构，占到这种致使结构的46.3%，可以说是主要表达方式。从另一个角度看，汉语译语文本和汉语创作文本把零对应结构作为主要的表达手段（分别为31.7%和28%），说明汉语表达习惯也在很大程度上限制着汉语译文。但这种情况对“得”字结构不适用，关于这一点，我们还要在下文分析。

4.“so...that”结构在非文学（百科）子语料库中的分布

下面是英汉和汉英两个非文学（百科）子语料库中“so...that”结构及其对应结构的分布情况。

表3　英汉非文学子语料库中so...that的对应结构

	频次	构成比例（%）	出现频率（次/百万字）	考察字/词（万）
前对应	12	42.8	9.2	130
后对应	3	10.7	2.3	
前后对应	8	28.6	6.2	
零对应	5	17.9	2.9	
“得”字结构	0	0	0	
合计	28	100		

表4　汉英非文学子库中so...that的对应结构

	频次	构成比例（%）	出现频率（次/百万字）	考察字/词（万）
前对应	8	80	8	100
后对应	0	0	0	
前后对应	0	0	0	
零对应	2	20	2	
“得”字结构	0	0	0	
合计	10	100		

So...that 结构在非文学语料库中的分布显示，其使用频率远远低于它在文学库中的使用频率（只有文学库使用频率的四分之一）。在英汉非文学库中，汉语译文中的“前后对应”结构出现频率要远远高于英汉文学子库（28.5%：6.1%），这可能是因为非文学翻译更注重直译，更形式化所致；而且，在非文学语料库的汉语原文部分，没有检索到“前后对应”和“后对应”结构。非文学文本没有发现与“so...that”，这也说明“得”字结构更口语化、更倾向于主观评价，在非文学文本中使用频率因而会很低。非文学（百科）语料再次验证了汉语原创文本一般不用“前后对应”结构（统计结果为0）。

四、“So...that”与“到”字结构和“得”字结构

1.“V/Adj./Adv.+到”

汉语中的“V/Adj./Adv.+到”结构后面可以跟名词，表示动作或性质状态达到某种程度；后面加动词或小句时表示状态达到的程度（吕叔湘 1994：128）。朱德熙（1982：131-132）举了两个例子。

（9）糊涂到连自己的名字也忘了。

（10）删到只剩下五百字。

这一类格式表示程度高，其中的宾语可以换成“这样”“这个样子”“这种程度”等体词性成分。这种结构形式是较为地道的汉语表达，在汉英库中有四个。

（11）这都是刹那间的事，——快到不容冯云卿有所审择，有所决定。

All this passed through his mind in a flash–*so* quickly *that* he had no chance to weigh the alternatives and decide what to do.

（12）就可惜荪甫厂里的女工已经穷到只剩一张要饭吃的嘴！

The only trouble is that the women employed in Sun–fu's factory are *so* poor *that* they've nothing left to call their own except their ever–hungry mouths!

（13）大副揣摩着老板们的心理，开了慢车，甲板上平稳到简直可以

竖立一个鸡蛋。

The skipper, sensing the mood of the party on deck, had cut down the speed to please them, and the boat was now*so* steady *that* one could have balanced an egg on one end on the deck.

(14)藏香的青烟在空中袅绕,四小姐嘴里默诵那《太上感应篇》,心里便觉得已不在上海而在故乡老屋那书斋,老太爷生前的道貌就唤回到她眼前,她忽然感动到几乎滴眼泪。

As she sat there intoning the verses of the book with the blue smoke from the incense curling round her, she could imagine herself back in the study of her old home. Her father's pious face floated before her, and she was *so* overcome *that* her eyes filled with tears.

例(11)、(12)、(13)都是"Adj./Adv.+到"结构,例(14)是"V+到"结构。英汉翻译时,有些表示程度高的表达可以用这种结构。语料显示,"到"字结构的使用范围有限,"到"字前面的形容词或副词不能用程度副词修饰,如果到前面是副词,该副词必须单说,如例(11);如果是形容词,则必须是作表语,如例(12)、(13);如果是动词,它必是不及物的,不能在谓语和"到"之间有宾语。而且,就"Adj./Adv.+到"结构来说,"到"前面的形容词(或副词)在意念上不能表示频率。例如:

(15)于是他时不时地找姨妈要药吃,结果弄得她烦起来,最后她干脆让汤姆自己动手爱拿多少就拿多少,不要再来烦她就行。

He asked for it *so* often *that* he became a nuisance, and his aunt ended by telling him to help himself and quit bothering her.

句中的"时不时"表示频率,若套到"到"字结构里,成为:"于是他找姨妈要药吃,时不时(经常)到让人烦……",这样表达的可接受性就比较差。

"到"字结构使用频率不高,但它是一种地道的汉语表达方式,在英汉翻译时恰当运用有助于增强表达效果。

2."得"字结构

朱德熙(1982:132)指出:只要把其中的"到"换成动词后缀"得",这类格式就转换成表示状态的述补结构了。这就是说,"得"字结构引导的是一个表示状态的补语。根据何善芬(2002:291),“得”字结构既可以引导结果补语也可以引导程度补语,这种结构是动补结构。但我们从汉英语料库中发现,“得”的前面既可以是动词,也可以是形容词,二者使用频次大致相当。如:

(16)他那时候窘得似乎甲板上人都在注意他,心里怪鲍小姐太做得出,恨不能说她几句。

At that moment he was *so* embarrassed *that* it seemed to him that everybody on deck was watching him. Inwardly he blamed Miss Pao for being too overt in her behavior and wished he could have said something to her about it.

(17)结果鸿渐睡了竹榻,刚夹在两床之间,躺了下去,局促得只想翻来覆去,又拘谨得动都不敢动。

He felt *so* cramped *that* when he lay down all he wanted to do was toss and turn, yet he was so restricted he didn't dare make a move.

我们先看看“得”字结构在英汉和汉英两个文学子库中的使用情况。

表 5　“得”字结构在英汉文学子库中的分布情况

“得”之后的成分	状态形容词		动词或动词性结构		主谓结构	
结构类型	V+得+	Adj.+得+	V+得+	Adj.+得+	V+得+	Adj.+得+
频次	1	1	3	7	5	4
频次小计	2		10		9	
构成比例(%)	9.5		47.7		42.8	
频率(次/百万字词)	1.2		5.8		5.3	

表 6　“得”字结构在汉英文学子库中的分布情况

“得”之后的成分	状态形容词		动词或动词性结构		主谓结构	
结构类型	V+得+	Adj.+得+	V+得	Adj.+得	V+得	Adj.+得
频次	2	2	16	25	14	15
频次小计	4		41		29	
构成比例(%)	5.4		55.4		39.1	
频率(次/百万字词)	2.7		27.3		19.3	

统计结果显示,“得”字结构的三个类型在英汉/汉英两个文学子库中的

构成比例大致相当。“得+形容词”结构所占比例在这两个子库中都很小，表明这种结构并不常用；但该结构在两个子库中出现的频率却有天壤之别，在英汉文学库中每百万字只出现 12.3 句，而在汉英文学库中每百万字却高达 49.3 句。这说明，汉语原创文本更多地使用较为简捷的“得”字结构，而英汉翻译时“得”字结构的使用频率偏低。

3.“得”在汉语译文中使用频率偏低的原因

语料分析显示，英汉翻译时“得”字结构使用频率过低与“得”字结构使用受到较多限制有关。尽管“得”字结构可以跟主谓结构，但这个主谓结构一般都是简单句，不是一个复杂结构，所以不能说“我们给抢得、逼得、刮得我爸爸对我们说生孩子很可怕……”。

而且，如果有两个或更多由 so 引导的词组并列，也不宜使用“得”字结构，这样的排比结构在英语里有很多，这也是译文使用“得”字结构较少的原因。如：

(18)我说，我们给抢得、逼得、刮得太苦了，我爸爸对我们说生孩子很可怕，我们最应当祈祷的就是让我们的妇女不要生育，让我们惨的种族灭绝！

I say, we were *so* robbed, and hunted, and were made so poor, *that* our father told us it was a dreadful thing to bring a child into the world, and *that* what we should most pray for, was, that our women might be barren and our miserable race die out!

(19)这儿的一切我都从来没见过，变化很大，很突然，很不公正，我完全给弄糊涂了。

All here is *so* unprecedented, *so* changed, *so* sudden and unfair, *that* I am absolutely lost.

还有一个原因：英语 so...that 结构中，that 引导的小句既可以表达某一行为和状态达到的程度，又可以表示某一状态导致的结果；这时就不能用“得”和“到”字结构，因为它们只表达程度意念。如：

(20)但在其他方面他仍然十分平静，因此罗瑞先生决定寻求他所需要的帮助——那帮助来自医生自己。

In all other respects, however, he was *so* composedly himself, *that* Mr. Lorry determined to have the aid he sought. And that aid was his own.

本文发现,英汉文学子库中大量使用连词(因此)、动词(弄)和副词性连词(如“竟”)来表达后果和结果的意义,原因就在这里。

五、从零对应结构的运用看汉语语言的特征

在英汉文学库中,使用零对应结构的比例为 31.7%;在汉英文学子库中,使用零标记的比例为 28%。二者比例大致相当,但零对应结构是英汉文学库中的首选项,在汉英文学库中则是第二选择。在汉英语料中,零对应与“so...that”对应的概率要低于“得”字结构和“so...that”的对应,但比其他选择项要高,说明零对应仍是一个重要的处理手段。一般认为,汉语是意合语言,较少使用逻辑联结词。零对应结构使用的情况是否与我们的期待相反呢?回答是否定的。这是因为,我们考察这一现象时并没有把“前后对应”“后对应”这些使用逻辑联结词的情形考虑在内。如果把这两类情形也考虑在内,我们就会发现:表 1 显示“前对应”和“前后对应”两项百分比之和为 33.3%,而表 2 显示两项相加仅有 8;二者相比,英汉翻译中使用关联词的比率要比汉语原创文本高出 25.3%。从这个角度说,汉语还是典型的意合语言。英汉文学翻译时大量使用零对应也反映出:汉语意合特征对译文也起着重要的影响。

但在非文学语料库中,我们发现,英汉翻译文本中“前”和“前后”两项的构成比例之和为 39.2%,而在汉语原创文本中的构成比例则为 0,差异十分显著。表明英汉非文学文本的翻译更倾向于将逻辑关系的外显(explicit)。而且,“前后对应”项所占比例最高,说明非文学译文更注重结构的对应。

六、应用:so...that 汉译时对应结构灵活处理

在对语料进行统计分析时,我们还发现了许多结构,这些结构虽不是汉语

常用的结构,但运用起来也相当有表现力。有些是独创的临时性结构,但用起来很自然。例(21)就是这样的结构。

(21)我老爱玩青蛙,所以我老是长出许许多多的疣子。

I play with frogs so much that I've always got considerable many warts.

原文 so much 在上下文里表达的是频次,意思是"经常",而汉语的副词"老"正能表达"一直;再三"的意思(见吕叔湘 1994:313)。译文中使用"老"和"所以"呼应虽不常见,但也能顺畅地表达原意。

下面的"so...that"结构中间有逗号,但 that 引导的从句并不表达"严格"的程度,而只是某种状态带来的结果,这种情况下可以用表达因果关系的连词,如"因此"。

(22)对人的检查很严格,因此,人们通过路障十分缓慢。

...but,the previous identification was so strict,that they filtered through the barrier very slowly.

例(23)也是用逗号隔开的"so...that"结构,但表达的是一种状况立即导致了另一种状况的出现,所以用副词"便"。

(23)有的人知道距离检查到自己的时间还长,便索性倒在地上睡觉,或是抽烟,其他的人则有的谈话,有的走来走去。

Some of these people knew their turn for examination to be so far off,that they lay down on the ground to sleep or smoke,while others talked together,or loitered about.

有些情况下,与 that 对应的汉译部分如果没有任何标记,如例(24)。若照原文翻译为"我完全糊涂了",它与前一分句的关系就会很松散,不明确;这时可运用"弄"来表达"致使"意义,前后两个表述之间的关系就非常明确了。

(24)这儿的一切我都从来没见过,变化很大,很突然,很不公正,我完全给弄糊涂了。

All here is so unprecedented,so changed,so sudden and unfair,that I am absolutely lost.

这些例证也说明,"so...that"结构的意义随着语境有细微的差异,在汉语中没有任何一个能承担这么多的功能和意义。因此,根据使用的场景作灵活处理是必要的。上述例证正能说明这一点。

七、结语

陈定安(1998:190)指出,“so…that”译成汉语时,“都可加‘就’、‘得’、‘便’、‘以’、‘能’、‘使’、‘因而’、‘因此’等词。但有时也可不加任何词,直接译出”。本文的描写和分析证实了这一结论。但语料检索结果显示,可能的对等译法比这还要灵活。本文描写、归类并分析了该结构的各种可能对应形式,结果如下。

1.“如此……以致”及与之相似的“前后对应”式结构不是英汉翻译中常见的结构形式,零对应才是主要对应形式;

2. 就“so…that”结构的汉译而言,统计结果显示,非文学文本比文学文本更倾向于结构上的对应;

3. 汉英文学语料显示,“得”字句与“so…that”对应的比率最高,但“得”字结构的使用受制于多种因素,统计分析不支持把“得”字结构视为“so…that”结构的首选对应形式;

4. 汉语中没有固定的结构与so…that对应,so…that在汉语译文中有多种对应形式,“前后对应”结构大都是临时性结构,运用的是汉语原有的修饰和关联成分,但它们的搭配使用却是受源语结构影响的结果,应视之为结构上的借用或异化。

(本文原载《中国英语教育》2003年第1期。作者为王克非、秦洪武)

参考文献

D.Biber, *et al*, *Longman Grammar of Spoken and Written English*, Beijing: Foreign Language Teaching and Research Press, 1999.

C.James, *Contrastive Analysis*, Essex: Longman Group Ltd., 1980.

G. Toury, *Descriptive Translation Studies and Beyond*, Amsterdam/Philadelphia: John

Benjamins Publishing Company, 1995.

M.Tymoczko, "Computerized Corpora and the Future of Translation Studies", *Meta*, 1998, Vol.43, No.4, pp.1-8.

陈定安:《英汉比较与翻译》(增订版),中国对外翻译出版公司 1998 年版。

何善芬:《英汉语言对比研究》,上海外语教育出版社 2002 年版。

吕叔湘:《现代汉语八百词》,商务印书馆 1994 年版。

思果:《翻译研究》,中国对外翻译出版公司 2001 年版。

王克非:《英汉/汉英语句对应的语料考察》,《外语教学与研究》2003 年第 6 期。

吴广义:《That 用法初探》,《浙江师大学报(社会科学版)》2000 年第 3 期。

吴竞存、侯学超:《现代汉语句法分析》,北京大学出版社 1982 年版。

赵元任:《汉语口语语法》,吕叔湘译,商务印书馆 1979 年版。

朱德熙:《语法讲义》,商务印书馆 1982 年版。

A Parallel Corpus-based Study of Translational Chinese

This paper, based on a Chinese-English parallel corpus, probes into the features of translational Chinese, and has made the following findings: 1) Different from what is generally believed, translational Chinese, compared with original Chinese, has higher type-token ratio and longer sentence segments; 2) there is difference between original Chinese and translational Chinese in POS distribution; the former uses more function words and fewer content words; 3) translational Chinese tends to exaggerate the compositional potentiality of some words or morphemes, which results in high-frequency use of some lexical bundles. The above features specific to translational Chinese cannot find full expression in universals of translation. Considering this, we need to look to interference from source language (English) for an adequate explanation.

1. INTRODUCTION

Translational language (TL) retains, to varying degrees, some features of its source language (SL), and it is "a non-standard version of the target language that is [...] affected by the source language" (Hopkinson 2007). By 'non-standard', we mean the language used in translation is not as idiomatic and prototypical as it is in original texts in the same language, because the former contains deviations from the typical patterns of TL, with SL being its origin (Toury 1995:208).

Features of translational language can be observed in many ways. According to Santos (1995:60), we can go into 1) properties of all translation, i.e. the universals of translation (Baker 1993), 2) properties of translations particular to a source language and target language, i.e. translationese, and 3) properties of particular translated texts (with the author and the translator taken into consideration). This study focuses on the second set of properties.

The use of parallel corpus in the study of translational Chinese has emerged in recent years in China, as has been done by Ke Fei (2003), Qin & Wang (2004). However, studies in this field are rare and inconsistent, owing to the lack of reasonable methodology and appropriate tools. For a better inquiry into translational Chinese, this study attempts a multilevel analysis.

2. UNIVERSALS OF TRANSLATION

Baker (1993, 1998a) reports that all translational languages share some features, namely, i) simplification (including lexical simplification, syntactic simplification, stylistic simplification); ii) explicitation (what is implied in original text gets explicit, so are the cohesion markers); and iii) normalization (source-text textemes tend to be converted into target-language repertoremes and diversity is lost).

Baker (1998b: 225) does acknowledge that in translation, some stylistic features of the source text tend to be transferred to the target text; however, her findings are made mainly on the basis of monolingual comparable corpus, without duly taking into account the influence of source language (see Hansen & Teich 2001; Wu & Huang 2006; Huang & Wang 2006). Moreover, Baker's study revolves around shallow linguistic features such as word length, type/token ratio, sentence length, lexical density, etc.; as a result, many abstract features peculiar to the languages in translation pair have been blinked.

Considering the empirical data on which the universals are based, it is questionable whether they are applicable to all translational languages, especially to languages of different types. For instance, we are quite concerned whether they are applicable to translational Chinese. To observe their applicability, we employ a multilevel analysis approach to translational Chinese. On the one hand, we make use of Baker's analytic techniques; on the other hand, we conduct micro-level analysis (like POS distribution, compositionality and load capacity) so as to arrive at an adequate description.

3. NORMALITY, CORPUS AND MULTILEVEL ANALYSIS

3.1 Normality

Chinese has its own typical linguistic patterns, and this typicality is termed "normality" (Yu 2002: 151). Normality is not a set of rules, but a language intuition which cannot be precisely measured or defined. However, we can assume its presence in a certain amount of original Chinese texts, because, compared with translated Chinese texts, the former is closer to the normality.

3.2 Corpus

The comparable corpus we use for description and analysis are from the General Chinese-English Parallel Corpus (GCEPC)[①] created by Beijing Foreign Studies University (BFSU). GCPEC has four subcorpora, namely Chinese-English Literature, Chinese-English Non-literature, English-Chinese Literature, English-Chinese Non-literature. The Chinese texts taken from CE and EC corpora can form comparable corpus, and the same is true for English texts. Besides, GCEPC enables us to take into account the English source texts in analysing trans-

① GCEPC is a Chinese-English bidirectional parallel corpus. The corpus-building project was led by Professor Wang Kefei and was completed in 2004. It contains about 20 million words and characters which are stored in XML format. The corpus for this study is about 3.5 million words and characters.

lational Chinese.

3.3 Multilevel analysis

This study first analyses translational Chinese at a macro level (TTR, word length, sentence length), and then turns to micro-level analysis (POS distribution, keywords analysis, compositionality and lexical bundles).

4. MACRO-LEVEL DESCRIPTION

The Macro-level description mainly concerns type-token ratio (TTR), word length count and sentence length count that reflect the difference between translated and original Chinese texts. Chinese words for TTR and sentence length calculations are segmented by ICTCLAS. Below is the data extracted from Wordlist in WordSmith 4.0.

Table 1 Macro-level description of translated and non-translated Chinese texts

	TOKENS (Counted)	TYPES	STTR	Word Length	S Length	SS Length
OCT(lit)	466,414	23,047	46.72	1.36	25.46	6.02
OCT(non-lit)	222,758	11,066	41.92	1.76	27.05	7.20
OCT	689,172	28,437	45.19	1.49	25.95	6.35
TCT(lit)	578,148	24,213	47.36	1.44	25.81	7.00
TCT(non-lit)	496,218	26,174	47.65	1.64	31.52	8.58
TCT	1,074,366	36,354	47.49	1.53	28.27	7.65
ESTQit)	546,632	22,409	43.21	4.26	16.76	6.79
EST(non-lit)	487,673	25,739	44.37	4.87	20.24	9.32
EST	1,034,305	35,695	43.75	4.54	18.23	7.78

As shown in Figure 1, OCT (Original Chinese Texts), TCT (Translated Chinese

Texts) and EST (English Source Texts) are different in type-token ration, word length, and sentence segment length (*SS Length* for short). What follows are details.

4.1 STTR

Generally, the larger the corpus is, the smaller the TTR. Given the obvious difference of the subcorpora in size, we cannot stop at a simplified TTR count, what we really need is STTR (standardized type-token ratio)① count.

Higher STTR indicates more different lexical items, while lower STTR suggests that fewer specific words are used and the more general ones are frequent (Westin 2002:75). As is shown in Table 1, STTR for OCT is 2.3 percent lower than that for TCT (47.49 vs 45.19), however, they are higher than that for EST (43.75). This difference suggests TCT, in comparison with OCT, is not so "simplified" in terms of lexical diversity. This may serve as counter evidence of lexical simplification which states translational language tends to use simple words for ease of understanding.

4.2 Word Length

For English and for many other alphabetic languages, word length is a way of measuring lexical specificity and diversity. For Chinese, however, word length count can reflect idiomaticity of language use: in Mandarin Chinese, most words used in Chinese discourse are disyllabic and monosyllabic, but "monosyllabic words are most frequently used" (Lü 1981:9).

The mean word length of TCT and OCT are similar, only that the former is 0.04 longer than the latter. Moreover, in contrast with TCT (53.16% words being monosyllabic, and 41.72% words disyllabic), OCT uses more monosyllabic words (56.96%), and fewer disyllabic words (38.58%). This suggests that TCT is not as idiomatic as OCT in word length.

4.3 Sentence Length (S Length) and Sentence Segment Length (SS Length)

Sentence length measures sentences that begin with capital letters (for English

---

① i.e. the ratio is calculated for the first 1,000 running words, then calculated afresh for the next 1,000, and so on to the end of the subcorpus in question.

but not for Chinese) and ends in full stops, exclamation marks, question marks or colons. We hereby note that Chinese sentences are calculated in words, but not in characters.

The calculation of mean S length yields the following results: TCT uses longer sentences (2.32 more words on average) than OCT; in addition, TCT uses much longer sentences than EST (18.23 for EST, while 25.81 and 28.27 respectively for OCT and TCT). The following instances can show why Chinese uses longer sentences than English does.

(1) And Pinkerton—Pinkerton—he has collected ten cents that he thought he was going to lose.

那么/c 平克顿/nr —/x 平克顿/nr —/x 他/r 一定/d 是/u 要/v 回来/dg 一/m 角/q 钱/n 的/u 老/a 账/n ,/w 这笔/r 钱/n 他/r 本来/d 以为/v 没有/v 盼头/n 了/y 。/w(16 : 22)

then_c Pinkedun_nr—_x Pinkedun_nr —_x he_r surely_d is_u claim_v back _dg one_m cent_q money_n DE(gen)_u old_a debt_n,_w this_r sum_c money_n he_r originally_d believe_v not-have_v prospect_n LE(crs)_y。_w

(2) You speak collectedly, and you—are collected.

你/r 这/r 话/n 倒/y 还有/v 自制力/n ,/w 而/c 你/r —/x 也/y 确实/d 镇静/a 。/w(7 : 10)

your_r this_r utterance_n nevertheless_y have_v forbearance_n,_w but_c you _r —_x also_y really_d calm_a。_w

Chinese, an isolating language, usually resorts to lexical means to express what is expressed grammatically in English. For example, the relative pronoun*that* in sentence (1) is replaced by a noun phrase 这笔钱 (literally *this sum money*), and the added expression 本来 (literally *originally*) serves to express the temporal meaning in *thought* (past tense).

The above amplification is to some degree compulsory, while a lot other amplifications are optional. For instance, as shown in example 2, there is shift of part of speech in translation [e.g. form*speak* to 这话 (lit. *this utterance*); from *collectively* to

有自制力(lit.*have forbearance*),and this shift forces the other sentential elements to change accordingly.More than that,modality implied in the original is made explicit in translation [such as 倒(*nevertheless*);也(also);确实(really)].Of whatever type,amplification contributes to the expansion of sentence length,and it is just this amplification that makes sentences in TCT much longer than their counterparts in EST,a support for explicitation in translation.

A simple S length calculation could not reveal intro-sentence properties of a language,so the result it derives might prove to be mistaken if we take sentence segment into account.

As Chen(1994)reports,"about 75% of Chinese sentences are composed of more than two sentence segments① separated by commas or semicolons".If this is true,SS length calculation might tell us more about the organization of Chinese sentences.For ease of data retrieval,we also use <s></s> tags to delimit sentence segments.Table 1 tells us that 1)SS length in CTC and OCT are shorter than their counterparts in EST,2)SS in TCT are significantly longer than those in OCT,and 3)mean SS length of TCT is very similar to that of EST.

Obviously,results of S length count are different from those of SS length count,yet they are not in conflict.For example,a Chinese sentence can be longer than an English one,but the former may contain more segments than the latter.Put differently,Chinese sentences contain more but shorter clauses or phrases than English sentences do,and this can explain why English,compared with Chinese,is shorter sententially but longer segmentally.

The greater sentence length of TCT supports explicitation in translation,but the greater SS length of TCT(compared with OCT)does not support normalization,because it is more like EST than OCT in this respect.

① A segment can be a clause or a phrase,with commas,semi-colons,colons being delimiters.

5. POS DISTRIBUTION

5.1 Statistical Results

POS(part of speech) distribution partially reflects typological features of a language. For POS distribution analysis of Chinese and English, we use ICTCLAS and CLAWS to tag CTC/OCT and EST. In addition, to ensure the representativeness of normality, we single out literature subcorpora for analysis.

Table 2 POS Distribution in OCT, TCT and EST(lit.)

POS \ Distribution		Original Chinese(lit)		Translational Chinese(lit)		Original English(lit)	
		Number	Frequency	Number	Frequency	Number	Frequency
1	Verbs	110391	23. 64	133762	22. 93	108340	19. 88
2	Nouns	100827	21. 59	113823	19. 52	112536	20. 65
3	Adjectives	24948	5. 34	24672	4. 23	35846	6. 58
4	Adverbs	48676	10. 42	52266	8. 96	42065	7. 72
5	Pronouns	41259	8. 83	68859	11. 81	64433	11. 82
6	Prepositions	14536	3. 11	25932	4. 45	58743	10. 78
7	Conjunctions	9687	2. 07	15252	2. 61	39304	7. 21
8	Numerals	17322	3. 71	20174	3. 45	8463	1. 5
9	Classifiers (Ch)	14209	3. 04	16337	2. 80	0	0
10	Particles (Ch)	39370	8. 51	57372	9. 84	0	0
11	Articles(En)	0	0	0	0	52325	9. 60
12	Determiners (En)	0	0	0	0	17132	3. 14
Total	421225	90. 26	528449	90. 6	539187	98. 88	

As is illustrated in Table 2, EST has a lower frequency of verb use, about 4% lower than OCT. This difference confirms our belief that English is prominently "nominal" while Chinese is more "verbal"(Si 2002:55-58;Shao 2005:24).

In addition, Table 2 displays difference in the use of pronouns, prepositions and conjunctions. On the one hand, TCT is very similar to OET but quite different from OCT in the use of pronouns, which suggests TCT has undergone interference from EST; on the other hand, TCT uses much fewer prepositions and conjunctions than EST(their source texts), which means TCT seems to have gone through less interference from EST in the use of prepositions and conjunctions.

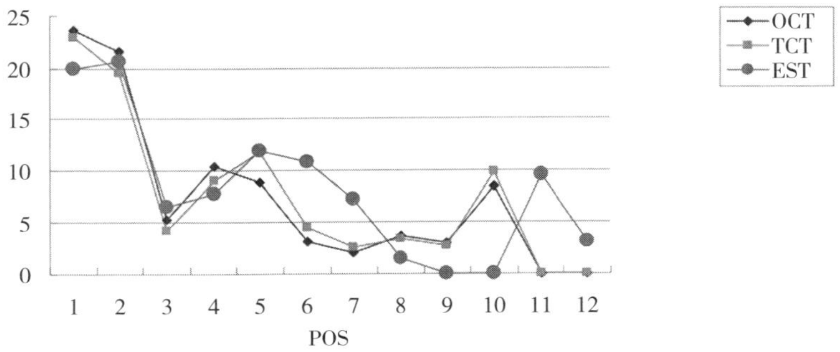

Figure 1 A broken line graph of POS distribution

Numbers along x-axis: 1=V; 2=N; 3=AJ; 4=AD; 5=PR; 6=CON; 7=PP; 8=NUM; 9=CLA; 10=PAR; 11=ART(En); 12=DET(En)

Figure 1 shows that TCT and OCT are very similar in line shape, but they are quite different from OEC. That suggests, as far as POS distribution is concerned, the difference between TCT and OCT is smaller than that between TCT and EST, and translational Chinese largely conforms to the normality of Chinese.

In sum, compared with OCT, TCT uses fewer verbs, nouns, adjectives and adverbs, but more pronouns, prepositions and conjunctions. In line with these facts, we have good reason to assume that POS distribution in TCT has received interference from English, the source language.

The analysis made so far shows TCT and OCT are similar in POS distribution, but it is still uncertain if this is true for the distribution of specific lexical items. For a close look at the behaviors of specific lexical items, we employ Keywords tool in

WordSmith 4.0 to extract words that have statistically significant difference in frequency in TCT and OCT(the reference corpus).In what follows,we observe content words in Section 5.2,and function words in Section 5.3.

5.2 Content Words

Nouns

We find that TCT and OCT are different in using nominal expressions.Lexically,the frequency of some words like 上帝(*God*),绅士(*gentleman*),牧师(*priest*) are unusually high in TCT in comparison with OCT, while OCT marks an higher frequency in the use of nouns like 当差(*lower official or servant in ancient China*),洋车(*rickshaw*),饺子(*jiaozi*),表姐(*a daughter of father's sister or of mother's brother or sister,who is older than oneself*),姑奶奶(*sister of one's paternal grandfather,sometimes refers to speaker herself,arrogantly*),旗袍(*chi-pao*),夜壶(*chamber pot*),to name just a few.

Morphologically,morphemes like 兄(*brother*),时(*time*),妇女(*woman,mother*),氏(*surname*),帖(*document or notes*),斋(*studio*),etc.to form the words like 令堂(*your mother*),午时(*at midday*) and 白塔寺(*Baita Temple*) are almost only found in OCT.

Apparently,the difference in using nouns is attributed largely to cultural and social differences between the two language communities.

Verbs

In TCT,the following verbs are used with unusually high frequency:a) aspectual verbs:开始(*begin*),结束(*finish*);b)"happen" verbs:发生(*happen*),产生(*produce*);c)"find" verbs:表现(*represent*),发现(*discover*);d) causative verbs:让(*let,make*);e)"judge" verbs:认为(*think*),相信(*believe*),感觉(*feel*);f) psychological verbs:害怕(*afraid*),怀疑(*doubt*);g) others:具有(*have*),存在(*exist, there be*). Certainly, these words also occur in OCT, but their frequency is remarkably lower. The major reason for this difference is that their counterparts (verbs,prepositional phrases,and adjectives) are used with usually high frequency in EST.

We also find OCT uses more monosyllabic verbs than TCT. The frequency of verbs such as 凑(*gahter*), 搁(*place*), 甭(*don't*), 傍(*depend on*), 嚷(*shout*), 嫌(*dislike*), 吵(*quarrel*), 捧(*hold in both hands*), 混(*mix, make trouble, lurk*), 怔(*daze*) is usually high in TCT compared to OCT, which tells us that, from a monosyllable-idiomaticity correlation perspective, TCT is less idiomatic than OCT.

Adjectives

As keywords extraction shows, OCT frequently uses more monosyllabic adjectives than TCT, which are 脆(*crisp*), 高(*high*), 贵(*expensive*), 好(*good*), 红(*red*), 厚(*thick*), 慌(*nervous*), 紧(*tight*), 老(*old*), 俏(*charming*), 小(*small*), 饱(*full*), 苦(*bitter*), etc.. In contrast, TCT only frequently uses a tiny number of adjectives like 大(*big*), 久(*long*), 多(*many*), 快(*fast*), but it frequently uses more disyllabic adjectives. This is another evidence of less idiomaticity in language use in TCT.

Locative Particle

In OCT, only 里(*inside*), 外边(*outside*), 内(*within*) are more frequently used in comparison with TCT. In TCT, however, there are more such high-frequency locative particles, such as 以前(*before*), 之前(*before*), 之间(*between*), 之后(*after*), 之中(*in*), 之外(*outside*), 周围(*around*). The unusual frequency of locative particles in TCT results from interference from EST, for the latter frequently uses prepositions such as *before*, *after*, *between*, *in*, *under*, *near*, *around*, etc., and this high frequency in use is reflected in rather frequent use of locative particles in Chinese translations.

Adverbs

In TCT, some time-related adverbs, such as 正(*in the process of*), 已(*already*), 已经(*already*), 一直(*always*), are much frequently found to co-occur with aspectual markers (ZHE, LE, GUO) to unify their temporal features. The reason for this is that TCT has a strong tendency to explicitate by lexical means the perfective and imperfective senses inherent respectively in *have v-en* and *have been v-ing* constructions.

Modal adverbs express speaker's attitude towards a proposition. In TCT, some modal adverbs are used with a strikingly high frequency, which are 必须(*must*), 或许(*perhaps*), 竟然(*actually*), 大约(*about*), 如此(*so*), etc. OCT, in contrast, frequently uses other words to perform the function, such as 得(*have to*), 兴许(*perhaps*), 原来(*actually*), 却(*actually*), 来(*about*), 这么(*so*). So, the difference is not only in frequency, but also in word choice: Modal adverbs used in TCT seem to be more formal, far from being spoken and spontaneous as those used in OCT.

5.3 Function Words

Pronominals

In OCT, the following pronominals① show an usually high frequency: 大家(*we*, *us*), 她们(*they*, *them*), 怎(*what*), 怎样(*what*), 这(*this*), 自己(*self*), etc.

In contrast, TCT uses the following pronominals in usually high frequency, such as 她(*she/her*), 他(*he/him*), 他们(*they/them*), 它(*it*), 它们(*them*), 我(*i/me*), 我们(*we/us*), 那(*that*), 那儿(*there*), 那个(*that one*), 那时(*then*), 那种(*that kind of*), 这个(*this*), 这时(*at the time*), 这种(*this kind of*), 这样(*in this way*), 其他(*other*), 另(*the other*), 别的(*other*), 任何(*anyone*), 每个(*everyone*), 一切(*all*). Obviously, in contrast with OCT, TCT seems to have exaggerated the use of 1st and 3rd personal pronouns, some demonstrative pronouns and some classifiers. In sum, the use of pronominals contributes to the uniqueness of translational Chinese. For more analysis, see Section 6.2.

Conjunctions

A major difference between TCT and OCT is found in the use of conjunctions. The statistics show that there are 16 conjunctions occurring with usually high frequency in TCT, such as 不过(*but*), 但(*but*), 但是(*but*), 尽管(*though*), 或者(*or*), 不仅(*not only*), 而且(*moreover*), 另外(*in addition*), 哪怕(*even if*), 即使

① In Chinese linguistic literature, pronouns belong to content words, however, they form a closed set, so we prefer to say they are function words.

(*even though*),如果(*if*),然后(*then*),因此(*so*),于是(*upon that*)and 和(*and*). In contrast, only 7 conjunctions are used frequently in OCT, which are 可是(*but*), 并且(*and*),况且(*besides*),不但(*not only*),所以(*so*),假若(*if*),愈……愈(*the more...the more*), etc. This difference in number and frequency only confirms our belief that logical relations are more implicit in Chinese than in English.

The POS distribution analysis made so far suggests many features characteristic of TCT can look to interference from EST for explanation. In short, compared with OCT, TCT uses more function words and more disyllabic words.

6. COMPOSITIONALITY

TCT may exaggerate the compositional potentiality of some morphemes or words in Chinese. The exaggeration can be observed in the following three ways.

6.1 Nominal Morphemes

Take for example the Chinese morpheme 性(*-xing*; meaning *property*, similar to *-ness*, *-ity*). It occurs 2.9 times per ten thousand words in original Chinese literary texts; in contrast, its frequency hits 5.2 in translated Chinese literary texts. Moreover, its diversity in composition increases in TCT. For example, there are 71 types of *-xing* combinations in translated Chinese literary texts, of which 42 are not used or rarely used in Chinese original literary texts, such as 独创性(*creativity*), 决定性(*decisiveness*), 可信性(*reliability*), 坚定性(*firmness*), 实质性(*substantiality*), 强制性(*compulsiveness*), etc. In the original Chinese literary texts, however, -xing is found more often to occur with monosyllabic words, forming words like 爽性(*straightforwardness*), 火性(*bad temper*), 牛性(*obstinacy*), 癖性(*natural inclination*), 韧性(*tenacity*), etc.

In translation, a translator consciously or subconsciously follow and imitate some features of source language (Kefei 2005). The active and diverse use of *-xing* morpheme in TCT is a good case in point. In TCT, *-xing* imitates the corresponding suffixes such as -*ity*, -*ness*, -*dom*, etc. in English, hence more active than it is in OCT. Interestingly, -*xing* is now a regular morpheme in Mandarin Chinese.

The phenomenon mentioned above is true for morphemes such as -力(*force*, *ability*), -度(*degree*, *extent*) in TCT where they are very frequently used to form technical terms.

In a word, the high-frequency use of these morphemes in TCT suggests an imitation of their compositionality in English.

6.2 Composition of "Dem + Num + Cla"

The construction "demonstrative pronoun (Dem) + numeral (Num) + classifier (Cla)" occurs more frequently in TCT than in OCT. Listed below are three constructions with such high frequency.

Table 3 Distributions of "Dem + Num + Cla" Constructions

	TCT		OCT	
	Frequency	**MI**	**Frequency**	**MI**
这 一	1010	0. 035	334	0. 019
这 种	491	0. 09	39	0. 012
这件事	123	0. 017		

In OCT, the Dem-Num composition 这一(*zheyi*; literally, *this one*) typically co-occurs with monosyllabic words such as 点(point), 条(item), 天(day), 次(time), 年(year); but in TCT, the construction's compositional potentiality is dramatically enhanced in that it also frequently co-occurs with disyllabic words like 问题(problem), 条款(article, clause, item), 事实(fact), 目标(aim), 领域(field), 计划(plan), 过程(process) and 观点(viewpoint). This enhancement contributes partially to high-frequency use of disyllabic words in TCT.

Another case in point is 这种(*zhe zhong*; literally, *this kind*), this Dem-Num phrase is weak in compositionality in OCT because it almost exclusively co-occurs with 人(*person*). Even so, the combination "这种-人" is far less frequently used in OCT than in TCT (39 vs. 295). In TCT, *zhe zhong* is extremely active, and it can yield diversified compositions, as can be seen in its composition with 药(*medicine*),病(*disease*),事(*matter*),做法(*practice*),想法(*idea*),现象(*phenomenon*),感觉(*feeling*),情况(*situation*),方式(*way*),方法(*method*),and with many other nominals that are not frequently or typically used in OCT.

The search in GCEPC shows the frequent use of 这一 and 这种 in TCT corresponds to the frequent use of articles and demonstrative (such as *the/this/that*) in EST.

For the same reason, other such phrases as 一个(*an-individual*),一件(*an-item*),一位(*a-position*),一片(*a-slice*) occur more frequently in TCT than in OCT. The major reason for this difference is that indefinite articles in English strongly tend to be rendered into Chinese Num-Cla phrases.

It should be noted that many Num-Cla-N bundles used in TCT are not always the direct translations of NPs in EST; in fact, some of them are renderings of pronouns or demonstratives. For example, 这件事 in TCT might be an equivalent of *it*, *this* or *that*, but not necessarily *the matter* or *the thing*.

(3) a. It had happened at last.

这件事终于发生-了。

This matter eventually happen-LE(crs)

b. "Nobody knows about this but us?"

"除了咱们,没人知道这件事-吧?"

"except us, no man know this matter-BA?"

c. "Humph! We'll see about that."

"嗯,这件事我们得管一管-了。"

"Er, this matter we have to take care of-LE(cr)"

d. There must 'a' been an angel there.

这件事一定有个高手在-帮你的忙。

This matter must have one master-hand ZAI-help your busy-work.

The examples above demonstrate changes of cohesive devices in E-C translation, i. e. a change from pronouns, demonstratives or demonstrative adverbs in

English to NPs in Chinese version. These changes reflect the difference between Chinese and English: the former employs more lexical devices to realize textual coherence. However, the changes are not frequently found in TCT; in fact, compared with OCT, TCT resorts more to the use of pronominals to achieve textual cohesion, which means translational Chinese is very similar to English source texts in the use of cohesive devices.

All in all, some grammatical devices typically used in English are prone to being imitated in E-C translation, which leads to the overuse of the compositionality of some morphemes, phrases and cohesive devices and which makes TCT less idiomatic than OCT.

6.3 Relative Fixedness of Some Expressions

It is argued that some phrasal discourse markers such as comment clauses*I think*, *it seems* and conversational routines (such as *thank you*), are to some degree lexicalized, because they are relatively fixed usages (see Brinton & Traugott 2005: 67). In TCT, we do find some lexical bundles that are rather frequently used. They might not be very 'Chinese', but they tend to be "institutionalized" and become rather fixed. Below are two examples.

随着时间的推移

The expression 随着时间的推移 (lit. along with time's running) denotes the passage of time. It is often used in Chinese, yet it is borrowed from English (perhaps an imitation of *with the passage of time*). What interests us here is the fact that the expression can be used in dealing with many similar expression in English, such as *as time went on*, *moment by moment*, *over time*, *as time drifted along*, *with a long-term time horizon*, *in the course of time*, *as time went by*, or even *eventually*.

Actually, the expression is now a regular expression in Chinese, and is even more popular than the very "Chinese" expressions like 光阴荏苒 (*time elapses quickly*), 日复一日 (*day after day*), 岁月流转 (*with the passage of time*). Perhaps it is due to translation that the expression 随着时间的推移 becomes an expression frequently used in Chinese.

是(不)可能(的)

The expression 是(不)可能(的)(lit.(is not) possible) conveys speaker's attitude toward a proposition. In TCT, this frequently-used expression is an equivalent to many expressions in EST. Below is a list of the possible equivalents.

Table 4 Expressions equivalent to 是(不)可能(的)

English Equivalents	POSSIBLE	CAN	LIKELY	WILL	Might	Probable	Incapable	No Equivalent	Total
Frequency	41	10	5	2	2	1	1	3	67

In OCT, the expression 是(不)可能(的) appears only 17 times, all of which being found in political texts; in addition, it is usually put at the end of a sentence, hence not used frequently and diversely. In TCT, its use is diversified because it can appear at different positions in a clause (quite like the use of 'possibility' expressions in English).

What's more, in TCT, the load capacity of 是不可能[…]的 is expanded. As in the example below, where the capacity of [...] is expanded to 34 Chinese characters (in Chinese version, parts in italics are equivalent to the part following "the impossibility that" in English):

(4) [...], but had long since recognized the impossibility that *any mission of divine and mysterious truth should be confided to a woman stained with sin, bowed down with shame, or even burdened with a life-long sorrow.*

[...],但从那以后,她早已承认了:任何上界的神秘真理的使命是不可能委托给一个为罪孽所玷污、为耻辱所压倒或者甚至为终生的忧愁而沉闷的女人的。

Through N-gram search within TCT, we find many other expressions behaving like the above two expressions, which are 目的是为了(*for the purpose of*),在某种程度/意义上(*to some degree, in a sense*),是必要的(*it is necessary that*),一遍又一遍(*time and again*),很久很久以前(*long, long ago*),更确切地说(*precisely*),

一般情况下(*generally*).

The fixedness of expressions in TCT suggests that once an expression enters into the target language through translation, it might become relatively fixed and frequently used in translational language or even grow into a popular expression in target language. TCT has a stronger tendency to use relatively fixed expressions to deal with diverse expressions (with same or similar functions) in EST, which can serve as a support for lexical simplification, but at the same time a denial of normalization in translation universals.

7. CONCLUSION

Translational Chinese has the following features: 1) TCT uses fewer monosyllabic words than OCT does; 2) TCT tends to expand the normal load capacity of some Chinese constructions, which leads to longer sentence segments; 3) compared with OCT, TCT uses more function words; 4) TCT can change or expand the compositionality of some words or morphemes in Chinese.

The features mentioned-above do not fully support the translation universals.

Firstly, TCT use more types and longer segments than OCT. This does not support lexical and syntactic simplification;

Secondly, explicitation in TCT runs in parallel with implicitation, such as the implicitation of logical relations and co-reference devices. In this sense, explicitation is a relative notion. As far as English-Chinese translation is concerned, TCT is more explicit than OCT, but more implicit than EST. This relativity suggests explicitation and implicitation co-exist in any translation pair; it is not always unidirectional.

Thirdly, TCT exaggerates the compositional potentiality of some morphemes and words inChinese, and it has expanded some Chinese constructions' load capacity. Considering this, TCT does not fully support normalization.

It can be concluded that the so-called translation universals might be a shifting phenomenon between specific languages or just some features in local translated discourse.It is by no means the only phenomenon applicable to all translational languages.

（本文原载 Richard Xiao（ed），*Using Corpora in Contrastive and Translation Studies*，Newcastle：Cambridge Scholars Publishing，2010，pp.164－181。作者为王克非、秦洪武）

References

M.Baker，"Corpus Linguistics and Translation Studies：Implications and Applications"，M.Baker，G.Francis and E.Tognini－Bonelli（eds.），*Text and Technology：In Honour of John Sinclair*，Amsterdam，Philadelphia：John Benjamins，1993，pp.233－250.

M.Baker，"Réexplorer la Langue de la Traduction：une Approche par Corpus"，*Meta*，1998a，Vol 43，No.4，pp.480－485.

M.Baker，*Routledge Encyclopedia of Translation Studies*，London：Routledge，1998b.

L.J. Brinton & E. C. Traugott，*Lexicalization and Language Change*，Cambridge：Cambridge University Press，2005.

H.Chen，"The Contextual Analysis of Chinese Sentences with Punctuation Marks"，*Literary and Linguistic Computing*，1994，Vol 9，No.4，pp.281－289.

S.Hansen & E.Teich，"Multi－layer Analysis of Translation Corpora：Methodological Issues and Practical Implications"，D.Cristea，N.Ide.D.Marcu and M.Poesio（eds.），*Proceedings of EUROLAN* 2001 *Workshop on Multi－layer Corpus－based Analysis*，Iasi，Romania，2001，pp.44－55.

C.Hopkinson，"Factors in Linguistic Interference：A Case of Study in Translation"，*Skase Journal of Translation and Interpretation*，2007，Vol 2，No.1，pp.13－23.

Libo Huang & Kefei Wang，"Fanyi Pubianxing Yanjiu Fansi"（"Reflections on the Corpus－based Studies of Translation Universals"），*Chinese Translators Journal*，2006，No.5，pp.36－40.

Kefei Wang，"Hanyu Ba Zi Ju Tedian，Fenbu Ji Yingyi"（"Chinese BA－construction and its English Translation"），*Foreign Languages and Their Teaching*，2003，No.12，pp.1－5.

Kefei Wang, "Fanyi Zhong De Yin He Xian" ("Implicitation and Explicitation in Translation"), *Foreign Language Teaching and Research*, 2005, No.4, pp.303-307.

Lü Shuxiang (ed.), *Xiandai Hanyu Ba Bai Ci* (*Eight Hundred Words in Mandarin Chinese*). Beijing: The Commercial Press, 1980.

Hongwu Qin, & Kefei Wang, "Jiyu Yuliaoku De Fanyi Yuyan Fenxi" ("Parallel corpora-based Analysis of Translationese"), *Modern Foreign Languages*, 2004, No. 1, pp. 44-52.

D.Santos, "On Grammatical Translationese", Kimmo Koskenniemi (ed.), *Short papers presented at the Tenth Scandinavian Conference on Computational Linguistics*, Helsinki, 1995, pp.59-66.

Zhihong Shao, *Han Ying Duibi Fanyi Daolun* (*Chinese-English Contrastive Analysis and Translation*), Shanghai: Huadong University of Technology Press, 2005.

Guo Si, *Yi Dao Tanwei* (*Looking into Translation*), Beijing: China Translation & Publishing Corporation, 2002.

G.Toury. *Descriptive Translation Studies and Beyond*, Amsterdam/Philadelphia: John Benjamins Publishing Company, 1995.

I.Westin, *Language and Computers: Studies in Practical Linguistics*, New York: Rodopi, 2002.

Ang Wu & Libo Huang, "Guanyu Fanyi Gongxing De Yanjiu" ("On Corpus-based Studies of Translation Universals"), *Foreign Language Teaching and Research*, 2006, No.5, pp.296-302.

Guangzhong Yu, *Yu Guangzhong Tan Fanyi* (*On Translation*), Beijing: China Translation & Publishing Corporation, 2002.

What is peculiar to translational Mandarin Chinese? A corpus-based study of Chinese constructions' load capacity

It is generally held that the sentence length (hereafter S-Length) provides useful information about the reading level of a text. However, it does not work very well as an indicator in studying translational Mandarin Chinese. To improve reliability of the length measurement, this article seeks to give an alternative account from the perspective of the sentence segment length (henceforth SS-Length), which is closely correlated with the construction load capacity (CLC) to which Mandarin Chinese is sensitive. The study demonstrates that, as far as Mandarin Chinese is concerned, the SS-Length account is more revealing than the S-Length counterpart, because the former is more relevant to language use in Chinese. It is also found that CLC, which is related to the SS-Length, is one of the determinants that contribute to the readability of a Chinese text. Hence it should be a staple part in translation assessment and translator training.

1. INTRODUCTION

Corpus-based studies over the past two decades have shown that translated texts have a number of recurrent common features independent of the languages involved in translation, including simplification. For example, translational language has been shown to use simpler syntax(Baker 1993;Puurtinen 2003:148).This feature is also related to the mean sentence length(S-Length)as there is a dominant belief that the S-Length is an index of readability.For instance,it has been found that translations have a lower mean sentence length than comparable non-translational texts(Laviosa 2002:60-62).However,the explanatory power of the sentence length account is only tested in newspaper texts;whether it is also applicable to literary translation is a question that remains unanswered(Olohan 2004:100);and whether it applies to translational Mandarin Chinese is unknown either.Wang and Qin(2009)shows that translational Mandarin generally uses longer sentences(2.32 words longer on average than those in original Mandarin texts), but such an obvious difference is not found in translated and non-translated literary Chinese texts(which show a difference of only 0.35 words on average).The first finding is a counterexample of the alleged syntactic simplification, while the second does not seem to support the very existence of a significant difference in the mean sentence length between translated and nontranslated Chinese.

The very similar S-Lengths in translated and non-translated Chinese literary texts mask a key fact, i.e. in English-to-Chinese translation, translated Chinese sentences, owing to the different degrees of adherence to the source language norms, are prone to be wordy and lengthy(Wu 1984:648).To uncover the hidden cause of wordiness, we need go deeper into the internal structure of a sentence, and see if there are other accounts that help to better describe the features of translational Chinese.

Recently, studies by Wang(2003), Hu(2007) and Huang(2008) suggest that translational Mandarin Chinese supports such translation universals as explicitation, simplification, and normalization and so on(Baker 1998).There are, however, still some issues left unaddressed.For example, there are no adequate descriptions of the features unique to translational Mandarin Chinese; nor has a proper way been proposed to identify such unique features.To flesh out these features, the present study will focus on the construction load capacity(CLC)and the mean sentence segment length(SS-Length).

2. CLC AND SS-LENGTH

2.1 What is CLC?

We use the acronym CLC for the construction load capacity. A 'construction', as has been used in Goldberg(1995:4), refers to a basic unit of language, which can be either a clause or an independent phrasal pattern like V-NP or P-NP that pairs form with meaning. A construction has meaning, but such a property has little to do with the number of words or the complexity of expressions in it. In this article, however, we will not address the semantic aspect of a construction; instead, we focus on its grammatical attributes.

English and Mandarin Chinese have very few or no case inflections, so the meaning of a sentence in these languages depends heavily on word order(Baker 1992:110). However, English and Mandarin Chinese are quite different in the linear order of peripheral syntactic elements(such as prepositional phrases, attributives and participles). For instance, in English, a modifying element can be post-positioned by using such grammatical devices as relative clauses, participle phrases and prepositional phrases. In contrast, Mandarin Chinese lacks such devices, which leads to its left-branching feature(Liu 2006:205), i.e. the rejection of post-modification. Therefore, Mandarin Chinese clauses and phrases are typically close-ending, with objects or head nouns being the end points.

Being left-branching and close-ending, a Mandarin Chinese construction is sensitive to its load capacity; or as Lian(2006:34) puts it, it "resents" the insertion of long modifiers. Thus, a Mandarin Chinese clause tends to be short; and theoretically, a Mandarin Chinese sentence may contain more segments than does its English equivalent.

2.2 SS-Length

According to Chen(1994),75% of Mandarin Chinese sentences are composed of two or more sentence segments.A sentence segment is much like a Chinese term 读 *dou* 'a pause in a sentence',and it can be a single sentence or a part of a sentence divided by a comma or a colon.Be it a phrase,a clause or one-segment sentence,a sentence segment(SS)is a syntactic unit that is semantically independent, which means it can be taken as a unit of analysis for translational Chinese.Considering the sensitivity of Mandarin Chinese to its construction load capacity(CLC),it can be assumed that,other things being equal,the larger the CLC,the longer the SS.In turn,the SS-Length can in most cases mirror the read ability of language use in a text.

As has been observed in Qin(2010),for Chinese original texts,the S-Length is positively correlated with the number of sentence segments,and it has little to do with the SS-Length,as little variation in length is found in the use of sentence segments in original Chinese texts.For translational Mandarin Chinese,however,that is not the case.The S-Length(which is relatively stable)has little to do with the number of sentence segments,but the number of SS is negatively correlated with the SS-Length.Given the above features,we have strong reasons for supposing that the SS-Length and its load capacity are leading factors in determining the quality of language use in English-Chinese translation.

With the above concepts,we will examine the interrelations among the S-Length,the SS-Length,and the CLC,with a view to pinpointing the reason underlying the difference in the SS-Length.

3. RESEARCH METHOD AND DATA

3.1 Methodology

The present study takes a quantitative approach to investigating the features of translational Mandarin Chinese. As has already been noted, the effectiveness of the SS-Length observation is only theoretical, which means it needs support from empirical language data. For that purpose, we use the SS-Length account to seek data support in the hope that, with the help of POS-tagged corpus analysis, the account will equip us with more detailed evidence in delving into the internal composition of the segments.

3.2 Corpus data

The comparable corpus data we use for description and analysis are from the General Chinese - English Parallel Corpus (GCEPC), a Chinese - English bidirectional parallel corpus developed by Beijing Foreign Studies University (BFSU) that contains about 20 million English words and Chinese characters marked up in the XML format (Wang 2003). GCPEC has four subcorpora, namely Chinese-English Literature (CHOL), Chinese-English Non-literature (CHONL), English - Chinese Literature (CHTL), and English - Chinese Non - literature (CHNL). Therefore, the corpus for this study includes the Chinese-English and English-Chinese subcorpora, forming a comparable corpus of approximately 3.5 million English words and Chinese characters. Now we have two comparable components for original and translational Chinese: the original Chinese corpus (684,988 characters, including original Chinese texts from CHOL and CHONL), the translational Chinese corpus (700,931 characters, including translated Chinese texts from CHTL and CHTNL). In addition to this scaled-down comparable corpus, GCEPC also enables us to take into account the influence of English source texts on translational Chinese.

In addition, we choose for reference and comparison a text entitled *Ernü Yingxiong Zhuan* (*The Tale of Heroic Sons and Daughters*, HERO for short), which was written by Wen Kang in mid-19th century Qing Dynasty and was translated into English by Fei Zhide. The novel, written in the Beijing dialect, has generally been referred to in Chinese linguistic literature as a work featuring the transition from Chinese *wenyan* (ancient Chinese) to modem *baihua* (modern Chinese). With such a distinctive feature, the text is used in this study as a reference corpus, from which we can observe the features of CLC at the early stage of modern *baihua* and explores the way in which the CLC is expanded in translation.

For the ease of data retrieval, all the texts in the corpus are annotated with part-of-speech information while the English-Chinese parallel texts are aligned at the sentence level. It should be noted that all the texts in GCEPC's translation pairs are from the modern times (1940–2004).

In what follows, we will first discuss the computation of the S-Length and the SS-Length, which is followed by an analysis of translational Chinese. We will then move on to focus on microscopic analysis, i.e. syntactic complexity demonstrated in sentence segments.

3.3 Data collection

The data used in computing the SS-Length are drawn from each subcorpus, and the raw frequency counts are normalized to a common base (per 10,000 running words) for factor analysis with the aim of deriving dimensions that account for the difference among the subcorpora. Finally we go into the factors that have correlations with the capacity of Chinese constructions.

To get an exact measure of the SS-Length, we use regular expression search built in Antconc (3.3.0w.). The regular expression used in identifying sentence segments in the POS tagged Chinese corpus is given as follows.

```
[(。|;|:|!|?|,)/w)|(\n)]\s{1,}(\b[^\x00-\xff]+/[\x00-\xff]+\b\s{1,}){1,30}[,|。|?|;|:|!]/w
```

The regular expressions uses [^\x00-\xff] as a metacharacter for a Chinese character, and [\x00-\xff] for an English letter (the tags attached to Chinese words in the corpus use one or two English letters). The sequence (。|;|:|!|?|,)/w) means the beginning of a sentence of a clause, with (\n) standing for the beginning of a paragraph while \s means that every word is followed by a space. The string [,|。|?|;|!]/w means the end of a sentence segment, be it a sentence ending punctuation mark, a colon, or a quotation mark. "{1,30}" denotes the number of Chinese words in SS, from one word to 30 words. We use "\s{1,}" because in the corpus, there may be spaces larger than 2.

In the expression, {1,30} means that the SS-Length is within the range from the one-word segment to the 30-word segment.① In addition, we also make a search of SS with the length of 31 words or more (as shown by 31+word in Table 1). It should be noted that sentence segments of different lengths are concordanced separately.

Regular expressions are also used to obtain information about the internal composition of Mandarin Chinese sentence structures. As will be seen in the following sections, a proper account of modifiers can well reflect the composition of sentence segments, as Chinese SS-Length is sensitive to pre-modifiers. While it may be difficult to identify the internal structure of a Chinese sentence segment, Mandarin Chinese typically uses the structural particle 的 (DE) to mark an attributive modifier,② which makes it possible to extract nominal modifiers by searching for DE. Based on such a cue, the following regular expressions are used in this study to measure the SS-Length.

a. Regex used in extracting sentence segments with one occurrence of DE:

\b 的/u\b\s(\b[^\x00-\xff]+/[^w]\b\s){1,}

b. Regex used in extracting sentence segments with two occurrences of DE:

(\b[^\x00-\xff]+/[\x00-\xff]+\b\s){1,}\b 的/u\b\s(\b[^\

① Sentence segments with the length of 31 or more words are very rare in the corpus (usually no hit in some subcorpora), so we just search SS with that number of words at one time by using the regular expression given below: [(。|;|:|! |? |,)/w)|(\n)]\s{1,}(\b[^\x00-\xff]+/[\x00-\xff]+\b\s{1,}){1,30}[,|。|? |;|:|!]/w.

② In this article several abbreviations are used in grammatical glosses of Chinese examples, including ASP for aspect marker; CL for classifier, DE for structure particle de which is a marker of modification between the modifier and the modified, LOC for locative, PAR for particle, and PL for plural suffix-men.

x00-\xff]+/[\x00-\xff]+\b\s){1,}\b 的/u\b\s(\b[^\x00-\xff]+/[\x00-\xff]+\b\s){1,}

In b),"(\b[^\x00-\xff]+/[\x00-\xff]+\b\s){1,}\b 的/u\b" means any number of words (at least one) before the auxiliary "的/u", and "\b 的/u\b\s(\b[^\x00-\xff]+/[\x00-\xff]+\b\s){1,}" means any number of words following "的/u". Searching with the regular expression returned concordances exemplified below, where there are two modifiers in each clause:

规定/n 了/y 对/p 证券/n 投资/v 的/u 新/a 的/u 限制/v 办法/n

regulate ASP to stock investment DE new DE restriction method

官员/n 们/k 非常/d 熟悉/v 他们/r 调控/vn 的/u 企业/n 的/u 情况/n

official men(pl.) very familiar their readjust DE enterprise DE situation

Table 1: Standardized frequencies of sentence segments ofvarious lengths

SS-Length	Chinese Original Texts			Chinese Translated Texts	
	HERO	CHOL	CHNL	CHTL	CHTNL
1-word	52.41628	48.32079	30.34225	47.86367	37.99655
2-word	85.16475	66.07731	39.47885	55.07481	28.34363
3-word	123.546	98.32867	61.87201	67.60172	39.54622
4-word	137.45	120.4857	74.15917	81.91507	48.60766
5-word	126.5027	122.9319	76.48573	86.59904	52.22751
6-word	117.5577	110.1945	71.05708	81.719	53.20936
7-word	99.29338	91.25699	62.28401	73.02641	51.97909
8-word	76.5753	69.97166	51.57213	62.48203	49.29378
9-word	58.66656	50.65459	40.76331	50.3037	41.29699
10-word	41.8432	36.75023	31.0693	37.95108	36.86091
11-word	29.77304	26.75428	23.58068	29.75957	32.10543
12-word	21.42686	18.62818	16.79487	22.23253	25.88308
13-word	14.35319	12.6531	12.8688	17.27624	20.67807
14-word	9.637409	8.477579	9.185073	12.57048	16.06454

续表

SS-Length	Chinese Original Texts			Chinese Translated Texts	
	HERO	CHOL	CHNL	CHTL	CHTNL
15-word	5. 707592	5. 876663	6. 858511	9. 335268	12. 58665
16-word	4. 042098	4. 105229	4. 192659	6. 808101	9. 806705
17-word	2. 619878	2. 333794	3. 029378	5. 359337	7. 606407
18-word	1. 628067	1. 658962	2. 011507	3. 485748	5. 417938
19-word	1. 010524	1. 237192	1. 502571	2. 374666	3. 915584
20-word	0. 65497	0. 801363	0. 848226	1. 688409	2. 981049
21-word	0. 598829	0. 548301	0. 678581	1. 154654	2. 259446
22-word	0. 392982	0. 379593	0. 29082	0. 762507	1. 596991
23-word	0. 261988	0. 295239	0. 24235	0. 653578	1. 206615
24-word	0. 130994	0. 126531	0. 169645	0. 533755	0. 970024
25-word	0	0. 084354	0. 121175	0. 381254	0. 591478
26-word	0. 037427	0. 098413	0. 121175	0. 272324	0. 319398
27-word	0. 074854	0. 056236	0. 072705	0. 239645	0. 224762
28-word	0	0. 070295	0. 04847	0. 130716	0. 212932
29-word	0. 037427	0. 014059	0. 024235	0. 054465	0. 118296
30-word	0	0. 014059	0	0. 076251	0. 118296
31+word	0. 018713	0. 028118	0. 121175	0. 239645	0. 283909

Regular expressions constructed in similar ways can be used to extract sentence segments with more occurrences of DE from the corpus.

4. COMPUTATION OF THE SS-LENGTH

Regular expression searches enable us to get the frequency counts from the subcorpora of sentence segments within the length range (1 – 30 words) and segments with the length of 31 or more words(31+) ,which in turn are standardized (in every 10,000 running words).The standardized frequency list is given in Table

1, where the number in the left-most column denotes the length (in words) of sentence segments, and the numbers in other columns denote its relative frequencies in the subcorpora.

Figure 1 illustrates the difference in the distribution of sentence segments of various lengths in each subcorpus. As can be seen, in terms of SS-Length distribution, Chinese original literature (CHOL) is very similar to the mid-19th century Mandarin Chinese novel (HERO). That fact is hard to overlook: in terms of SS-Length, the Chinese literature norm remains unchanged. Does it mean that Mandarin Chinese remains the same over such a long period of time? Certainly not. But what has been changed? We will try to answer this question by looking into the internal structure of sentence segments (see Section 5).

Another point worth noticing in Figure 1 is the obvious difference in the frequency of sentence segments of 3-9 words. Yet that description might be misleading, in that there is difference at every length point in the graph, and the graph itself cannot reflect the extent to which the subcorpora differ from each other. For a better account, we will describe the variability among observed variables in terms of a potentially lower number of unobserved variables (called factors). In other words we will use factor analysis to observe the variations in the five variables.

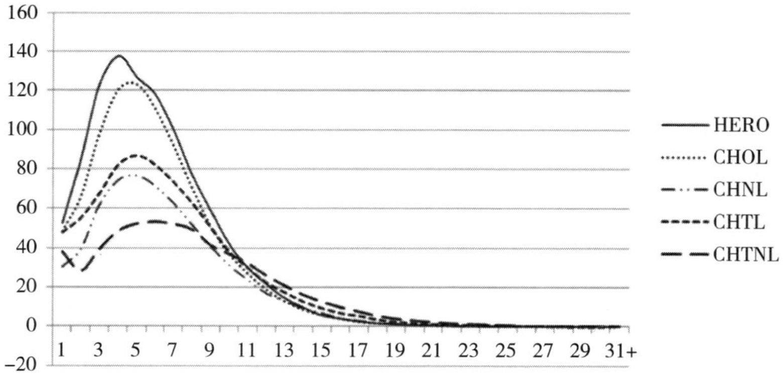

Fig.1: Distribution of sentence segments of various lengths in five subcorpora

Table 2: Rotated component matrix

SS-Length	Component		SS-Length	Component	
	1	2		1	2
tw4(24)	.999	-.018	tw8(28)	.947	-.138
sxtn(16)	.999	.002	tw6(26)	.937	-.159
eitn(18)	.998	-.065	tw7(27)	.894	.101
svtn(17)	.997	-.041	telv(12)	.872	.467
twty(20)	.994	-.053	Fiv(5)	-.798	.579
fortn(14)	.993	.058	Fou(4)	-.784	.613
fiftn(15)	.993	-.118	six(6)	-.771	.625
tw3(23)	.992	.034	thr(3)	-.763	.635
nitn(19)	.989	-.131	ele(11)	.729	.676
twl(21)	.985	-.049	sev(7)	-.728	.679
thity(30)	.983	.065	ten(10)	.048	.991
tw5(25)	.982	-.121	one(1)	-.225	.944
thrtn(13)	.980	,166	nin(9)	-.474	.868
tw2(22)	.979	.065	eit(8)	-.618	.782
tw9(29)	.964	.078	two(2)	-.680	.729

Table 2 and the component plot in the rotated space in Figure 2 suggest that there are two components representing the difference among the subcorpora. The method of factor extraction in factor analysis is Principal Component Analysis while the method is of rotation is Quartimax with Kaiser Normalization (with rotation converged in three iterations). What is striking about the statistical data is the explanatory power of longer sentence segments: longer segments can better illustrate the difference between original and translational Chinese.

As can be seen in Figure 2, in Component 1, sentence segments of lengths such as 24, 16, 18, 17, 20, 14, 23, 19, 21, 30, 25, 13, 22, 29, 28, 26 words are extracted as factors, all of which are segments longer than 13 words, hence unusually long segments. In Component 2, only segments as long as 1, 10, 9 words are extracted. Considering the gap in length, it is difficult to name the component. Yet, we can still describe them by comparing them with the length of sentence segments in typical Chinese novels found by Qin(2010), i.e.5.51 words on average. Even with this value as a reference, the factors in Component 2 are still much longer segments (10,9) and the shortest segment(1) falls far below the average SS-Length.

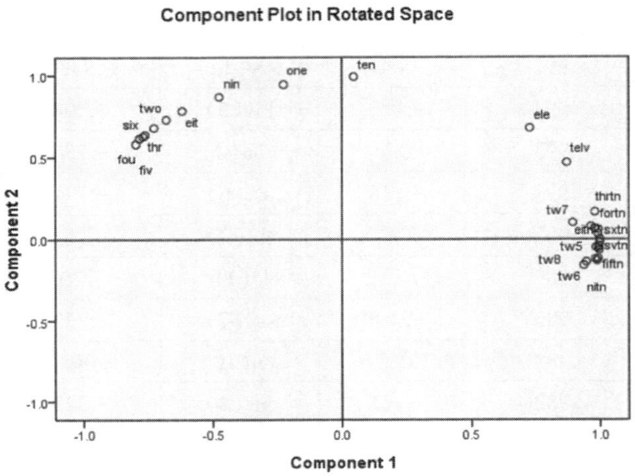

Fig.2: Principal Component Analysis of SS-Length variables in the five subcorpora

The statistical analysis helps us to identify the factors contributing to the difference between original and translational Chinese texts. It is clear that the longer, especially the unusually long segments should be taken into research focus.

5. CONSTRUCTION LOAD CAPACITY

In light of the above analysis, the SS-Length can be taken as the major factor affecting the S-Length in translational Mandarin Chinese. In what follows, we will first explore the correlations between the SS-Length and the CLC in terms of the number of pre-modifiers introduced by DE, an auxiliary marker standing between a modifier and the nominal it modifies.

5.1 Correlations between the SS-Length and the number of modifiers

Before moving on to examine the role played by the Chinese 'x-DE' construction in building fairly lengthy sentence segments (x refers to a syntactic element serving as a modifier), we will first justify our decision to select the construction for analysis. Based on the above findings, we assume that given close-endedness and left-branching modification of Chinese constructions, 'x-DE' as a pre-modifier plays a crucial role, to the degree that the longer a sentence segment is, the more likely the 'x-DE' construction will be used. For limited space, we will focus on three types of sentence segments, namely those containing two, three and more 'x-DE' constructions.

To test this assumption, we use the Correlate tool in SPSS 16.0 to undertake a correlation analysis between the SS-Length, two 'x-DE' pre-modifiers and three 'x-DE' pre-modifiers on the basis of the relative frequency of pre-modifiers for sentence segment of each size. The relative frequency is obtained by dividing the frequency of sentence segments of each length by the number of 'x-DE' premodifiers used in them.

Table 3: Correlation Analysis of SS-Length and SS complexity

		Single 'x-DE'	SS-Length	Double 'x-DE'	Triple 'x-DE'
Single 'x-DE'	Pearson correlation	1	.787**	.615**	.893**
	Sig. (2-tailed)	—	.000	.000	.000
	N	140	140	140	140
SS-Length	Pearson correlation	.787**	1	.567**	.702**
	Sig. (2-tailed)	.000	—	.000	.000
	N	140	140	140	140
Double 'x-DE'	Pearson correlation	.615**	.567**	1	.258**
	Sig. (2-tailed)	,000	,000	—	.002
	N	140	140	140	140
Triple 'x-DE'	Pearson correlation	.893**	.702**	.258**	1
	Sig. (2-tailed)	.000	.000	.002	-
	N	140	140	140	140

Note: ** means that correlation is significant at the 0.01 level (2-tailed).

Table 3 shows the result of the correlation analysis. As can be seen, the significance level of each correlation coefficient is very small (less than 0.01), which means that the correlation is highly significant and each pair of variables are linearly related. Hence the hypothesis is validated that the SS-Length, the number of DE constructions used in the sentence segment, and the use of multiple 'x-DE' pre-modifiers are positively correlated, in both original and translational Chinese texts. Based on the statistical results, we will examine more closely the use of 'x-DE' pre-modifiers in original and translational Chinese texts.

The analysis made thus far reveals the SS-Length can be taken as a major contributor to the S-Length in translational Mandarin Chinese. Considering that longer sentence segments better reveal the difference among the five subcorpora, we will focus on the use of triple 'x-DE' constructions used in long sentence segments.

6. LOAD CAPACITY ANALYSIS

Before we do the analysis, it is necessary to give a classification of the 'x-DE' structure, which can be done in terms of structural composition. Modifiers can be classified according to their complexity: it can be a word, hence a simple modifier; it can also be a phrase or a clause-like expression which takes a verb, hence a complex one. When there are many modifiers modifying one constituent, they are modifiers in parallelism, hence parallel modifiers; when modifiers are not all in parallelism, with at least one modifier being embedded in another, which we call embedded modifiers. In what follows, we use these concepts to observe the behavior of CLC related modification in the five subcorpora.

6.1 Simple parallel modifiers

In original Chinese, simple parallel modifiers are frequently used, yet the use of three or more parallel modifiers is rarely found, as illustrated in example (1).

(1) ST:……只有小风扇的单调的嗬嗬的声响(CHOL)

zhiyou xiao fengshan de dandiao de hehe de shengxiang.

only-have small electric-fan DE monotonous DE whir DE sound

TT:...only by the monotonous whir of the electric fan...

In this segment, the elements 小风扇 *xiao fengshan* 'small electric fan', 单调 *dandiao* 'monotonous' and 荷荷 *hehe* 'whir' all modify the head noun 声响 *shengxiang* 'sound'. So the segment has three modifiers between the verb 有 *you* 'have' and its object 声响 *shengxiang* 'sound'; moreover, the construction does not seem to be heavy-loaded because the modifiers are very short. Such multiple modifiers, however, are not frequently found in original Chinese literary texts, where double simple parallel modifiers are more often used instead.

6.2 Parallel modification with embedded simple modifiers

In the target text (TT) in example (2), the modifier 洁白的 *jiebai de* 'clean-white DE' is embedded in the modifier 混凝土构成的 *hunningtu goucheng de* 'concrete compose DE' that modifies the head noun 世界 *shijie* 'world'. The modifier is simple and short, therefore it does not reduce the readability of the segment.

(2) ST: a glittering antiseptic world of glass and steel and snow-white concrete(CHTL)

TT:这是一个由玻璃、钢筋、洁白的混凝土构成的晶莹夺目的世界

zhe shi yige you boli gangjin jiebai de hunningtu goucheng de jingying duomu

this is a with glass steel clean-white DE concrete compose DE antiseptic glittering

de shijie

DE world

Sometimes descriptive adjectives in the English source text are rendered into clausal modifiers in Chinese, as shown in (3), where the adjective 'fruitful' in the source text is translated into Chinese as a clausal element 结着果实的 *jie-zhe guoshi de* 'bear-ZHE fruits DE', which reduces readability.

(3) ST: along the fruitful banks of the broad rivers [CHTL]

TT:沿着广阔的河流的结着果实的河岸

yanzhe guangkuo de heliu de jie-zhe guoshi de he'an

along broad DE river DE bear-ASP fruits DE bank

6.3 Parallel modification with clausal modifiers

Example(4) from HERO illustrates the use of a clausal modifier

(4) ST:竟是来救我一家儿的性命的一位恩深义重的姐姐

jingshi lai jiu wo yi jiar de xingming de yi wei enshenyizhong de jiejie

unexpectedly is come save my one family DE life DE a CL beneficent DE sister

TT: Now I understand! You are the sister of great beneficence who has saved the lives of the three of us.

In this segment 来救我一家儿的性命 *lai jiu wo yi jiar de xingming* 'come to save the life of my family' is an expression very similar to a relative clause in English, where there is a verb and an object. Such a clausal modifier contributes to the complexity of the identifier-identified construction with the linking verb (是 *shi* 'is' and the predicative (姐姐 *jiejie* 'sister'), because the prepositioned clausal modifier delays the processing of major information (the identified), thus overloading the construction capacity. It is surprising to find such complex modification in a Chinese novel written more than a century ago, though in modern times, this usage is frequently found, as exemplified below.

(5) ST:是范博文的冷冷的带着讥讽的声音(CHOL)

shi Fan Bowen de lengleng de dai zhe jifeng de shengyin

is Fan Po-Wen DE cold DE have ASP sarcasm DE voice

TT: ...came Fan Po-wen's sarcastic voice

In the segment, 带着讥讽的 *dai-zhe jifeng de* 'with sarcasm' is a clausal modifier, slightly complex yet very short, which does not make the construction overloaded. Sometimes there are two clausal modifiers in a segment, as shown in (6) below.

(6)ST:突然变为了戏场上所有的那种夹着哄笑和叹息的闹哄哄的人声了(CHOL)

turan bianwei le xichang-shang suoyou de nazhong jia zhe hongxiao he tanxi de naohonghong de rensheng le

suddenly change-into-LE theatre-LOC have DE that-sort mix ASP laugher and sigh

DE babel DE voice PAR

TT:...had given way to the sort of babel of voices, interspersed with roars of laughters and sighs that one hears in a theatre.

In the segment, the construction composed of the verb 变为 *bianwei* 'become' and the noun 人声 *rensheng* 'human voice' is loaded with two clausal modifiers, one being 戏场上所有的 *xichang-shang suoyou de* 'characteristic of the theatre', and the other being 夹着哄笑和叹息的 *jia-zhe hongxiao he tanxi de* 'mixed with laughters and sighs'. Such complex modifiers make the construction heavily loaded and reduce the readability of the expression. But the corpus search suggests that such multiple clausal modifications are rarely found in original Chinese texts.

A look into the CHONL corpus suggests the non-literature original Chinese text also uses clausal modifiers, yet it uses them in a very compressed manner. For instance:

(7)ST:最近通过的以城市为重点的改革的决定(CHONL)

zuijin tongguo de yi chengshi wei zhongdian de gaige de jueding

recently approve DE take city as focus DE reform DE decision

TT:The recently adopted decision to focus reform on the cities...

In the example, modifiers 最近通过的 *zuijin tongguo de* 'recently approved' and 以城市为重点的 *yi chengshi wei zhongdian de* 'taking city as a focus') are modifying clauses, yet they are short and compact, which explains why they are more readable than(6). Here is another example:

(8) ST: Lucie sat in the still house in the tranquilly resounding corner,

listening to the echoing footsteps of years.

TT:她常坐在平静的反响着回音的安谧的屋子里听着岁月的脚步回响(CHTL)

ta chang zuo zai pingjing de fanxiang-zhe huiyin de anmi de wuzi LOC listen-ASP

she often sit in still DE resound-ASP echo DE tranquil DE house li ting-zhe

suiyue de jiaobu huixiang

time DE footstep resound

In the Chinese translation the segment 反响着回音 *fanxiang-zhe huiyin* 'resounding the echo', which is an adjective('resounding') in the source text, is now a clausal element acting as a modifier in parallel with other modifiers.

6.4 Parallel modification with an embedded clausal modifier

For Chinese, the most complex case of modification is that a modifier is embedded in another one, which may make short-term memory overloaded. The usage could be found in original Chinese text, as shown in example(9).

(9)ST:总之是最能吸引二十岁左右多愁善感的女郎们的爱怜的一张脸(CHOL)

zongzhi shi zui neng xiyin ershi sui zuoyou duochoushangan de girl-PL de

in-short is most able attract twenty year-old around sentimental DE nülang-men DE

ailian de yi zhang lian

love DE one CL face

TT:In short, it was a face to win the love and sympathy of a sentimental girl of, say, twenty.

In this segment, the DE modifiers are not in parallelism; in fact they are sequentially nested in larger modifiers as analyzed below.

'*in short is* [*most able to attract* [[*twenty year around sentimental DE*] *girls DE*] *love DE*] *one-CL face*'

Structurally, the noun phrase 'one-CL face' is modified by the modifier 'most able to attract...love', but the head 'love' in the modifier is in turn modified by another nested modifier('girls'), which in turn is modified by still another nested modifier('twenty year around sentimental'). Such a complex use of modifiers is rarely found in original Chinese texts, but it is not uncommon in translated Chinese texts, as the relative clauses in English source texts are often treated as prepositioned clausal modifiers in translated Chinese texts.

(10) ST: A loud or low expression of anguish — the whisper, or the shriek, as it might be conceived, of suffering humanity

TT: 那听起来时而如低语,时而如高叫的忽低忽高地表达出来的极度痛苦和受难的人生(CHTL)

na ting qilai shier ru diyu shier ru gaojiao de hudihugao de biaoda

that sound up sometimes like whisper, sometimes like shriek DE loud-or-low DE express

chulai de jidu tongku he shounan de rensheng

out DE extremely painful and suffering DE humanity

For example, in the English segment(in fact a sentence) in(10), the nominalized actions such as 'expression', 'whisper' and 'shriek' are all rendered into verbs or prepositional phrases in the Chinese translation. As a result, there is a long embedded clausal modifier 听起来时而如低语,时而如高叫的忽低忽高地表达出来的 *ting qilai shier ru diyu shier ru gaojiao de hudihugao de biaoda chulai de* 'that sounds sometimes like a whisper, sometimes like a shriek, which is expressed sometimes in a loud and sometimes in a low voice', which describes the modifier 极度痛苦和受难 *jidu tongku he shounan* 'extreme anguish and suffering'. The segment in(10) is a demonstrative construction with a pronoun(那 *na* 'that') followed by a noun(人生 *rensheng* 'human life'), very simple indeed. But with such a long modifier embedded in the construction, it immediately becomes structurally complicated and difficult to follow, because readers have to wait for a long while before they can identify the modified element.

In example(11), 'a sugar' in the source text is rendered into a clause 一块

糖做的 *yi kuai tang zuo de* ‘made with a lump of sugar’),which is embedded in the modifier 玫瑰蓓蕾一样的 *meigui beileiyiyangde* ‘rosebud-like’,making the translation much more complex than the expression ‘sugar rosebud’ in the source text.

That treatment is clearly not ideal;however,if the modifier is prepositioned,it has to be translated in an alternative way as exemplified in(11).

(11)ST:The fragment of coral,a tiny crinkle of pink like a sugar rosebud from a cake,rolled across the mat.

TT:珊瑚碎片,像蛋糕上的一块糖做的玫瑰蓓蕾一样的小红粒,滚过了地席(CHTL)

shanhu suipian xiang dangao shang de yi-kuai tang zuo de meigui beilei yiyang de

coral fragment,like cake LOC DE a-CL sugar make DE rose bud like DE

xiao hong li gun guo-le dixi

tiny red crinkle,roll across ASP mat

In translational Chinese,there are also cases where a clausal modifier has an embedded modifier,which is often found in non-literary translational Chinese texts.

(12)ST:The most ambitious effort to implement a marketable permit system

TT:执行可出售的许可证制度的最具雄心的努力(CHTNL)

zhixing ke chushou de xukezheng zhidu de zui ju xiongxin de nuli

implement can sell DE licence system DE most have ambition DE effort

In this segment,the first modifier(modifying 努力 *nuli* ‘effort’) is a long clausal expression:执行可出售的许可证制度的 *zhixing ke chushou de xukezheng zhidu de* ‘implement marketable DE permit system DE’,where the modifier 可出售的 *ke chushou de* ‘marketable’ is embedded. Obviously,a clausal modifier embedding another modifier adds to the complexity of the construction,which substantially affects the readability of the segment.

A more excessive use of complex modifiers is found in translational Chinese, as is shown in example(13).

(13) ST: But Choi was impressed several years by the words of a Chicago black leader being quoted in a Korean-American newspaper.

TT:但是,他曾看到一份朝鲜裔美国人办的报纸上援引的一位芝加哥黑人领袖的话几年来给崔留下了深刻的印象。(CHTNL)

danshi ta ceng kandao yi-fen Chaoxianyi Meiguoren ban de baozhi shang yuanyin de

but he once find one-CL Korean American run DE newspaper LOG quote DE

yi-wei zhijiage heiren lingxiu de hua jinian lai gei cui liuxia le shenke de

one-CL Chicago black leader DE words years during give Cui leave ASP deep DE

yinxiang

impression

In the long segment in the Chinese translation, the clausal modifier 一份[...]报纸上援引的 *yi-wei* [...] *baozhi shang yuanyin de* 'quoted in a newspaper' contains another nested clausal modifier 一份朝鲜裔美国人办的 *yi-fen Chaoxianyi Meiguoren ban de* 'run by a Korean-American'. This treatment certainly makes the segment structurally complicated and more difficult to read.

Obviously, the good control over the load capacity involves the proper use of specific translation techniques. In example (14), there are five words contained in "number-classifier...NP' construction in TT1, while in TT2 no character is contained. However, that does not mean TT2 fails to give a full transference of the meaning conveyed by the attributive clause in ST; in fact, it has done so quite well, as can be found in the second half of the sentence. In contrast to TT1, TT2 successfully deals with the attributive clause by using another dislocated segment.

(14) ST: She gave me one piece of intelligence which affected me very much.

TT1:她报告了我一项使我非常难过的消息(CHTL)

ta baogao le wo yi-xiang shi wo feichang nanguo de xiaoxi

she report-ASP me one-CL make me very sad DE message

TT2:她告诉我一个消息,使我感触很深(trans.Zhuang Yichuan)

ta gaosu wo yi-ge xiaoxi shi wo ganchu hen shen

she tell me one-CL message, make me feel very deeply

The analysis above confirms our belief that it is beneficial to make good use of segments in translational Chinese, so that a sentence segment with proper load capacity will ensure or enhance the readability of a translation.

7. INTERPRETATION OF CLC

Since the inception of vernacular Mandarin Chinese (*baihuawen*) in the early 20th century, translation has assumed the task of molding modern Mandarin Chinese by *borrowing* new expressions or even structures. While "it is easier to borrow words than to borrow syntax" (Gao 1984:533), considerable efforts have been made in grammar imitation. The proliferation of such imitations makes Mandarin Chinese sentences longer than they used to be prior to the introduction of Western literature into China via translation. But it should be noted that along with the positive role translation has played in language change, translational Chinese has also had some adverse effects. A notorious one is the frequent use of long pre-modifiers, of which the inappropriate use may make language use dull, stiff, wordy and awkward (Zhang 2007:286-287). Then in what way does CLC affect the terseness and smoothness of Mandarin Chinese?

The answer to this question can be found in the psychology of reading literature. It has been noted that it may take the reader longer reading time to interpret sentences with embedded clauses (Peng 1997:346). For example, it will add an extra burden to the reader's memory by processing a sentence like "the juice *that the child spilled* stained the rug", because there is in the sentence an embedded constituent *that the child spilled*. In contrast, 'The child spilled the juice *that stained the rug*' can be processed more easily, for the linear distance between 'juice' and 'stained' is short. In fact, the requirement for a short linear distance among the main sentential elements S, V and O is a common feature in English and Chinese. However, this requirement may not be satisfied in some translated Chinese texts, where prepositional phrases are overused to translate attributes in English source texts. Translation in this way displays a high propensity for overexpansion of CLC, which makes a difficult reading.

8. CONCLUSION

The discussions in this article suggest that the S-Length cannot tell much in the context of translational Mandarin Chinese. In view of the non-morphological and paratactic features peculiar to Chinese, the SS-Length and CLC account can better reflect the quality of language use in Mandarin Chinese. We find that there are significant differences between original and translational Mandarin Chinese in terms of SS-length, but in original Mandarin Chinese texts there is no such significant difference, which suggests that translational Mandarin Chinese deviates from the norms of the target language in CLC. In other words, CLC exerts an enormous influence on the quality of translation. To enhance the quality of language use in translational Chinese, a good translation is apt to use non-prepositional devices to avoid the over-load of CLC or to keep the SS-Length decently short. This is both an important translation technique and a key factor in assessing translation quality.

（原载 *Corpus Linguistics and Linguistic Theory* 2014-1（AACI & A&HCI），作者为王克非、秦洪武）

References

M. Baker, *In Other Words: A Coursebook on Translation*, London: Routledge, 1992.

M. Baker, "CorpusLinguistics and Translation Studies: Implications and Applications", M. Baker, G. Francis & E. Tognini-Bonelli (eds.), *Text and Technology: In Honour of John*

Sinclair, Amsterdam and Philadelphia: John Benjamins, 1993, pp.233-250.

M.Baker, Towards a Methodology for Investigating the Style of Literary Translator, *Target*, 2000, No.12, pp.241-266.

Hsin-Hsi Chen, "The Contextual Analysis of Chinese Sentences with Punctuation Marks", *Literary and Linguistic Computing*, 1994, Vol 9, No.4, pp.281-289.

Zhi Gao, "Fanyi zai yuwen fangmian de renwu" ("Role of Translation in Chinese Language and Literature"), Luo Xinzhang (ed.), *Fanyi Lun Ji* (*Collected Papers in Translation Studies*), Beijing: The Commercial Press, 1984, pp.532-535.

A.Goldberg, *Constructions: A Construction Grammar Approach to Argument Structure*, Chicago: The University of Chicago Press, 1994.

Xianyao Hu, "Jiyu yuliaoku de Hanyu fanyi xiaoshuo ciyu tezheng yanjiu" ("A Corpus-based Study on the Lexical Features of Chinese Translated Fiction"), *Foreign Language Teaching and Research*, 2007, No.3, pp.214-220.

Libo Huang, "Ying-Han fanyi zhong rencheng daici zhuyu de xianhua" ("Explicitation ofPersonal Pronoun Subjects in English-Chinese Translation: A Corpus-based Investigation"), *Foreign Language Teaching and Research*, 2008, No.6, pp.454-460.

S.Laviosa, *Corpus-based Translation Studies: Theory, Findings, Applications*, Amsterdam: Rodopi, 2002.

Shuneng Lian, *Ying Yi Han Jiaocheng* (*A Course of English-Chinese Translation*), Beijing: Higher Education Press, 2006.

Miqing Liu, *Xinbian Han-Ying Duibi yu Fanyi* (*Chinese-English Comparison and Translation*), Beijing: Higher Education Press, 2006.

M.Olohan, *Introducing Corpora in Translation Studies*, London and New York: Routledge, 2004.

Danling Peng, *Hanyu Renzhi Yanjiu* (*A Cognitive Study of Chinese*), Jinan: Shandong Education Press, 1997.

T. Puurtinen, "Nonfinite Constructions in Finnish Children's Literature: Features of Translationese Contradicting Translation Universals", S. Granger, J. Lerot & S. Petech-Tyson (eds.), *Corpus-based Approaches to Contrastive Linguistics and Translation Studies*, Amsterdam: Rodopi, 2003, pp.141-154.

Hongwu Qin, & Kefei Wang, "Jiyu duiying yuliaoku de Ying yi Han yuyan tezheng fenxi" ("A Parallel Corpus-based Study of Chinese as Target Language in E-C Translation"), *Foreign Language Teaching and Research*, 2009, No.2, pp.131-136.

D.Santos, "On Grammatical Translationese", K.Koskenniemi (ed.), *Short Papers Presented at the Tenth Scandinavian Conference on Computational Linguistics*, Helsinki, 1995a, pp. 59-66.

D.Santos, "On the Use of Parallel Texts in the Comparison of Languages", *Actas do XI Encontro da Associação Portugesa de Linguistica*, Lisbon, 1995b, pp.217-239.

J.Sinclair, "Corpus Creation", G. Sampson & D. McCarthy (eds.), *Corpus Linguistics: Readings in a Widening Discipline*, London: Continuum, 2004.

A.F.Tytler, *Essay on the Principles of Translation*, New York: E.P. Dutton & Co. Inc., 1907.

Kefei Wang, & Hongwu Qin, "Ying yi Han yuyan tezheng tantao: Jiyu duiying yuliaoku de hongguan fenxi" ("A Parallel Corpus-based Study of General Features of Translated Chinese"), *Journal of Foreign Language Research*, 2009, No.1, pp.102-104.

Kefei Wang, "Ying-Han/Han-Ying yuliao duiying de yuliaoku kaocha" ("Sentence Parallelism in English-Chinese/Chinese-English: A Corpus-based Investigation"), *Foreign Language Teaching and Research*, 2003, No.6, pp.410-416.

Kang Wen, *Ernü Yingxiong Zhuan* (*The Tale of Heroic Sons and Daughters*, Trans. by Zhide Fei), Beijing: New World Publishing House, 2003.

Yan Wu, "Cong suowei 'fanyi ti' shuoqi" ("On Translationese"), Luo Xinzhang (ed.), *Fanyi Lun Ji* (*Collected Papers in Translation Studies*), Beijing: The Commercial Press, 1984, pp.647-650.

双语语料库及其应用研究

本文首先介绍语料库的发展历程和语料库的主要类型及其应用研究领域,然后综述了基于双语语料库的语言对比分析和翻译研究,并讨论了研究方法和今后课题。

随着计算机技术和语料库语言学的快速发展,大规模语料的收集、整理和标注加工已经实现。在此基础上,如何将描述与分析、定性与定量有机结合起来以求充分解释各种语言现象,是语料库语言学的重要课题。本文主要探讨了双语语料库在语言对比分析、翻译研究等方面的应用问题。

一、Corpus 的含义及语料库发展

英文 corpus 一词源于拉丁语,本意为"body"(身体、躯体)。18 世纪后,该词开始用于指称"关于某一主题文字形式的汇编、全集";到 20 世纪 50 年代,corpus 一词逐渐具有现代意义上的"语料库"的含义,指"用于进行语言分析而收集的大量书面语或口语资料"(*OED* 1989:959);60 年代第一个机读语料库——布朗语料库(*the Brown Corpus*)(Kennedy 2000:23;Kenny 2001:24)在美国创建,标志着现代计算机语料库的诞生,corpus 一词也演化到了现在的意义①,成为

① "corpus"一词在意义上大致经历了这样一个变化过程:"身体"→"尸体"→"汇编、全集"→"(口语或书面语的)语料"→"语料库"(参见 OED 1989:959)。《牛津高阶英汉双解词典》(第 6 版)中对"corpus"一词的释义为"(书面或口语的)文集,文献;汇编;语料库"(p.376),由此也可以看出语料库的发展过程。

"语料库"。

人们通常误以为语料库是伴随计算机的发明而逐步出现的,其实原始意义上的手工语料库出现得更早,甚至可以追溯到中世纪(杨惠中 2002:46)。按照 Kennedy 的说法,最早涉及语言研究性质的语料库始于 18 世纪,是为基督教《圣经》所作的词汇索引,用于语汇检索和证明《圣经》各章节间的一致性(Kennedy 2000:13-14)。Francis(1992)认为计算机出现之前的最早的语料库开始于 1775 年 Dr. Johnson 编写的《英语词典》(*A Dictionary of the English Language*)(见 Kenny 2001:23-24),因为这部词典不仅收词丰富,释义准确,还大量引用著名作家及其经典作品中的语言来说明词义和用法。然而,第一个现代意义上的语料库却应当毫无争议地归功于 Randolph Quirk 于 20 世纪 50 年代末在伦敦大学建立的"英语用法调查"(Survey of English Usage)语料库①(Kenny 2001:24;王克非 2004:3)。语料库从本质上讲,就是"依照某种原则方式所收集的大量文本总汇"(Kenny 2001:22)。而今天我们在语言学研究中所谈到的语料库,是指运用计算机技术,按照一定的语言学原则,为了特定的研究目的而大规模收集并贮存的真实语料,这些语料经过一定程度的标注,便于检索,可应用于描述和实证研究。由此可见,以计算机技术的应用为标志,语料库的发展经历了三个阶段:原始语料库、现代语料库和当代语料库。原始意义上的语料库主要指计算机出现之前以语汇索引、词典编纂、方言研究、语言教学研究和语法研究为主要代表的原始手工语料库,其最显著的特点就是对经典文本语料的手工收集。现代意义上的语料库包括运用计算机技术大规模收集多种文本语料的电子语料库,其主要有三个特点:大规模的真实语料;经过一定的标注处理;便于检索。当代语料库是指 20 世纪 90 年代以 COBUILD 英语语料库、朗文语料库(LONGMAN)、英国国家语料库(BNC)以及国际英语语料库(ICE)为代表的超级语料库(mega-corpora),它们规模庞大,大都有上亿词的容量,覆盖面更宽,应用范围更广(见表 1)。

---

① "英语用法调查"语料库仍以人工收集为主,既包括书面语也包括口语,建立该语料库的初衷是要编写一部'标准'英语语法,起初没有计划借助计算机技术。但其中的口语部分经过计算机处理包括在伦敦—隆德语料库中(Svartvik 1990,转引自 Kenny 2001:24),因此它是语料库由人工处理向计算机处理过渡阶段的代表。

表 1　语料库发展的三个发展阶段

发展阶段	时期	特点及应用	典型代表
原始语料库	18 世纪—20 世纪初	手工收集原语料;无标注。 主要应用于语汇索引、词典编纂、方言研究、语言教学研究和语法研究。	Alexander Cruden 于 1736 年出版的钦定版《圣经》语汇检索;Dr.Johnson 于 1755 年出版的《英语词典》(A Dictionary of the English Language)。
现代语料库	20 世纪 50 — 80 年代	由手工收集向计算机语料库过渡;初步依照一定语言学原则进行标注。主要用于语法分析和语言对比研究,逐渐涉及其他领域。	Randolph Quirk 的"英语用法调查"(the Survey of English Usage)语料库;布朗语料库(the Brown Corpus);兰卡斯特-奥斯陆-卑尔根(LOB)语料库等。
当代语料库	20 世纪 90 年代至今	语料库呈现超大规模趋势;类型更加丰富,应用更加广泛,包括:语言研究、对比研究、翻译研究、教学研究词典编纂,以及机器翻译和软件开发等。	共建英语语料库(the Cobuild Bank of English);朗文语料库(Longman);英国国家语料库(BNC);国际英语语料库(ICE)等。

需要指出:第一,语料库的演变过程说明"语料库"这一概念由来已久,其雏形早在 18 世纪甚至更早就已经出现,今天语料库语言学中所讲的"语料库"是一个以计算机技术应用为标志的现代概念,也就是说"corpus"或"corpora"并不一定等于现代意义上的"语料库";第二,早期的语料库主要是对原语料(raw material)的人工收集,以书面语为主,这些材料用于语汇索引、词典编纂、语法研究、方言研究和语言教学研究;现代意义上的语料库种类繁多,主要借助计算机手段,在一定的语言学理论的指导下对语料在各个层次上进行了标注,应用范围涉及语言研究、对比研究、翻译研究、教学研究以及词典编纂等众多领域;第三,当代语料库的设计、研制和应用以印欧语系内部语种(尤其是英语)为主,尚未普及到世界各种语言。

二、语料库的分类与应用

语料库是一个多角度、多层次的研究工具,因此对其分类也显得纷繁复杂,没有统一的划分。从语料内容上可分为:书面语与口语、共时与历时,以及原创语言与翻译语言;从选材方式上可分为:抽样型和监控型;按照语言数量可分为:

单语的、双语/平行的和多语的;从用途方面又可分为:普通语料和专门用途语料。而且每个语料库还可进一步细分成一些子库。一般来说,研究目的与方法是语料库类型的根本决定因素,基于此,我们可以对语料库做一分类(见图1)。

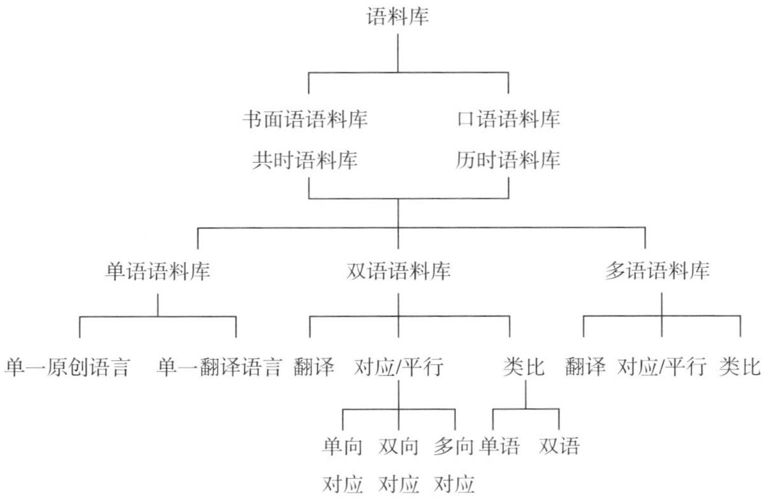

图1 语料库的简单分类(参见 Granger 2003;王克非 2004:8)

以上分类主要依据语言数量、文本间是否具有翻译关系或对齐关系(王克非 2004:6-9)。大体上说,语料库的应用涉及以下几个方面:语言研究、对比研究、翻译研究、语言/翻译教学研究,单语/双语词典研编以及机助/机器翻译与翻译软件开发等(如表2)。

表2 语料库的应用

语料库类型		语言研究	对比研究	翻译研究	语言/翻译教学	单/双语词典研编	机助/机器翻译与翻译软件开发
单语语料库	单一原创语言	√		√			
	单一翻译语言	√		√			
双语语料库	翻译	√	√	√	√		
	对应/平行	√	√	√	√	√	√
	类比		√	√			

续表

语料库类型		语言研究	对比研究	翻译研究	语言/翻译教学	单/双语词典研编	机助/机器翻译与翻译软件开发
多语语料库	翻译	√	√	√	√		
	对应/平行	√	√	√	√	√	√
	类比		√	√			

从表2可以看出，与翻译研究有关的语料库主要包括三类：翻译语料库，对应/平行语料库，其中以平行语料库最为突出，其最大的特点在于包括了两种原创语言文本和与之对应的两种翻译语言文本，可以有多种用途。语言研究和翻译研究向来重视语言材料的收集，而基于大规模电子语料文本库的语言与翻译研究更具有以下四个特点：第一，大规模的真实语料；第二，共时与历时的结合；第三，定性研究与定量研究的结合；第四，理论与实践的结合。这些特点集中体现了理论研究中的继承性与创造性。

三、基于双语库的语言对比分析

对比语言学的源头大约可以追溯到19世纪末20世纪初的对比分析①研究，但最早提出"对比语言学"的通常被认为是20世纪美国的语言学家Benjamin Lee Whorf（王宗炎 2000：112），而后这一学科经历了一个盛衰起伏的过程。对比语言学与翻译研究有着一种不解之缘，二者统一于两种不同语言之间的相互关系当中。两种研究的最终目标不尽相同，但两个领域却存在一种互补关系。对比分析是翻译实践不可或缺的步骤，翻译实践是对比分析的重要手段，在一定程度上二者互为研究方法和对象。对语料的关注是对比语言

① "对比语言学"（contrastive linguistics）与"对比分析"（contrastive analysis）二者可以互换使用，王宗炎先生还指出："对比分析或对比语言学不同于比较语言学（comparative linguistics）。比较语言学是历时性研究，它要追究语言之间的谱系关系；对比分析是共时性研究，它要追究语言之间的一致性和分歧性——尤其是分歧性。"（王宗炎 2000：111）

学和翻译研究最大的共同之处,近年来语料库语言学与计算机技术的结合和飞速发展,使得对大量真实语料(尤其是双语/多语平行语料)的对比分析成为可能,这为对比语言学和翻译研究提供了新的契机。

基于单一语言语料库的语言研究成果非常丰富,基于双语语料库开展的语言对比分析还不多见。这主要是因双语库的建设难度较大,相对滞后。不过随着双语库逐渐为学界所重视,这类研究也开始兴起。其中涉及汉语的双语对比分析有肖忠华、王克非、熊学亮、曹大峰、施建军、柏晓静和詹卫东等(见王克非等 2004),论及语言的体、被动句、把字句、致使结构、动词结构等。国外在印欧语系各语言之间也开展了一些研究。例如 Kristin Davidse 和 Liesbet Heyvaert(见 Granger *et al*.2003)的“论英语与荷兰语中的中动结构”(On the middle construction in English and Dutch)一文,将语料库和对比研究结合起来,从微观角度针对现有英语与荷兰语中有关中动结构的理论提出了新的假设。作者指出对中动结构的现有分析方法主要有两种:1)作格法(the ergative view),此种观点认为,中动结构中不存在明确的施事者(Agent),因此结构中只有一个参与者,施事行为归于主语,属于唯动格结构的范畴;2)及物法(the transitive approach),该种观点认为中动结构包含两个参与者——隐含的施事者和受事者性质的主语,强调主语的受事者性质。由此可以看出,前一种观点认为中动结构属于包含一个施事主语的主动语态结构,而后者视其为主语为受事者的被动结构。两位作者指出以上两种观点均存在缺陷,提出中动结构本身赋予了主语与动词短语之间一种内在的配价关系,由中动结构所建立的非施事主语与主动动词短语之间的关系从根本说是情态性(modal)的。André Hantson 在其“英语动名词结构与挪威语限定词+不定式/at 从句结构”(English gerund clauses and Norwegian det + infinitive/at clause constructions)一文(见 Granger *et al*.2003)中从英语—挪威语对比的角度入手,探讨了两种语言特定结构之间的特点及其翻译问题。文中既有对传统观点的维护,也有借助语料库分析方法对两种语言进行相关统计分析和翻译转换问题的探讨。但是这类语言对比分析的研究还不丰富,有待进一步开展。

四、基于双语库的翻译研究

纵观翻译理论发展的历史，到 20 世纪 90 年代初为止，翻译研究经历了语文研究、语言学研究、文化研究、哲学研究和认知研究五个范式。早期的翻译理论以文学翻译为主要研究对象，以词汇与语义的关系、是否忠实于原作、译文风格取向以及译者的创造力等因素来建立翻译的方法论体系，这一研究范式开创了翻译理论的先河，为后来翻译理论的发展奠定了基础。然而这些理论大多局限于评论或批评性质的个人经验总结，既抽象又模糊。到了 20 世纪 50—60 年代，以 Eugene A.Nida 和 J.C.Catford 为代表的学者建立了翻译研究的语言学方法体系。他们以语言学理论为指导，采用形式分析的方法从词汇、语法、句法、语义、语用、语篇、功能等层面对原语文本和译语文本进行分析，期望对翻译问题进行所谓的'科学'解释。这一范式一直延续到今天，依然是翻译研究的主流方法之一。翻译的文化研究范式出现于 80 年代末，以 James Holmes（1988）的"翻译研究的名与实"（The Name and Nature of Translation Studies）一文为起点，Susan Bassnet 和 André Lefevere 提出了翻译研究的文化转向，将研究的重心转向了翻译活动所涉及的诸多社会和文化因素。其中以 Evan Zohar 多元系统理论最为突出，改变了以往以"对等"为核心的视角，使翻译研究取得了新的突破。翻译的哲学研究范式由来已久，早在 19 世纪的 Schleiermacher 和 Walter Benjamin 所创立的诠释学（hermeneutic）翻译研究方法就已经为后期的解构主义翻译观奠定了基础。翻译认知研究范式以认知科学的研究为基础，旨在探究翻译过程中译者头脑中的"黑匣子"（black box）；这个领域的研究方兴未艾。以上这五种范式依然渗透于今天的翻译研究当中，使翻译研究呈现一种跨学科的态势。然而目前翻译研究最为突出的一个问题就是定性研究与定量研究相脱节，理论研究与语言转换的实践相脱节，缺乏客观的量化标准和评估模式。建立基于语料库的翻译研究新方法可以弥补上述不足。

基于语料库的翻译研究方法是建立在以上各种方法论基础之上的，是各种研究方法的整合与延续。它以语言学理论和科学统计方法为指导，以对双语文本转换的真实语料为研究对象，兼及翻译活动中的各种超语言因素，对翻译进行历时与共时的研究，使得翻译理论的研究与语言转换中语料实例重新科学地结合起来。从本质上看，语料库与翻译研究之间存在一定的内在联系。因为翻译研究不外乎涉及文本、文化、译者、翻译过程等语言及超语言因素，而语料库，尤其是双语对应/平行语料库不仅包括了语言信息，也包括了翻译过程涉及的各种超语言因素。

Johansson 认为语料库方法的最大优势在于它可以将理论研究与教学实践真正结合起来。在文末，他对未来的研究方向提出了三点建议：第一，多语语料库研究；第二，翻译语料库和学习者语料库研究；第三，新一代语法书和词典研编。Sara Laviosa 以“语料库与翻译研究”（Corpora and translation studies）为题，提出了“基于语料库的翻译研究”（corpus-based translation studies）范式。她从 Gideon Toury 提出的“描述翻译研究”（Descriptive Translation Studies）与基于语料库的翻译研究之间的联系入手，指出了二者的共性：第一，注重从实证的角度对真实语料进行直接观察；第二，对语料库文本的选择并非基于某个固定的定义，而是建立在共识性标准和外部分类的基础上，必要时采取随机抽样的方式；第三，两种方法都坚持认为从实证性研究中得出的一般性结论只有建立在对大量文本语料研究的基础之上才能保证其效度；第四，适用于研究对象的各种原则都要经过大量系统的研究来发现，并以概率原则为表述形式。由此可见，翻译研究的领域尚未最终划定，基于语料库的翻译研究范式是在原有研究范式的基础上孕育产生的，其最大的优势在于其新颖灵活的研究方法和关于不同语言及翻译现象的大量真实语料。

按照 Toury 的观点，翻译理论研究与描述性翻译研究之间是一种互惠的关系，“换句话说：描述性翻译研究所积累的发现将有助于一系列连贯‘法则’的制定，这些‘法则’能够说明与翻译活动相关的各个变量之间的内在关系”（Toury 2001：16）。而这样一种互惠的关系是建立在对双语文本的转换进行描述的基础之上。他同时指出，纯翻译研究与翻译应用研究之间是一种单向关系，即纯粹的翻译研究只服务于翻译应用研究（Toury 2001：17-18）。事实上翻译理论研究、描述性翻译研究和翻译应用研究三者之间存在一种内在的联系:翻译理论提出某种假设或方法论,通过描述性研究对其进行验证,产生完善的方法论体系,然后将其投入具体应用领域。在整个过程中,对语料的实证性分析与描写起着举足轻重的作用。基于语料库的翻译研究是指将原语/翻译文本语料库应用于对翻译产品或过程的实证性研究、对理论建构的阐述以及译员培训等方面的学科分支,它的最大特点就在于借助实证基础上的方法和理论原则,使用归纳和演绎的方法来研究翻译产品和翻译过程。这种新研究方法促进了理论研究、实证研究和应用研究之间的对话(Laviosa 2003,参见 Granger *et al*.2003:45)。因此,基于语料库的翻译研究方法使翻译理论的模式更加科学和完善,这一方法的继承性集中体现在其与描述性翻译研究的共性方面:第一,注重从实证的角度对真实语料进行直接观察;第二,对语料库文本的选择并非基于某个固定的定义,而是建立在共识性标准和外部分类的基础上,必要时采取随机抽样的方式;第三,两种方法都坚持认为从实证性研究中得出的一般性结论只有建立在对大量文本语料研究的基础之上才能保证其有效性;第四,适用于研究对象的各种原则都是经过大量系统的研究来发现,并以概率性规则作为表述形式。(Toury 2001:49-50)这样的研究方法具有三个优势,第一,建立不同语言之间在语义层次上的真实对应(这里的"对应"是一个宽泛的概念)。第二,对先前的翻译理论和假设进行重新验证。第三,提出新的假设并加以验证。

Olohan(2003)指出语料库语言学的研究对象不是语言能力(linguistic competence)而是语言应用(linguistic performance),所以基于语料库的翻译研究就是以文本语料为基础,从直觉出发产生关于翻译现象的假设,并对这些假设进行系统的研究。她继而提出了翻译研究中语料库研究方法的理论框架,第一,描写研究。显然,语料库的方法是从真实的文本语料出发,是对翻译中语言运用的描写;第二,普遍性研究。基于语料库的研究方法以认同/原型的翻译概念为基本概念工具,以多元系统理论(the Polysystem Theory)为指导研究翻译活动中的普遍现象;第三,翻译的语境化研究,即借助翻译文本来重新构建特定社会文化环境中的各种规范和限制性因素。作者同时指出,尽管语料库的研究方法涉及大量的量化数据,但不应过分强调这一方法的"客观性"或"科学性",因为基于语料库的翻译研究方法同样离不开主观的定性分析。

五、小结

以上着重讨论了双语语料库的发展、功用以及在语言对比、翻译研究等方面的应用研究。将语料库应用于翻译研究的优势不言而喻,但语料库也不是万能的。因此,我们在利用语料库的同时,也要注意其不完善之处。第一,文本语料不可能穷尽。基于语料库的语言分析和翻译研究主要是建立在对真实语料直接观察基础之上的归纳性研究,那么,语料库要多大才称得上有代表性、才能依据它得出有普遍意义的结论?第二,语料库(尤其是平行语料库)的选材过程通常以建库者的母语语言系统为出发点(Granger *et al*.2003:47),那么选材的标准难免会受到本族语价值体系的干扰,这使得文本选择带有一定的主观性和偶然性。应当用什么标准来最大限度地摆脱这种影响?第三,原创语言作品以及翻译作品的质量应当以什么样的标准来衡量?第四,双语文本的对应问题。上文已经提到对应/平行语料库相对而言与翻译研究的关系最紧密,双语文本间的对应除了词级、句级、段级或篇章级等形式对应之外,语义对应方式的研究是否应当作为翻译研究的重点呢?因为对应语料库的最大特征就在于双语的平行对应,使我们对两种不同语言之间的"一一对应"有了重新的认识,这一点正好应验了雅柯布森(1959)的观点:"语言之间真正的区别不在于说话者可以或者不可以表达什么,而在于说话者必须或者决不能表达什么"。(钱军等译 2001:266)。第五,目前世界上印欧语系之外语言(如汉语、日语、朝鲜语、马来语、泰语等)的基于双语库的对比分析和翻译研究成果都还很少,有待我们努力。拿汉语来说,英汉两种语言同为世界上的两大语种,分属不同的语系,基于英汉/汉英平行语料库的研究一定会深化我们对许多语言问题的认识。

(本文原载《中国英语教育》2005年第2期,作者为王克非、黄立波)

参考文献

S.Granger, J. Lerot and S. Petch-Tyson (eds), *Corpus-based Approaches to Contrastive Linguistics and Translation Studies*, Amsterdam: Rodopi, 2003.

G.Kennedy, *An Introduction to Corpus Linguistics*, Beijing: Foreign Language Teaching and Research Press, 2000.

D.Kenny, *Lexis and Creativity in Translation: A Corpus-based Study*, Manchester: St. Jerome Publishing, 2001.

S.Laviosa, *Corpus-based Translation Studies: Theory, Findings and Applications*, Amsterdam: Rodopi, 2002.

M.Olohan, *Introducing Corpora in Translation Studies*, London and New York: Routledge, 2004.

K.Popper, *Objective Knowledge: An Evolutionary Approach* (revised edition), Oxford: Oxford University Press, 1979.

J.Sinclair, *Corpus, Concordance, Collocation*, Shanghai: Shanghai Foreign Language Education Press, 1999.

G.Toury, *Descriptive Translation Studies and Beyond*, Shanghai: Shanghai Foreign Language Education Press, 2001.

黄立波、柯飞:《从多个视角探究翻译》,《外语与翻译》2005 年第 2 期。

王克非等:《双语对应语料库:研制与应用》,外语教学与研究出版社 2004 年版。

王宗炎:《语言问题探索》,上海外语教育出版社 1985/2000 年版。

雅柯布森:《雅柯布森文集》,钱军等译注,湖南教育出版社 2001 年版。

杨惠中:《语料库语言学导论》,上海外语教育出版社 2002 年版。

大规模英汉平行语料库的检索与应用：大数据视角

本研究从大数据视角报告“大规模英汉平行语料库检索平台”的设计开发及其应用。首先，梳理了语料库检索问题中方法和技术的发展脉络；其次，介绍了面向一亿词级别英汉平行语料库检索的“大规模英汉平行语料库检索平台 V2.0”的功能，该平台不仅具备单语检索、双语检索和搭配分析等基本功能，也提供元信息过滤、词形还原、模糊检索和支持正则表达式和通配符的ProConc 语言的半结构化复杂检索等功能，可快速准确地从语料库中抽取信息，为基于英汉平行与历时类比语料库的翻译研究、翻译教学和双语词典编纂提供数据基础；第三，对比分析本研究所设计的方法与技术较之传统平行语料库检索技术的优势，分析了平台在实际语料库检索中的信度，借此为大数据背景下语料库的信息抽取研究提供借鉴。

一、引言

自 20 世纪 90 年代中后期以来，国内外翻译语料库的研制逐步形成热潮，语料库被广泛应用于探索翻译的语言特征、普遍性、规范性、文体与译者风格以及翻译教学和双语词典编纂，为翻译研究提供了新的观察模式与经验依据，促进了语料库翻译学理论地位的确立（Baker 1993；McEnery & Xiao 2007；王克非、黄立波 2008；黄立波、王克非 2011；王克非 2012；秦洪武等 2014）。此外，平行语料库也为机器翻译系统提供长期翻译记忆、翻译实例和训练数据，在提升机器翻译系统效能的研究中发挥着关键作用(Och & Ney 2002;刘群 2009;冯志伟 2010)。

近年来,随着计算机技术的发展和语料库研制方法和自动化技术的逐渐成熟,获取、加工和利用大规模双语资源变得更加方便快捷。超大型双语库体量巨大,语料来源真实有效,采样均衡,设计合理,涉及的语言对、语体、语域、年代和语言变体种类繁多,规模也从过去的十万、百万词级跃升至千万乃至数亿词级。现今的双语库已具备大数据的“5V”特性(孟小峰、慈祥 2013:147),即规模性(volume)、多样性(variety)、高速性(velocity)、价值性(value)和真实性(veracity)。

双语语料的规模化效应不仅为平行语料库的研制与应用提供了新的思路,也对双语库检索和信息抽取技术提出了更高的要求。近年来语料库检索与统计分析软件的开发取得了一些成果,但面向较大规模语料库的处理能力仍然存在问题。特别是面向双语对应语料库检索与分析软件的开发较之单语语料库工具相对滞后,无论是功能还是检索效率都无法满足大规模双语文本应用的实际需求。本研究以北京外国语大学中国外语与教育研究中心在国家社科重大项目资助下建成的上亿词级“大规模英汉平行语料库”为例,介绍面向该双语库检索平台“大规模英汉平行语料库检索平台 V2.0”,对该平台的信度进行考察,并通过实例来介绍如何利用该平台开展语料库翻译研究,以期研究者未来能利用该平台对大型语料库进行有效和充分地使用。

二、面向翻译语料库的检索研究概述

检索是从语料库中批量提取、观察、统计和分析语言现象的重要途径(梁茂成等 2010:57),也是呈现模式化数据的主要方法,属于语料库“展示和应用工具”(王克非 2004a:61)。“没有良好的语料库工具支持,语料库研究便难以有效开展”(许家金、贾云龙 2013:57)。因此,自平行语料库兴建之始,检索技术便受到重视,研究人员相继开发出多种双语检索工具与软件平台,以支撑翻译研究、语言教学和词典编纂等。较之单语库,英汉平行语料库不仅包含英、汉两种语言的语料,还包含英、汉语言间的翻译关系,因此,英汉平行语料库的检索不仅需要从英汉语料库文档中分别抽取信息,还需要观察和抽取两种语言间的翻译对应关系。根据上述的特点,面向平行语料库的检索工具可依据语言类型、载体和用途三个基本维度进行区分。依据语言类型,可分为单语和双语;按照检索载体,可分为基于网络和基于单机;根据用途,可分为通用和专用两类。

我们对当前国内典型的可用于双语平行语料库检索的软件工具和平台进行了调查,结果如表 1 所示:国内基于语料库的翻译研究和语言对比研究分别使用面向单语的检索软件与双语检索软件来实现对平行语料库的单语信息和双语对应信息的抽取和统计分析。其中,比较常用的单语检索软件有英国利物浦大学 Mike Scott 团队开发的 Wordsmith 和日本早稻田大学 Laurence Anthony 开发的 AntConc,这两款软件是开放工具,支持 TEXT 和带标记的 xml 文件,包含索引行提取、词频统计和主题分析三个模块。ParaConc 是面向平行语料库对应信息提取的检索软件,由新西兰奥克兰大学 Michael Barlow 主持研制,支持双语对应行的提取和简单的搭配分析界面,支持 text 和 xml 文档两种存储格式。BFSU ParaConc 是北京外国语大学梁茂成研制的双语对应文本信息检索工具,支持固定格式 TEXT 文本库的检索。GCEPCC(王克非 2004b)是北京外国语大学为"通用汉英对应语料库"开发的专用检索平台,面向 Text 格式平行语料库的检索,支持索引,具备较高的检索效率。ECPCC(黄万丽、秦洪武 2015)是以关系数据库作为数据结构、面向"英汉平行历时语料库"的双语在线检索系统,具备"第四代"语料库检索工具的特点(许家金、吴良平 2013)。CEO 是为"通用汉英对应语料库"开发、具备单机和 Web 界面的双语检索软件,后台使用关系数据库对语料库进行管理,因而具有较好的平台兼容性。

当前,面向单语语料库研究的工具主要有 Word-Smith、AntConc 和 PowerConc(许家金、贾云龙 2013)。这类检索软件功能相对完善,无论是索引行提取与词频分析,还是主题词和搭配,都有在线或者单机专用工具。但这类工具并未针对平行语料库的研究需求进行设计,对 xml 的支持不完善,难以处理篇头和语料库文档中的标注信息,对汉语的支持也不完善,特别是在处理超过千万词级别的语料库时，会出现不兼容和效率低问题。双语库的检索一直是平行语料库研究的难点，当前多数平行库研究者采用 ParaConc 和 BFSU ParaConc 进行检索，前者可以提供类似单语检索工具的索引行提取功能，并支持完整的正则表达式和通配符检索功能，后者可以进行一对一的双语检索，支持较为强大的正则表达式，但不支持元信息的提取，也不支持中英文双向检索功能。ParaConc 支持用户自定义对篇头信息实现过滤，但功能简单，无法使用组合式的篇头筛选，在加载约 1000 万 XML 语料库的过程中会出现软件崩溃的情况。此外，国内一些大型平行语料库的研制也开发了基于 B/S 架构的网络平台，并使用关系数据库对平行库进行管理，方便用户随时随地对平行语料库进行操作。但采用关系数据库的 B/S 结构在处理海量语料信息时检索缓慢（黄万丽、秦洪武 2015：20），在没有网络的环境下，特别是在当前绝大多数平行语料库都没有完全解决版权问题的前提下，也难以推广。

因此，在借鉴上述检索工具和平台的基础上，本研究从大数据视角出发，开发面向一亿字词以上语料的"大规模英汉平行语料库检索平台 V2.0"，对传统的双语检索软件进行了扩充，融合了单语检索、篇头信息抽取、搭配分析、N-gram 分析、词汇归元等功能，并对软件的可用性和检索效率进行了优化，在面对超大规模的平行语料库时，依然具有很高的检索效率。

表 1　面向平行语料库的检索工具与平台

检索工具	语言	载体	用途	编码	双向	元信息	词性	搭配	词元	数据组织	文件
WordSmith	单语	单机	通用	Unicode	—	否	否	是	是	TEXT，XML	是
AntConc	单语	单机	通用	Unicode	—	否	是	是	是	TEXT，XML	是
ParaConc	双语	单机	通用	ANSI	否	是*	是	是	否	TEXT，XML	是
BFSU ParaConc	双语	单机	通用	ANSI	否	否	是	否	是	TEXT	是
GCEPCC	双语	单机	通用	Unicode	是	是	是	否	否	TEXT	是
ECPCC	双语	Web	专用	Unicode	是	是	是	否	是	RDB	否
CEO	双语	单机/Web	通用	Unicode	是	是	是	否	是	RDB	否

* ParaConc 的元信息和词性检索需要经过复杂的定义。

三、平行语料库检索平台的设计与应用实例

考虑到实际运用,本研究所设计的检索方案试图融合原创文本与翻译文本的类比语料库和双语平行语料库的检索功能,更好地支持汉语检索,为语料库翻译研究和教学提供一体化的解决方案。本检索平台(以下简称“平台”)适应容量超亿词级别的大规模平行语料库的单机检索,有效利用并行计算技术和索引技术对检索效率进行了充分的改进,图形框架使用 Python 语言进行开发,核心搜索算法使用 C 语言编写以改善效率,支持 Windows 系统;由于 Python 的跨平台特性,未来可移植到 Mac OS 和 Linux 平台运行。

1. 数据格式、基本模块与检索方法

“大规模英汉平行语料库检索平台 V2.0”是运行于单机的双语平行语料库检索平台。底层数据采用 UTF-8 编码的 XML 格式语料库通用文档组织,兼容多种语言,可完整保存语料库文本、标注和元信息,数据无需导入导出,方便语料交换,供其他检索工具和平台使用,平行库中文档实例如图 1 所示。数据管理模块、索引模块和检索引擎均自主设计,采用高效索引结构及全文检索技术和并行计算技术,即便语料规模非常大,也可以在短时间内检索到所需内容。

该平台具有单语检索、双语对应检索和搭配分析三个基本模块。单语检索模块针对平行语料库英、汉原创文本和翻译文本的单语语料库以及单语类比语料库的信息进行提取;双语对应检索模块则对双语句对齐语料库进行信息抽取。单语和双语检索模块都支持复杂搭配和类连接等词汇共现特征的抽取,但考虑到搭配强度分析的需要,平台也单独设计了搭配分析模块。

平行语料库检索通常需要抽取复杂信息,大多数工具采用通配符、正则表达式或者基于关系数据库的 SQL 语句实现。但是,前两者无法实现元信息的提取,不支持 XML 文档读取;而 SQL 中的文本搜索须依赖数据库管理软件的全文检索引擎,效率较低。此外,正则表达式具有强大描述能力,但编写困难,搜索效率不高。一些检索工具通过将通配符在算法中转换为正则表达式来执

行最终的检索，虽降低编写难度，但检索效率无法有效提高。本研究的检索算法结合正则表达式、界面化的元信息查询，并自主实现支持索引和基于有限状态自动机的原生通配符搜索。提高效率的同时，兼顾强大的描述能力。本研究设计的 ProConc 语言不仅可以描述具体的语言单位（单词、短语、语块、词类、类连接等），还可提取词类码、还原词形、提取翻译对应信息、计算搭配强度等。ProConc 语言也同时支持与、或、非三种检索逻辑，并同时适用英汉语言。

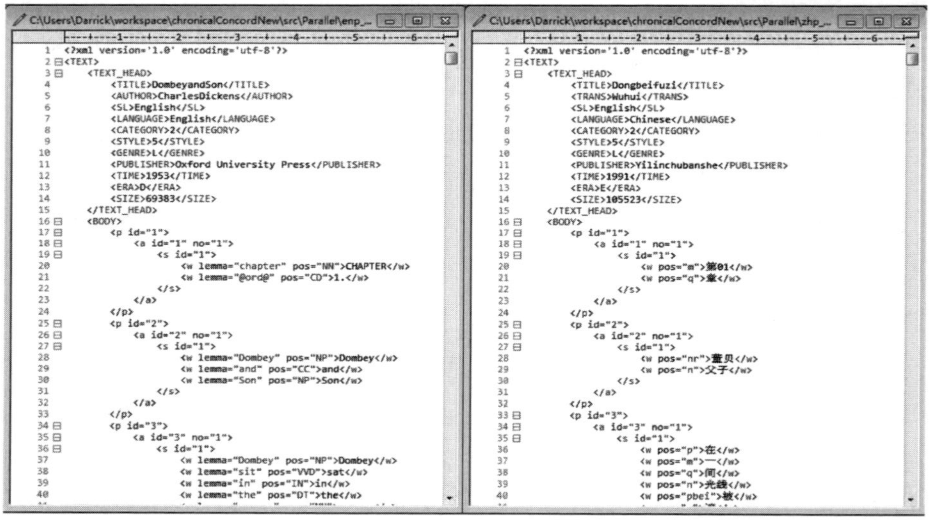

图 1　大规模英汉平行语料库数据组织

2. 英汉平行语料库检索功能

"平台"目前提供多达一亿字词的英汉双语语料检索，包括单语、双语和搭配分析三个模块，并在文本头过滤、简单与复杂检索、英汉双向检索、检索结果过滤、汉语分拆检索和搭配强度分析等方面做了精心设计，可以取得精准的检索结果。上述功能简述如下。

（1）基于界面的篇头信息检索：语料库的篇头信息又称元信息，用于描述语料库文档信息，包括文本作者/译者、语体、文体类型、年代、语言和翻译关系等信息。"平台"可以对上述这些信息进行过滤以便选取合适的文本进行检索，可便于使用者展开以语言、历时、共时、文体、体裁、原创与翻译作为区别单位的单双语考察,筛选界面如图 2 所示。

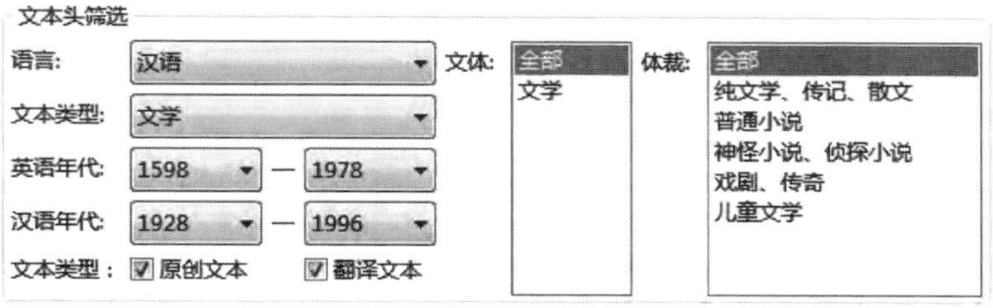

图 2　检索平台篇头元信息筛选

(2)基于 ProConc 语言的简单检索:本研究设计了 ProConc 检索语言的简化版本,使用通配符编写检索表达式,可降低检索表达式编写难度。检索通配符包括字符通配符和词例通配符,字符通配符包括“ * ”、“?”和“+”三个符号,“ * ”表示匹配单词内零个或者多个字符,“?”表示匹配单词内任意一个字符,“+”表示匹配单词内任意一个或者多个字符;词例通配符包括“#”和“@”,前者匹配任意一个单词,后者匹配任意零个或一个单词。例如:检索“会?”,可检出“会议”、“会场”、“会面”等,检索可检出“on behalf of”、“on account of”等,字符通配符和词例通配符也可混合使用,从而描述更为复杂的查询。简单检索功能也提供了表达式级别的大小写区分和英语词形还原功能,在界面可以选择。

(3)基于 ProConc 语言的复杂检索:本研究所设计开发的 ProConc 语言,借鉴并融合了正则表达式与通配符的特点,支持对标注信息、词形还原、大小写转换等结构化信息的检索,同时也增加了“否定”查询语义。为了兼顾正则表达式较高的描述能力与通配符的编写简便的优点,ProConc 语言在词例的匹配上使用通配符,在符号匹配部分则使用正则表达式。检索规则与查询详见表 2。

由表 2 可见,“平台”支持复杂表达式的抽取,通过使用包含上述符号的混合查询表达式,可以描述更为复杂的检索。

(4)英汉、汉英双向检索:双向检索是平行语料库特有的检索模式,允许用户根据研究目的在语料库中搜索源语与目标语之间配对。例如希望搜索将“解决问题”翻译为“solve the problem”的所有对应检索行时,就可以使用双向检索这一模式。此外,双向检索功能支持篇头、简单和复杂检索模式所有功能。

表 2　ProConc 复杂检索语言语法规则

类型	形式	释义	示例与含义
形符定界	“< … >”	形符定界符号	< word = great > < word = idea >匹配短语 great idea
词形匹配	“< word =…>”	检索词形	< word = better > < word = than >匹配短语 better than
	“< lemma = …>”	词形还原	< lemma = be > < word = . * ing >匹配“系动词 + 动词 ing”形式的短语,如:are going
	“<…> % c”	区分大小写	< word = China > % c < word = Airline > % c 匹配短语 China Airline 且区分大小写
词类匹配	“< pos =…>”	查找词类	< lemma = get > < pos = VVN >匹配 get 的原形及各种曲折形式与动词过去分词的结构构成的被动语态,如:get shocked
范围查询	“< … > {3, 5}”	匹配次数	< lemma = be > < pos = RB > {0,3} < pos = VVN > 匹配 be + 0~3 个副词 + 过去分词构成的被动语态,如 is well informed,are still constantly fragmented 等
通配符	“@”	匹配任意零个或者一个单词	< word =进行 > @ < word = 改革 > 匹配“进行改革”、“进行教育改革”、“进行经济改革”等
	“#”	匹配一个单词	< word =克服 > # < word = 困难 > 匹配“克服自身困难”、“克服外在困难”等
	“!”	排除满足条件的形符	< word =克服 > ! < word = 困难 > 不匹配“克服困难”,匹配“克服障碍”等
正则表达式	< word = REGX > < lemma = REGX > <pos = REGX >	应用于匹配 Word、Lemma 和 POS 标注中使用正则表达式	< word = . * lize,pos = v. * >匹配“lize”结尾的且词性为动词的所有单词

(5)检索结果过滤、抽样与排序:检索过滤这一功能允许用户对检索结果进行精细化筛选,可实现跨距搜索,例如在语料库中检索“不是……而是……”这一组合,可利用简单检索搜索“不是”一词,然后使用检索过滤模块,在检索结果的右侧跨距为 0 到 20R 的语境中搜索“而是”,进而实现近似复杂检索中的功能,这一功能中也可实现上述所有检索功能。由于语料库容

量较大,往往一次检索所产生的检索结果数量庞大,“平台”支持使用随机抽样或者分层抽样的方式对检索结果进行随机筛选指定的结果数,也可以按照文体等要素进行分层抽样。此外“平台”支持按照检索关键字和元信息的文本内容进行多级排序。

(6)汉语分拆检索:“平台”语料库中的汉语经过词汇切分,因而上述检索中对汉语的处理也以分词的结果为准。对于一些粒度较大的词,例如“孟加拉虎”,在语料库中很可能切分成两个词“孟加拉_NP”+“虎_NN”,因此在语料库中直接搜索“孟加拉虎”可能造成漏检。因此,“平台”提供汉语分拆检索模式,即将检索串拆分成由单个字符构成的串,如将“孟加拉虎”拆分成“孟 + 加 + 拉 + 虎”,以便获得较为全面的检索结果。

(7)搭配分析:该模块可使用上述所有的检索模式,并在库中的单语部分进行搭配强度的分析,分析指标包括 MI、MI^3、T-Score、Z-Score、Cha 和 Log-likelihood 指标。

除了上述功能外,“平台”检索的结果还可以输出为 Excel 或者 Word 文档,对检索结果进行定制化的显示,每一条检索记录都将其部分重要元信息一同展示出来,供研究者进一步甄别和筛选。此外,使用者还可根据需要在输出结果中选择“显示词性标记”或者“并保存”,便于在后续研究中使用文本编辑工具或者语料库工具进行进一步的筛选。

3. 英汉平行语料库检索应用

语料库检索工具提供强大的检索功能,但完成以特定目的的翻译研究则需要定制特定的检索方案,对语料库中的信息进行抽取和观察。一次检索任务往往需要组合运用语料库中的上述功能,才能完成目标。本文从实际个案出发,介绍如何利用本检索平台开展语料库翻译研究。

例如从汉语角度出发,考察汉译英方向原创语言中的虚义动词“进行”在英文中的对译情况。我们选取 2000—2002 年间社科文体汉译英文本作为语料来源,这部分语料包含英文约 51 万形符,汉语约 39 万形符,共计 90 万形符。首先,考察“进行”的汉英对译情况,如图 3(a)所示,在双语检索模块中文本头筛选模块选取“非文学”,将汉语年代设置为 2000—2002,文体选择“应用文”,体裁选定“哲学、社会科学”,在检索项一栏选中汉语,输入单词“进行”,通过检索,一共获得 407 条检索项,如图 3(b)所示。

（a）检索定义界面

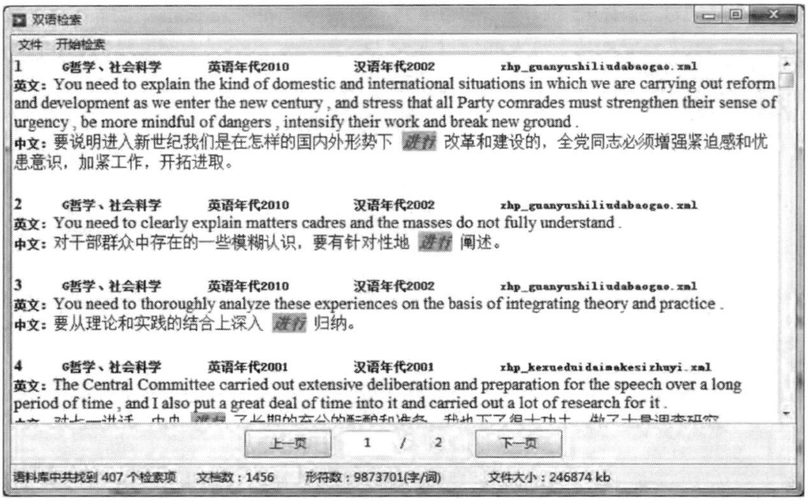

（b）检索结果展示界面

图 3 “进行”的双语汉译英单向检索

对上述407条检索结果进行初步分析发现,“进行”的对译情况可大体分为三类:

(1)无具体对译(隐化):

① 进行 + 名动→动词:

对干部群众中存在的一些模糊认识,要有针对性地进行阐述。

You need to clearly *explain* matters cadres and the masses do not fully understand.

要从理论和实践的结合上深入进行归纳。

You need to thoroughly *analyze* these experiences on the basis of integrating theory and practice.

② 进行 + 名动→名词

中国是世界上最大的发展中国家,人均资源不足,发展很不平衡,实现现代化的任务很繁重,需要进行长期的艰苦努力。

China is the largest developing country in the world, and it has insufficient resources per capita and uneven development. Thus, achieving modernization is an onerous task and will require great *efforts* over a long period of time.

(2)有具体对译:

① 进行 + 名动→动词 + 名词(显化)

要说明进入新世纪我们是在怎样的国内外形势下进行改革和建设的,全党同志必须增强紧迫感和忧患意识,加紧工作,开拓进取。

You need to explain the kind of domestic and international situations in which we are *carrying out* reform and development as we enter the new century, and stress that all Party comrades must strengthen their sense of urgency, be more mindful of dangers, intensify their work and break new ground.

广播、电视和报纸对此进行了一系列的追踪报道和分析。

The broadcast media and the papers *provided* a barrage of reports, updates, and analyses.

② 名词 + 进行 + 得→名词 + 动词(显化)

这个实验的第一部分进行得很顺利。

The first part of the test *progresses* smoothly.

③ 进行 + 的 + 名词→形容词 + 名词(显化)

每一个场景开始时都是一个小孩孤零零地站在一旁观看一些正在进行的集体活动。但最后,这个小孩主动加入到这些活动中,每个人都很快乐。

Each scene began by showing a different solitary child watching some *ongoing* social activity and then actively joining the activity,to everyone's enjoyment.

(3)无具体对译但存在语法转换(被动语态):

美国在对阿富汗采取行动的当晚,事先通过我国驻美国大使馆向我国进行了通报。

On the night the United States was to take action against Afghanistan,China *was notified* through our embassy in Washington of the impending action.

这其中的原因是多方面的,既有国际环境的原因也有国内的原因,既有历史的原因也有现实的原因,既有物质技术发展方面的原因也有精神文化领域的原因,要进行全面分析。

The reasons for these phenomena are many,and include both international and domestic factors,both historical and contemporary factors,factors involving material and technological development and intellectual and cultural factors, all of which need to *be comprehensively analyzed*.

对上述现象进行初步分类,可进一步对其中一类的转换展开研究。本文选取“进行”转换为被动语态的一类现象进行进一步的分析。由于检索行众多,要从中过滤出英语译文中转换为被动句的形式,以减少干扰项,缩小分析语料的范围。与第一步的检索一致,文本头筛选保留上次检索所限定的范围。勾选“英语”检索项,选择“词形还原”来忽略动词的曲折变化。在英文检索项中输入被动句的基本构造形式或者带有副词修饰词的构造形式“< lemma = be > < pos = rb > {0,5} < pos = vvn >”,中文检索项则保持“进行”不变,进行检索,同时勾选“显示词性标记”,从而可以进一步开展更加细致的分析。检索界面如图 4 所示,共检出 123 条双语索引行。

对这些进行人工甄别和分类之后,合乎条件的检索项共 19 条,并且满足两类形式,一类有具体对译,另一类无具体对译,具体情况如表 3 所示。

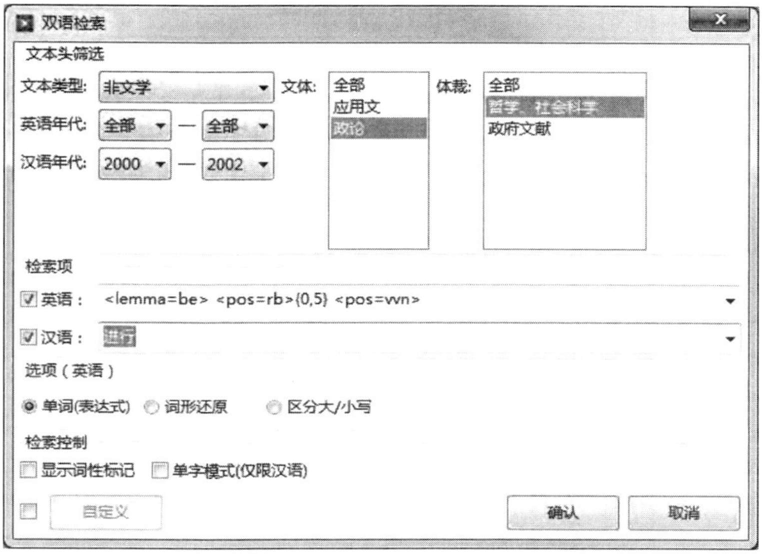

(a)检索定义界面

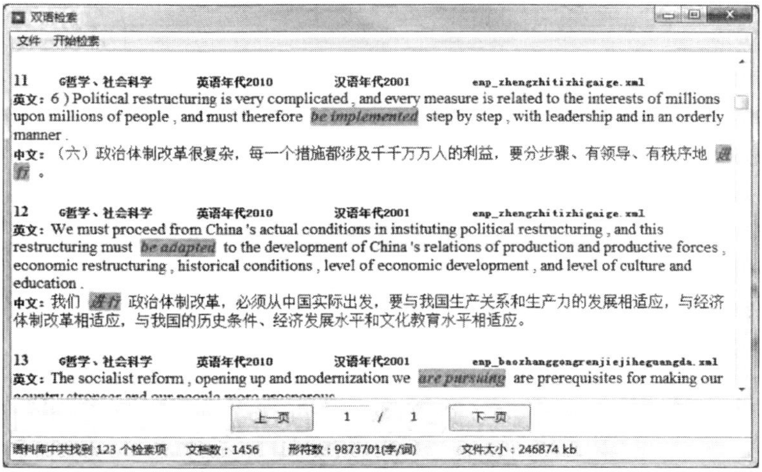

(b)检索结果展示界面

图 4 “进行”译为被动句式的双语汉译英双向检索

表 3 “进行”被动转换的对译情况

转换模式	英语对译	搭配	频次
进行→被动结构(译出)	be implemented(1), be carried out(6), be perpetrated(1), be made(3), be settled(1), be done(1)	改革、活动、犯罪、推进、交易、生产、流转、研究、全球化、创新、党建工作、规划	13
进行+名动→被动结构(未译出)	be(examined), be(explored)(1), be(notified)(1), be(reviewed), be (adjusted), be (criticized and corrected)	审批、探索、通报、总结、调节、批评与纠正	6

(1)进行→动词被动结构

政治体制改革很复杂,每一个措施都涉及千千万万人的利益,要分步骤、有领导、有秩序地进行。

Political restructuring is very complicated, and every measure is related to the interests of millions upon millions of people, and must therefore *be implemented* step by step, with leadership and in an orderly manner.

依法进行管理,就是要切实保障宗教信仰自由,保证正常宗教活动有序进行,保护宗教团体的合法利益。

Administering religious affairs in accordance with the law means effectively guaranteeing the freedom of religious belief, ensuring normal religious activities *are carried out* in an orderly manner and protecting the legitimate interests of religious organizations.

(2)进行+名动→动词被动结构

二是,社会主义实践的历史还比较短,从十月革命算起也只有八十多年,中国进行社会主义建设只有四十多年的历史,很多事情都要在实践中进行探索。

Second, the history of socialist praxis is short. It has been only 80 plus years since the October Revolution, and China started to build socialism little over 40 years ago, and many things still need to be *explored* through praxis.

需要进行行政审批的项目,要建立科学的机制,以堵塞漏洞,减少钱权交易的机会。

For projects that should *be examined* and approved through administrative channels,a scientific mechanism should be established in order to close loopholes and reduce the chances of the abuse of power for financial gain.

四、检索平台信度分析

本文通过对比 AntConc 3.44 与 ParaConc 2.69 这两款工具与“平台”单语检索部分和双语检索部分相同检索项的检索结果数量的一致性来分析“平台”检索结果的可信度。本文在 7,281,597 词英语语料和 14,430,485 字汉语语料中,随机抽样选取 30 组检索结果在 1000 以上的检索项来进行对比,具体检索词如表 4 所示:

表 4 语料库检索项

检索语言	检索项
英语	therefore, fund, energy, aggregate, unit, decline, small, monetary, Russia, must, rise, free, common, should, economic, yet, party, access, will, week, profit, balancer, never, various, security, almost, natural, portfolio, between, competition
汉语	出口、系列、方式、如今、降低、模型、以下、原因、工厂、进行、意义、假定、反应、这种、实现、事情、为什么、信息、中国政府、竞争、只要、监管、最低、总统、比率、储备、运动、单位、感到、理解

其中英文检索结果如表 5 所示:

可以看出,三款检索工具的英文结果基本一致,只有 AntConc 在实词检索项上的检索结果较之“平台”与 ParaConc 略多,这是由于 AntConc 对 XML 语料库文档仍然采取文本搜索方式,因此将带有连字符的单词检索出来,例如:Unit-sold、small-scale、momentary-policy、duty-free、must-go-up、must-have、profit-and-loss 等,而“平台”则采用了与 ParaConc 相同的搜索策略。为了对比不同检索工具在检索结果上的差异性,本文使用非参数假设检验方法中的符号检验来进行相同英文检索项的配对检验。“平台”与 ParaConc 的检验结果表明,在显著性水平为 0.05 上的 Z 值为 0,即两者在英文检索结果上完全不存在差异;此外,“平台”与 AntConc 的检索结果显示,在显著性水平为 0.05 上的 Z 值为 0,因而两者在英文检索结果上完全不存在差异。由上述分析可见,“平台”的英文检索结果是可靠的。

本文也对汉语作为检索项的检索结果进行了检验,结果如表 6 所示。

表 5 AntConc、ParaConc 与“平台”英文检索结果数量对比

检索项	平台	AntConc	ParaConc	检索项	平台	AntConc	ParaConc
therefore	3241	3241	3247	yet	2406	2420	2412
fund	2601	2768	2605	party	1841	1956	1841
energy	1786	1953	1837	access	1254	1257	1254
aggregate	2030	2032	2030	will	22570	22583	22574
unit	1062	1328	1062	week	1942	2055	1949
decline	1826	1827	1826	profit	2018	2171	2018
small	2947	3090	2948	balance	1651	1814	1653
monetary	3304	3340	3305	never	1538	1554	1538
Russia	1428	1441	1430	various	1269	1269	1269
must	6362	6380	6363	security	1869	1915	1872
rise	3354	3381	3357	almost	2291	2297	2293
free	1909	2683	1910	natural	1807	1837	1807
common	2262	2279	2265	portfolio	2521	2539	2524
should	6953	6950	6955	between	7550	7559	7553
economic	8685	8740	8699	competition	1539	1540	1540

表 6 AntConc、ParaConc 与“平台”中文检索结果数量对比

检索项	平台	AntConc	ParaConc	检索项	平台	AntConc	ParaConc
出口	5777	5777	5776	事情	1160	1160	1159
系列	1492	1492	1491	为什么	2025	2025	2006
方式	3995	3995	3995	信息	6181	6181	6179
如今	1194	1194	1193	中国政府	1301	1301	1301
降低	3772	3772	3771	竞争	3920	3920	3920
模型	4305	4305	4305	只要	1168	1168	1160
以下	1534	1534	1531	监管	2554	2554	2554

续表

检索项	平台	AntConc	ParaConc	检索项	平台	AntConc	ParaConc
原因	3899	3899	3898	最低	1389	1389	1389
工厂	1226	1226	1226	总统	1055	1055	1054
进行	11649	11649	11649	比率	1385	1385	1385
意义	1670	1670	1670	储备	2673	2673	2673
假定	1739	1739	1733	运动	1080	1080	1080
反应	1420	1420	1420	单位	1444	1444	1444
这种	11762	11762	11743	感到	1152	1152	1152
实现	2952	2952	2952	理解	1758	1758	1758

表6显示,三款检索工具的中文结果基本一致。为了对比不同检索工具在检索结果上的差异性,本文仍然使用非参数假设检验方法中的符号检验来进行相同英文检索项的配对检验,“平台”与ParaConc的检验结果表明,在显著性水平为0.05上的Z值为0,即两者在中文检索结果上完全不存在差异;此外,“平台”与AntConc的检索结果显示,在显著性水平为0.05上的Z值为0,因而两者在中文检索结果上完全不存在差异。由上述分析可见,“平台”的中文检索结果完全可靠。

由上述的可信度分析可见,使用“平台”进行语料库研究的结果可以信赖。从检索速率看,本文发现,在2000万字词双语语料内,英文平均检索时间,“平台”为30.94秒,AntConc为93.78秒,ParaConc为21秒,对于中文的平均检索时间,“平台”、AntConc与ParaConc分别为29.59秒、84.71秒、23.02秒,本平台和ParaConc速率较高,后者略快。但是,在加载超过2000万语料时,ParaConc会提示内存溢出,无法进行检索,可见“平台”在单机处理大数据时具有较大的优势。

五、结语

本文所研究的双语库检索技术面向超过一亿字词的大规模双语平行语料

库,可以在任何配置的计算机上运行,灵活可靠,简单易用。较之传统的双语库检索工具,“平台”具备一些明显的优势:①基于单机,但采用索引和搜索技术,可高效处理巨量语料数据;②支持提取双语双向元信息的搜索;③具备较为完备的检索功能,支持单语和双语双向的简单检索和复杂检索;④具有较高的可靠性,检索结果与主流平行语料库检索结果具备极高的一致性;⑤较高的可扩展性,兼容 XML 主流的语料格式,语料可随时扩展而无须导入;⑥同时支持双语和单语检索,免去用户使用不同检索软件所造成的数据结果的差异性,使研究结果更加可靠。本文所研制检索技术也具有一定局限性,本研究采用单机的形式,不适用于语料向上扩展至数十亿字词语料的处理。在未来的研究中,将继续为该语料库开发联机平台,并逐步实现汉语被动义和英汉词级对应单位的自动抽取。

（原载《外语电化教学》2017 年第 6 期,作者为王克非、刘鼎甲）

参考文献

M.Baker,“CorpusLinguistics and Translation Studies: Implications and Applications”, M.Baker, G.Grancis & E.Tognini-Bonelli (eds.), *Text and Technology: In Honour of John Sinclair*, Amsterdam: John Benjamins, 1993.

T.McEnery, & R.Xiao, “Parallel and Comparable Corpora: What is Happening?” M. Rogers & G.Anderman (eds.), *Incorporating Corpora: The Linguist and the Translator*, Clevedon: Multilingual Matters, 2007.

F. J. Och, & H. Ney, “Discriminative Training and Maximum Entropy Models for Statistical Machine Translation”, *Proceedings of the 40th Annual Meeting of the Association for Computational Linguistics*, Stroudsburg: ACL, 2002.

冯志伟:《基于语料库的机器翻译系统》,《术语标准化与信息技术》2010 年第 1 期。

黄立波、王克非:《语料库翻译学:课题与进展》,《外语教 学与研究》2011 年第 6 期。

黄万丽、秦洪武:《英汉平行历时语料库的创建与语料检索》,《当代外语研究》2015 年第 3 期。

梁茂成、李文中、许家金:《语料库应用教程》,外语教学与研究出版社 2010 年版。

刘群:《机器翻译研究新进展》,《当代语言学》2009 年第 2 期。

孟小峰、慈祥:《大数据管理:概念、技术与挑战》,《计算机研究与发展》2013 年第 1 期。

秦洪武、李婵、王玉:《基于语料库的汉语翻译语言研究十年回顾》,《解放军外国语学院学报》2014 年第 1 期。

王克非:《双语对应语料库:研制与应用》,外语教学与研究出版社 2004 年版。

王克非:《新型双语对应语料库的设计与构建》,《中国翻译》2004 年第 6 期。

王克非:《中国英汉平行语料库的设计与研制》,《中国外语》2012 年第 6 期。

王克非、黄立波:《语料库翻译学十五年》,《中国外语》2008 年第 6 期。

许家金、贾云龙:《基于 R-gram 的语料库分析软件 PowerConc 的设计与开发》,《外语电化教学》2013 年第 1 期。

许家金、吴良平:《基于网络的第四代语料库分析工具 CQPweb 及应用实例》,《外语电化教学》2014 年第 5 期。

双语对应语料库翻译教学平台的应用初探

本文通过语料呈现实验探讨双语对应语料库翻译教学平台的应用效果。实验显示,学生在观察语料后能够归纳和总结出有意义的翻译技巧,并能据此评估或反思自己的翻译行为。实验表明,在翻译课堂教学中使用语料资源有助于自主学习和发现式翻译教学环境的创建,也有助于学习者形成稳定的翻译技巧。

近 20 年来,语料库的创建和应用取得了长足发展。对应语料库大都在 20 世纪 90 年代开始创建,起步较晚,但已展现出广阔的应用前景。在欧美,这类语料库有十多个,涉及近 20 个语种,如 Hansard(法—英对应语料库)和 ENPC(英语—挪威语对应语料库)(Véronis 2000:14-15);在中国,有中科院计算所的大规模汉英对应语料库、北京大学的"BABLE 汉英平行语料库",以及北京外国语大学的"通用汉英对应语料库"(该库现有可检索语料 2 千万字/词以上,见王克非 2004a),后者是本项研究使用的主要工具。

对应语料库的创建有两个主要目的:一是用于语言与翻译研究,二是用于外语教学。用于前者的研究成果丰富,涉及语言对比、双语词典编纂和翻译研究(Laviosa 1997;Baker 1999;Serpellet 2000;Hunston 2002)。用于后者尤其是用于翻译教学的研究也已取得不少成果,如 Zanettin(1998)、Pearson(2003:15-24)和 Bernardini(2004b:97-111),但大都研究平行语料为翻译训练提供的可能的资源和手段,还没有研究探讨大型对应语料库在课堂教学中的实际应用问题。

一、研究内容

有关运用语料库提高翻译效率和质量的研究还没有全面展开，而将对应语料库应用于翻译教学的研究则是刚刚开始（Bowker 2003；Bernardini 2004b）。从理论上看，语料库用于教学有利于自主学习环境的创建（Bernardini 2004a：22；秦洪武、王克非 2007）。自主性学习主要表现在两个方面：研究性学习和发现式学习（learning as discovery）。前者假定学习者和教师研究兴趣相投、研究能力相当；后者则鼓励学习者自行调节兴趣点，并给他们提供机会来提高自己观察和处理问题的能力，使他们对两种语言的特征和差异有敏锐的觉识。本文认为，研究和发现虽不矛盾，但在以技能培养为核心的翻译教学中，不宜过分强调学生的研究能力，发现式学习这一提法更合适一些。

近年来，国内也有研究关注语料库在翻译教学中的应用问题。有些研究探讨了语料库在翻译教学中的用途（郭红 2004；于连江 2004；王克非 2004b），但还没有研究系统地探讨对应语料在课堂教学中的应用方式和应用效果，也没有研究关注学生对于语料使用的态度。鉴于此，我们以“通用汉英对应语料库”为翻译教学平台，探讨在现有技术条件下翻译语料用于翻译教学可能产生的积极效果。

二、研究设计及步骤

实验使用的翻译语料全部取自北京外国语大学“通用汉英对应语料库”。

语料呈现实验分为两步。第一步要求受试观察真实翻译语料；第二步让受试将自认为有意义的发现以书面形式表达出来，鼓励同学之间（一般为同桌）通过商讨共同完成观察报告。

1. 参与者

参加本次调查的是某大学外语学院英语专业本科四年级学生（3 个班，

136 人)和一年级研究生(35 人)。这些学生都在学习翻译,此前没有接触过语料库。本研究主要观察学生对语料呈现的整体反应,因此,个体和性别差异未列入考察范围。但是,鉴于语言水平可能影响到语料库的使用,在整理数据时将研究生和本科列为对比分析的对象。

实验分三次进行。第一次的受试是本科四年级 3 个自然班的学生,呈现的汉英对译语料涉及汉语动词与英语介词 in/at 间的对译关系(呈现给 1、5 班),以及汉语动词与 over/with 之间的互译①关系(呈现给 2 班)。为利于把握受试对语料的反应,实验使用的对应语料由教师课前筛选。在呈现语料时,教师不对学生做任何暗示,以保证学生自主做出判断。第二次的受试是本科四年级学生,第三次的受试是一年级研究生,这两次实验使用的翻译语料都是汉语句群的英译②。以上三次语料呈现方式相同。具体步骤为:

(1)语料呈现——刺激:将语言学习者的注意力集中于关键词或结构的翻译对应项。语料由教师挑选(也可以应学生要求或建议学生自行检索)。

(2)学生浏览语料:学生通过考察语料建立自认为有效的形式—意义关联。

(3)提示学生记录他们的心得和他们认为有意义的发现。

(4)要求学生回答一个开放性问题:观察语料后你有什么心得或发现?

让受试回答上面的开放性问题有两个目的:一是考查学生对语料呈现的态度;二是观察学生在浏览语料时关注了哪些对翻译教学有意义的问题。

2. 数据收集

本项研究呈现的语料量为 1500~1700 个汉英字词(汉语字与英语词比率

---

① 如:隔壁绍兴戏唱完了,你就打鼾,好厉害 After the Shaohsing opera was [over], you started snoring your head off;韩孟翔狡猾地笑着回答,把手杖一挥,就沿着那水门汀向南走,却故意放慢了脚步 he replied [with] a sly grin, then turned away down the street, swinging his stick, though he was careful not to walk too fast。

② 如:◆【4:1】

<s>是一条快船。</s>

<s>单趟直放,不过半天多,就到了。</s>

<s>就是颠得厉害。</s>

<s>骨头痛。</s>

<s> It's a fast boat and didn't stop on the way, and we did the journey in half a day, but it did roll terribly, and made my joints ache.</s>

为1.6∶1),学生可在10分钟左右浏览完毕。阅读完毕,教师要求受试回答一个开放性问题:观察语料后你有什么心得或发现?教师建议报告由两人或多人共同完成,长短不限。学生的回答以书面报告形式提交给老师,供下一步进行归类和分析。

3. 数据分类

鉴于学生回答的问题是开放式的,我们采用吴一安(2005)使用的主题一致分析方法对学生回答的内容进行分类,分类后再整理出受试关注的内容细节。这些内容以提及频数的形式呈现出来,形成附录中的六个统计表。

1　受试对语料呈现的态度

三次实验的对象都是英语专业的学习者,他们正在学习汉英翻译。报告显示学生对于汉英翻译时的处理技巧比较敏感,而且也表达了自己对于语料呈现的态度。如:

(1)英语介词很有用处,有时比一个句子表达得还要清楚。

(2)看似挺难的汉语句子,用英语的介词短语简简单单就译出来了,而且带有原文的韵味,其乐无穷。

(3)平时翻译时意识不到用英语介词使译文简洁。

(4)翻译不仅要靠大的英语词汇量,还要学会灵活使用我们已经掌握了的词汇和语法。

(5)看这些汉英对译很有趣,也感觉很有用。

可以看出,受试在观察语料后不仅能够意识到语言运用问题,还能够反思自己的语言能力和翻译能力,有的甚至指出需要调整自己的语言学习方式。总的说来,学生对翻译语料呈现的反应是正面的。

2　报告内容的分类

我们把受试告的内容分成四类:技巧觉识、功能认识、语言差异和评估(对翻译手段的评价)。

(1)技巧觉识:受试注意动词与介词之间的转换关系,也注意到汉语句群在英语译文中的组合方式。这说明受试具有从对应语料中觉识到翻译技巧的能力。

(2)功能认识:受试注意到一些英语的介词能够引入时间、状态、年龄、同时性等背景信息，还注意到英语连词、从句在语言组织上的独特作用。这说明受试对技巧的觉识与他们对词汇和语法功能的认识是相通的。

(3)语言差异：有些受试注意到英汉两种语言的差异。

(4)评估：学生注意到了某些翻译处理方式产生的文体效果和语言运用的灵活性，说明学生对翻译技巧有评价能力。

以上分类说明，在呈现汉英翻译语料后，受试对于翻译技巧、词汇—语法功能、语言差异比较敏感，同时也注意到了翻译技巧的运用效果。这些都表明，受试能够有效地观察和评价翻译语料，翻译语料呈现的作用是积极的。

三、结果与分析

1. 第一次呈现的语料

第一次语料呈现后，收到的 64 份报告中有 41 份(占 64%)提及汉语动词和英语介词短语在翻译中的转换问题(见(附录)表 1~3)。表中显示，有关技巧觉识方面的内容出现频率最高，也最集中。统计还显示，受试对于介词的功能也做了较为全面的归纳，但多停留于对共现词项的描述，不如对技巧的觉识那么集中。另外，表 1~3 显示，受试陈述个人对译文的评价时主要涉及文体效果(19 次)和介词使用的灵活性(6 次)。

统计还显示，受试对于不同类型的介词有不同的认识，这一点主要体现在对 over、with 这两个介词的表达功能上。表 3 显示受试注意到介词的功能是引入背景信息，说明部分受试在观察翻译时已发现汉英翻译时动词与介词转换的内在依据，同时也注意到英语在表达背景信息时可以使用与汉语不同的语言手段。上述内容表明多数受试能从呈现的语料中归纳出有意义的翻译内容，并能给予比较合理的解释。

当然，受试报告中对于译文的评估有失偏颇。如表 1 有 2 份报告、表 2 有 1 份报告认为，汉语生动、英语单调。做出这一概括的主要依据是：呈现语料中的汉语动词群都转换成了英语译文中的“介词 + 名物化”短语形式。但这是一种误解，教师需要对此做出分析和说明。

面对成批出现的语料，只有少数受试明确而具体地提及英汉语言之间差异，说明大多数受试还不能在更抽象的层面上思考语言差异问题。

2. 第二次呈现的语料

表1、表2、表3与(附录)表4、表5之间存在有趣的差异。表1、表2、表3中的主要内容是词的运用和功能，而表4、表5则主要涉及句子和句际关系。显然，观察语料的类型不同，受试关注的内容也就不同。比如，呈现的多为句对应语料时，受试关注的重点在词和词性（见表1、表2、表3）；当呈现内容为句群对应语料时，受试则将关注的重点调整到衔接手段的使用上（见表4、表5）。总之，受试能够根据呈现的材料来调整自己的注意焦点。但表4、表5也显示，个别受试的归纳和概括还有些问题。比如，有受试认为英语译文比汉语原文逻辑性更强。这一判断只是依据连接词使用的数量，但逻辑性的强弱不是凭连词使用的数量来判断的。

本科生受试的报告显示出他们对语料感兴趣，也能捕捉到潜藏在译文后面的翻译技巧。这至少可以说明，本科生能够通过观察翻译语料、归纳并通过讨论来学习翻译技巧。这些技能和心得在初期需要教师有针对性地提供语料，但归纳和总结都是学生自主完成的。从这个意义上说，翻译语料的呈现可以有效地帮助翻译学习者获得翻译技能、提高翻译水平。

此外，语料呈现还有助于学生调整学习方法，注意自身语言运用能力的培养。如有受试在报告中写道：

> 翻译不仅要靠大的单词量，还要学会灵活使用我们已经掌握了的词汇。

有个别受试甚至还觉察到自己的语言直觉和实际运用之间有距离。如：

> 我学了以前不知道的东西。发现一个简单的介词有不同的意思和功能。一个句子可以有不同的表达方式。这些译文处理技巧很精彩。看来我还要学更多的东西。这些技巧能够帮助我们译出好的译文。

分析真实文本可使学生在词汇和语法结构方面增长见识，这有利于学习者承担真实的翻译任务。观察语料不仅能够激发学习动机，还有助于学生适时调整翻译学习方式，提高对翻译技巧的认识和应用水平。一般说来，通过考察一个词或者结构的多个翻译例证，个别性的因素就会被规律性替代；有动因的翻译策略累积起来就可使学习者感知到一般的形式并形成有意义的概括。

3. 第三次呈现的语料

第三次呈现的语料与第二次相同,但受试不同。这一次的受试是一年级学习翻译理论与实践的研究生。表6(见附录)显示,受试对于翻译技巧细节的捕捉比本科生(表3、表4)受试更细腻。而且,他们对于语言事实抽象能力更强。比如,受试在报告中使用衔接手段、重构、从句这类术语来表述问题,而少用生动、地道等含混的字眼来表达自己的看法。

4. 报告反映出的问题

呈现语料可能引发不当的归纳和概括,原因主要来自两个方面:一是语料呈现的数量有限,无法涵盖与某一语言项目相关的所有情形;二是限于语言能力和分析能力,受试还无法深入思考语言和翻译问题。出现这些问题是正常的,但教师应该适时加以引导,鼓励学生尽可能全面地观察翻译和语言现象。

本次实验使用的语料是教师检索后筛选出来的,还不是由学生根据自己的需求自行检索。因此,这还不是真正意义上的自主性学习。要想充分挖掘学生的学习动机和潜力,就应鼓励学生按照自己的需求去检索、获得和研究真实语言素材,并提出自己的看法。这就为学生作为"研究者"去开辟新的研究领域带来了实实在在的希望,而不只是重复或者评估别人的研究(Leech 1997:10)。

目前在课堂上只是以电子文本或者检索软件的KWIC形式呈现翻译语料,这样的呈现方式完全由教师控制,过于机械、单调。鉴于此,创建方便、迅速的语料检索和应用环境,并实现学习者按照个人的需求检索、考察、探讨和使用语料,是对应语料库有效应用于翻译教学的关键。

四、小结

Bernardini(2004a:31-32)指出,语料库和语料分析工具似乎为发现式学习活动提供了强有力的辅助工具。规模较大的对应语料库能为翻译教学提供丰富多样的翻译素材,为灵活运用翻译技巧提供重要的参照资源,也为建立良性的课堂互动提供重要的物质环境，这些都有利于激发学生的学习兴趣，促使学生将注意力集中在与技巧密切相关的形式意义关联上。发现式学习本来不是基于语料库的，但语料库却能够有力地促进自主学习环境的建立。

学习者的观察结果可能是局部或者经验式的概括，但这一观察结果可以通过新的证据来检验、修改和丰富。从外语学习和翻译技巧觉识上看，学习者大量观察双语对应语料后可能对搭配、语义偏向和语义韵等现象更加敏感；翻译技巧和策略可以通过学生之间和师生之间的互动性讨论逐步形成，这有助于学生形成稳定、持久和灵活的翻译策略。传统上，教师在翻译教学过程中起主导作用，面对教材中数量有限且少有例外的零散范例，学生往往会盲目接受教师所陈述的规定性很强的翻译技巧，而翻译质量评估则完全依赖教师的直觉判断。这些都无助于培养学生灵活运用翻译技巧的能力。使用语料库可以弥补这一方面的不足，它允许学生（根据教师的建议）自主且有针对性地选择语料并借之做出概括或解释，充分发挥其自主捕捉翻译技巧和自主构建翻译策略的能力。从这个意义上说，对应语料库的应用有助于提升翻译教学的效果。

附录：受试报告的分类和统计

附 1.1　第一次呈现的语料：汉英翻译时介词短语的使用

表 1　汉语中的动词表达转换为英语 in、at 引导的介词短语（本科四年级 1 班，共收取报 24 份）

报告内容分类	技巧		功能					差异	评估			
	动词与介词转换	有些需要更大语境才明白	At 表同时性	At 表时间点，in 表时间段	At 引出一个行为	At/in 可以表达年龄/状况	In 可表方位、状态	英语多介词，汉语多动词	反思自己的翻译	英语介词用法灵活	汉语生动，英语单调	文体效果
频次	18	1	1	7	1	4	11	1	1	2	2	3

表 2 汉语中的动词表达转换为英语 in、at 引导的介词短语（本科四年级 5 班，共收取报告 21 份）

报告内容分类	技巧	功能			差异	评估		
	动词与介词转换	At 表时间点，in 表时间段	At/in 可表年龄/状况	In 可表方位、状态	英语多介词，汉语多动词	文体效果	英语介词用法灵活	汉语生动，英语单调
频次	10	3	5	6	1	8	2	1

表 3 汉语中的动词表达转换为英语 over、with 引导的介词短语（本科四年级 2 班，共收取报告 19 份）

报告内容分类	技巧	功能			评估	
	动词与介词转换	over 表时间	Over/with 可以表达状态	介词引入背景信息	文体效果	用法灵活
频次	13	2	1	7	13	4

附 1.2 第二次呈现的语料：汉语句群的英译

表 4 本科四年级 5 班，共收取报告 20 份

报告内容分类	技巧				语言差异		评估	
	汉语短句译为英语小句	英译文添加了连词	用介词引入从属性行为	用分词短语表达从属性行为	英语句子比汉语长	汉语省略多	英译文逻辑性更强	文体效果
频次	11	15	6	8	2		1	8

表 5 本科四年级 2 班，共收取报告 17 份

报告内容分类	技巧							语言差异			评估
	汉语短句译为英语小句	英译文添加了连词	用介词引入从属性行为	添加/改变主语	语序调整	重新组合	反思自己的翻译	英语句子比汉语长	汉语省略多	汉英比英汉使用技巧更多	英语译文逻辑性更强
频次	6	12	2	2	5	4	1	2	1	1	1

附 1.3　第三次呈现的语料:汉语句群的英译

表 6　研究生一年级,共收取报告 22 份

报告内容分类	技巧										语言差异		评估
	遣词	汉语短句译为英语小句	英译文添加了连词	译文使用副词表达原文的行为	汉语重复而译文使用代词	使用从句	使用了原文没有的衔接手段	调整语序/重构	背景与前景	添加/改变主语	英语句子比汉语长	汉语少用衔接手段	介词使英译文简洁
频次	1	11	11	5	3	6	4	4	1	4	6	4	9

(本文原载《外语电化教学》2007 年第 6 期,作者为王克非、秦洪武、王海霞)

参考文献

M.Baker,"The Role of Corpora in Investigating the Linguistic Behavior of Professional Translation",*International Journal of Corpus Linguistics*,1999,Vol 4,No.2,pp.281-298.

S.Bernardini,"Corpra in the Classroom:An Overview and some Reflection on Future Developments",J.Sinclair(ed.),*How to Use Corpora in Language Teaching*,Philadelphia:John Benjamins Publishing Company,2004a,pp.15-38.

S.Bernardini,"Corpus-aidedLanguage Pedagogy for Translator Education",K.Malmkjær (ed.),*Translation in Undergraduate Degree Programmes*,Amsterdam:John Benjamins Publishing Company,2004b,pp.97-112.

L.Bowker,"Corpus-based Applications for Translator Training:Exploring the Possibilities",S.Granger,J.Lerot & S.Peich-Tyson(eds.),*Corpus-based Approaches to Contrastive Linguistics and Translation Studies*,Amsterdam,New York:Rodopi,2003.

S.Hunston,*Corpora in Applied Linguistics*,Cambridge:CUP,2002.

S.Laviosa,"How Comparable can Comparable Corpora be",*Target*,199,Vol 9,No.2,pp.289-319.

G.Leech,"Teaching in Language Corpora:A Convergence",A.Wichmann,S.Fligelstone,T.McEnery & G.Knowles(eds.),*Teaching and Language Corpora*,London:Longman,

1997, pp.1–22.

J.Pearson, "Using Parallel Texts in the Translator Training Environment", F.Zanettin, S. Bernardini & D. Stewart (eds.), *Corpora in Translator Education*, Manchester: St. Jerome, 2003, pp.15–24.

N.Serpellet, "Mandative Constructions in English and their Equivalents in French: Applying a Bilingual Approach to the Theory and Practice of Translation", B.Kettemann & G. Marko(eds.), *Teaching and Learning by Doing Corpus Analysis*, *Proceeding of the Fourth International Conference on Teaching and Language Corpora*, Amsterdam, New York: Rodopi, 2000, pp.345–360.

J.Véronis, "From the Rosetta Sone to the Information Society: A Survey of Parallel Text Processing", J.Véronis(ed.), *Parallel Text Processing: Alignment and Use of Translation Corpus*, Cordrecht: Kluwer Academic Publishers, 2000.

F.Zanettin, "Bilingual Comparable Corpora and the Training of Translators", *Meta*, 1998, No.4, pp.4–14.

郭红:《计算机辅助翻译教学的一种尝试》,《外语界》2004 年第 5 期。

秦洪武、王克非:《对应语料库在翻译教学中的应用:理论依据和实施原则》,《中国翻译》2007 年第 5 期。

王克非:《双语对应语料库:研制与应用》,外语教学与研究出版社 2004 年版。

王克非:《双语对应语料库在翻译教学上的用途》,《外语电化教学》2004 年第 6 期。

吴一安:《优秀外语教师专业素质探究》,《外语教学与研究》2005 年第 3 期。

于连江:《基于语料库的翻译教学研究》,《外语电化教学》2004 年第 6 期。

论平行语料库在翻译教学中的应用

本文探讨了平行语料库在翻译教学中应用的依据、动因和方式。研究认为,平行语料库在课堂环境下使用的主要方式是呈现数据,让学习者面对充足、易筛选的双语数据,使翻译技巧和特定语言项目翻译的讲授相对集中,重点突出。作者指出,平行语料库的研究发现,如词性分布、句段长度和结构容量等,有助于改善译文评估方式,有些可以直接应用于教学过程,提升翻译学习效率和效果。再进一步,平行语料库数据运用得当,会有助于创建高质量的自主学习和发现式翻译教学环境。

一、引言

在教学中使用语料库,可以更为便利地获取语料。相关研究表明,语料库可以使学习者直接获得无限的语言数据(Johns 2002)。语料库和语料库工具在翻译教学中的作用不可估量(Pearson 1996:85)。语料库数据的主要运用方式有两类:语料库驱动的(corpus-driven)和基于语料库的(corpus-based)。前者和发现式学习(learning as discovery)契合;后者则可以提供纪实性证据(documentary evidence),为翻译过程提供辅助和参考。

在翻译教学和实践中,学习者较其他科目的学习更能积极参与教授过程,如评估译作,建立对等(翻译对等和语际对等)(Bernardini *et al*.2003:5)。因此,平行对应语料可以强化学生主动参与的效果,如通过观察双语对应句,学习优秀译文,学得翻译技巧;通过观察双语对应句,提升语言使用的准确性和地道程度；在真实翻译数据中解决实际问题，加深对翻译行为的认识。

平行语料库的创建在国外已有二十多年的历史，它在教学中的应用研究也有十余年；在国内，平行语料库在教学中的应用起步较晚。总体说来，语料库在翻译教学中的应用研究滞后于语料库翻译学研究，亟待开发出有效的应用方式以扩展其在翻译中的应用。本文主要探讨平行语料库在教学中的应用方式和相关发现，重点探索语料库翻译学研究成果在翻译教学中的应用问题。

二、语料库与翻译教学的契合

对翻译学习者而言，翻译学习过程就是通过学习成为翻译工作者的过程（李德凤、胡枚 2006）。简单说来，这个过程是通过学习学会制作翻译产品。那么，这些制作产品的知识从何而来？显然，它不是从教师那儿直接习得的，教师只是指导和协调，让学生通过翻译和评估翻译获得足够的翻译经验。按照这一理解，语料库提供的间接翻译经验是翻译教学中除个人实际翻译之外的另一主要资源。双语语料库与翻译教学存在天然契合点，语料库可为学习者提供经验数据，学习者可以藉之自主学习、发挥潜能，提升学习的效率和效果。

学习者自身的能动性在翻译教学中占据重要地位。以平行语料库为平台，其检索功能和提取功能可以让学生有机会参与教学内容和翻译材料的取舍，或提供课堂讨论和小组活动内容，以激发学生的参与意识。此外，平行语料库还有助于培养学生严谨的工作作风和批判性思维的能力，不拘泥于特定的译法或译者。这才是以学习者为中心①的翻译教学。

从翻译本身的性质看，翻译立足于实践，翻译教学也立足于实践、重视经验累积，双语平行库提供的间接翻译知识显然能够帮助学生累积翻译经验。教学重视学生自主学习能力的培养，平行语料库提供个性化的资料提取平台

① 以学习者为中心的教学指的是从教学目标的设定、教学材料的选择，一直到课堂教学、作业评估等环节充分考虑学生的因素（王宇 2003）。

能满足学生自主学习的环境要求;学生能够通过观察、分析形成翻译技巧,双语库可以为他们提供大量针对性强的观察对象。

三、双语库在翻译教学中的应用:方法问题

多年前,Bowker(2000)和 Bernardini(2004:97-112)说,对应语料库应用于翻译教学的研究刚刚起步。10 年过去了,双语语料库在翻译教学过程如何有效运用依旧有许多问题。核心的问题是平行语库如何与微观翻译教学环节有效衔接。

Baker(1993)和 Chesterman(2004)运用频率数据统计方法开展翻译语言研究,获取数据的方法是检索,这意味着语料库用于翻译教学也要靠频率和检索。除了这些语料库分析手段外,不存在基于双语语料库的全新教学环境和方法,只能在现有教学环境下让平行语料库进入翻译教学环节,发挥平行语料库的功用。因此,还要考虑学习者和双语对应的性质。国外语料库翻译教学研究提出了以下可能的语料使用方式。

1)刺激—认识:通过有针对性的语料观察,学生接受刺激,就可以提高一般意义上的语言认识(awareness;Hunston 2002:123);在翻译训练时,有针对性地集中探讨某翻译有助于发现新的翻译技巧,或者证实自己使用的翻译技巧。

2)功能同—编码异:译者总是倾向预先设定对等的翻译单位在意义上对等,这样,观察翻译对(translation pairs)就是观察两种语言是以何种方式来编码对应意义的(Barlow 2008:111);以这种方式获得的关于翻译技巧的认识显然有充分的理据,也更有助于形成稳定的翻译技巧。双语语料库还有助于翻译对等的研究,帮助研究者洞悉翻译的本质(Hunston 2002:128)。

3)翻译难点的教学:可借助双语语料库数据为译者提供不同语言中可能的翻译单位或对等篇章单元的集合,使译者对翻译难点的处理增加新的认识,这样有助于改进译作。

可以看出,基于语料库的翻译技巧分析是翻译教学中可以发挥较大潜能

的部分。比如,学习翻译中的拆分与合并技巧时可以先让学生观察一些实例,并根据源语—目的语之间的多层面对应关系观察翻译中发生的事情,这有助于他们对翻译技巧的理解,也会让他们意识到目标语中语言手段的多样性和灵活性。

双语语料库的创建目的和语料形态对于教学环境的使用构成挑战。从语料形态看,目前常见的对应语料库多为词性标注,这影响语言信息的提取深度,而且无法同时提供翻译所需的语义—句法信息。从检索技术上说,语料库使用者很难一次检索到适合课堂使用的语言材料。此外,语料库翻译学的一些描述方式不容易成为可以操作的翻译教学内容,如一些宏观描述的统计结果(如平均词长、平均句长)都是以数字性数据方式呈现的。这类数据抽象,在翻译教学中直接提供这类数字没有意义,让学生感受到这类数字背后的语言实例才是问题所在。

双语语料库在教学中的应用是基于实例的。语料库翻译学的研究成果应用于翻译教学需要的是支持理论发现的语言证据,再现理论发现的过程是语料库翻译学有效应用于翻译教学的关键。

四、双语库在翻译教学中的使用方式:数据呈现

根据王克非(2004)和秦洪武、王克非(2007)的研究,双语语料库在翻译教学中的积极作用十分明显。表现在以下两个方面:1)呈现对应语料能够提高学生对翻译技巧的觉识,而翻译技巧认识的提高有助于促进学生正确运用翻译技巧,进而提高翻译质量;2)技巧认识与翻译质量并不直接相关,说明语料呈现不一定形成有意义的概括。这说明,学习者的观察结果可能是局部或者经验式的概括,但这一观察结果可以通过新的证据来检验、修改和丰富。

为了让学生直接面对经验性语言数据,以便归纳和总结翻译规律,学得翻译技巧。这需要让翻译学习者能在特定时间或者特定场景下观察足量的、有针对性的语言运用实例,如翻译对或者类比文本(comparable texts),这个过程

就是语料呈现。根据王克非、秦洪武等(2007)的研究,语料呈现大致有以下五个步骤:

a.语料呈现——刺激:注意关键词/结构的翻译对应项。语料由教师挑选、应学生要求检索或学生自行检索。

b.学生浏览语料:通过考察语料,建立新的形式—意义关联。

c.学生报告观察心得并记录自己认为有意义的发现。

d.报告心得和发现:经验性地展示(或让学生自我发现)两种语言对应的多对多性质,建立翻译技巧觉识。

e.教师和学生共同讨论与所呈现语料相关的翻译策略。

五个步骤中,语料呈现是关键。首先是呈现的量和呈现环节,即需要明确翻译课堂教学中哪个环节分配多少时间呈现语料。如果翻译课堂采用发现式教学,就宜在靠前的课堂教学环节引入和呈现语料。由于呈现的语料通常要关联到翻译技巧的讲授,那么,供学生观察语料时间不能长于发现式教学需要的讨论时间,而且要考虑学生的注意力广度,以免出现学生精力不集中的问题。一般的做法是,供小技巧教授的语料观察时间以5—8分钟为宜,呈现的语料大约为10—15个翻译对(史汝波等2009)。如表1。

学生观察语料库后进行讨论,讨论的内容为汉译英中词性转换技能的运用。作为教师需要清楚词性转换并非单个词的转换,还需要调整句式和其他成分的表述方式,转换的内容也具有一定的规律,如语义上多为行为方式和手段。学生累积这类经验就有望形成较为稳定的翻译技巧使用意识,形成稳定的、可以灵活运用的翻译技能。

表1　呈现语料实例

呈现语料:双语对译句	讲授技巧:词性变换
1.他们一边喝粥一边谈这事。 They talked about it over their porridge.	动词→介词
2.会开完了,人散了。 People went away after the meeting./ The meeting being over,and the attendants left.	动词→介词
3.事业有成要靠努力工作,而不是投机钻营。 Success is through hard work,but not by securing personal gain.	动词→介词

续表

呈现语料:双语对译句	讲授技巧:词性变换
4.你想不想陪我去逛逛商店? Would you like to go shopping with me?	动词→介词
5.他笑着回答我说,…… He answered me smilingly(with a smile),…	动词→副词/介词
6.我们五点钟上完了一天的课。 The school is over at five o' clock.	动词→介词
7.他支支吾吾,最后还是说了。 Hesitatingly,he finally told the truth.	动词→副词
8.她连哭带喊,述说了自己的遭遇。 She cryingly recounted her sufferings.	动词→副词

注:此为汉英翻译,关联的教学内容为词性转换。

学生经过语料呈现和讨论之后报告他们观察语料后的感受。主要有以下看法:

a.英语介词很有用处,有时比一个句子表达得还要清楚。

b.平时翻译时意识不到用英语介词使译文简洁。

c.翻译不仅要靠大的英语词汇量,还要学会灵活使用我们已经掌握了的词汇。

d.看这些汉英对译很有趣,也感觉很有用。

e.看似挺难的汉语句子,用英语的介词短语简简单单地就译出来了,而且带有原文的韵味,其乐无穷。

从 a、b 所列的反应看,学习者对英语介词的使用有了新的认识,这更新、丰富了他们的语言运用知识;从反应 c 看,观察语料还促使学生反思自己学习和运用英语的方式,这有助于他们改善自己的学习观念;d、e 则说明,有针对性地语料呈现还能提高学生对翻译学习和语言学习的兴趣。这些反应清楚地表明,学生对教学过程中使用双语语料库态度是积极的。学生愿意使用现代技术来做翻译练习,愿意使用语料库来辅助翻译,因为它能够帮助他们改进翻译,同时又能把自己的翻译和专业译者进行对比(Awal *et al*.2014)。

五、语料库翻译学研究发现在翻译教学中的应用

平行语料库提供的多译文环境最直接的作用是提供比较,学生通过比较不同的译文获得对翻译技巧和翻译质量的认识(Yepes 2011)。Pearson(2003:15)指出,平行语料库对译员培训很有作用。基于语料库的研究发现能够也应该为专业翻译课程的设计和实施提供信息。那么,语料库翻译学研究成果在翻译教学中能提供哪些帮助呢,我们以汉语翻译语言研究为例探讨这个问题。

近年来,基于语料库的汉语翻译语言研究十分活跃。研究较多的是翻译共性,如黄立波、王克非(2006)、王克非、胡显耀(2008)、胡显耀、曾佳(2009,2011)及刘泽权、陈冬蕾(2010)等,他们发现,汉语翻译语料与原创汉语相比,表现出明显的简化、显化和范化特征;而且,无论是文学还是非文学语料,翻译汉语与原创汉语相比,具有词语变化度偏低、词汇密度偏低、虚词和指代方式显化、常用词频率增加等特征。这些发现对于翻译教学的启发意义是,译文语言同样需要挖掘汉语本身的表达手段和表现潜力,同时也要尊重汉语本身的意合倾向,这是提高汉语译文可读性的要点。

当然,汉语翻译语言的个性研究对翻译教学有非常重要的借鉴价值。如句段长度和结构容量的研究。Wang & Qin(2010,2014)基于 GCEPC 模拟汉语原创文本,发现英译汉文本语言的标准化类符/型符比较高,句段偏长。主要原因是汉语翻译语言扩大了汉语某些结构式的容量,导致汉语翻译语言不如汉语原创语言易读、易解。进一步分析发现,汉语翻译语言的整体特征虽然与汉语原创语言一致,但前者结构容量扩增,句子偏长,因此不完全支持规范化假说(秦洪武、王克非 2009;王克非 2011)。此外,研究显示,句长分析不适合描写汉语翻译语言,句段长度和结构容量更能反映汉语翻译语言的个性特征。因此,运用积极的语言手段调控结构容量有助于提高汉语翻译语言运用质量(秦洪武 2010)。

以下是将语料库翻译学研究发现运用于翻译教学中的案例。

1. 案例 1:译文中过度使用某些语言项目

使用语料库手段比较 *Robinson Crusoe*(《鲁滨孙漂流记》)徐霞村和郭建中的两个译本时,发现郭译和徐译在关键词的使用上差异很大(引自秦洪武、王克非 2013)。表 2 中两个译本在使用代词(它、它们、自己)上有显著差异,这提示我们以此为线索提取语料去探寻二者之间存在差异的原因以及翻译技巧使用上的差异。

表 2　徐译本、郭译本关键值比较

	功能词	徐译本	郭译本	关键值	显著性
1	已经	79	15	47.10	0.000
2	已	7	58	-46.37	0.000
3	时候	63	16	29.38	0.000
4	时	19	57	-20.38	0.000
5	它	140	34	68.27	0.000
6	它们	67	26	18.25	0.000
7	自己	60	107	-14.03	0.000
8	的	1345	1112	20.45	0.004

我们知道,"它"的对应词在英语里是 it,复数是 them,这提示我们提取英语 it 的汉语对译,然后观察 it 在不同译文中的处理方式。观察结果显示,这些差异其实意味着两个译本在翻译技巧和处理方式上存在巨大差异。在下面的译文中,徐译使用代词"它",而郭译则使用多种方式来建立互指关系。

a)使用"指示代词—量词—名词"形式,如:

(1)I could make it spread,but if it did not let down too,and draw in,it was not portable for me any way but just over my head,which would not do.(Defoe)

a.头顶上以外,没有别的法子携带<u>它</u>,那当然不合适。(徐译)

b.做一把撑开的伞不难,但如果不能收起来,就只能永远撑在头顶上,<u>这种伞</u>根本无法携带,当然不适用。(郭译)

b)使用指示代词,如:

(2)'A storm,you fool you,' replies he;'do you call that a storm? why,it was nothing at all; give us but a ...(Defoe)

a.“大风？傻瓜，你叫它大风吗？那算什么！只要……（徐译）

b.“风暴？你这傻瓜，”他回答说，“你把那也叫风暴？那算得了什么！只要……（郭译）

c)使用原词重复，如：

(3)...had it at home, I bound and splintered up its leg, which was broke.(Defoe)

a.牵了回来。到家之后，我把它的断腿绑起来。（徐译）

b.牵回家。到家后我把山羊的断腿绑了起来。（郭译）

d)使用零代词，如：

(4)...for when I had fish on my hook I would not pull them up, that he might not see them ...(Defoe)

a.鱼上钩时，我总不把它钓起来，让那摩耳人看到。（徐译）

b.因为即使鱼儿上钩，我也不钓上来，免得让那摩尔人看见。（郭译）

学生观察的结果是，汉语使用“它”的使用频率远远低于英语的 it，而多用指示代词、原词重复、零代词等衔接手段。过多使用“它”不如使用其他衔接手段更符合汉语的特点，为使行文自然流畅，衔接自如，使用非代词的其他手段来接应上文应是很好的选择。有了这些认识，学生在使用汉语译文时就可能注意到汉语代词使用的规范，提升译文质量。

2. 案例 2：汉语结构的封闭性和容量

近年来的汉语翻译语言研究显示，汉语是结构封闭型语言，结构式容量自然成了影响句段长度的关键因素（秦洪武、王克非 2009；王克非、秦洪武 2009；秦洪武 2010）。在汉语里，对容量比较敏感的结构式主要有以下几种：“介词 + 方位词”结构、“指示代词/数量短语 + 名词”结构、“谓语 + 宾语”结构、“形容词 + 名词”结构。译文里还有大量的语法“模仿”，这种做法流传日久，使汉语句子变长；使用不当会造成行文呆滞，繁复拘谨，不够平易。为了表达修饰与被修饰成分间的紧密关系，汉语译文常使用“……的”结构将修饰成分前置。这种处理方式会过度扩增结构容量，从而增加工作记忆负担和处理时间，句子的可接受性随之降低。鉴于此，我们把结构的容量列为汉语翻译行

文应关注的问题。可以通过比较译文,让学生观察容量控制的必要性和可行的方式。如下面的“数量短语 + 名词”封闭结构:

(5) We have no reason to doubt, Mr.Copperfield, that you are a young gentleman possessed of good qualities and honourable character.

a.我们没有理由来怀疑,科波菲尔先生啊,你是一位具有良好的品性和高尚的人格的年轻绅士。(对译_许译)

b.科波菲尔先生,我们没有理由怀疑,你这位年轻的先生品德优良,人格高尚……。(换译_庄译)

(6) I do not think I have ever experienced so strange a feeling in my life...

a.一种我生平似乎从未有过的奇异感觉……。(对译_许译)

b.有一种奇怪的感觉,这恐怕是以前从来没有过的……。(换译_庄译)

对译文本在使用处理技巧上往往有偏好,倾向于将修饰成分前置。再如:

(7) She gave me one piece of intelligence which affected me very much ...

a.她报告了我一项使我非常难过的消息……。(对译_许译)

b.她告诉我一个消息,使我感触很深……。(换译_庄译)

我们发现,学生能很快捕捉到译文在结构容量控制上的差异,且大都倾向于结构容量小的庄译文。看来,要相信学生会通过观察语料形成自己对翻译技巧运用的看法,而且,这样的看法一旦形成,会长久影响他的翻译行为。

六、小结

以上分析说明,在翻译教学中使用双语平行语料库有以下优点:1)有助于学生发现语言使用的复杂性和句子的型式;2)学生审读真实篇章中的例证,比依赖语法书和教科书中那些孤零零的范例更可取;3)对应语料库可以用作专家系统,把学习者的注意力转向成熟译者或专家译者所发现的典型问题的典型(或非典型)处理方法。传统上,教师在教学过程中起主导作用。学生面对的是教材中的零散范例,翻译质量评估几乎完全依赖教师的判断,学生自主构建策略的能力因之难以充分发挥。本研究表明,传统的翻译教学理念需要更新。一是需要从技巧传授转向技巧发现;二是要丰富评估方式。语料库平台可以把原文、范例译文和学生译文同时呈现,学生通过观察异常数值来判断译文中可能出现的问题。在大数据时代,随着数据使用在量、速度和多样性上的不断提高,平行语料库相关数据必将为翻译和翻译教学提供更广阔的拓展空间和更强大的支持。

(本文原载《外语教学与研究》2015年第5期。作者为王克非、秦洪武)

参考文献

N.Awal, I.Ho-Abdullah & I.Zainudin, "Parallel Corpus as a Tool in Teaching Translation: Translating English Phrasal Verbs into Malay", *Procedia: Social and Behavioral Sciences*, 2014, Vol.112, pp.882-887.

M.Baker, "Corpus Linguistics and Translation Studies: Implications and Applications", M.Baker, G.Francis & E.Tognini-Bonelli (eds.), *Text and Technology: In Honour of John Sinclair*, Amsterdam: John Benjamins, 1993, pp.233-250.

M.Barlow, "Parallel Texts and Corpus-based Contrastive Analysis", M.González, L.Mackenzie & E.Alvarez (eds.), *Current Trends in Contrastive Linguistics: Functional and Cognitive Perspectives*, Amsterdam: John Benjamins, 2008, pp.101-121.

S.Bernardini, "Corpus-aided Language Pedagogy for Translator Education", K.Malmjær (ed.), *Translation in Undergraduate Degree Programmes*, Amsterdam: John Benjamins, 2004, pp.97-112.

S.Bernardini, D.Stewart & F.Zanettin, "Corpora in Translator Education: An Introduction", F.Zanettin, S.Bernardini & D.Stewart (eds.), *Corpora in Translator Education*, Manchester: St.Jerome Publishing, 2003, pp.1-14.

L.Bowker, "A Corpus-based Approach to Evaluating Student Translations", *The Translator*, 2000, Vol.6, No.2, pp.183-210.

A.Chesterman, "Beyond the Particular", A.Mauranen & P.Kujamäki (eds.), *Translation Universals — Do They Exist?* Amsterdam: John Benjamins, 2004, pp.33-49.

S.Hunston, *Corpora in Applied Linguistics*, Cambridge: CUP, 2002.

T.Johns, "Data-driven Learning: The Perpetual Challenge", *Language and Computers*,

2002, Vol.1, pp.107–117.

J.Pearson, "Electronic Texts and Concordances in the Translation Classroom", *TEANGA: The Irish Yearbook of Applied Linguistics*, 1996, Vol.16, pp.85–95.

J.Pearson, "Using Parallel Texts in the Translator Training Environment", F.Zanettin, S. Bernardini & D.Stewart (eds.), *Corpora in Translator Education*, Manchester: St Jerome Publishing, 2003, pp.15–24.

K.Wang, & H.Qin, "A Parallel Corpus-based Study of Translational Chinese", R.Xiao (ed.), *Using Corpora in Contrastive and Translation Studies*, Newcastle: Cambridge Scholars Publishing, 2010, pp.164–181.

K. Wang, & H. Qin, "What is Peculiar to Translational Mandarin Chinese? A Corpus-based Study of Chinese Constructions' Load Capacity", *Corpus Linguistics and Linguistic Theory*, 2014, Vol.10, No.1, pp.57–77.

G. Yepes, "Parallel Corpora in Translator Education", *Redit: Revista Electrónica de Didáctica de la Traducción y la Interpretación*, 2011, Vol.7, pp.65–80.

胡显耀、曾佳:《用语料库考察汉语翻译小说定语的容量和结构》,《解放军外国语学院学报》2009 年第 3 期。

黄立波、王克非:《翻译普遍性研究反思》,《中国翻译》2006 年第 5 期。

李德凤、胡枚:《学习者为中心的翻译课程设置》,《外国语》2006 年第 2 期。

刘泽权、陈冬蕾:《英语小说汉译显化实证研究——以〈查泰莱夫人的情人〉三个中译本为例》,《外语与外语教学》2010 年第 4 期。

秦洪武:《英译汉翻译语言的结构容量:基于多译本语料库的研究》,《外国语》2010 年第 4 期。

秦洪武、王克非:《对应语料库在翻译教学中的应用:理论依据和实施原则》,《中国翻译》2007 年第 5 期。

秦洪武、王克非:《基于对应语料库的英译汉语言特征分析》,《外语教学与研究》2009 年第 2 期。

秦洪武、王克非:《重译评估的语料库方法:*Robinson Crusoe* 的两个中译本》,《燕山大学学报》(哲学社会科学版)2013 年第 4 期。

史汝波、郭乂、秦洪武:《平行语料在翻译教学中的应用:一项教学实验》,《外语电化教学》2009 年第 6 期。

王克非、胡显耀:《基于语料库的翻译汉语词汇特征研究》,《中国翻译》2008 年第

6 期。

王克非、秦洪武、王海霞:《双语对应语料库翻译教学平台的应用初探》,《外语电化教学》2007 年第 6 期。

王克非、秦洪武:《英译汉语言特征探讨——基于对应语料库的宏观分析》,《外语学刊》2009 年第 1 期。

王克非:《双语对应语料库在翻译教学上的用途》,《外语电化教学》2004 年第 6 期。

王克非:《语料库翻译学探索》,上海交通大学出版社 2011 年版。

王宇:《关于本科翻译教学的再思考——探索“以学习者为中心”的翻译教学模式的一次尝试》,《外语界》2003 年第 1 期。

双语对应语料库的翻译辅助功能探讨

本文比较机器翻译软件和翻译记忆软件对翻译的辅助作用，并探讨语料库尤其是汉英双语对应语料库在英汉翻译中的用法、用途和独特之处。研究认为，双语对应语料库能够实施英—汉和汉—英双向检索，提供针对性较强的参考译文，还能提供更大语境或者复合检索，帮助译者获得丰富的参考资源，高效高质地完成翻译任务。作者认为汉英双语对应语料库能够开发成为功能强大的机助翻译工具。

半个多世纪以前，人们对机器翻译（MT）寄予厚望，希望它能够借重信息技术提供的各种潜力成就高质量的翻译。但机器翻译至今还未开发出真正可靠的翻译工具。自20世纪90年代以来，机辅翻译（CAT）工具蓬勃发展，有许多翻译记忆（TM）软件相继得到开发和应用。此外，一些在线双语对译检索系统也出现在互联网上，展现出良好的应用前景。

与此同时，语料库的发展和应用给机助翻译注入了新的活力。近20年来，随着各种语料库的创建和应用，双语语料库正以其独特的方式进入人们的视野，其辅助功能日益凸显。本文以北京外国语大学汉英双语对应语料库（CEPC）为例，对比语料库与其他翻译辅助工具在翻译实务上的用途，重点探讨了CEPC的翻译辅助功能。

一、机辅翻译工具：类型和特点

信息技术发展到今天，联网计算机犹如一个工作间，可以从那里存贮和调用翻译所需的各种资源,其数量、类型、内容及获取速度远胜过其他传统资源。除了电子词典和搜索引擎外,目前常用的英汉机辅翻译工具软件还有四类:机器翻译软件、翻译记忆软件、双语对译句搜索引擎、双语对应语料库。这些软件对翻译都有辅助作用,但辅助方式不同,作用各异,这是本文要探讨的问题。

二、机器翻译软件

机器翻译软件很多,常见的在线工具有 Babylon Pro、华建翻译、Google 翻译工具、Free Online Language Translator、Babel Fish、Yahoo、有道,等等。这些软件都能产出完整的译文,但目前看来译文质量差强人意。表现在以下几个方面。

1)一次只提供一种译文。如果不同软件给出的译文不一致,译者难以做出选择。比如“垃圾邮件”既对应 spam(Google),又对应 junk mail(华建/Yahoo/Worldlingo)。“体制改革”里的“体制”对应 institutional(Babylon、Google)、system(华建/有道)和 organizational(Worldlingo、Yahoo)。究竟该选用哪个?软件本身无法提供更多的信息。这时机器翻译对译者助益不大。

2)词库更新不够及时。一些较新的词语组合找不到合适的译文,如,“山寨(手)机”有多个对应词:Mountain fastness machine(华建)、Village in a mountainous area machine(Yahoo)以及“山寨 machine”(Google)。而“群体事件”的翻译更是鱼龙混杂,有 groups events,colony incident,mass incidents,community event。没有其他信息做参照,面对这么多的对应词,译者无所适从。

3)不易处理结构较复杂的汉语表达形式。比如,有的软件在翻译“踩踏事件”时只是根据原文将词机械拼凑起来,加上冠词,如 trample the incident,steps on the event。译文合乎语法,但没有意义。其实“踩踏事件”这个词组是定中结构,不是动宾结构,由于踩踏容易看作动词,故出现一些误解和错译。再如,在处理“你真记性坏”这个句子时,出现下面两种译文:

a.You really bad memory.(Babylon/Google)

b.Your real memory is bad.(华建/Worldlingo/Yahoo)

“你真记性坏”这个句子的特点是:小句主语(记性)隶属于大句主语代表的事物(你)。句 b 显示,软件翻译能通过语义运算识别出“记性”和“你”之间的关系,但不能处理好副词“真”。而能处理副词“真”的 a 句却不能处理好“记性”和“你”的隶属关系。可见,机器翻译对于汉语句法关系的判断能力还比较弱,语义运算能力有限。

4)语序调整能力差,对于汉语话题句的处理能力很低。比如,“无线电我是门外汉”是汉语常见的话题句,大句主语(无线电)前边隐含“对于、关于”的意思。英语没有这种句式,翻译时要做出添加或调整。但现有的机器翻译软件均无法对此做出恰当的调整,于是产生下面的译文。

a.Radio I am a layman.(Babylon/Wbrldlingo/Yahoo)

b.Radio I layman.(华建)

c.I am a layman radio.(Google)

简言之,现有的翻译软件主要靠词对应实施翻译,内容更新不及时,语义运算能力差,句法识别和转换能力有限。机器翻译主要关注源语,而人工翻译的目标是理解目的语,所以前者译文自然难以准确。正如冯志伟(1996:424)所言,机器翻译软件对于一些复杂的句子的分析依然很困难,多义词和歧异问题尚未找到切实有效的解决办法。

三、翻译记忆软件

面对机器翻译难以逾越的语义瓶颈,美国政府曾责成 ALPAC 于 1966 年对这类系统进行评估,结果显示,机器翻译速度慢、效率低,比人工翻译贵一倍,所以,这类软件的开发得不偿失(Craciunescu 2004)。在沉寂了多年之后,从 20 世纪 90 年代开始,机器翻译领域发生了重大转向:从基于语法规则的翻译转变为基于翻译实例的翻译,翻译记忆的设计理念应时而生。人们对基于翻译实例的翻译记忆工具兴趣渐浓,可以想见,若能将由语料库转化而成的语言知识库同基于规则的机器翻译结合起来,机辅翻译前景光明(Bernardini *et al*.2003:3)。

目前不少翻译记忆软件已具备商业用途，如 Déjà Vu，Trados，还有我国的雅信 CAT。这类软件具有自动记忆和匹配功能，可根据译者需要自行建库，还可以有效地进行术语管理，确保科技翻译中术语一致。另外，此类软件能实施多语种双向互译。现以 Trados 为例考察它的检索功能。

Trados 翻译记忆软件的检索功能和在线对译句检索程序工作机制相似，它能建立句库，帮助使用者有效地应对专业翻译。例如，从 Trados 句对齐库中可以检索到"垃圾邮件"的两个对应项，对应部分底色为黄色。

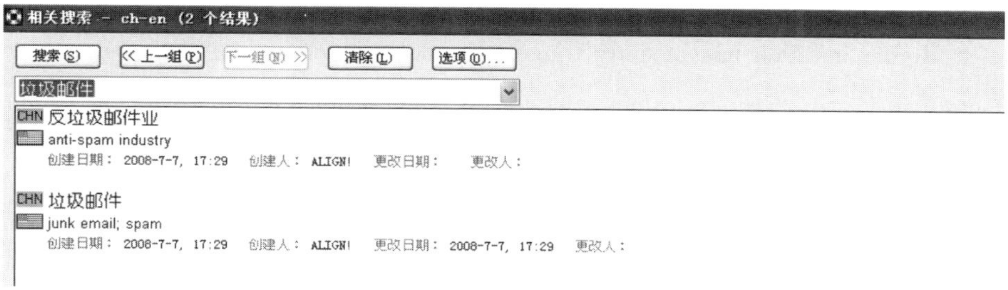

要像普通对译句检索那样提供丰富的对译，翻译记忆软件就需建立相当规模的句库。但对于个体译者而言，限于时间、精力和经济条件，大规模建库不太现实。但不管怎么说，翻译记忆软件有助于提高翻译质量和效率，适合专业文献翻译。（用 spam 和 junk mail 为例，也存在 3.1 提到的那个难以选择的问题。）

四、在线英汉双语对译句子检索平台

在线英汉双语对译句子检索工具出现时间不长，近来比较活跃的有句酷、金山爱词霸和融合句酷及网络释义的灵格斯对译句搜索引擎。支持这些在线工具的句库已具备相当规模，且检索方便。此类工具的辅助能力表现在以下几个方面。

1）一次检索多个例证。比如，"群体事件"在灵格斯中有很多在句子中出现的对应项，有 mass incident/event/disturbance；group affair/event/accident；

colony event，甚至还有 mass emergency。这显然要比机器翻译能提供更多的参考。只是对应项太多，不容易做出选择。

2）多源检索和呈现。现有的许多在线句对译搜索工具附有词典或百科搜索，多有较高的参考价值。比如，爱词霸附带的“百科”搜索显示，“山寨机”的英文翻译是 emulational mobile phone。这样翻译是否合适还可商榷，但它意思上还说得通。

3）时能检索到较好译文。如“踩踏事件”在灵格斯（句酷）和爱词霸百科中均发现对应项“stampede”。甚至还有对译句，如：

Higher inflation has recently triggered popular reaction in Asia ranging from factory strikes in Vietnam tostampedes for discounted items at some Chinese supermarkets.

近来，通胀加剧已在亚洲引发普遍反应，例如，从越南的工厂罢工，到中国一些超市促销引发的踩踏事件等。

4）译文例句参照价值高。如“我真记性坏。”也能巧遇相近的句子：

My memory is really dreadful—manager's daughter?（句酷、灵格斯）

我记性真坏——经理的小姐？

有些译例提供的翻译方式还很丰富，可以帮助我们产出高质量的译文。这是机器翻译软件难以企及的。如“无线电我是门外汉。”可以检索到不少值得参照的对译词和句。

When it comes to mathematics，I' m completely at sea.（句酷、爱词霸）

说到数学，我完全是门外汉。

Where the law is concerned，I am only a layman.（句酷、灵格斯）

谈到法律，我不过是门外汉。

All that form of life was outside him.（灵格斯）

对于那种生活方式，他全然是个门外汉。

有些译文大同小异，甚至可以直接使用现成的翻译。如检索“你这种事做不得。”可以直接得到下面的译文：

You must never do this.（句酷）

这件事你做不得。

You must not do it.（句酷）

你不得做这件事。

尽管如此，对译句检索平台的辅助功能还是十分有限。首先，语境信息不够充分，只考察句子对译不足以应对各种复杂的情形。其次，现有对译句检索平台没有系统地区分源语和目的语，对译成分的选择比较盲目，难以保证译文地道。再次，对译句只是陈列多个译句，难以考察影响语言运用的其他因素（如语域、文体、搭配能力等）。

五、双语对应语料库

现有的在线翻译辅助资源只是句对齐文本，没有更大的语境参照，也没有进行语法或其他功能标注。而且，现有的句对齐检索仅能显示非常笼统的元信息（metainformation，如该句来自"词典"或来自"网友提供"），参考信息不充分。在检索功能上，翻译记忆工具虽能提供词精确和模糊检索，但不能进行词性检索，更不能检索到翻译方向、文体等重要信息。

要避免上述问题，双语对应语料库是一个很好的选择。北京外国语大学双语对应语料库（CEPC）创建于2003年，该语料库语料规模还在不断扩充之中。其主要特点是：1）语料规模大，目前的可检索语料达2000多万字词，检索内容丰富。2）汉英双向，既有汉英翻译语料，也有英汉翻译语料。3）语料制作过程复杂，涉及句对齐，xml编码，有用的元信息和英汉语词性标注。4）分类细致，有题材、语域、翻译时间等详细标注。5）检索方式多样，既有分类的在线检索，又有复杂的研究用检索。

对应语料库已广泛应用于翻译研究，但有关它在翻译实践上的应用研究还很少，有关使用者如何有效使用该类语料库的研究更少（见Santos & Frankenberg-Garcia 2007）。因此，有必要介绍汉英双语对应语料库在翻译中可能的用途和应用方式。

1. 参考译文针对性强

CEPC可以根据词汇使用的语域和语境检索对应词。比如，在"只要不动摇、不懈怠、不折腾”中“折腾”并不指具体的动作,而是一类社会现象。从其他资源中得到的多是具体的动作,如“turn from side to side,toss,do something again and again”。但在 CEPC 中,可以检索到更有针对性的例证。如:

如果搞资产阶级自由化,就是再来一次折腾(汉—英:非文学)

Bourgeois liberalization would plunge the country into turmoil once more.

因为中国不能再折腾,不能再动荡(汉—英:非文学)

Because China could not afford any more disorder or unrest.

因为萨利已经开始瞎折腾了(英—汉:文学)

For Sally was crumbling.

在自己的宅子里头瞎折腾(英—汉:文学)

defiling his own palace with it;

不难看出,作为一种社会行为的“折腾”,在英语里的对译可以是 plunge... into turmoil 或者 disorder 等。

2. 双向检索例证

双向检索指可以根据不同的源语和目的语关系检索例证,好处是多向验证。比如,“我真记性坏。”的英译可以从汉英和英汉两个方向寻找翻译对应项,这样有望检索到适切的对应词或对应结构。

我记性真坏——经理的小姐?(汉—英)

My memory is really dreadful—manager's daughter?

文纨,你记性真好!(汉—英)

What a good memory you have,Wen-wan!

You've neither sense nor memory,and I leave it to fancy where your mothers was that let you come to sea.(英—汉)

你们既没有头脑也没有记性,我真不明白你们的母亲怎么会让你们出海。

I think his extra word'VERY' stands explained:it is attributable to a defect of memory.(英—汉)

这多出来的一个字就已经说明问题:这是因为[记性]差了那么一点儿。

通过英汉翻译,我们可以确定 memory 对应“记性”;通过汉英翻译,我们可以确认“你真记性坏”可能使用 you really have [...],或者 how adj.[...],或者 what a …结构形式，据此可形成下面的译文：You really have a bad memory./ How bad your memory is! / What a bad memory you have!

3. 提供更地道的译文

根据秦洪武、王克非（2004，2009），英汉翻译时，译者会过度使用汉语里的某一表达式或者结构来翻译英语里的某类表达式。如过度使用汉语数量短语“这种、这一、这个”来翻译英语指示代词 this/such。实际上，“这种”在汉语里用得不多，且与之共现的词项有时有贬义。英译汉时过度使用这个短语是受英语影响造成的。要选择多样的表达，译者可以在汉英翻译库中检索 this/such 的汉语对译文，这可能找到更符合汉语表达习惯的处理方式。

我们要抓住时机，现在是改革的最好时机。

We must seize [this] highly opportune moment for reform.

又是范博文的刻薄的声调。

[This] was another cut from Fan Po-wen.

这么，我们公司眼前既有事业好做，将来‘东方大港’之类完成了的时候，我们的事业就更多了。

In [this] way, we'll have something solid to get on with, and then one day, when the Great Eastern Harbour and so on have been completed, we'll be able to expand even more.

这样做不会也不可能破坏社会主义经济。

[This] cannot and will not undermine the socialist economy.

由此反推，英语里好多使用指示（如 this, that, such）的地方在译成汉语时不需要任何指示语；而且，“这么”“这样做”“此”都可能对应 this。总之，译者通过观察这类语料反思自己的翻译行为（王克非等 2007；秦洪武、王克非 2007），避免在翻译时过度使用“这种”。

4. 提供更多的语境信息

使用较大的语境有助于我们弄清一个词在具体语境下的用法，以及这些用法的语用含义。如，根据语境，第一个例证里的“外行”有自谦的口吻，而第二个例证里有调侃他人的意味。这些信息在翻译时有很好的参照作用。

我想你对新话颇有学术上的兴趣吧？	You take a scholarly interest in Newspeak, I believe?'
温斯顿已恢复了他的一部分自信	Winston had recovered part of his self-possession. '
他说，“谈不上什么学术上的兴趣	Hardly scholarly,' he said.
我是个外行，这不是我的专业	'I'm only an amateur.It's not my subject.
我从来没有参加过这一语言的实际创作工作。	I have never had anything to do with the actual construction of the language.'
“但是你的文章写得很漂亮，”奥勃良说	'But you write it very elegantly,' said O'Brien. '

CEPC 还可以使用通配符检索、词性检索，并提供检索词的搭配信息，其他检索工具都不能实施此类检索。这些检索能够从多个角度确定一个词的用法。

5. 复合检索功能

复合检索功能即运用语料提供的元信息，使用多个检索限制条件提取译者需要的信息。CEPC 目前推出的在线检索程序（“中英双语在线”）能够实施此类检索。检索方式如下：

该图显示，在线检索系统可以执行严格匹配和模糊匹配，模糊匹配有助于许多结构式的检索。更重要的是，该检索系统较完整地实施了复合检索：如源语设定（英语或者汉语）、类型选择（有文学和非文学）、领域区分（文学、人文、社科、自然）、文体分类，等等。比如，若设定了检索条件，可得到“与其……不如”的索引项：

1. 波克一面大声擤鼻子，一面流露出有些感兴趣的目光，不过，与其说他感兴趣，不如说他是出自礼貌。
A little interest flickered in Pork 's eyes as he blew his nose loudly but it was more politeness than interest.

检索结果显示，在 20 世纪上半期的英汉翻译里，对应英语 rather…than/more adj.…than/not as adj.as 的很少使用“与其……不如”（1 次）；而在二十世纪后半期的英汉翻译中，则出现了 5 次。而汉语原创语言中这类结构没有出现。看来，现代汉语有更灵活的方式来表达“与其不如”的意思。检索源语言为汉语的子库，我们可以方便地检索到对应的目标语英语 rather... than/ more...than/not as adj.as 的汉语表达式。如：

"赠人以车，不如赠人以言。"

"A gift of a cart is not as good as a gift of words."

"跟车铺打印子，还不如给我一分利呢！"

"Better to pay me ten per cent than pay the shop installment."

"我以为这一点的可能性很大，他马上就会看到独角戏不如搭班子好。"

"Not at all: I'm sure there's every possibility that he'll soon realize that it's better to play a part in a big show than try to run a one-man show."

与其热枕头上翻来覆去，还是甲板上坐坐吧。

Rather than toss and turn on his warm pillow, Hung-chien would just as soon sit for a while longer on the deck.

他叹着气说："唉，与其因为他有才能而被夺，我宁愿他是一个一无所长的没出息的人呵。"

He said with a sigh, "I would rather he be a mediocrity than a talented person and lose his life."

故此主张"与其忠实而使人'看不懂'，毋宁不很忠实而'看得懂'。"

Thus, they argue: "'Unintelligibility' resulting from faithfulness is worse than faithlessness that makes translation 'intelligible'."

很明显，"与其……不如"这么完整又有点机械的结构只有在英汉翻译里使用，汉语里还有更多的组合方式可供选择，这也是英汉翻译时译者应参考这些表达方式，以避免译文流于单调、机械。

以上检索功能的最大优点是，在语料库足够大且分类明晰的情况下，译者可以从中得到分类明确、针对性较强的参考译文，这些十分有用的功能其他翻译辅助工具都不具备。随着语库规模的扩大和检索功能的完善，CEPC 的翻译辅助功能会更加突出。

六、单语语料库

翻译时常常遇到难以把握的词汇运用(词汇选择、词汇搭配、句法关系),这时可以参考目标语原创语料库,因为原创单语语料库可以提供更丰富的语言使用信息。

前文说过,爱词霸“百科”搜索可以查到“山寨机”的英文对应表达 emulational mobile phone,而灵格斯的“网络释义”提供了“山寨”的对应词 copycatting。这两个词是否都合适呢?我们在 COCA 中没有发现 emulational。emulation 的意思是仿真,它本身就是一种计算机技术,不是侵权仿制。但在 COCA 上检索到 copycat 的使用。如:

Illegal sales over the phone and the Internet have been reported,andcopycat products have already appeared.

Audiences might now expect to seecopycat movies."Once one movie hits,everybody usually tries to make a lot of them,"says Adam Schroeder.

这两个例子里的 copycat products 和 copycat movies 可以分别译成“山寨产品”和“山寨版电影”。如此看来,“山寨机”译为“copycat mobile phone”应不会有问题。

再如,“垃圾邮件”有 junk mail 和 spam 两个对应项。COCA 的检索结果显示,spam 使用的频率远远高于 junk mail。而且,Yahoo 英文网站的邮件系统里就是用 Spam 指垃圾邮件。这样,“垃圾邮件”的典型对应词应该是 spam。

面对“群体事件”令人眼花缭乱的对应项(mass incident/event/disturbance;group affair/event/accident;colony event,mass emergency)。我们进入 COCA 语料库尝试检索,发现,group event 常用,但意思是集体项目;只有“mass incident”被认可,尽管它还不是正式的用语;其他均无参考价值。百度和 Google 搜索常见的是 group event 和 colony event,这主要与 CNKI 知识搜索有关,是汉语学术文献的译法,同样不可取。以下是 COCA 中检索到的用法:

1. Popular discontent is bubbling in China. Last year, there were 58,000 "mass indents" across China, according to government statistics cited in the Chinese magazine Outlook.

2. Chinese government's own figures, last year there were more than 80,000 "mass incidents" throughout the country. It is commonly believed that a great number of these.

3. Erupt on a regular basis. The Ministry of Public Security reported 17,900 "mass incidents" in the first nine months of 2006. They are almost always snuffed out.

1. 47与其负债起床，不如空腹睡觉。
   47 Better go to bed supperless than rise in debt.
2. 但是匈奴人比早期希腊人更加执着于游牧生活，早期希腊人与其说是真正的游牧部落，还不如说是流动的养牛农夫。
   But the Huns were much more wedded to the nomadic life than the early Greeks, who were rather migratory cattle farmers than true nomads.
3. 人们认为，伊斯兰教帝国的真正创立者与其说是穆罕默德，不如说是他的朋友兼助手阿布_贝克。

在实际翻译时,汉英双向对应语料库中的原创文本库本身就可以用作单语库,常用词的组合和搭配可以在这类库中检索。如果对应库解决不了,就需要通过检索更大的单语库来确定用法。由此看来,单语和双语语料库在翻译实务中的用途是其他各类翻译辅助软件无法替代的。

七、小结

机器翻译在翻译辅助方面的功用有限;基于翻译实例的翻译记忆对翻译的辅助作用高于机器翻译,但由于检索功能过于单调,辅助作用也有限。相比而言,双向双语对应语料库对翻译辅助作用较为突出,它可能提供其他工具无法提供的丰富的翻译对应信息。因此,在双语对应语料库这个操作平台上,译者可以充分利用其各种潜能,高效高质地完成翻译任务。我们相信,随着制作和检索技术日趋完善,汉英双语对应语料库将成为功能强大的机助翻译工具。

(本文原载《中国英语教育》2011 年第 4 期,作者为王克非、熊文新)

参考文献

S.Bernardini,*et al.*"An Introduction",F.Zanettin *et al.*(eds.),*Corpora in Translator Education*,Manchester:St.Jerome Publishing,2003.

O.Craciunescu,*et al*,"Machine Translation and Computer-Assisted Translation:A New Way of Translating?"*Translation Journal*,2004,Vol.8,No.3.

D. Santos, & A. Frankenberg - Garcia, "The Corpus, its Users and Their Needs, a User-oriented Evaluation of COMPARA",*International Journal of Corpus Linguistics*,2007,Vol.12,No.3,pp.335-374.

冯志伟:《自然语言的计算机处理》,上海外语教育出版社 1996 年版。

秦洪武、王克非:《基于语料库的翻译语言分析——以"so...that"的汉语对应结构为例》,《现代外语》2004 年第 1 期。

秦洪武、王克非:《对应语料库在翻译教学中的应用:理论依据和实施原则》,《中国翻译》2007 年第 5 期。

王克非、秦洪武、王海霞:《双语对应语料库翻译教学平台的应用初探》,《外语电化教学》2007 年第 6 期。

王克非、秦洪武:《英译汉语言特征探讨——基于对应语料库的宏观分析》,《外语学刊》2009 年第 1 期。

附:在线机器翻译软件:

Babylon Pro:http://translation.babyIon.com/

华建翻译:http://www.hjtrans,com/

Google 语言工具:http://translate.google.cn/translate_t? hl=zh-CN#

Free Online Language Translator: http://www. worldlingo. com/en/products _ services/worldlingo_translator.html

Babel Fish:http://babelfish.yahoo.com/

Yahoo 翻译:http://fanyi.yahoo.com.cn/translate_txt

有道翻译：http://fanyi.youdao.cnm/

在线双语句对齐检索平台：

北外中英双语在线（CEO）：http://202.204.128.82/ceo/indexl.html

句酷：http://www.jukuu.com/

金山爱词霸：http://www.iciba.com/

下编　语言与翻译研究

察言观世:从语言生活看社会万象①

语言是人类社会最基本的生存要素之一,也是人类社会发展的最重要因素,这一点在全球化、信息化、媒体化时代尤为突出,它关涉各国各民族政治、经济、文化以及人们生活和交往的各个方面。关注和考察语言生活状况,有助于我们掌握各国语言发展及其与政治、经济、文化等的关系和动态,有助于及时调整语言战略、改进语言布局和提高语言教育质量,也有助于了解我国语言在世界发展格局中的地位和变化。可以说,观察语言变化也是观察世界动态的一个重要的、敏感的和及时的窗口。

一、引言

在迈向世界并面临全方位激烈竞争的新世纪,发展文化软实力是国家的一个战略决策,对于与此相关的语言问题和语言生活的重要性,我们也必须从国家意识和国际视野来认识。

语言是人类社会最基本的生存要素之一,也是人类社会发展的重要因素之一,这一点在全球化、信息化和媒体化的时代尤为突出。它关涉各国各民族政治、经济、文化以及人们生活和交往的各个方面。社科院 7 年前组建队伍编

① 本研究得到教育部人文社会科学重点研究基地重大项目“国外语言生活状况调研”(11JJD740002)、国家语委“十二五”科研规划 2011 年度重点项目“国外语言生活状况综合考察”(ZDI125-7)、国家社会科学基金项目“国家利益视角下的语言规划研究:中美个案对比”(11BYY030)的资助,并获北京外国语大学中国外语教育研究中心学术资助,特此鸣谢。

辑出版了《中国语言生活状况》，每年出一本，对中国语言包括汉语、少数民族语言和各地方言等的动态变化实施全方位的描写和分析，受到学界、社会和政府部门的高度重视。但是，作为一个走向国际的大国，中国的政治地位、经济利益、文化影响等已逐步延伸到世界各地，而我们对国外语言生活状况还缺乏应有的和足够的关注，是亟待提升的一个重要方面。

了解国外语言生活的各个方面和各种状况，有助于我们准确把握世界语言发展动态，能为国家确定语言战略、制定语言政策、实施语言规划，尤其是确定外语战略、制定外语政策、实施外语规划，并由此提升国际地位和话语权，提供直接、及时、全面的信息和资讯。通过了解国外语言生活，掌握世界语言发展动态，也会有助于拓宽我们语言研究的领域，加深对语言的认识，提高全民的语言意识和素质。因此可以说，观察语言变化也是观察世界动态的一个重要的、敏感的和及时的窗口。

二、语言生活

根据李宇明（2010a：91）的定义，语言生活是指“运用和应用语言文字的各种社会活动和个人活动。”他认为，“说话、作文、命名、看书、听广播、做广告、语言教学等等，都属于语言生活范畴”。由此可见，语言生活几乎同人类社会所有的活动相关，而且贯穿始终。人类活动，无论是群体还是个体活动，都离不开语言。这是由语言的功能和作用所决定的。

语言的功能很多，主要有三项。首先，语言是人类交往的首要工具，这是语言在人类活动中的最显著的作用与功能。李宇明所说的“说话、作文、命名、看书、听广播”等都属于言语交往活动，离开了语言，这些活动都无法想象。在言语交往中，人们通过语言了解和理解对方所表达的意义，同时通过语言表达思想与观点。言语交际学者把前者称作“解码”（decoding），后者“置码”（encoding）。二者的共同基础是语言（Zufferey，2010：5）。

其次，语言是人们认知外界的途径和进行思维的机制，这一点已被认知语言学所证实。研究表明，不同的语言会导致不同的认知结果，失去语言就会失去认知能力及思维能力(Jonides,2000:87-104;Elgin,2001:49-72;Ebersole,2002:88-125;Fuhrman and Boroditsky,2007:1007-1010)。可见,人们认识外界、接受新知、总结归纳、分析推理、判断是非等认知和思维活动离不开语言。

再者,人们通过语言认知外界、解读意义、表达思想的同时,还用语言确认地位、界定身份,区分你我,这些也是人类社会活动的重要内容,语言此项功能称作社会功能(Halliday,2006:309;Arwood et.al,2009:125)。言语交际活动从说话人来说是一个不断选择恰当的语言形式表达意义的过程,从受话人来说是不断准确解读不同语言形式、理解其意义的过程,语言形式的选择还会受制于各种社会因素,不同的语言形式表达不同的社会意义(Ishihara and Torane,2009:117)。所谓"什么人说什么话,什么场合说什么话"就是这个道理。因此,语言活动能够充分体现人们社会活动中细微而又复杂的关系和变化。

语言的交际、认知、思维以及社会功能决定了语言对人类社会的重要性,同时决定了语言与人类社会活动的紧密关系,因此,也决定了语言生活的重要意义。语言生活不仅仅是人们生活的某一部分,而且贯穿于生活的全部;语言生活不仅仅反映语言本身,在很大程度上也反映人类生活的全部。所以语言生活状况以及动态特征,一方面可以提供关于语言本身的状况和动态,一方面也可以提供关于人类社会的状况与动态。

三、对语言生活的关注

对语言生活的关注,国内与国外不尽相同。国内关于语言生活状况的研究和关注相对比较弱,长期以来对语言生活状况的观察、语言信息的汇集和统计,没有得到应有的重视。自新中国成立以来进行了六次人口普查,没有一次把语言生活状况列入调查范围,相对频率较快的全国经济普查(四年一次),迄今也未将语言信息列入调查范围。新中国成立以来,我国全国范围的语言普查仅有两次:一次是 1956 年进行的"汉语和少数民族语言调查",一次是 2000 年展开的"中国语言文字使用情况调查"。这两次较大规模的语言普查为摸清我国语言国底、制定相关语言国策作出了贡献,但是类似语言普查的活动没有系统化和常规化,以致信息数据滞后于实际情况的问题时有发生,影响研究的准确性和决策的科学性。我国对国内语言生活信息的把握尚且如此,对国外语言生活状况的掌握更加薄弱。

构成这一现状的主要原因之一是我国对诸如语言战略、语言规划与政策等语言宏观方面的研究重视不够,对语言的认识停留在“工具”概念上,未能上升至“资源、软实力”等比较宏观的层面。学者潜心研究语言本体,除此之外很少关心;决策者缺乏数据和理念支撑,所以作为调整语言战略,修订语言政策基本依据的语言生活状况得不到重视。所幸21世纪以来,尤其是最近五六年,这一现状正在改变,我国出现了一批语言规划以及语言战略的研究成果,如周玉忠,王辉(2004)、张西平,柳若梅(2008)等人对国外研究的理论与流派的介绍和评析;蔡永良(2003,2007)、吴英成(2010)、戴曼纯,刘润清(2011)、王克非(2012)、沈骑(2012)、赵蓉晖(2012)等人对欧美以及一些非英语国家的语言规划与政策较为深入的研究;戴庆厦(2004)、陈章太(2005)、李宇明(2010a,2010b)、周庆生(2006,2007),姚亚平(2006)、薄守生,赖慧玲(2009)等人对本国的语言规划富有见地的探讨;特别是李宇明、周庆生等领衔主持的《中国语言生活状况》(绿皮书)项目,自2005年起编辑出版,每年一集,不仅为国家相关部门以及专家学者提供了我国比较全面系统及时的语言生活状况信息,填补了国内语言生活状况调查的空白,也为本项研究提供了有益的借鉴。

无论是对语言生活状况的关注还是对语言的宏观研究,国外较我见长。在掌握语言生活状况方面,美国和加拿大做得尤其出色。美、加两国是移民国家,语言资源丰富。为及时掌握这方面信息,政府统计机构人口普查时提供了包含语言信息的“长表”,要求民众回答关于语言生活状况的问题。为使语言信息更加精确及时,2010年两国采取了不同的处理策略。加拿大把原来“长表”中的语言调查项放到“短表”中作为全体调查对象的必填项。美国则把这部分内容放到另一个比全国人口普查更频繁的项目“美国社区调查”中进行。除美、加之外,欧盟各国,亚洲的日本、新加坡、印度、韩国等对此也十分关注。

欧美等发达国家对语言生活状况的关注得益于语言规划与政策的深入研究和语言战略思想的深化。这方面研究历史悠久,现已形成了影响很大的学科,著述十分丰富,体例也比较齐全,比如学科的定义、分类、内涵和外延(Haugen,1972;Cooper,1989)、学科研究的思想原则(Kaplan & Baldauf,2003;Spolsky,2004,2012;Canagarajah,2005),经济价值(Das Gupter and Ferguson,1977;Fieman,1991;Webb,2002;Djité,2011),社会功能(Tollefson,1990;Schiffman,1993;Mühlhäusler,1996;Skutnabb-Kangas,2000;Bang & Døør,2007;Liddicoat,2008;Blommaert,2010)等。这些研究加深了对语言功能与价值的认识,提高了“语言资源”意识,从而促进了对语言生活状况的关注和研究。

四、察言观世的意义

关注国外语言生活,有以下几方面价值和意义。

1. 有助于了解国外语言生活状况,掌握世界语言发展动态

首先,关注国外语言生活可以帮助我们了解国外语言生活的状况并掌握世界语言发展动态。

直接与语言关联的社会活动有许多,这些活动能够清晰地反映语言的状况与动态。比如语言教育,学校确定一门语言作为需要教学的语言,很大程度上确定了这门语言的基本现状和发展前景,特别是少数民族语言和外语。世界上除极个别的国家以外,如冰岛,绝大部分都属于多民族多语言的国家。限于政治经济、历史文化等多方面的原因,少数民族语言的教学大多数都是有所选择的,不可能将所有少数民族的语言列为学校教育的语言,设置课程进行系统教学,有的选择若干门,有的可能只选一门,有的甚至除国家通用语言之外,什么也不选。被选中的语言,便有了发展的余地和空间,未被选中的语言可能就会失去发展的空间和余地。外语也是如此,外语教育同样会选择一些外语而舍弃另外一些外语,一门外语能否进入外语教育行列一方面说明它的用途大小,另一方面反过来影响甚至决定它的作用的发挥。从整个国际社会角度看,一门外语是否被其他国家外语教育所接受,关系到这门语言的国际影响和国际发展的前景。由于语言与语言之间存在着相互依赖和影响的关系,无论是民族语言教育还是外语教育存在着选择单语、双语、多语进行教育的问题,

而每一种选择都会对一个地区、一个国家，乃至整个世界的语言格局构成影响。语言生态学的研究说明，语言个体的存亡强弱会影响到整个生态的持续健康发展。David Crystal 指出，当今世界有三大因素影响了世界语言生态，其中最主要的两个是：一、英语在世界范围内的广泛传播；二、因特网的普及（Crystal，2004：2-4）。事实上，英语在世界范围内的广泛传播主要得益于世界各国普遍实施的英语教育（Phan and Le，2013：221）。

语言同人的活动联系在一起，主要体现于语言的使用。语言使用构成语言生活，语言使用影响和决定语言的生存与发展。语言教育是语言使用的一种途径，语言使用更多的途径存在于人们的日常生活。因此，一个家庭、一个社区、一个地区，乃至一个国家使用什么语言对语言个体和群体都会产生重大影响。David Crystal 因特网的例子就是一个典型。因特网所用的语言主要是英语，无疑这对英语的广泛而又深入地传播起到了很大的推动作用（Shay，2008：166；Greiffenstern，2010：76）。因特网媒体的语言使用空间由英语所占据的现实引起了其他国家的关注和担忧，为此，许多国家纷纷开发本国语言的网站，以此来争取本国语言在因特网媒体的语言使用空间，维护和保障在国际交流中的地位和权益，拓展其功能和作用。类似因特网语言使用空间的矛盾与冲突充斥着当今国际社会的语言生活，这些矛盾与冲突及时而又准确地反映了世界语言的发展与走向。

此外，语言生活是人类活动的主要方面，语言与社会关系紧密，是社会生存与发展的一个十分重要的因素和宝贵的资源。了解语言生活状况，观察语言与社会活动各个层面和因素的互动情况，不仅能够更加深入地了解语言本身的功能和作用以及发展规律，也不仅能够充分掌握世界语言发展的动态，而且通过语言生活和发展动态，洞悉国际社会政治、经济、文化的变化与发展。目前我们处在一个快速变化发展的年代，我国又处在和平崛起、走向国际的关键时期，及时了解国外语言生活状况，准确掌握世界发展动态，有利于我们审时度势，把握时机，操纵胜局。

2. 有助于及时调整语言战略，合理修订语言政策

随着世界全球化、信息化、媒体化的迅速发展，语言的重要性越来越凸显，传统的以解决语言矛盾与问题为目的的语言规划与语言政策已经转变为以强

化文化软实力、提升国家在国际社会整体竞争能力为目标的语言战略。无论作为语言规划与政策宏观决策的语言战略还是具体安排处理语言格局以及相关问题的语言规划与政策本身都必须及时调整和修订,而语言战略的及时调整和语言政策的不断修订必须建立在对语言生活状况和语言发展动态充分把握的基础之上。

“语言战略”这一术语在学术界尚未普及,但在语言政策制定者中间已经是一个熟词。2001 年英国政府推出“国家语言战略”(National Languages Strategy),直言不讳,用了语言战略这一术语。此后,加拿大、南非等国相继推出他们的国家语言战略。“911”之后,美国政府推出了“国家安全语言计划”(National Security Languages Initiative),本质上是一项重大的国家语言战略(王淳,2010:41-45)。欧盟长期以来实行多语言多文化的语言政策,目的在于建构一个多元文化的欧洲,这是欧盟的语言战略(傅荣、王克非,2008)。从概念上说,语言战略是一个国家关于语言的总体规划和大计方针,关系到国家语言本身的健康发展,关系到语言格局的合理和科学,也关系到语言生活和谐和健康。由于语言是一个国家的重要资源,也是国家软实力的关键要素,语言战略的良莠也会直接影响到国家发展,尤其是在语言功能与作用凸显的当下,更是如此,因此,语言战略已成为当今世界国家发展战略的重要组成部分,这是欧美等发达国家近期频频调整国家语言战略的主要原因。

语言战略体现于多个方面,其中最为重要的是语言规划与语言政策。后者是前者的实现途径。当今世界诸多国家语言战略的调整也主要体现于语言政策和规划的调整。美国国家安全语言战略具体的落脚点在于“唯英语政策”至“多语言政策”的转变;英国一向是“语言输出国”,将英语推广到世界每一个角落,视其他语言为草芥,进入 21 世纪以来,一改“独尊英语”的常态,将国家语言战略的目标确定在“提高全民多语言的水平和能力”上面。显而易见,这是一项国家语言政策和规划的重大调整。

任何战略、规划以及政策的调整都是审时度势的结果,调整得当与否取决于对时势的把握,因此,充分了解事态,准确把握时势是调整包括确立战略规划目标、制定方针政策的前提。当今社会进展迅速,语言生活内容与形式以及世界语言格局与态势都在发生根本性的快速变化。唯有及时充分了解国外语言生活,适时准确把握世界语言动态,方能准时准确地调整国家语言战略,合理科学地制定语言政策与规划。

3. 有助于语言教育改革,提高语言教育质量

语言教育不仅是语言生活的重要方面,也是语言战略以及语言政策与规划的重要部分。语言教育是影响语言格局变化和发展的重要因素,因此,也就成为语言战略以及语言政策和规划的重要落脚点之一,具有重要的战略意义。21 世纪是国际交流空前广泛和深入的世纪,因此,也是不同语言与文化接触和交往空前年广泛和深入的世纪。外语教育地位和作用愈加重要,其战略意义不断凸显。传统的语言教育思想与方法要求更新与突破,原有格局需要调整,政策需要修订,方向需要进一步明确,质量有待于提高。全面了解国内外语言生活状况、准确掌握世界语言发展动态是完成这些任务的前提和基础,同时又是实施上述各项改革不可多得的经验与借鉴。

语言教育,包括外语教育,已经成为当世界语言生活的重要部分。这是时代发展使然。国际间不断加深的交往需要外语的强有力支撑。外语的不断引进,加大并加速不同语言之间接触与交流,同时又不同程度地引发各种语言矛盾与问题,甚至冲突,促使民族语言教育地位与作用的提升与显现。所有这一切正在充实和改变当今社会语言生活的内容和方式,同时正在影响和改变世界语言的动态和走向。另一方面,语言教育是语言规划的重要内容。语言规划分地位、本体和习得三个方面,习得规划就是语言教育规划,语言政策里面,语言教育政策占据重要地位。事实上语言教育规划与政策要比语言规划的其他两个方面,内容更加充实,问题更加复杂,尤其是在外语教育功能与作用十分凸显的当今社会。因此,语言战略与语言政策的调整,很大程度上就是外语教育规划和政策的调整。美国安全语言战略如此,英国国家语言战略亦然,焦点均在外语教育,前者将十多种外语列为国家外语教育的关键语言(critical languages),(王建勤,2012)后者提倡"全民学外语;终身学外语"(Languages for all;languages for life)。所有这些既是当今社会语言生活的重要方面,也是语言教育所面临的新的挑战。

所以,毫无疑问,充分了解国外语言生活能够使我们准确把握语言教育,尤其是外语教育的发展现状和动态走向,有效地应对新的挑战,使我国的语言

教育以及外语教育改革更为清醒、科学、合理和富有成效。

4. 有助于拓展语言研究范围,提高语言意识和素质

从语言研究角度看,关注国外语言生活,把握世界语言动态,能够拓宽语言研究的范围,改变语言观念,强化语言意识,提高语言素质。

语言意识指的是民众关注语言、珍视语言的态度和观念。语言意识可以是个人的,在双语言和多语言社区,个人对两种或多种语言的态度,语言态度直接影响到语言的选择和使用。在外语教育可能提供多种外语学习的情况下,个人的语言态度很大程度上决定选学某些语言而放弃其他语言,比如学习英语而不学法语。语言意识也可以是社会的,个人的语言意识一方面作为内容构成社会语言意识,另一方面作为部分受制于社会语言意识。社会语言意识是社会文化意识形态的重要部分。Schiffman 把它称作“语言文化”(linguistic culture),并指出,语言文化影响甚至决定个人的语言选择和使用,同时左右甚至决定国家语言战略规划与政策的制定(Schiffman,1996:121)。在 Haugen(1972:325)看来,个人语言意识是语言生态的心理基础,社会语言意识是社会基础。因此,看似多样无序的语言生活一方面受制于语言意识,另一方面反映“语言文化”。社会个体和群体的语言意识又是他们语言素质的反映。

语言意识的强弱和语言素质的高低很大程度上取决于人们对语言本身的认识。语言的认识同语言研究息息相关,随着研究的不断广泛与深入,人们对语言本身的认识不断提高。当今世界对语言的认识已经摆脱了“工具”观的束缚,看到了语言的社会认同、文化实力、经济资源等方面的本质特征。这是当下国际社会对语言的关注和珍视达到空前程度的原因,同时也是当今世界语言意识形态新的基础和内涵。相比之下,我国在这一方面较为滞后,语言的“同化观”“实力观”以及“资源观”尚未深入人心,人们还普遍认为语言是交际工具,仅此而已。这是我国语言意识比较薄弱的主要原因之一。事实上,大至国家语言战略规划与政策,小到家庭个人外语语种的选择,盲目有余而理性不足,个中缘由均与此有关。这也是对我国语言学研究提出的新的挑战。

因此,关注国外语言生活不仅能为国家相关部门决策以及相关研究部门与学者提供第一手信息与资料,不仅能够促进语言研究领域的拓宽和视野的扩展,而且还能够加强和提高我国民众的语言意识和素质。语言研究不仅要

研究本体，而且要研究语言与社会文化、政治经济、国家安全等方面的关系。语言研究的范围包括了整个人类社会的所有活动。语言不是需要时拿起用过后放下的工具，而是贯穿人类活动挥之不去的要素，必须时刻加以关注和珍视。掌握语言也不仅听说读写四种能力，而需具有熟知并驾驭语言社会功能及战略作用的素养。

五、结语

察言观世，由国外语言生活把握国外语言动态、考察社会万象，是一项艰巨复杂的工程，也是一项需要长期努力、坚持不懈的任务。语言生活千姿百态，包含了社会活动的所有方面；语言动态瞬息万变，涵盖了社会变化的纵横交叉。而唯有长期及时准确全面了解和把握它们，才有真正意义上的理论和实践价值，才能促进语言意识和素质的提升，语言研究领域的拓展，语言教育的改革以及语言战略规划与政策的调整。

（本文原载《中国外语》2013 年第 6 期，作者为王克非、蔡永良）

参考文献

E.Arwood, et. al, *Visual Thinking Strategies for Individuals with Autism Disorder: Language of Pictures*, Shawnee Mission, Kansas: Autism Asperger Publishing Co., 2009.

J.C.Bang & J. Døør, *Language, Ecology and Society: A Dialectical Approach*, London: Continuum, 2007.

J. Blommaert, *The Sociolinguistics of Globalization*, Cambridge: Cambridge University Press, 2010.

A.S.Canagarajah, (ed.), *Reclaiming the Local in Language Policy and Practice*, Mahwah, NJ: Lawrence Erlbaum, 2005.

R.L.Cooper, *Language Planning and Social Change*, Cambridge: Cambridge University Press, 1989.

D.Crystal, *The Language Revolution*, Cambridge: Polity Press Ltd., 2004.

J.Das Gupta, and C.A.Ferguson, "Problems of Language Planning", Rubin, J.(ed.), *Language Planning Processes*, The Hague: Mouton Publishers, 1977, pp.3-8.

D.Di Cesare, *Utopia of Understanding between Babel and Auschwitz*, Translated by N. Keane, Albany: The State University of New York Press, 2012.

P.G.Djité, *The Language Difference: Language and Development in the Greater Mekong Sub-Region*, Bristol: Multilingual Matters, 2011.

F.Ebersole, *Language and Perception: Essays in the Philosophy of Language*, Lanham, ML: The University Press of America, 2002.

S.H. Elgin, *The Language Imperative*, Cambridge, Massachusetts: Persues Publishing, 2001.

W.Fierman, *Language Planning and National Development: The Uzbek Experience*, Berlin: Walter de Gruyter, 1991.

O.Fuhrman, and L.Boroditsky, "Mental Time-lines Follow Writing Direction: Comparing English and Hebrew Speakers", *Proceedings of the 29th Annual Conference of the Cognitive Science Society*, 2007, pp.1007-1010.

S.Greiffenstern, *The Influence of Computers, Internet and Computer-Mediated Communication on Everyday English*, Berlin: Logos Verlag Berlin GmbH, 2010.

M.A.K.Halliday, *On Language and Linguistics*, New York: Continuum, 2006.

E.Haugen, *The Ecology of Language: Essays by Einar Haugen*, Stanford, CF: Stanford University Press, 1972.

N.Ishihara, and E.Tarone, "Emulating and Resisting Pragmatic Norms", N.Taguchi, (ed.), *Pragmatic Competence*.Berlin: Mouton de Gruyter, 2009.

J.Jonides, "Mechanism of Verbal Working Memory Revealed by Neuroimage Studies", Landau, J.et.al (eds.), *Perception, Cognition, and Language: Essays in Horner of Henry and Lila Gleitman*, Boston: MIT Press, 2000.

R.B.Kaplan, and R.B.Baldauf, Jr.*Language and Language-in-Education Planning in Pacific Basin*, Norwell, MA: Kluwer Academic Publishers, 2003.

C.Knight, et. al (eds.), *The Evolutionary Emergence of Language: The Social Function and the Origins of Linguistic Form*, Cambridge: Cambridge University Press, 2000.

A.J. Liddicoat & R. A. Jr. Baldauf, (eds.), *Language Planning and Policy: Language*

Planning in Local Contexts, Clevedon: Multilingual Matters, 2008.

P.Mühlhäusler, *Language Ecology: Linguistic Imperialism* and *Language Change in the Pacific Region*, London: Routledge, 1996.

L.H.Phan and T.L.Le, "Moral Dilemma of English Language Teaching", in T.Seddon, and J. Levin (eds.), *Educators, Professionalism and Politics: Global Transitions, National Spaces and Professional Projects*, London and New York: Routledge, 2013, pp.220–247.

S.Shay, *The History of English: A Linguistic Introduction*, San Francisco, CA: Wardja Press, 2008.

T.Skutnabb-Kangas, *Linguistic Genocide in Education or Worldwide Diversity and Human Rights?*, Mahwah, NJ: Lawrence Erlbaum Associates, Inc.Publishers, 2000.

B.Spolsky, *Language Policy: Key Topics in Sociolinguistics*, Cambridge: Cambridge University Press, 2004.

J.W.Tollefson, *Language Policies in Education: Critical Issues*, Mahwah, NJ: Lawrence Erlbaum Associates, Inc.Publishers, 2002.

V.N.Webb, *Language in South Africa: The Role of Language in National Transformation, Reconstruction and Development*, Amsterdam and Philadelphia, PA: John Benjamins Co., 2002.

S.Zufferey, *Lexical Pragmatics and Theory of Mind: The Acquisition of Connectives*, Philadelphia, PA: John Benjamins Publishing Company, 2010.

薄守生、赖慧玲:《当代中国语言规划研究——侧重于区域学的视角》,中国社会科学出版社 2009 年版。

蔡永良:《美国的语言教育与语言政策》,上海三联书店 2007 年版。

蔡永良:《语言・教育・同化——美国印第安语言政策研究》,中国社会科出版社 2003 年版。

陈章太:《语言规划研究》,商务印书馆 2005 年版。

戴曼纯、刘润清:《国外语言规划的理论与实践研究》,外语教学与研究出版社 2011 年版。

戴庆厦:《中国濒危语言个案研究》,民族出版社 2004 年版。

傅荣、王克非:《欧盟语言多元化政策及相关外语教育政策分析》,《外语教学与研究》2008 年第 1 期。

李宇明:《中国语言规划论》,商务印书馆 2010 年版。

李宇明:《中国语言规划续论》,商务印书馆 2010 年版。

沈骑:《当代东亚外语教育政策发展研究》,北京大学出版社 2012 年版。

王淳:《安全诉求于认同危机:论美国国家语言战略的重塑》,《国外理论动态》2010 年第 9 期。

王建勤:《美国“关键语言”战略与我国国家安全语言战略》,载赵蓉晖编:《国家略视角下的外语与外语政策》,北京大学出版社 2012 年版。

王克非:《国外外语教育研究》,外语教学与研究出版社 2012 年版。

吴英成:《汉语国际传播:新加坡视角》,商务印书馆 2010 年版。

姚亚平:《中国语言规划研究》,商务印书馆 2006 年版。

张西平、柳若梅:《世界主要国家语言推广政策概览》,外语教学与研究出版社 2008 年版。

赵蓉晖编:《国家略视角下的外语与外语政策》,北京大学出版社 2012 年版。

周庆生编:《中国语言生活报告(2005)上编》,商务印书馆 2006 年版。

周庆生编:《中国语言生活报告(2006)上编》,商务印书馆 2007 年版。

周玉忠、王辉:《语言规划与语言政策:理论与国别研究》,中国社会科学出版社 2004 年版。

“十五”期间外国语言研究综述

“十五”是迈进新世纪的第一个五年，也是我国改革开放二十年后进入持续发展的一个新阶段。外国语言研究同各个学术领域一样，在“十五”期间取得了长足的进步。我们从研究概貌、重要成果和突出进展等方面可以略见一斑。

一、研究概貌

目前我国外国语言研究类学术期刊有 26 种，若加上刊登这方面论文的各种学报，则有数百种之多。据初步统计，自 2000 年至 2004 年上半年在各种期刊上发表的外语研究与外语教学论文约 13200 多篇，即年均发表论文近 3000 篇。若按普通语言学、应用语言学（外语教学）和翻译研究三大类划分，则大致比例是普通语言学研究论文占 41%，外语教学类论文占 39%，翻译研究占 20%。这与前 5—10 年的研究总况相仿（我们曾对 20 世纪 90 年代本领域研究做过调研（参看王克非，1996），发现九十年代前半期发表论文约 12000 篇，年均 2400 篇，三类研究比例分别是 40%、41% 和 19%；90 年代后半期发表论文近 14000 篇，年均 2800 篇，三类研究比例分别是 39%、39% 和 22%），论文总量上持续缓慢增长。

二、重要成果

近五年国内外语界除了介绍和引进国外语言学理论之外，出现了更多的独立研究，如在功能语言学（包括语用学）、认知语言学、形式语言学、应用语言学、翻译学等方面（后两方面我们另文讨论）的开拓。

首先看功能语言学，包括系统功能语言学及其他功能语言学（如语用学）的论著。

就总体研究看，有胡壮麟的《功能主义纵横谈》（2000；33 万字），一部内容广博的文集，包括作者在过去数年间引介和创作的 30 篇著述，主要内容涉及 1）系统功能语法，2）美国的功能主义，3）语篇分析，4）汉英对比研究，以及 5）符号学和认知研究。

又如朱永生和严世清的《系统功能语言学多维思考》（2001；21 万字）。该书从理论上对经典系统功能语言学的全面反思和修正。彭宣维的《英汉语篇综合对比》（2000；31 万字）试图通过英汉语的对比，为全面描写汉语做准备；作者采用专题的方式加以论述，尝试建立自己的理论模式。同一作者在《语言过程与维度》（2002；44 万字）中，从文化语境、到情景语境、语篇语境、语义、语法和语音，以语言的认知属性为出发点，对经典系统功能语言学提出值得注意的修正。罗选民的《话语分析的英汉语比较研究》（2001；32 万字）则从话语分析的方方面面对英汉语言进行对比研究。此外还有两部介绍性成果。一是刘辰诞的《教学篇章语言学》（1999；24 万字），二是钱敏汝的《篇章语用学概论》（2001；27 万字）。

就具体研究看，本阶段较早出现的成果是黄国文的《英语语言问题研究》（1999；24 万字）。该作者的《语篇分析的理论与实践——广告语篇研究》（2001；34 万字）是应用性语篇研究成果；其另一著作《英语语法结构的功能分析》（2003；36 万字）是专题研究的代表性成果。此外，辛斌的《语篇互文性的批评性分析》（2000；20 万字）采用系统功能语言学批评语言学的方法探讨互文性以及语言、权力和意识形态之间的关系。朱永生和郑立信、苗兴伟所著《英汉语篇衔接手段对比研究》（2001；21 万字），从照应、替代、省略、连接、重复、同义、反义、上下义关系和搭配等角度，对英汉语的相关现象进行了系统比较。同一类型著作还有张德禄和刘汝山的《语篇连贯与衔接理论的发展及应用》（2003；28 万字），它与早期胡壮麟的《语篇的衔接与连贯》（1994）以及以上朱、郑、苗三人的著作一起，对经典系统功能语言学衔接和连贯理论的发展作出了贡献。

李战子的《话语的人际意义研究》(2002;37 万字)主要从传记话语的角度探讨语言的人际功能,并提出了自己的理论模式。苗兴伟的《语用预设的语篇功能》(2000;20 万字)则是从语用学中的“预设”为着眼点探讨语篇功能,是语用学和系统功能语言学相融合的有益尝试。钱军的《句法语义学——关系与视点》(2001;44 万字)以功能为总体原则,研究句法结构中成分之间、以及句法结构和语义结构之间的相互关系;作者试图说明英语的结构不是任意的,而是和意义的表达密切相关。

这方面的研究论文也不少,主要有:黄国文“韩礼德系统功能语言学 40 年发展述评”(《外语教学与研究》2000.1)、王嘉龄“优选论与功能主义”(《外语教学与研究》2002.1)、卓勇光“等式主谓与信息对应的功能分析”(《现代外语》2004.3)、姜望琪“也谈新格赖斯照应理论”(《外语教学与研究》2001.1)、何伟“系统功能语法时态系统概观”(《外语教学与研究》2003.6)等。

自 20 世纪 80 年代末以来,外语界的语用学研究持续不衰,这是因为语用研究同外语教学密切相关。语用学论文主要有理论方面的研究和面向外语教学的应用研究。前者如徐盛桓:“理论语用学研究中的假说:研海一楫之四”(《外语与外语教学》2002.6);蒋严:“论语用推理的逻辑属性:形式语用学初探”(《外国语》2002.3);高军、戴炜华:“语码转换和社会语用学因素”(《外国语》2000.6);辛斌:“体裁互文性与主体位置的语用分析”(《外语教学与研究》2001.5)、彭建武:“语言转述现象的认知语用分析”(《外语教学与研究》2001.5)、王欣:“九十年代语用学研究的新视野:历史语用学、历时语用学和文学语用学”(《外语教学与研究》2002.5);胡壮麟:“语境研究的多元化”(《外语教学与研究》2002.3);熊学亮、刘国辉:“格赖斯会话合作原则的默契内涵”(《外语与翻译》2001.1);何自然、申智奇:“刻意曲解的语用研究”(《外语教学与研究》2004.3)。后者如:匡方涛、文旭:“隐喻的认知语用研究”(《外语学刊》2002.4);涂靖:“幽默的关联理论阐释”(《四川外国语学院学报》2003.5);张新红、何自然:“语用翻译:语用学理论在翻译中的应用”(《现代外语》2001.3);莫爱屏:“关联理论与口译”(《外语与翻译》2002.1)等。

“十五”期间认知语言学研究得到进一步开展。这方面研究有:赵艳芳著

《认知语言学概论》(2001;20 万字),是一本系统介绍国外认知语言学理论的入门著述;高原的《照应词的认知分析》(2003;23 万字),是同时以英语和汉语照应词为对象的专论。作者将语篇中的照应词的使用过程作为一种认知现象、从句子内部、语篇结构、语篇特征等角度考察照应词的使用情况;蓝纯的《从认知角度看汉语和英语的空间隐喻》(2003;22 万字),以汉语的"上"、"下"和英语的 up 和 down 为研究对象,从定性和定量的角度研究指出上述四个概念均与状态、数量、时间和社会等级四个抽象的目标认知域有关。最近又有吴一安在荷兰 John Benjamins 出版社出版的具有很高学术含量的英文著作《英汉空间指示语研究》。得到著名语言学家、剑桥大学教授 Gillian Brown 的肯定。

另有程琪龙编著的《认知语言学概论——语言的神经认知基础》(2001),主要介绍美国语言学家兰姆的神经认知语言学观点。陈忠华、刘心全和杨春苑所著《知识与语篇理解:话语分析认知科学方法论》(2004;20 万字),是一部具有方法论意义的书;作者把认知心理学的分析方法应用于知识类型、知识表征以及知识构型的解析,进而探讨语篇意义的建构以及对语篇宏观结构的理解。

在刊物上发表的认知语言学论文也很丰富,有理论研究的和应用研究的。前者如沈家煊:"认知语法的概括性"(《外语教学与研究》2000.1)和"人工智能中的联接主义和语法理论"(《外国语》2004.3);程琪龙:"认知功能语言观及其理论"(《外语与外语教学》2000.4)和"双宾结构及其相关概念网络"(《外国语》2004.3);周榕:"隐喻认知基础的心理现实性"(《外语教学与研究》2001.2);刘润清、刘正光:"Vi+NP 的非范畴化解释"(《外语教学与研究》2003.4);朱永生:"功能语言学对文体分析的贡献"《外语与外语教学》2001.5);王寅:"认知语言学的哲学基础:体验哲学"(《外语教学与研究》2002.2);文旭:"认知语言学的研究目标、原则和方法"(《外语教学与研究》2002.2);束定芳:"语言的认知研究"(《外国语言文学》2003.3);陈勇:"认知语义学视野下的俄语词汇语义研究"(《中国俄语教学》2003.2);冉永平:"认知语用学探微"(《外语学刊》2002.4);彭宣维:"以社会—认知为基础的'过程—维度'语言模式"(《外语教学与研究》2004.3)等。后者如沈黎:"运用认知语言学理论编学教材练习"(《外语与外语教学》2001.10);许余龙:"语篇回指的认知语言学探讨"(《外国语》2002.1);梁晓波:"认知语言学对英语词汇教学的启示"

(《外语与外语教学》2002.2);熊学亮:“认知语言学与外语教学”(《国外外语教学》2002.4);李战子:“学术话语中认知型情态的多重人际意义”(《外语教学与研究》2001.5);赵学凯:“认知学习理论与外语电化教学实践”(《外语电化教学》2001.1);邹智勇:“语义范畴的认知语言学诠释”(《外语学刊》2000.3);谢应光:“认知语义学与英语成语的意义研究”(《四川外国语学院学报》2002.2);周利娟:“从认知角度看交际中的误解”(《外语学刊》2003.3);吴红云、刘润清:“二语写作元认知理论构成的因子分析”(《外语教学与研究》2004.3)等。

外国语言研究的其他分支学科也产出了不少值得注意的研究成果。如方立的《逻辑语义学》(2000;31 万字),李绍山的《语言研究中的统计学》(2001;21.5 万字),张绍杰的《语言符号任意性研究——索绪尔语言哲学思想探索》(2004;20 万字),都有一定价值。方立所著对逻辑语义学的发展历史有清楚的描述。词典学方面出现几部较有价值的著作:雍和明的《交际词典学》(2003;22.8 万字)、赵彦春所著的《认知词典学探索》(2003;31 万字)、章宜华的《计算词典学与新型词典》(2004;38 万字),其中赵彦春的著述是从认知的角度进行词典研究。此外,钱冠连所著《语言全息论》(2002;24 万字)以及《语言:人类最后的家园——人类基本行为的哲学和语用学研究》(商务印书馆即出)是我国为数不多的语言哲学专论。朱文俊著的《人类语言学论题研究》(2000;35.8 万字)为以汉语为出发点的相关研究奠定了基础。“清华语言论丛”中的朱雪龙著《应用信息论基础》、钱冠连的《汉语文化语用学》(修订版)、杨永林的《中国学生英语色彩语码认知模式研究》和《中国学生汉语色彩语码认知模式研究》、封宗信的《文学语篇的语用文体学研究》等,也都是相关领域里较出色的研究成果。

另外值得一提的是形式语言学方面的研究,这也是汉语界和外语界打破所谓“两张皮”隔阂做得比较成功的方面。过去外语界在形式语言学上的研究多止于介绍或转述加点评论,近几年已出现借鉴国外语言学理论和方法、结合汉语语言现象加以讨论的论著。如程工的《语言共性论》(1999;26 万字)阐述语言共性和个性的关系之后,又从心理学、生理学、学习理论、跨语言比较研究以及汉语研究等角度,提供证据,并且 1)从跨语言的角度看汉语中主语对语类的选择，2）对比汉语“自己”与英语反身代词的差异，3）讨论把字句和动词复制句，对学界许多似乎已成定论的观点提出了自己不同的看法。石毓智的《语法的形式和理据》（2001；近20万字）则从多个角度逐一探讨了现代汉语句子信息组织的原则、现代汉语动补结构的类型学特征、主语与话题关系、汉语的句法结构和词汇标记之间的关系、限定与非限定动词和语序的关系、语法、语音和词汇的关系、陈述语气和虚拟语气的句法差异、时间的一维性对介词衍生的影响等。其另一著作《肯定和否定的对称与不对称》（2001；29万字）所用方法包括定量和定性方法以及连续性和离散性视角，结合英语对汉语肯定和否定的对称与不对称进行了多方面的考察。近年又有戴曼纯著《最简方案框架下的广义左向合并理论研究》（2003）、王立弟《论元结构新论》（2003）相继出版，都提出不少有创见的观点。

这方面论文也不少，重要的有潘海华、胡建华“汉语复合反身代词与英语反身代词比较研究”（《外语教学与研究》2002.4）、李梅“话题之功能短语分析”（《外语教学与研究》2002.4）、韩景泉“英语中间结构的生成”（《外语教学与研究》2003.3）、温宾利“自然语言中的关系结构”（《外语教学与研究》2001.4）、刘爱英、韩景泉“提升结构的句法研究”（《外国语》2004.5）、宋文辉“再论现代汉语动结式的句法核心”（《现代外语》2004.2）、何晓炜“核心功能语类与汉英两种语言的结构差异研究”（《外国语》2004.5）等。现在外语界不少硕士和博士研究生在选题方面向汉外语对比、以及直接从事汉语研究这一大方向靠拢。像北外这样的传统上讲究用外语撰写学位论文的学校都已在鼓励研究生结合汉语语言文学进行研究并用汉语撰写论文。

综观外语界的研究，系统功能语言学和认知语言学方面成绩比较突出。前者结合汉语，但总的倾向是英语研究，具有普通语言学意义；后者则更多的是以相关原则和方法探讨汉语；同时表现出多学科综合的趋势。

三、突出进展

与前期相比，“十五”期间本领域比较突出的进步表现在两个方面：

一是认知语言学,特别是关于隐喻的研究,发展很快。隐喻是和认知联系在一起的,但并非必然。例如,严世清的《隐喻论》(2000;20 万字)重新审视隐喻的性质、机制和功能,对主流学派的词汇隐喻理论和系统语言学的语法隐喻理论之间的异同和互补性展开讨论。胡壮麟的《认知隐喻学》(2003;23 万字)则是一部从多角度研究隐喻问题的专著,具体涉及隐喻的实质、理解、应用以及中国的隐喻研究等方面。束定芳的《隐喻学研究》(2000;21 万字)主要探讨隐喻的本质、隐喻的类型及句法和语义特征、隐喻的产生机制、功能、工作机制、理解以及其普通语言学意义和哲学意义。此外,束定芳还选编了国内近十余年间发表的有关认知研究的论文集《语言的认知研究——认知语言学论文精选》(2004;50 万字),从中可以看出我国认知语言学研究的发展和现况。隐喻方面的重要论文有胡壮麟“评语法隐喻的韩礼德模式”(《外语教学与研究》2000.2)、朱永生、严世清“语法隐喻理论的理据和贡献”(《外语教学与研究》2000.2)、周榕“隐喻表征性质研究”(《外语教学与研究》2002.4)、束定芳“论隐喻的运作机制”(《外语教学与研究》2002.2)和“论隐喻与明喻的结构及认知特点”(《外语教学与研究》2003.2)、程琪龙“语言认知与隐喻”(《外国语》2002.1)、金娜娜、陈自力“语法隐喻的认知效果”(《外语教学与研究》2004.1)、常晨光“语法隐喻与经验的重新建构”(《外语教学与研究》2004.1)等。

二是语料库语言学研究。语料库语言学在国际上的发展也只是近二三十年的事情。我国在九十年代开始介绍国外语料库的建设和相关研究,近些年则不单单是介绍,已开始进行实质性研究,特别是在双语平行语料库方面已有迎头赶上的趋势。如北京外国语大学的教育部重点研究基地“中国外语教育研究中心”研制的通用型汉英双语对应语料库和中日对译语料库规模都在两千多万字/词以上,北大计算语言学研究所的双语平行语料库也具有相当大的规模(目前国际上尚未见到同样规模的双语库研制报道),并在相关软件的研制(如汉外语句对齐、汉语分词)上取得领先水平。利用双语库开展语言对比、翻译转换、翻译教学、双语词典编纂等相关的研究工作也在进行之中,如徐一平主编《中日对译语料库的研制与应用研究论文集》(2002;35 万字)、王克非等著《双语对应语料库:研制与应用》(2004;24 万字)等。近年由桂诗春、杨惠中主持编制的《中国英语学习者语料库》(光盘)收集了一百多万词的中国大学生英语书面语语篇材料,是研究我国学生英语中介语的重要材料,实际上已有数十篇利用该语料库开展的实证研究成果发表在各种外语刊物中。新近出版的何安平著《语料库语言学与英语教学》(2004;20 万字)和她主编的《语料库在外语教育中的应用——理论与实践》(2004;约 48 万字),对语料库在英语课堂教学中的应用方法和应用前景作了详尽的探讨,其中包括基于语料库的教材研究、课堂话语研究和中介语研究,很有价值。

四、研究现状与问题

本领域研究近五年取得较大进步得益于以下几个方面:

其一,与国际学界的交往增加,如大批引进国外重要学术著作,外研社的“当代国外语言学与应用语言学文库”两批影印出版 114 种经过专家委员会认真挑选的书籍,上海外语教育出版社引进应用语言学系列和翻译学系列书籍近 100 种,还有北京大学出版社“西方语言学原版影印系列丛书”出版十余种当代语言学著作。这些著作的引进,不仅为我国相关研究者、教师和研究生解决了不易购得原版书的困难,为师生们使用和查阅文献带来了方便,而且绝大部分引进著作都有我国学者为之撰写“导读”,这既是对国外理论的内化,也便于读者了解和把握书中要旨。

国际学术交往的增加还表现在举办了更多的国际学术会议和邀请国际知名学者来我国参加研讨和讲学,如北京外国语大学近几年举办三次中国英语教学研讨会、中国英汉语比较研究会的第五次研讨会、湖南大学举办的形式语言学研讨会和语言习得研讨会、清华大学和中国译协举办的第四届亚洲翻译家论坛等学术会议。一些全国性学术会议也逐渐转向国际会议或邀请外国学者参加,如全国口译研讨会前三届都只是国内学者参会,2002 年起,由北外主办的第四届和 2004 年由上外主办的第五届都邀请了不少国际知名口译教学和研究的专家前来研讨。这些都有力地促进了我国外语界学者同国际学术的沟通和接轨。

其二,研究经费的大幅度增加。过去经常被提出的图书购置经费不足、科研经费不足、学术成果出版困难等问题,随着我国综合国力的提高和科教兴国战略的实施,已在很大程度上得到改善。不少研究成果都得到国家或省部级科研项目的资助。图书资料的购置经费更是大有改观,如北外的中国外语教育研究中心、广外的外国语言学与应用语言学研究中心、湖南大学的语言学系等单位都常年订购国外相关学术期刊 60 种以上。与国际学术界交往的扩大也得益于研究经费的充实。

其三,研究方法和论文规范上较之从前进步。七年前,桂诗春、宁春岩撰文论述研究方法时曾指出,外语界的语言学和应用语言学论文 54%以上的研究使用简单的思辨性方法,80%以上的研究不依靠数据;这一状况在近年已有所改观,从《外语教学与研究》《外国语》《现代外语》等几家重要学刊发表的论文看,约 70%以上的论文属于有理有据的研究。

我国语言学领域现存主要问题,我们认为有如下几点:

1)学科名称:外国语言学名称不太合适,因为语言学研究不按国别区分。我们认为宜改为国外语言学,其含义是中国以外的语言学研究和各语言(如英语、日语等)的语言学研究。

2)学术分量:从每年发表的大量论文看,相当一部分论文或是转述、或是重复、或是内容干枯,原创性研究不够。

3)学科分布:从外语界看,从事功能语言学、语用学研究的人数和论文数量远超出从事形式语言学和语言对比研究的;讨论翻译问题的论文过多,尤其是与国外相比时更显突出。

4)学术规范:许多论文中英文摘要不全,或不得要领,论文章节不清晰,条理性较差;参考文献也常有不够完备、不够规范的。

五、今后研究重点与建议

“十五”期间,我国外语研究和外语教学领域的学术活动呈现良好的发展态势,为下一个五年的进一步发展奠定了基础。学术研究有自己的生长规律,研究者们有各自的学问兴趣,除了上述各主要领域的研究会继续发展外,我们以为,今后的研究重点可以放在:1)以汉语学生为本的外语教学模式的研究(包括听说能力的提高、教材的研编、课程的调整、测试的改进以及师资的提升);2)基于认知语言学和双语平行语料库的语言对比研究。

综上所述,我们建议:

1)充分借鉴国外语言教育新理论、新模式,在开展较大规模的全国性外语教育调研(包括大学外语专业和非外语专业,以及中小学英语教学)的基础上,进行适应中国外语学习者的外语教学模式研究、习得特点研究,并将研究结果应用于教学实践中进行检验和修正,最终提出比较适合汉语环境下的外语教育理论和模式。同时应注重远程的网络外语教育的新方法与新模式研究。

2)加强对语料库建设的投入和对语料库语言学的重视,使这项研究较快走到国际前沿。积累大量语言素材是观察、分析语言与翻译问题的必要条件;创建大型双语语料库,储存大量的真实语料,对语料做各种带有研究目的的标注,利用研制的检索工具对标注语料进行快捷的搜寻和分析,可以发现已往因条件所限而未能注意的语言现象。这是利用现代技术进行语言研究和语言对比研究以及翻译、教学、词典研编等相关研究的好途径,也为进一步开展从形式、功能和认知等方面探究语言提供新的视角和材料。

3)“十五”期间通过影印引进了许多原版国外语言学和应用语言学方面的学术著作,今后可以更多地翻译相关重要著作,或编译某些重点研究领域的学术论文集,使更多的语言研究者接触到国外理论和研究方法,促进我国的学术发展。

4)学术刊物建设是学术发展的重要保证;许多年前,我们曾提出应调整学刊朝专业化、专门化方向转型,减少雷同的综合性刊物,创办如认知语言学、语用学、社会语言学等专门期刊,使学术向更精细更专深的方面发展。同时也应积极努力创办英文的语言学期刊,将我国的语言研究更好地推向国际,接受国际学界的评价,并促使我国的语言研究和语言教学研究更有深度和更加规范。

5)国家有关部门对专业学术刊物和学术团体的设置管制过紧,这不利于学术活动的开展，建议试行学术刊物登记制，以鼓励和促进学术的繁荣。

（本文原载《外语学刊》2005年第6期。原为给国家社科基金规划办撰写的十一五规划咨询报告中的一部分，发表时作了修补，但刊物做了些删减，现在予以补回；资料截至2004年。作者为王克非、王福祥、彭宣维）

参考文献

蔡金亭：《语言因素对英语过渡语中使用一般过去时的影响》，外语教学与研究出版社2003年版。

常晨光：《语法隐喻与经验的重新建构》，《外语教学与研究》2004年第1期。

陈勇：《认知语义学视野下的俄语词汇语义研究》，《中国俄语教学》2003年第2期。

陈忠华、刘心全、杨春苑：《知识与语篇理解：话语分析认知科学方法论》，外语教学与研究出版社2004年版。

程琪龙：《认知功能语言观及其理论》，《外语与外语教学》2000年第4期。

程琪龙：《认知语言学导论》，外语教学与研究出版社2001年版。

程琪龙：《语言认知与隐喻》，《外国语》2002年第1期。

程琪龙：《双宾结构及其相关概念网络》，《外国语》2004年第3期。

戴曼纯：《最简方案框架下的广义左向合并理论研究》，外语教学与研究出版社2003年版。

丁尔苏：《语言的符号性》，外语教学与研究出版社2000年版。

董宏乐：《科学语篇的隐喻性》，复旦大学出版社2005年版。

方立：《逻辑语义学》，北京语言文化大学出版社2000年版。

封宗信：《文学语篇的语用文体学研究》，清华大学出版社2003年版。

高军、戴炜：《语码转换和社会语言学因素》，《外国语》2000年第6期。

高一虹：《语言文化差异的认识与超越》，外语教学与研究出版社2000年版。

高一虹：《“1+1>2”外语学习模式》，北京大学出版社2001年版。

高一虹等：《中国大学生英语学习社会心理——学习动机与自我认同研究》，外语教学与研究出版社2004年版。

高原：《照应词的认知分析》，外语教学与研究出版社2003年版。

顾曰国:《会话分析》,外语教学与研究出版社 2000 年版。

韩宝成:《外语教学科研中的统计方法》,外语教学与研究出版社 2000 年版。

韩景泉:《英语中间结构的生成》,《外语教学与研究》2003 年第 3 期。

何伟:《系统功能语法时态系统概观》,《外语教学与研究》2003 年第 6 期。

何晓炜:《核心功能语类与汉英两种语言的结构差异研究》,《外国语》2004 年第 5 期。

何自然、申智奇:《刻意曲解的语用研究》,《外语教学与研究》2004 年第 3 期。

胡壮麟:《语篇的衔接与连贯》,上海外语教育出版社 1994 年版。

胡壮麟:《理论文体学》,外语教学与研究出版社 2000 年版。

胡壮麟:《功能主义纵横谈》,外语教学与研究出版社 2000 年版。

胡壮麟:《评语法隐喻的韩礼德模式》,《外语教学与研究》2000 年第 2 期。

胡壮麟:《语境研究的多元化》,《外语教学与研究》2002 年第 3 期。

胡壮麟:《认知隐喻学》,北京大学出版社 2003 年版。

黄国文:《英语语言问题研究》,中山大学出版社 1999 年版。

黄国文:《韩礼德系统功能语言学 40 年发展述评》,《外语教学与研究》2000 年第 1 期。

黄国文:《语篇分析的理论与实践——广告语篇研究》,上海外语教育出版社 2001 年版。

姜望琪:《也谈新格莱斯照应理论》,《外语教学与研究》2001 年第 1 期。

蒋严:《论语用推理的逻辑属性——形式语用学初探》,《外国语》2002 年第 3 期。

蒋祖康:《第二语言习得研究》,外语教学与研究出版社 2000 年版。

金娜娜、陈自力:《语法隐喻的认知效果》,《外语教学与研究》2004 年第 1 期。

匡方涛、文旭:《隐喻的认知语用学研究》,《外语学刊》2002 年第 4 期。

蓝纯:《从认知角度看汉语和英语的空间隐喻》,外语教学与研究出版社 2003 年版。

李梅:《话题之功能短语分析》,《外语教学与研究》2002 年第 4 期。

李绍山:《语言研究中的统计学》,西安交通大学出版社 2001 年版。

李战子:《学术话语中认知型情态的多重人际意义》,《外语教学与研究》2001 年第 5 期。

李战子:《话语的人际意义研究》,上海外语教育出版社 2002 年版。

梁晓波:《认知语言学对英语词汇教学的启示》,《外语与外语教学》2002 年第 2 期。

刘爱英、韩景泉:《提升结构的句法研究》,《外国语》2004 年第 5 期。

刘辰诞:《教学篇章语言学》,上海外语教育出版社 1999 年版。

刘润清:《外语教学中的科研方法》。外语教学与研究出版社 2000 年版。

刘润清、吴一安等:《中国英语教育研究》,外语教学与研究出版社 2000 年版。

刘润清、刘正光:《Vi+NP 的非范畴化解释》,《外语教学与研究》2003 年第 4 期。

刘润清、戴曼纯:《中国高校外语教学改革现状与发展策略研究》,外语教学与研究出版社 2003 年版。

罗选民:《话语分析的英汉语比较研究》,湖南人民出版社 2001 年版。

苗兴伟:《语用预设的语篇功能》,苏州大学出版社 2000 年版。

莫爱屏:《关联理论与口译》,《外语与翻译》2002 年第 1 期。

潘海华、胡建华:《汉语复合反身代词与英语反身代词比较研究》,《外语教学与研究》2002 年第 4 期。

彭建武:《语言转述现象的认知语用分析》,《外语教学与研究》2001 年第 5 期。

彭宣维:《英汉语篇综合对比》,上海外语教育出版社 2000 年版。

彭宣维:《语言过程与维度》,清华大学出版社 2002 年版。

彭宣维:《语言导论新编》,清华大学出版社 2003 年版。

彭宣维:《English Text 导读》,[澳]James Martin 原著,北京大学出版社 2004 年版。

彭宣维:《以社会—认知为基础的“过程—维度”语言模式》,《外语教学与研究》2004 年第 3 期。

钱冠连:《语言全息论》,商务印书馆 2002 年版。

钱冠连:《语言:人类最后的家园——人类基本行为的哲学和语用学研究》,商务印书馆 2005 年版。

钱军:《句法语义学——关系与视点》,人民教育出版社 2001 年版。

钱敏汝:《篇章语用学概论》,外语教学与研究出版社 2001 年版。

冉永平:《认知语用学探微》,《外语学刊》2002 年第 4 期。

沈家煊:《认知语法的概括性》,《外语教学与研究》2000 年第 1 期。

沈家煊:《人工智能中的联接主义和语法理论》,《外国语》2004 年第 3 期。

沈黎:《运用认知语言学理论编学教材练习》,《外语与外语教学》2001 年第 10 期。

石毓智:《语法的认知语义基础》,江西教育出版社 2000 年版。

石毓智:《肯定和否定的对称与不对称》,北京语言文化大学出版社 2001 年版。

石毓智:《语法的形式和理据》,江西教育出版社 2001 年版。

束定芳:《隐喻学研究》,上海外语教育出版社2000年版。

束定芳:《论隐喻的运作机制》,《外语教学与研究》2002年第2期。

束定芳:《论隐喻与明喻的结构及认知特点》,《外语教学与研究》2003年第2期。

束定芳:《语言的认知研究》,《外国语言文学》2003年第3期。

束定芳主编:《语言的认知研究——认知语言学论文精选》,上海外语教育出版社2004年版。

宋文辉:《再论现代汉语动结式的句法核心》,《现代外语》2004年第2期。

涂靖:《幽默的关联理论阐释》,《四川外国语学院学报》2003年第5期。

王福祥:《文化语言学》,外语教学与研究出版社2000年版。

王嘉龄:《优选论与功能主义》,《外语教学与研究》2002年第1期。

王克非:《语言学近况分析与我们的科研设想》,《外语研究》1996年第3期。

王克非等:《双语平行语料库:研制与应用》,外语教学与研究出版社2003年版。

王立弟:《论元结构新论》,外语教学与研究出版社2003年版。

王欣:《九十年代语用学研究的新视野:历史语用学、历时语用学和文学语用学》,《外语教学与研究》2002年第5期。

王寅:《认知语言学的哲学基础:体验哲学》,《外语教学与研究》2002年第2期。

王志军:《英汉被动句认知对比研究》,上海外语教育出版社2004年版。

温宾利:《自然语言中的关系结构》,《外语教学与研究》2001年版。

文旭:《认知语言学的研究目标、原则和方法》,《外语教学与研究》2002年第2期。

吴红云、刘润清:《二语写作元认知理论构成的因子分析》,《外语教学与研究》2004年第3期。

谢应光:《认知语义学与英语成语的意义研究》,《四川外国语学院学报》2002年第2期。

辛斌:《语篇互文性的批评性分析》,苏州大学出版社2001年版。

辛斌:《体裁互文性与主体位置的语用分析》,《外语教学与研究》2001年第5期。

徐盛桓:《理论语用学研究中的假说:研海一楫之四》,《外语与外语教学》2002年第6期。

许余龙:《语篇回指的认知语言学探索》,《外国语》2002年第1期。

熊学亮:《认知语言学与外语教学》,《国外外语教学》2002年第4期。

严世清:《隐喻论》,苏州大学出版社2000年版。

杨永林:《中国学生英语色彩语码认知模式研究》,清华大学出版社2002年版。

杨永林:《中国学生汉语色彩语码认知模式研究》,清华大学出版社 2002 年版。

雍和明:《交际词典学》,上海外语教育出版社 2003 年版。

张德禄、刘汝山:《语篇连贯与衔接理论的发展及应用》,上海外语教育出版社 2003 年版。

张绍杰:《语言符号任意性研究——索绪尔语言哲学思想探索》,上海外语教育出版社 2004 年版。

张新红、何自然:《语用翻译:语用学理论在翻译中的应用》,《现代外语》2001 年第 3 期。

章宜华:《计算词典学与新型词典》,上海辞书出版社 2004 年版。

赵学凯:《认知学习理论与外语电化教学实践》,《外语电化教学》2001 年第 1 期。

赵彦春:《认知词典学探索》,上海外语教育出版社 2003 年版。

赵艳芳:《认知语言学概论》,上海外语教育出版社 2001 年版。

周利娟:《从认知角度看交际中的误解》,《外语学刊》2003 年第 3 期。

周榕:《隐喻认知基础的心理现实性——时间的空间隐喻表征的实验证据》,《外语教学与研究》2005 年第 2 期。

周榕:《隐喻表征性质研究》,《外语教学与研究》2002 年第 4 期。

朱文俊:《人类语言学论题研究》,北京语言文化大学出版社 2000 年版。

朱永生:《功能语言学对文体分析的贡献》,《外语与外语教学》2001 年第 5 期。

朱永生:《语境动态研究》,北京大学出版社 2005 年版。

朱永生、严世清:《语法隐喻理论的理据和贡献》,《外语教学与研究》2000 年第 2 期。

朱永生、严世清:《系统功能语言学多维思考》,上海外语教育出版社 2001 年版。

朱永生、郑立信、苗兴伟:《英汉语篇衔接手段对比研究》,上海外语教育出版社 2001 年版。

卓勇光:《等式主谓与信息对应的功能分析》,《现代外语》2004 年第 3 期。

邹智勇:《语义范畴的认知语言学诠释》,《外语学刊》2000 年第 3 期。

社会经济发展与外语教育的互动

外语教育政策是国家教育政策的重要组成部分。外语教育政策的恰当与否不仅关系到国家的政治、经济、科技发展，而且关系到国家的安全、文化传统的传承以及下一代整体素质的提高。一个合适的外语教育政策的制定需要综合多种因素，从宏观到微观多层面、多方位地权衡利弊。例如，外语教育投资的成本与产出、社会对外语人才的实际需求、国家安全与国际关系的需要、学习外语的最佳年龄、外语教育与其他各课程教育的关系，以及外语教育对于拓宽学习者的国际视野、增强其跨文化沟通能力和外语对年轻一代民族认同感的影响等，都是制定恰当的外语教育政策时必须考虑的因素。

世界上许多国家对本国的语言政策包括外语教育政策都非常重视，有丰富的研究成果和文献资料，他们的经验和教训非常值得我国教育主管部门借鉴。我国一直没有专门机构从事类似工作，对于国外的外语教育政策和措施缺乏了解，以致我们的外语教育政策的制定带有一定的盲目性。从近半个世纪的历史看，我国的外语教育规划和政策曾有过几次失误，而对当前的外语政策和现状，也有不少学者已经从不同角度撰文表示忧虑（参阅胡文仲，2001）。

本书就是一项对多国外语教育现状及政策的调研，以及在此基础上的一些初步分析，以填补我国在这方面的空白。我们相信这一调研和比较分析的成果将有助于我国制订出既切合当前经济、文化发展需要又符合外语教学特点和教育规律的改革方略，同时也为我国对外汉语教学在世界范围内的推广提供一定依据。

一、外语教育政策的调研

在历时近四年的调研工作中，我们考察和比较了有一定代表性的十三个国家和地区的社会经济现状和外语教育政策，以及相关措施、基本数据、现实情况等，并加以比较、分析。这些国家既有发达国家，也有发展中国家，既有操印欧语系语言的国家，也有非印欧语系语言的国家。

我们主要关注的是：(1)不同国家的外语教育政策模式及各自的利弊，不只是外语教育政策内容的一般性介绍；(2)考察与分析时特别注意外语教育与该国社会经济发展之间的关系；(3)研究涉及的国家为非英语国家，重点考察其英语教育，兼及其他语种教育，使考察结果对我国更具借鉴价值。

调研所涉领域的研究主要有五个方面：各国外语教育大环境（基本情况），各国的语言政策，各国的教育政策，各国的外语教育政策以及各国的外语教学。具体内容包括：

对象国的历史、地理、政治、经济、文化、教育等社会发展总况；

对象国的语言政策、双语教育政策和实践、外语教育规划及其成效得失；

国家颁发的官方文件（如相关法律法规、教学大纲，或课程标准、指导框架等）；

学生正式学习外语的年龄，不同阶段（小学、中学、大学）外语学习在课程设置中所占的教学时数及教学目标；

主要外语教学策略、教学方法、培养模式等方面的实践与创新；

外语教学中综合运用现代科学技术的情况；

有代表性的或主要的大学、中学外语教材及其教学内容；

普通高校开设外语的语种和学习不同外语语种的人数及比例；

外语教师队伍及教师教育情况；

外语教育评价体系、评测方法；

其他相关内容等。

二、语言、社会、教育

我们谈外语教育政策与社会发展，离不开语言、教育、社会这几个关键词。

近十多年，特别是进入21世纪以来，世界已进入全球化和信息化时代。全球化和信息化意味着世界各地人民更密切更广泛地相互交往，而这一交往最重要的工具和最突出的特点，就是语言，包括本族语和外国语。因此，在全球化时代，语言的作用比以往任何时候都更加凸显。语言和教育所代表的软实力在成长，重要性日益凸显，值得密切关注。

就语言而言，语言是工具，是身份，是资源，是力量。

人们通过语言进行思维和认知，交流信息和情感，传承文化和知识，因此是重要的交往工具。这是人们最容易认识到的一种语言特性。

人总是生活在某个文化社团中，操表达某种文化和习俗的语言，因此最简单有效的表明自己身份和判断他人身份的手段就是语言。无数例证表明，正由于这种身份性，语言成为民族系连和认同的重要标志。同时，人可以通过学习一门新的语言改变或提高自己的身份。

我们知道土地、森林、石油等有形的自然资源、物质资源，但人类社会还有无形的社会资源、精神资源，它对于人类社会同样重要，同样值得开发。语言就是这样的无形资源。因为每种语言背后都蕴涵着一个民族的文化和思维等社会或精神的资源，因此，学习和掌握一门语言就可能获得一种资源。任何语言都具有自身价值和作用，但语言越强势，使用范围越广，其资源价值体现就越大。

长期以来人们谈到实力，总会想到经济、军事、科学技术、物质资源等方面，但现代社会，人们认识到还有同样不可不重视的软实力，那就是语言、文化、教育、信息、关系、价值观等。比之于农牧时代、工业时代，在全球化的今天，软实力的竞争更加重要，如同没有硝烟的战争。从软实力的主要代表看，语言可以说是软实力的基础，因为它是其他软实力的构成要素，是文化或意识形态影响力的保证。

对于一个社会,人是最重要的,一个会思想、会用语言表述思想的人是最重要的。那么培育这样的人,也就是我们常说的一个高素质的人,就是教育的神圣职责,也是社会和谐发展的需要。在这里,我们可以看到,语言、社会、教育三者紧密相连,是人类社会进步的真正保障。

同时,由上述简要的相互关联的解说,我们也会清楚地看到外语教育对于文明社会里的人的真正意义,那就是,多了一个交流工具,多了一种社会身份,多了一些无形资源,多了一分生存实力。

三、经济社会发展与外语教育的互动

在全球一体化的国际交往中,外语,特别是相当于国际通用语的英语,扮演着日益重要的角色,受到世界各国的重视。不仅非英语国家更加强调英语,美国等英语国家也开始重视外语。联合国教科文组织(UNESCO 2003)出版了《多语世界中的教育》,分三部分论述多语言教育的重要性,特别是多语言的世界对教育体系带来的挑战。书中强调,在数字化时代,在全球经济和社会文化交往日益频繁的今天,语言和教育问题更加突出。如何既保留各自不同的语言和文化,用母语进行教育和传播知识,又能使接受优质教育的人们具备与世界沟通的语言能力,是全世界各国都面临的挑战。各国如何应对,如何制定外语和外语教育的政策,往往反映出国家实力、国家政策、教育理念等的变化。因为,社会经济的发展需要强化外语和外语教育,外语教育的发展反过来会支持社会经济的进步和全球一体化进程。

具体到一个国家,根据自己的政治、经济、军事、外交和科技发展的需要,做出关于外语在本国教育体系中的地位、比重等问题的规定,就是为本国制定了一个特定时期的外语教育政策。

以亚洲新兴的工业国韩国为例。

韩国的外语教育始于对中国汉字的借用,历经了照搬日本的日语教育体系以及仿效美国的英语教育体系的艰辛路程。直至1955年才开始韩国外语教育的自主发展进程。过去50多年来,韩国教育试图通过制定合理的教育政策来实现人才资源的合理开发。其制定教育政策的立足点在于自由民主主义和市场经济。

韩国外语教育起步较晚,但发展迅速。近50多年中,韩国外语教育得到国民政府和全体国民的热心支持,发生了巨大变化。历届政府根据来自各方面的要求,尤其是来自政策、经济、学术以及现实各方面的要求,适时调整外语教育政策,不断进行外语教育改革,以适应不断增长的经济社会发展之需。

在21世纪全球一体化大背景下,韩国为了培养具有多元语言文化和国际竞争力的人才,更加重视外语教育,加大对外语教育的投入,把外语教育放在战略发展的高度,制定一系列积极的外语教育政策,推动外语教育迅速有效地开展。所以韩国人常把经济视为第一经济,而把促进经济发展的教育视为第二经济。外语教育则是第二经济的重要组成部分。韩国五十年经济崛起为亚洲四小龙,既促进了外语教育事业,也伴随有外语教育的提升。[①]

看经济强国日本的英语教育对策。

日本有悠久的学习外国学习外语的传统,明治维新之后一百多年里,外语教育特别是英语教育发展极快。进入21世纪,日本政府痛感英语教育对于日本全面持续发展和国际化公民培养的重要,对英语教育提出了更多更高的要求。2002年4月,日本全国开始实行新的英语学习指导要领(相当于我国的英语课程标准)。同年7月,文部科学省在"改进英语教学圆桌会议"和"改革英语教育圆桌会议"的意见基础上,提出了"培养能使用英语的日本人的战略构想"行动计划,并对该构想的具体目标、实施步骤等做了详细的说明。

2003年3月31日,文部科学省正式开始实施"培养具有英语能力的日本人"的行动计划。文部科学大臣远山敦子亲自撰文论述这一计划的意义和要点。她指出,世界已进入一个高度全球化大竞争的时代,从经济或资本投资的角度,从国际交往的角度,从知识信息交流和获取的角度,人们都需要与外部世界更多的沟通,在这样的情形下,英语这个国际通用语起到了将不同地区不同语言的人们联系起来的作用。这对于日本更好地与世界各国沟通,相互理解和信任也是至关重要的。但是日本的现实情况是,许多日本人由于英语能

① 参阅本书第九部分。

力的局限，还不能有效地与外国人交流思想，表达情感。因此，文部科学省采取各种措施包括修改文部科学省的“指导要领”，以提高日本学生的基本英语交流能力，包括改善教师的英语教学能力等。

这一行动计划有详细的目标描述，对初中学生、高中学生、大学生以及一般公民的英语水平都有明确的要求，对实质性地改进英语教学的能力和设施也有具体的步骤，是一个五年甚至更长时间内的提升日本国民整体英语水平的纲领性文件（MEXT 2003）。

配合培养具有英语能力的日本人的行动计划，日本教育当局 2003 年开始实施“超级英语（Super-English）”教学项目，即不仅把英语作为必修课进行日常教学，还把英语作为授课语言来进行其他学科的教学，这种类似于我国英汉双语教学的模式于 2005 年已在日本 100 所中学进行试点。为此日本仅以政府名义聘请的以英语为母语的正规教师每年就达 1000 名以上，进行“团队教学（Team-teaching）”，即课堂由一位外籍英语教师和一位日本本国英语教师来合作进行的教学活动，并配套投资 1 亿 8 千万日元进行本土英语教师的培训。

从这些措施，我们可以清楚地看到，日本英语教育随着社会的发展有了新的更高的目标，以适应日本经济、政治、文化各方面进一步走向国际的广泛需要。

看近 30 年风云变幻的俄国。

近 30 年里，俄罗斯社会大变革。《2010 年俄罗斯教育现代化纲要》将教育纳入国家社会经济的互动体系中，使教育政策的发展变化能够与政治、经济发展相呼应、相协调，成为服务国家、服务国民的重要措施。这种教育发展观念及相应举措也深深地影响了俄罗斯的外语政策及外语教育发展，为其发展和演变提供了宽阔的背景。

从俄罗斯外语教育简史看，18 世纪前俄国社会比较封闭，因而几乎没什么人学习外语。此后由于社会发展、生活和交流的需要，人们开始重视学习外语。18 世纪前 25 年是俄罗斯外语教育快速发展的时期，在莫斯科成立了一批新型（教会）学校，对外国人子弟和俄国贵族青年开设拉丁语、希腊语、德语。19 世纪上半期成立了一系列专门学校和普通教育机构，把拉丁语、希腊语、德语、法语欧洲语言作为必修课程,英语只在军事学校、公务和商业化学校中开设,意大利语和丹麦语只针对军事和海军学校的学生。随着时代的发展,近些年俄罗斯外语教育呈现出一种多元态势,学校教育不再推行单一的外语制,虽然英语仍为俄罗斯最主要的外语学习语种,德语、法语等欧洲语言次之,汉语、日语等东方语言也开始进入俄罗斯广阔的外语教育市场。

俄罗斯外语教育的另一个特点是,高度中央集权的国家体制决定了俄罗斯的外语教育发展与国家意志紧密相连。苏联一直对教育包括语言教育实施全面的中央集权领导,曾成功地通过各种手段向其他国家推广俄语,特别是东欧和其他社会主义国家,包括中国和朝鲜。在俄语一统天下的情况下,俄罗斯的外语教育的规模和语种数量处于相对停滞状态,少量的外语学习也是为了国家的政治需要。但开始逐渐走出中央高度集权的俄罗斯外语教育,现在也融入国际社会的大潮,表现出更灵活的外语教育政策。

再看发达的欧洲国家:法国。

法国是欧洲大国,是欧洲联盟重要成员国,因此,其外语教育与国家乃至世界的经济、政治、科技和社会文化发展息息相关。无论当局还是民众,对外语和外语教育都有高度的认识和需求。十多年前,法国参议院文化事务委员会对法国外语教育情况进行全面调研后认为,1)在"全球化"的大环境下,外语教育要以面向国际和跨文化的理念为中心;2)利用欧洲发展趋势,提供语言多元选择;3)学习外语要从"娃娃"抓起,并同国外建立直接联系,利用互联网资源并最大限度地聘用外国助教。在法国民众中,越来越多的人认为,掌握外语已成为进入世界市场的有效工具,而"只懂一门语言,就好像一条腿走路"。

法国的经验也表明,外语教育与社会经济发展是双赢互利的事情。一方面,世界和国家的发展影响了外语教育。首先,由于全球化的发展,法国对外联系日益频繁,外语在教育体制中的地位提高了,从不受重视而逐渐"转正",成为学校教育的正式学科。其次,随着欧洲一体化进程的深入,欧盟的外语政策全面渗透着法国外语教育政策的走向。再次,由于英语国家尤其是美国在世界经济中的"霸主"作用,英语成为学习人数最多的语种;而新兴国家在国际舞台上的崛起,给法国带来了新的就业机会,也促使这些国家的语言在法国

“人气兴旺”。

另一方面，外语教学的发展也对国家的方方面面产生了影响。比如，公众的外语学习需求、语种选择也从不同角度影响着国家政策的制定。英语以近乎百分之百的学习率成为法国第一大外语，国家必须培养、选拔相应的师资以满足英语学习的需要。而法国的“老牌”外语——德语教学则受到了很大的冲击，以至于德语教师失业，国家因此出台专门政策来重振德语“雄风”。汉语则在中国长盛不衰的持续发展的大背景下，前所未有地在法国“火”了起来。

法国的汉语热明显有社会政治经济关系的影响。首先，中法关系良好，法国官方重视同中国的关系，从而重视汉语教学。法国教育部的网站上还介绍汉语有锻炼记忆力、严密思维和组合能力的种种好处。法国学习汉语的人数在1993至2003年十年间增幅达172%。第二，法国媒体近年频繁报道中国的各个方面，改变了民众的眼光，而且正面、具体和近距离的报道越来越多。第三，中国作为一个大国在国际舞台的崛起给了法国人想象未来的空间。中国经济飞速发展，与法国境况不如从前形成鲜明对比。法国就业形势严峻，法国家长纷纷寄希望于汉语，希望它为子女未来找到好工作提供便利。第四，中国文化的感召力长年不衰。几千年的文化、神秘的异国情调等足以让好奇的法国人关注中国。第五，中国的开放也给了法国了解中国的机会。一方面，中国官方注意对外宣传、中国文化年在法举办和中国文化中心在巴黎的建立对汉语在法国的发展也起到了一定的促进作用，而另一方面，中国地方政府、民间机构的对法交往便利、频繁，也起到了为法国汉语学习加温的作用。

四、各国外语教育政策和外语教育发展给我们的启示

无论东方和西方，发达国家或发展中国家，其外语教育发展的历史、现状以及有关外语教育的政策演变，其共同的特点或启示是：

1）外语教育不是单纯的语言教学，它折射出时代的需求、国家的开放程度和经济社会的发展水平，也因此而消长。

2)一国公民的外语普及程度,往往反映公民的国际意识,国家的国际化程度,预示国家未来的发展前景;因此,外语教育是现代化教育、世界公民养成的一个重要元素。

3)外语的教学、培训、考试,关系到全社会公民的个人发展、求职就业,涉及面广,关注度高,是民间和政府都十分重视的社会行为,也是日益增长的第三产业和市场。

4)外语教育不是单纯地培养外国语言文学人才或翻译人才,应当着力结合专业来培育精通外语的高级专业人才;重视口头和书面交流能力、打造各专业的国际型人才,是各国目前外语教育的重点。

5)外语教育的发展与国家外语政策密切相关,政府高层高屋建瓴地适时引导和支持,是外语教育发展的关键性保障;从各国情况看,提前在小学即开设外语课程、注意多语种人才培养、鼓励国际教育交流等,是当前政策导向的一些重要方面。

总之,我们的多国外语教育及其政策的调研,已清晰地表明外语教育是如何与社会经济发展良性互动,互为需求的。因势利导,根据政治、经济、学术以及现实各方面的要求,重视以英语通用语为主的外语教育,把外语教育放在国家战略发展的高度,着重提高公民的文化素质和国际意识,培养具有多元语言文化和国际竞争力的人才,才是我们今天应该走的道路,才有利于国家软实力的提升,适应持续增长的经济社会发展的需要。

(本文原载《外语界》2011 年第 1 期)

参考文献

1.《2010 年俄罗斯教育现代化纲要》。

2. 胡文仲:《我国外语教育规划的得与失》,《外语教学与研究》2001 年第 4 期。

3. 王克非:《日本英语教育动向探知》,《中国英语教育》2010 年第 2 期。

4. Deth, Jean-Pierre Van. *L'enseignement scolaire des langues vivantes dans les pays membres de la Communauté européenne. Bilan. réflexions et proposition*. Bruxelles: AIMAV-Didier, 1979.

5. Herras, José Carlos. *Le bilinguisme dans l'Union européenne: un objectif à atteindre.// L'enseignement des langues étrangères dans les pays de l' Union européenne.Peeters Louvain-la-Neuve*, 1998.

汉语把字句特点、分布及英译

汉语把字句的主要功能或语法意义是“处置”。该句式的特点和作用有三：一是将宾语提至动词前，解决该宾语无法后置的问题；二是突出宾语，同时也突出动作及其后果；三是便于语句衔接。本文通过大量语料考察，发现翻译的汉语作品比原创的汉语作品使用更多的把字句，文学类作品比非文学类作品使用更多的把字句；这一发现进一步证明把字句适用于表达复杂和细微的意思。文中还讨论了英译把字句的方法。

一、把字句的结构特点及语义重心

汉语有许多独特的结构式，把字句即其中一例。对把字句的研究始于王力先生，已有 70 年历史，至今仍在继续。早期的讨论以王力（1943，1944）、吕叔湘（1948）、丁声树（1980）、朱德熙（1980）等为代表，近期的讨论，邵敬敏（1985，2001）、范晓（1998）、张旺熹（1991）、张伯江（2000）等可为代表。这些论述分别从句法、语义、语用及对外汉语教学等多方面分析了把字句的使用、构成条件、动宾关系等。本文主要关注把字句的特点、其使用与分布情况，以及与英译有关的一些问题。

把字句的基本部分或结构是：

1）把字前面部分（主语或零主语）；

2）把字及其宾语（宾语为后面动词的受事或施事）；

3）把字句中的动词（主要为具有处置或致使意义的动词）；

4）动词前后的修饰成分（状语或补语）

其中，第3）项动词最为关键，2）、4）项必不可少。

把字句中的“把”字，有论者认为是助动词，或副动词，或次动词，不过更多的人还是倾向于将“把”字视作介词。把字也确实在其宾语与动词之间起到了中介作用。3）项之所以关键，是因为把字句中的动词有其特殊性，即它一般只能由具有处置（包括致使、描述）意义的动词承担，从而对其前面的宾语（多为受事，较少为施事）发生影响，引发某一结果或状态。因此，通常情况下，能愿动词、心理动词和“有”、“没有”等动词不会出现在把字句中做谓语动词。

2）、4）项之必不可少也是把字句的特点。因把字句总表示某种广义的处置的结果或状态，仅一个动词不能完整表达，需要带上状语、补语等与之构成一个结构式。

语言的功能是表达，任何句式的产生和发展都有语义上的需要。把字句也是如此。把字句的使用，主要是因为宾语很难安排在动词之后（如下节例句1—5均很难不使用把字句），这一点前人有不少论述，也确实如此。我们想说的是，除了此消极因素之外，恐怕还有（1）强调的作用，或者说把字句起着一个双重强调的作用。一般地说，汉语是尾重心，即语句的重心在句子末尾。“作为外语系的学生，我们不仅要学好外语，也要学好汉语。”这句话强调了尾部的“外语”和“汉语”。这句话如果换个说法：“作为外语系的学生，我们不仅要把外语学好，还要把汉语学好。”这时强调的就不仅是“外语”和“汉语”，还有“学好”。又如下节例句3）、4）；“把买食品的钱省下来”同“省下买食品的钱”，语义重心是不同的。（2）便于与后面的语句衔接，如下节例句2）、3）等；“装扮自己”后面已不容易连接其他成分，而“把自己装扮成”后面就可以有连接成分；又如下节例1），“转移”若用在前面，一是不便将宾语与另一宾语相区隔，二是不便两次使用。概括地说，该句式的特点和作用有三：其一，将宾语提至动词前，解决该宾语无法后置的问题；其二，突出宾语，同时也突出动作及其后果；其三，便于语句衔接，并将（把字后面的）宾语与动词所涉及的其他成分相区隔。

从把字句的使用频率看，其最重要的用途是表现处置的结果或状态，因此动补式的把字句占把字句的绝大部分。邵敬敏(1985/2001:234)的考察是:《骆驼祥子》中共有419个把字句,动补式的有353句,占84.3%,动宾式的有48句,占11.3%;再加上动补动宾式连用的5句,419个把字句里就有406个使用动补或动宾句式。可见,动补式是把字句最常用的句式,其次是动宾式,这两者占把字句的97%。这也同把字句的特殊语义重心有相关性。

二、把字句的使用与分布情况

把字句是现代汉语中普遍使用的一个句式,原因是具有特殊功能,如上所述。本节考察它的使用分布情况。

王力经考察认为(1958:中413),把字句是后起句式,中晚唐以后逐渐多用。祝敏彻(1957)和邵敬敏(1985/2001:247)进而提出,由于把字句将原在动词后面的宾语提前,使谓语部分得到解放,即由封闭式结构变成开放式结构,各种词和短语得以与V构成新的结构,表达更为复杂细微的意思,从而使把字句获得发展。我们赞同这一观点,并再进一步提出假设:翻译复杂的外文句子时,常常可能导致译文语句的表达相应复杂而细微,从而增加把字句的使用。先看一下有关考察。

张旺熹(1991)曾调查了532700个汉字的中国现当代文学语料,发现1188个把字结构(见表1)。

表1　中国现当代文学语料中把字句使用情况

统计项 / 体裁	语料字数出现率	把字结构数	把字结构千字出现率
诗歌	20700	52	2.51
戏剧	63200	153	2.42
散文	98300	166	1.69
小说	350500	817	2.33
合计	532700	1188	2.23

从表 1 可见,除散文类语料中把字句出现频率稍低之外,其他几种体裁的语料中把字句出现频率大致为每千字 2 句略多,平均 2. 23 句/千字。这是汉语文学作品中的情况。

为了扩大考察范围,并对上述关于翻译可能导致把字句增多的假设加以验证,我们参照表 1,据中国外语教育研究中心汉英双语平行语料库(参看王克非,2003),对把字句的使用做了一个初步考察。与张的考察不同的是,我们不仅考察汉语原创语料,也考察汉语翻译语料;不仅考察文学语料,也考察非文学语料。本文通过汉译英部分考察汉语原创语料,英译汉部分考察汉语翻译语料(见表 2;语料字数只算汉语的,不包括英语)。

表 2　各种汉语语料中把字句使用情况

种类 \ 统计项	语料字数出现率	把字句数	把字句千字出现率
汉译英(文学)	632000	1280	2. 02
骆驼祥子	148600	419	2. 82
林家铺子	12690	35	2. 75
汉译英(非文学)	352000	357	1. 01
白皮书(1)	20310	4	0. 19
科尔沁沙地	3350	3	0. 89
英译汉(文学)	765000	2696	3. 52
廊桥遗梦	63220	230	3. 63
老人与海	43800	336	7. 67
英译汉(非文学)	351000	728	2. 07
共产党宣言	19505	42	2. 15
第三帝国的灭亡	48100	98	2. 03

将表 2 的汉译英部分及小说语料中把字句出现频率同表 1 的小说部分相比,可以看出二者比较接近,也就是说,汉语原创文学语料中,平均每千字中出现的把字句不少于 2 句。我们在表 2 列出了四类汉语语料总的考察情况,以及各类的两个抽样数据。分析表明,把字句的使用和分布有如下主要特点:

1)汉语原创作品中的把字句少于翻译作品中的(在文学语料中是 2. 02

比 3.52，在非文学语料中是 1.01 比 2.07）；

2）同质语言中，非文学作品中的把字句少于文学作品中的（在汉语原创语料中是 1.01 比 2.02，在汉语翻译语料中是 2.07 比 3.52）；

3）在上述两种比较中，后者分别是前者的 1.75 至 2 倍；其中每千字中把字句出现频率最高者为英译汉文学作品《老人与海》：7.67 句/千字，最低者为汉译英非文学作品《白皮书》（中国的少数民族）：0.19 句/千字，两者相差近 40 倍。

这些考察数据证明，翻译的汉语作品比原创的汉语作品使用更多的把字句；同时也表明，文学类作品比非文学类作品使用更多的把字句，而且差别相当大。这两点发现进一步证实把字句适用于表达复杂和细微的意思，反过来，表达复杂或细微的意思时，把字句比较胜任，因而使用渐多，特别是翻译较复杂的外文语句时。例如以下一些实例：

1）If the artist attempts to change his or her style of writing or dancing or singing, etc., the audience may turn away and look to confer fleeting fickle fame on another and then, in time, on another, and so on and so on.

如果这位艺术家企图改变笔调、舞步、唱腔的话，听众观众就会舍他而去，把那飘忽不定的称誉转移给别人随后又转移给另一人，这样不停地转来转去。

2）To make himself the one trusted friend, to whom should be confided all the fear, the remorse, the agony, the ineffectual repentance, the backward rush of sinful thoughts, expelled in vain!

他把自己装扮成那人的可信赖的朋友，让对方向他吐露一切恐惧、自责、烦恼、徒劳的懊悔、回潮的负罪感，而且丝毫不能苟且。

3）Some argue that even families whose incomes are as much as 18.5 percent of the poverty level sometimes go hungry, skimping on food to pay for such things as housing, medical care or clothing.

有人认为收入相当于贫困线标准 18.5%的家庭有时还挨饿，把买食品的钱省下来交纳房租、医疗费或买衣服。

4）In San Antonio, Texas, recently, a 13-years-old girl allegedly beat and then held down another girl...

据说最近在得克萨斯州的圣安东尼奥,一个 13 岁的女孩殴打另一女孩,然后把她按倒在地……

5) She amused herself with gathering handfuls of wild flowers, and flinging them, one by one, at her mother's bosom.

她采集了一把野花自己玩着,把野花一朵接一朵地掷到母亲胸口上。

上述句子若不用把字句就不容易表达。如例 4),“按倒她”可以说,“按倒她在地”或“按她倒在地”就不成句子;例 5)更是不能换成其他表述(若说“将野花……”,此时的“将”与“把”同义)。

三、把字宾语的有定、无定问题

由于“把”的出现,动词后的宾语挪到了前面,或者说将陈述对象前置,句式发生了很大变化,并对句子的构造产生影响(因并非所有把字句都是宾语前置后形成的),因此,把字句中介词把的宾语就引人注目,其中一个值得探讨的问题就是该宾语的有定、无定。我们从语料中观察到一些情况,与前人的论断有所不同,因此,在本节提出讨论。

王力(1944)、吕叔湘(1948)等均指出把字句中介词“把”的宾语具“有定”特点。吕叔湘(1948)说:“宾语代表无定的事物,不能用‘把’。”王还(1957,1985)等不赞成此说,曾举例证明其宾语也可以是“无定”的。邵敬敏(2001:234-235)认为有定、无定是句法范畴里的一对概念,与语义范畴里的确指、泛指是不同概念。“有定的形式必然为语义上的确指,而无定的形式却既可能是泛指,也可能是确指,甚至无所谓‘有定’‘无定’形式,在语义上也可分为确指和泛指。”他实际上是认为,有些把字的宾语在形式上看似无定,在语义上却是有所指的,因此王力、吕叔湘等的宾语有定说大体成立,或毋宁说其宾语应是确指的。这符合绝大多数把字句的情况。

但是仍然有些把字句中把字的宾语在形式上无定,在语义上似乎也是泛指的例子。邵敬敏提到只有疑问句里有这样的现象,如“你把哪本书拿走了?”我们从语料库考察看,这一现象也不仅限于疑问句。例如:

6)不知他把谁给骗了。

7)天知道这小子把哪个人得罪了。

8)把哪个提上来,把哪个撸下去,那还不是他一句话的事儿。

9)"把一支烟烧完,祥子还是想不出道理来"。(老舍:《骆驼祥子》)

再结合这类把字句的英译文观察一下。

10)大家都说,刘先生跟韩先生可以讲和了,把一个历史系的助教换一个外文系的教授。

Everyone's saying now Mr. Liu and Mr. Han can come to terms by trading a teaching assistant in the History Department for a professor in the Foreign Languages Department.

11)把一个什么样的世界带入21世纪,是国际社会深切关注的重大问题。

What kind of world will enter the 21st century is an important issue of great concern to the international community.

12)把一个国家、一个党的稳定建立在一两个人的威望上,是靠不住的,很容易出问题。

The stability of a country and a party cannot be based merely on the prestige of one or two persons. That tends to create problems.

13)钱会把人引进恶劣的社会中去,把高尚的理想撇开,而甘心走入地狱中去。[此处"人"近似泛指]

Money will lure people to the evils of society, cause them to forget their high ideals and willingly follow the path to hell.

14)她以自己的闪烁不定的光辉,使忧郁的人群欢快起来,就像是一只长着光彩夺目的羽毛的鸟儿跳来跳去,在幽暗的叶簇中时隐时现,把一棵树的枝枝叶叶全都照亮了。

She made the sombre crowd cheerful by her erratic and glistening ray, even as a bird of bright plumage illuminates a whole tree of dusky foliage by darting to and fro, half seen and half concealed amid the twilight of the clustering leaves.

15)尽管如此,那一阵惊异他还是几乎按捺不住——在帮那姑娘起身的两三秒钟内,她竟把个什么东西塞在他手里。

Nevertheless it had been very difficult not to betray a momentary surprise, for in the two or three seconds while he was helping her up the girl had slipped something into his hand.

16)她这样年轻,对生活还有期望,她不懂把个把烦人的人推下悬崖,根本不解决任何问题。

She was very young, he thought, she still expected something from life, she did not understand that to push an inconvenient person over a cliff solves nothing.

17)她无数次扯着嗓门大喊大叫,要把个什么人处死刑,其实这人的名字她听也没听过,他犯的罪行她也根本不相信。

Times beyond number, she had shouted at the top of her voice for the execution of people whose names she had never heard and in whose supposed crimes she had not the faintest belief.

由这些例句可见,把字句中把字的宾语所受限制可能没有前人断定的那么严格。

四、把字句的英译

讨论了把字句的一些特点和分布等情况后,我们来关注一下将汉语把字句翻译成英语(可参看陈宏薇,1998)的问题(有时我们会结合一些英译汉来反观汉译英)。

把字句通常有如下几种形式:

(甲)宾语为后面动词受事的把字句(广义的处置义)

把+宾语+动词+补语(地点、方位或趋向;如,把书包放下。把敌人吓跑了。)或+介词短语(表方位或描述;如,把改革放在头等重要的位置。我们都把他当作学习的榜样。)

把+宾语+副词+动词(如,把他狠狠地揍了一顿。她把眼睛一瞪。)

把+宾语+副词+动词+补语(如,他把双手高高地举过了头。)

(乙)宾语为后面动词施事的把字句(多含致使义)

把+宾语+动词+补语(如,把姐姐乐得跳了起来。)

(丙)其他类(如带双宾语等)把字句

根据以上不同形式的把字句,翻译成英语时,需采用不同的方法,主要有:

1)选择适当的英语使动动词,包括用 make / have / get 等相关搭配;

2)仿汉语形式:英语动词+宾语+补语,或动词+宾语+介词短语;

3)其他变通方式。

以下从语料库收集的例句分别予以说明。

1. *以适当英语使动动词翻译*

18)她把头扭了两扭,斜着眼睛,扑哧一笑。

She *shook* her head, looked askance at him and snorted.

19)如果中国在一九九七年,也就是中华人民共和国成立四十八年后还不把香港收回,任何一个中国领导人和政府都不能向中国人民交代,甚至也不能向世界人民交代。

If China failed to *recover* Hong Kong in 1997, when the People's Republic will have been established for 48 years, no Chinese leaders or government would be able to justify themselves for that failure before the Chinese people or before the people of the world.

20)他们把他想象成传达上天智慧、谴责和博爱的代言人。

They *fancied* him the mouth-piece of Heaven's messages of wisdom, and rebuke, and love.

21)美国把它的制度吹得那么好,可是总统竞选时一个说法,刚上任一个说法,中期选举一个说法,临近下一届大选时又是一个说法。

The United States *brags about* its political system. But politicians there say one thing during a presidential election, another after taking office, another at mid-term elections and still another with the approach of the next presidential election.

22)他悄悄地径直向门口走去,走时还把门给闩好了。

He straightway made his stealthy exit, *latching* the door behind him.

动词前以"一"为副词的把字句翻译成英语时通常只能用相应的动词表述,该副词意义不易保留:

23)很娇媚地把头一扭,她又吃吃地笑着。

She *tilted* her head coquettishly and giggled.

24)杜竹斋把舌头一伸,嘻嘻地笑了。

Tu-Chu-chaff *stuck out* his tongue, withdrew it, and grinned.

25)没有回答,桂长林把身体一摇,两只手叉在腰里,凶狠狠地看了屠维岳一眼。

Instead of answering, Kuei Chang-lin *shook* himself, put his hands on his hips, and glared at Tu Wei-yueh.

26)范博文忽然叹一口气,把脚一跺,走到四小姐跟前。

Fan Powers sighed and *stamped* his foot, then went up to Huei-fang.

27)冯眉卿恨恨地把两腿一伸,就在床上翻身滚开了尺多远,似乎刘玉英身上有刺。

Feng Mei-ching angrily *straightened* her legs and rolled over so, that she put a foot or so between Liu Yu-ying and herself, as if her friend were covered with prickles.

宾语为施事的把字句,通常去掉"把"字后基本意义不变(个别宾语为受事的如例28也如此;前有副词时可能例外),因此翻译成英语时多当作没有"把"字的普通句子处理:

28)轻蔑、狠毒、无缘无故的恶言秽行和歹意对善良和神圣的事物妄加嘲弄,这一切全都会唤醒起来,虽说把他吓得要命,却仍在诱惑着他。

Scorn, bitterness, unprovoked malignity, gratuitous desire of ill, ridicule of whatever wasgood and holy, all awoke to tempt, even while they *frightened* him.

29)正在这节骨眼上,偏偏把他给累病了。

It was right at the moment we needed him most that he *fell ill with hard work*.

30)整理这些报纸,把我整整忙乎了一天。

I *was busy* all day rearranging the newspapers.

31)这一趟差把可我累坏了。

The trip tired me out too much.

32)雪沉,不甚好扫,一时又找不到大的竹帚,他把腰弯得很低,用力去刮揸。

It was heavy and not easy to sweep, for he didn't know where the large bamboo broom was kept and so had to *bend* very low and sweep hard.

33)日本制造商又看到机会了,纷纷把上面所说的廉价产品,渗透进东南亚和其他亚洲市场。

Sensing the opportunities, the Japanese manufacturers decided to penetrate these South-east Asian and other Asian markets with their cheap range of products as highlighted in the previous paragraph.

34)大自然从沉睡中醒来,精神抖擞地把一片奇景展现在这惊奇的孩子的眼底。

The marvel of Nature shaking off sleep and going to work *unfolded* itself to the musing boy.

用 make / have / get 等+适当的词或短语翻译:

35)我们把恐怖分子打得抱头鼠窜。

We *have* the terrorists *on the run*.

36)都穿上大褂,谁短撅撅的进来把谁踢出去。

You're all to wear long gowns, anyone who shows up in a short jacket *gets kicked out*.

2. 仿汉语形式翻译:英语动词+宾语+补语 / 介词短语

37)其次,在天气不佳的星期日他又习惯于以这家的朋友身份跟他们在一起谈天、读书、看看窗外的景色,把一天打发过去。

Secondly, because, on unfavourable Sundays, he was accustomed to be with them as the family friend, talking, reading, looking out of window, and generally *getting through* the day.

38)十一届三中全会以来,全党把工作重点转移到社会主义现代化建设上来,在坚持四项基本原则的基础上,集中力量发展社会生产力。

Since the Third Plenary Session of the Eleventh Central Committee, the Party*has shifted* the focus of all its work *to* the drive for socialist modernization and, while adhering to the Four Cardinal Principles, has concentrated on developing the productive forces.

39）他估计可以趴着挤进去时，就把头先伸进去……

He judged he might squeeze through on his knees; so he *put* his head *through*…

40）和大家一齐坐下，大家把对刘四的不满意都撒到他身上来。

But as soon as he sat down the others *transferred* their resentment toward Fourth Master Liu *to* him.

41）甚至当他还是个年轻的孩子时，就能把表拆开又装上。

Even when he was still a young boy, he could *take* a watch *apart* and *put* it *together* again.

42）希望大家放开手脚，把经济搞上去，把生产力搞上去。

I hope that you will boldly *push* the economy *ahead* and *expand* the productive forces.

（句中两处把……搞上去，一处仿汉语形式，另一处以使动动词译之）

43）他把一支香烟放在嘴里，一半烟丝就掉在舌上。

He *put* a cigarette *in* his mouth. Half the tobacco promptly fell out on to his tongue.

44）一个小孩不愿上床睡觉，会故意把杯中牛奶泼到地毯上，于是造成忙乱引起斥责，要他马上睡觉的事便给忘了。

A young child who is reluctant to go to bed deliberately *spills* milk from a cup *on to* the carpet so that in the ensuing fuss and scolding the immediacy of his bedtime will be forgotten.

45）国际上好多国家把对华政策放在我是不是病倒了或者死去了上面。

Many countries *base* their China policies *on* the prospect of my illness or death.

46）他把自己形容成一个软心肠的人。

He *describes* himself *as* an old softie.

47）经济调研把这一点归因于劳动力市场日益灵活。

Economic research *puts* this *down to* increased flexibility in the labour market.

48）在这种时候，他能沉睡一天，把苦恼交给了梦。

At such times, he'd stay in bed for a whole day, trying to *drown* his unhappiness *in* dreams.

49）上帝把这孩子交给了我来抚养。

God *gave* her *into* my keeping.

50）二强子在去年夏天把女儿小福子——十九岁——卖给了一个军人卖了二百块钱。

The summer before, he had *sold* his nineteen-year-old daughter Joy *to* an army officer *for* two hundred silver dollars.

3. 用其他变通方式翻译

51）他们喜欢把自己打扮成一无所有的愣头小子。

They *prefer an image of* penniless tough guys.

52）中国人把"谦虚"引以为荣，美国人因"率直"而自豪。

The Chinese *take pride in* "modesty" and the Americans in "straightforwardness".

53）他愿意快快把这一天过去，不再受这个罪。

So he wished the day would *end* quickly to end his discomfort.

54）十月革命的胜利也是列宁把马克思主义的原理同俄国革命的实践相结合的结果。

Similarly, the victory of the October Revolution was a product of Lenin's *integration of* the principles of Marxism *with* Russian revolutionary practice.

55）但是把开展批评同"双百"方针对立起来，却是一种严重的误解或曲解。

To *place* criticism *in contradiction to* that policy is a gross misunderstanding or distortion.

56）要把地方上和社会上的钱，转一部分用于基础建设。

Part of the funds collected by the local authorities and idle capital collected from society at large should *be put into* infrastructure projects.

将零主语把字句（多为祈使句）翻译成英语时，或以祈使句对应，或补出语义中的主语：

57）把鞭子递给我。

Hand me that switch.

58）把上衣的纽扣解开！

Unbutton your jacket!

59）把孩子们集中起来，也许今晚就举行入伙仪式。

We'll *get* the boys *together* and have the initiation to-night, maybe.

五、小结

把字句最主要的功能或语法意义是“处置”（包括“致使”和“描述”）。该句式的特点和作用有三：一是将宾语提至动词前，解决该宾语无法后置的问题；二是突出宾语，同时也突出动作及其后果；三是便于语句的衔接，并将（把字后面的）宾语与动词所涉及的其他成分相区隔。本文经语料考察，发现翻译的汉语作品比原创的汉语作品使用更多的把字句，文学类作品比非文学类作品使用更多的把字句；这一发现进一步证明把字句适用于表达复杂和细微的意思。将相应的把字句译成英语时，多根据实际情况，选择适当方法应对：1）相应的英语使动动词，包括用 make/have/get +动词或形容词；2）英语动词+宾语+补语，或动词+宾语+介词短语；3）其他变通方法。

（本文原载《外语与外语教学》2003 年第 6 期）

参考文献

陈宏薇主编：《汉英翻译基础》，上海外语教育出版社 1998 年版。

丁声树等：《现代汉语语法讲话》，商务印书馆 1980 年版。

范晓：《汉语的句子类型》，书海出版社 1998 年版。

吕叔湘：《把字用法的研究》，载吕叔湘：《汉语语法论文集》，商务印书馆 1984 年版。

邵敬敏:《汉语语法的立体研究》,商务印书馆 2001 年版。

王克非:《语言与翻译研究并重的双语平行语料库》,载屠国元主编:《外语/翻译/文化》第三辑,湖南科技出版社 2003 年版。

王还:《"把"字句与"被"字句》,新知识出版社 1957 年版。

王还:《"把"字句中"把"的宾语》,《中国语文》1985 年第 1 期。

王力:《中国现代语法》,商务印书馆 1943 年版。

王力:《中国语法理论》,商务印书馆 1944 年版。

王力:《汉语史稿》(中册),科学出版社 1958 年版。

张伯江:《论"把"字句的语义句式》,《语言研究》2000 年第 1 期。

张旺熹:《把字结构的语义及其语用分析》,《语言教学研究》1991 年第 1 期。

朱德熙:《语法讲义》,商务印书馆 1980 年版。

祝敏彻:《论初期处置式》,载《语言学论丛》(北京大学编)第一辑,新知识出版社 1957 年版。

语法研究的方法论新探

——《语料库语言学的多因分析》述介

一

《语料库语言学的多因分析》是收录在卡迪夫(Cardiff)大学 Robin Fawcett 教授主编的一套语言学系列丛书中的一本。作者为南丹麦大学副教授,此书是他三年前在德国汉堡大学语言科学学院所做博士学位论文的基础上修订而成。

此书具体研究的语言现象是"小词置位"(particle placement)问题,即详尽分析英语及物性短语动词的词序变化(小词移动),书的副标题也表明了这一点。概括地说,此书有三大特点:一是在材料上依据 BNC(英国国家语料库)语料,二是在理论上借助认知—功能语言学和心理语言学,三是在方法论上实行多因素综合分析。

全书论述部分有九章,分别是:第一章导论,介绍研究范围、理论设想和全书的研究框架;第二章作文献综述,主要是介绍语音、句法、语义、话语等变量及其研究;第三章描述此书的研究目标;第四章就此研究所涉及的关键概念和假说加以讨论;第五章是关键的数据问题,即本书所涉语料库数据的来源及其处理;第六章对语料库研究结果进行详细的分析和讨论;第七章作进一步的语言学讨论,从原型角度、变化性与语法、句法变化等方面作深入的探讨;第八章专题论述结构的激活;第九章是此项研究的总括和研究展望。最后的附录部分也有不少重要信息,特别是作者收集整理的"英语及物性短语动词"一览表。此外,书末还附有全书征引作者索引和主题索引。以下我们对此书的要点作一简要述介。

二

J.R.Firth 曾指出,词语的结伴/共现关系是词语的重要表现形式;“变异句”(allo-sentences)也含有这种词语共现关系,是语言学界一直感兴趣的一个语言现象。“变异句”即“语义相似而形式和语用相异的句对”,也称“语法变异”“句法变异”“构造变异”等。这类变异有多种(如主题化、左向移位、与格换位、属格等)。此书集中研究英语多词动词(短语动词)的词序变化这一句法变异问题(p.1),即:

(1)a.Fred picked up the book.　　[结构 0]

b.Fred picked the book up.　　[结构 1]

显然,句对(1)之变异发生在动词短语中,该短语含有一个动词、一个无形态变化的词,即小词,以及一个直接宾语 NP。但是当直接宾语为代词(如 it)时,就只能出现 b,而不会出现 a(书中 a 为结构 0,即动词与小词不分离;b 为结构 1,动词与小词之间被直接宾语分开,动词在其前,小词在其后)。

再者,在与句对(1)相似的句对(2)中,(2)a 不能转换为(2)b:

(2)a.Fred went into the forest.

*b.Fred went the forest into.

此外,句对(1)的句末小词可强调(重读),句对(2)的句末小词不可;句对(1)的小词可倒装于句首,句对(2)的小词不可。

诸如此类的问题都很值得研究,不过,此书只讨论导致(1)类句对发生词序变化的支配因素,亦即小词移动或其置位问题。

作者在材料上依据 BNC 语料,是为了确保研究结果是基于说话者实际使用的语言,确保研究合乎客观性、信度、效度等科学研究标准。他强调语言解释应充分,这就需要综合考察多种独立的因素,而不是只根据单一因素;要依据(概率上)足够的语料,而不是以往以直觉推断句子是否合语法或是否可接受。他在理论上采用认知—功能语言学视角，因为他认为语言是与人的其他认知机能密切相关的一个认知机能，同时，认为语言并非只受认知过程影响，语言的结构在很大程度上也受到语言交往过程中的相互作用等因素的影响。

在分析上，他主要采用心理语言学角度研究小词置位问题，从即时言语产生(online speech production)来考察。其分析模式是：

1)词序的选择通常依赖与不同结构选项相关的处理努力；

2)互动激活模式(interactive activition model)；

3)以功能为导向的竞争模式(competition model)。

三

小词置位的语言学研究已有一百多年历史。现有的研究成果显示，影响小词置位的变量(pp.9-21)有多种：

(a)语音变量：如果直接宾语重读，则很有可能使用结构0。没有首音重读的动词倾向于结构1。也就是说，TPV(及物短语动词)在(1)中不如在(2)中更能被接受：

(3)Fred divided up the cake.

(4)Fred divided the cake up.

(b)形态句法变量：TPV(及物短语动词)直接宾语的NP类型：(1)若是代名词(pronominal)，则代名词必须在动词和小词之间；(2)若是半代名词性名词，如matters或things之类，也倾向于在结构1中使用，如They talked matters over.(3)直接宾语的限定词在结构选择上也起一定作用。具体说来，非限定性限定语倾向于在结构0中出现，而限定性限定语倾向于在结构1中出现；(4)直接宾语的长度问题，长宾语适合于结构0，但长度是多少不易把握，因此有人提出与小词置放相关的是直接宾语的复杂程度。或者说，长度与复杂性可能高度相关。

(c)语义变量：动词短语的习语意义是第一语义变量。如果是习语意义，则采用结构0，如果是字面意义，则会导致结构1的产生。当然，一个动词短语不可能划分为完全习语性的或完全字面性的。

另一个语义变量是短语的习惯意义。如果动词短语表达的是习惯意义，则可能优先考虑结构 0。还有小词的语义修饰问题。有些小词(特别是 up)可以带 all,all the way,completely 这类完成标记词(perfective markers),或者体标记词 right。有这样的标记存在时,小词就跟在宾语后面。如:

(5)I will clean all/right up the room.

(6)I will clean the room all/right up.

另外,对一个直接宾语所指的认知熟悉程度也影响小词的置放(positioning),即越是熟悉就越倾向于结构 1,反之则倾向于结构 0。

(d)话语—功能变量:语段的语境可以影响结构的选择。核心问题之一是直接宾语的新闻价值。其新闻价值新(指前面未提及),则多使用结构 0,旧则多使用结构 1。距上次提及直接宾语的远近(或早晚)和提及的次数也会影响结构的选择:距上次提及越近,或提及次数越多,则可能用结构 0,反之则可能用结构 1。

但作者以其认知—功能语言学观点从新审视语料,并综合考察种种变量后,提出了新的解释,在权重上也与上述相反,即依次为话语—功能变量、语义变量、句法变量和语音变量。他认为两个非常相似的结构并非单纯与转换相关;像 VPC(动词小词结构)的变化就可能是由于说话者认知处理的需要:对于带直接宾语的动词小词结构,结构 0 需要较大的处理努力,结构 1 只需要很小的处理努力。他提出的理论假设是"认知处理假说"(processing hypothesis)。其假说基于一些认知—心理学概念,如处理努力、注意力分配、概念的存储、检索和激活,以及语言表达式的结构复杂性等。

其认知处理假说可描述为:通过给语段(U)选择其中一个结构,说话者(S)在两方面满足这两个结构的处理要求:一方面是他产生出语段,另一方面是听话者(H)对语段的理解。

关于话语—功能变量,他的解释是:概念的可识别性、概念—激活(直接与间接)对概念识别和激活的分类,容易把话语功能变量和由可识别性与激活来决定的处理努力联系在一起,包括"直接宾语所指在前文提到"这一变量,"直接宾语所指在前文提到的次数","直接宾语所指上次提及距现在多远”,“直接宾语所指与话语前文间的连贯性”(如上下义关系)。

关于语义变量,由于英语表达通常把新的或重要的所指放在句末(成为尾焦),他认为尾焦与认知处理的关系是:

○焦点成分需要更多的处理努力。

○不论是强调直接宾语还是小词,都要把强调部分放在句末,以便听话者在接收了必要的信息后处理即将到来的信息。

○可以看出,结构 0 会将直接宾语的所指在长时记忆中以更强烈的方式激活,持续时间更长。

结构 1 是有因移动的结构(caused-motion construction)的次类型。从中可以看出,直接宾语的具体所指更适合在结构 1 中使用。因为具体的、可以想象的所指较抽象,不易想象的所指更易检索。

对于结构 0 而言,带有习语性的 TPV 的句子更依赖动词与小词的共现,二者在语义上相互依赖。这也与处理努力有关,我们可以这样解释:

对于习语性 VPC 而言,动词和小词紧密依赖,在实际话语中二者紧紧依靠,可以更经济的方式来处理,换言之,对于字面义短语动词而言,不期待在语义依赖基础上更倾向于某一结构,因为低程度的相互依赖不需要组成部分之间距离特别短,这也就允许两种语序都可行。

关于形态—句法变量,作者指出,与多个结构相关的形态—句法因素是:复合动词和直接宾语名词短语。

如复合动词:结构 0 使结构处理简捷,而结构 1 在发出时,说话者心里必须记住直接宾语后面要加上特定的小词,而听话者需要等待更长的时间才能对即将到来的表达式进行正确的语法分析。

在英语里,一个概念的可识别地位涉及有定性、代词化和指称句法关系(即激活程度)等问题,还与声音、词序和句韵有关。首先是直接宾语的类型、人称代词的所指、实义名词短语的所指等,前者倾向于在结构 1 中使用,后者倾向于结构 0,因为代词的所指要求前文提及,高度突出。同理,直接宾语的限定语,即限制性直接宾语的所指为标记话题,说话者认定受话者对此非常熟悉;而非限定性直接宾语的所指通常都是说话者首次引入的话题,受话者对此并不熟悉,并不是说话者可随时调用的内容。直接宾语的长度和复杂程度同样可从处理努力上解释。

关于语音变量,他认为与动词短语的重读模式相关。英语句子中的信息结构的功能分析时应区分已知信息和新信息。已知信息不重读,新信息通常重读以表示“新”或“重要”。说话者引导受话者注意相关的所指,因此,便增加了与该所指相关的处理负担。对语言表达式的重读与尾焦原则相关联。

书中对其他变量也作了很多有意思的分析。这些内容有助于我们了解整个研究的实质。在第六章里,作者进一步分析各种考察结果。他证明了包括在认知处理假说中的所有变量都确实与小词移动有关,而未包括于其中的变量则与其无关。这也表明,先前的分析未能注意到各变量之间的相互关系,以及各变量同语域的互动性。他进而发现,各变量与结构的选择呈高度相关性。他还证明了区别性分析可以确定哪些变量对于说话者决定选择某一结构最为重要。语料数据有力地支持了作者提出的认知处理假说。第七章和第八章则主要讨论此项研究在方法论上的更为广泛的意义或应用价值。作者认为此书的研究发现与一般语言学中收集各种数据的其他研究方法(如社会语言学分析也要使用各种规则,还有近些年来的变异研究,当代基于语料库的研究等)是相关联的。他还将此书的研究发现与互动激活模式结合起来讨论,详细描述了结构选择背后的激活过程,并以图形模式显示。

四

仅就研究小词置位来说,此书也许显得比较窄小,但却是“小题大做”的成功一例。全书也基本实现了作者的两个主要研究目标:语言学目标和方法论目标。从其语言学目标来说,作者对影响结构 0 和结构 1 的运用的各种变量作了穷尽性描述,通过检验和分析实际预测力验证了前人的一些假说,又因为考察了这种结构在具体运用中的复杂性(变量多达二十个),对说话者在特定交际情景中可能采用哪种结构能做出较为准确的预测。从方法论目标来说,作者展示了小词置位或更广意义上的句法变体应该如何研究,即不能仅从单一的因果视角来透视原本多因的问题。他将多因统计步骤同认知—功能研究方法相结合，给语言研究者许多有益的启示。例如，影响小词置位的各个变量性质不同，但高度相关；又如，与以往研究不同，作者认为功能变量十分重要，因为它会激发句法变量的值。

此书为研究者提供了新的语法研究方法论，是指作者对语法现象进行基于语料库的多因素的、概率性的研究，而不只是传统的根据可接受性和最小句对试验的研究。就此书所做小词移动的多因分析来看，采用这种语料库语言学方法，可以在前所未有的详尽水平上描述小词移动，并将所有可能支配其变化选择的限制条件都结合到一个假说（如认知处理假说）之中加以解释。

（本文原载《外语教学与研究》2004 年第 4 期）

新中国翻译学科发展历程

本文提出,新中国翻译学科的 70 年发展是一个从萌芽到逐渐成长,再到充分发展的过程:1)在萌芽期,翻译作为学科发展的条件尚不充分;2)成长期的标志是国外译论涌入、学科意识提升、学术机构创建、翻译教学系统化;3)在发展期,翻译学科在国家层面获得认可,国内的翻译研究迅速发展,逐渐形成两大取向,即接轨国际的研究和中国特色的研究。翻译研究的发展促进了中国翻译学科体系的建构。

一、绪言

翻译因不同民族、不同语言社群的交流之需而产生,也为多元文化的融会发挥桥梁作用。翻译既是文化沟通的过程,也是文明交流的产物。

千百年来,无论东方西方,都见证了翻译对于文化传播与沟通的重大作用。仅从圣经为代表的文化翻译,就可清晰地看到一条由希伯来文到希腊文(亚历山大城),后由希腊文到阿拉伯文(巴格达),再经阿拉伯文译入拉丁文(托莱多)以至欧洲各国语言的文化典籍传播路径。这就是翻译开辟的文化沟通路径。

在中国,西汉末年的佛教传入,使佛经翻译成为中国翻译史上最初的重要一环。后来又有传教士的译介,以及更大规模的近代西学译入,给古老中国文化带来生生不息的活力。诚如季羡林(2007:10)所说:"中华文化这一条长河,有水满的时候,也有水少的时候,但却从未枯竭。原因就是有新水注入。

注入的次数大大小小是颇多的。最大的有两次，一次是从印度来的水，一次是从西方来的水。而这两次的大注入依靠的都是翻译。中华文化之所以能长葆青春，万应灵药就是翻译”。

翻译的史实丰富，作用巨大，但人们对翻译的认识和论述却远远不够。如在勒弗维尔所编《翻译 · 历史 · 文化》(*Translation/History/Culture*:*A Sourcebook*, Lefevere,1992)和罗新璋所编《翻译论集》(1984)中，中外历史上关于翻译的认识和观点，在现代以前基本处于议多论少的前理论阶段。新中国成立之后，翻译学科才逐渐从无到有、由小到大，一步步走上健康发展的道路。纵观这一成长历程，可清晰地看到三个时期：一是萌芽期(1949—1978 年)，起点是新中国的成立，百废待兴，终点是“文革”的终结，百衰待振，翻译学科亦然；二是成长期(1978—1999 年)，起点是改革兴起，终点是世纪末，标志是中国翻译工作者协会和重要学刊《翻译通讯》(后更名《中国翻译》)等的创立等；三是发展期(2000 年至今)，起点是学科意识的提升，如二级学科点的设立和翻译学博士点的开办。下面逐一评析。

二、萌芽期

翻译是跨语言跨文化的活动，表现为双语转换技能，具有实践属性和艺术特性；而翻译学则是对翻译这一特殊语言现象的研究，具有学术属性和复杂特性。新中国早期，翻译主要被视为一种跨语言技能，服务于培养国家建设所需的翻译和外事人才，跻身于新中国文学文化建设的行列。这体现在培养了一大批以英语、俄语为主的外事和翻译干部，更重要的是大量译介了国外的经典文学作品和学术著作，并将中国的政治文献和中国古代、现当代文学作品翻译成英、俄、日等多种语言，介绍给世界。

但作为学科，此时尚未得到发展。早期有董秋斯、茅盾等对翻译的讨论，甚至呼吁将翻译视为一门科学，如 1951 年，董秋斯发表了题为《论翻译理论的建设》的论文；在 1954 年全国文学翻译工作会议上，茅盾做了题为《为发展文学翻译事业和提高翻译质量而奋斗》的长篇报告。但由于时代局限，这些学科建设的声音并未受到重视。国际上的情况相仿,理论建设基本上也是在这个时期起步,如著名翻译学者奈达(E.Nida)1964 年出版《翻译科学探索》,霍姆斯(J.Holmes)1972 年在哥本哈根召开的国际应用语言学大会上发表《翻译研究的名与实》,被视为翻译学科的创建宣言。也就是说,到 20 世纪中叶,国际上才开始对翻译研究的性质、范畴和学科目标等进行科学、深入的探讨。由于时代的局限,国际上的这些理论探讨未能及时引入,国内翻译界谈论最多的还是严复的"信、达、雅"三原则。如王佐良(1987)在《新时期的翻译观》中总结说:信、达、雅是很好的经验总结,说法精练之至,所以能持久地吸引人。此外,学界讨论较多的还有鲁迅的"丰姿"说、钱钟书的"化境"说、傅雷的"神似"说,等等。这些论说都非常有见地,如罗新璋(1984)所言,是"我国自成体系的翻译理论"。但从严格意义上说,这些还不是一个学科的真正构建。

学术期刊往往是学术发展的一面旗帜。从这点来看,此时期几乎没有成系列的翻译学刊。1950 年曾创办了《翻译通报》,多在翻译实务层面讨论问题,很少从学科层面论述翻译。而该刊断断续续,才办两年,就在 1952 年休刊,第二年又复刊,维持了一年,最终还是在 1954 年停刊了。这也说明在这个时期,翻译作为学术或学科发展的条件还很不充分。

三、成长期

翻译学科的真正成长是在中国全面改革开放之后,有如下几个标志:

1　国外译论涌入

1978 年的改革开放,不仅是政治经济层面的改革开放,也是全方位的包括学术研究的改革开放。与外部十年以上的隔绝之后,中国的自然科学和人文社会学科均如饥似渴地学习国际先进的理论、方法、技术和管理等。翻译学科也一样,以开放的心态拥抱世界。

引进、融汇和争鸣,是这个时期的几个特征。1983 年,中国对外翻译出版公司出版了《外国翻译理论评介文集》,成为国内最早的译介国外翻译理论的书籍。随之而来的是更多国外翻译理论的涌入,如奈达的《奈达论翻译》(谭载喜译介)、巴尔胡达罗夫的《语言与翻译》、卡特福德的《翻译的语言学理论》、穆南的《翻译理论问题》、斯坦纳的《通天塔:文学翻译理论研究》、纽马克的《翻译教程》等,纷纷译介到中国。一时间,国内译界十分活跃,有力地激发了学科建设的理论意识。如许钧(2018:5)所言:此时的"译论引介的全面性、多样性、系统性和批判性,引介方式由翻译和转述变为评述和阐释,引介重点逐渐由语言学翻译理论转为文化翻译理论和解构主义翻译理论,理论来源地也从英美扩及德国、法国和低地国家,并开始从宏观层次关注西方翻译理论发展的整体脉络"。

除了译介国外翻译理论,也有学者开始梳理中国自己的翻译论述,如1981年香港翻译学会刘靖之编出《翻译论集》,1984年罗新璋编出一本流传更广的《翻译论集》,此外还有一系列翻译研究论集等。这些理论书籍,特别是从国外引进的众多译论,令人耳目一新,当时的年轻学子无不争相选读。

2　学科意识提升

随着大批国外译论的引入,关于翻译学科认识的争论此起彼伏,间接促进了学科意识的提升。前辈学者也发表了许多新见。例如,许国璋(1983/1991)提出"阐译"说,认为学术著作的翻译,不仅立言,还要立解,要为自己的文化引进一种概念系统。王佐良(1989)认为翻译背后是两大片文化,因此翻译不只是语言的转换,更有文化的融入。许渊冲也发表了关于音美、意美、形美的翻译观。中青年学者除了前面提到的谭载喜和许钧,还有王克非(1994)的翻译文化史论,刘宓庆(1995)的翻译美学思想,等等。当时,翻译是科学还是艺术之争,以及翻译学的目标、性质、定位、途径和方法等,都引发了广泛的讨论。争论的焦点是翻译学的学科性质、翻译学的中国特色、如何引进和看待西方翻译理论等问题。大讨论的实际结果是学科意识的提升。

3　学术机构创建

翻译学科进入成长期后,1980年《翻译通讯》创刊,它不同于早年的《翻译通报》,是翻译的理论与实践并重的学术期刊。1982年中国翻译工作者协会建立,更加有力地推动了翻译学科队伍的建立。1987年5月在南京,许钧等青年学生在南京开办了青年翻译家论坛,继而在当年7月,全国第一次翻译理论研讨会在青岛召开,这是最具规模、最有影响的一次翻译理论研讨会,对翻译学科建设的贡献度极高。会上谭载喜等人开始提出建立“翻译学”。十多年后的2000年，翻译界学者再次聚首青岛，则更是将学科建设作为会议的主题。1996年，中国译协新增翻译理论与翻译教学委员会，显示出对翻译学科的高度重视。

4 翻译教学系统化

张培基（1983）编写的《英汉翻译教程》和吕瑞昌等（1983）编写的《汉英翻译教程》等，对翻译教学改革有很大促进，使教学更加系统化。后来接连出现包括柯平（1991）《英汉与汉英翻译教程》在内的一批新型翻译教程，添加了更多理论色彩。

这是一个百家引进、百花竞放的时代，充满了奋发向上的勃勃生机。翻译学科得到前所未有的发展。

四、发展期

进入21世纪以来，中国翻译学者学科意识更强，发展步伐更大。主要的标志是翻译学科在国家层面获得认可，学术活动广泛开展，翻译研究走向国际前沿。

1 学科建立

外国语言文学学科的硕士招生同全国其他学科一样始于改革开放初期的1981年，随后开始博士招生。第一批外语学科博士生导师为季羡林、陈嘉、许国璋、王佐良等八位。招收翻译研究博士生是在其后几年，如1985年许国璋在北外开始在语言学科下招收翻译理论博士生。2004年初，上海外国语大学获批“外国语言文学”一级学科博士授权点，自主设置“翻译学”二级学科硕士、博士授权点。但长期以来，翻译学被归入外国语言学及应用语言学二级学科之下，相当于三级学科，发展受到一定限制。在翻译研究大发展的带动和外语界专家学者的呼吁下，教育部门在2006年批准设立翻译专业硕士学位（MTI），翻译专业研究生大幅度扩招，并在2009年批准将翻译学列为二级学科。这是对翻译研究的认可，对翻译学发展起到了促进作用。翻译学学科建设跨入一个崭新阶段。

此后，翻译学在全球化的大气候下，应国家发展战略需求，配合“讲好中国故事”“中国文化走出去”“一带一路”倡议等重大部署，获得更大的发展。例如在成长期里，在标志性的国家社科基金项目上，语言学科组里，外语立项仅占20%左右，翻译立项则在外语立项中仅占20%。十多年后，外语及翻译方面立项逐渐增多，如2015年的语言学国家项目，外语占比达三分之一，其中翻译立项也增长至外语立项中的三分之一以上，且相当大一部分是中译外研究。国家级的科研和教学奖励中，翻译学也占了较大比重，这都是先前未有的新局面。

2　研究长进

除上述之外，翻译学的大发展在著述、译丛、讲座、会议等方面也充分体现出来。2001年，上海外语教育出版社率先开始引进并陆续出版“国外翻译研究丛书”40种。自2006年起，外语教学与研究出版社也引进并陆续出版了“外研社翻译研究文库”30余种。同年，朱志瑜、王克非主编了一套“当代西方翻译研究译丛”（共10种），由外研社出版。这些引进著作为翻译研究者提供了一手文献，开阔了学术视野，为我国翻译学发展注入了强劲的推动力。翻译学术队伍逐渐扩大，学术产出迅速增长，在数量和质量上与前期相比都有显著的提高。国内的翻译研究逐渐形成两大取向，即接轨国际的研究和中国特色的研究。

接轨国际的研究，就是紧盯国际研究前沿，奋起直追。这方面起步早、进步大的是双语语料库的研制与应用研究，翻译文化史和中外翻译交流研究，双向翻译能力测评研究，利用键盘记录、眼动仪、ERP/EEG/fMRI等现代仪器来观测翻译过程的研究，口译及其教学的研究，等等，都产生了令国际学界为之侧目的研究成果，在国际学术期刊以及国际出版机构里出现更多中国翻译学者的身影。一些研究的层次和质量与国际水平不相上下，局部甚至有所超越。

特色研究指的是与中国相关的、具有中国独特视角或特有资源的翻译研究。进入发展期以来，中国特色的翻译研究，大多是对中国经典文学英译、外译的研究，以及这些翻译在世界上的传播、接受和影响。近些年，相关研究又扩展到中国特色话语包括外交话语、政治话语的建构和外译，以及其中展现的中国国家形象研究。国家社科基金还特别开设了中华学术外译项目。

3 译论出新

新中国70年来的大发展,特别是面向国际的拓展,成就了翻译学科,在发展期里尤为明显。除了前述翻译理论探讨,我国学者逐渐推出新的研究成果和理论探索。例如大型历时复合语料库构建及相关语言、翻译研究,黄忠廉提出的变译论,胡庚申提出的生态翻译观,周领顺的译者行为批评,以及王克非在多次会议上阐述的翻译路径研究。这些新论借鉴国外的相关理论,结合本国国情,探索中国译学话语体系,在一定程度上促进了中国翻译学科的构建与完善。

五、结语

新中国翻译学科的70年发展经历,是学科从萌芽到逐渐成长和发展的过程,也将迎来翻译学科繁荣的新时期。我们预期在新的繁荣发展阶段,中国的翻译新论逐渐为国际所认可和接受,中国的翻译资源逐渐为国际学者所发掘和进行比较,中国学者在国际会议、国际组织和国际学术期刊里更加活跃,担负起更重要的学术职责。同时也可促进中国的翻译研究进一步受到世界关注,让世界更好地认识和理解中国语言、文化与社会。

(本文原载《外语教学与研究》2019年第6期)

参考文献

E.Gutt,*Translation and Relevance:Cognition and Context*,Oxford:Basil Blackwell,1991.

J.Holmes,"The Name and Nature of Translation Studies",L.Venuti(ed.),*The Translation Studies Reader*,London:Routledge,2000,pp.172-185.

A.Lefevere,*Translation/History/Culture,A Sourcebook*.London:Routledge,1992.

E.Nida,*Toward a Science of Translating*,Leiden:E.J.Brill,1964.

G.Toury,*Descriptive Translation Studies and Beyond*,Amsterdam:John Benjamins,1995.

董秋斯:《论翻译理论的建设》,《翻译通报》1951 年第 4 期。

季羡林:《季羡林谈翻译》,当代中国出版社 2007 年版。

柯平编:《英汉与汉英翻译教程》,北京大学出版社 1991 年版。

刘靖之编:《翻译论集》,生活・读书・新知三联书店 1981 年版。

刘宓庆:《翻译美学导论》,书林出版社 1995 年版。

罗新璋编:《翻译论集》,商务印书馆 1984 年版。

吕瑞昌、喻云根、张复星、李嘉祜、张燮泉编:《汉英翻译教程》,陕西人民出版社 1983 年版。

谭载喜编译:《奈达论翻译》,中国对外翻译出版公司 1984 年版。

王克非:《论翻译文化史研究》,《外语教学与研究》1994 年第 4 期。

王克非:《关于翻译本质的认识》,《外语与外语教学》1997 年第 4 期。

王佐良:《新时期的翻译观——一次专题翻译讨论会上的发言》,《中国翻译》1987 年第 5 期。

王佐良:《翻译:思考与试笔》,外语教学与研究出版社 1989 年版。

许国璋:《许国璋论语言》,外语教学与研究出版社 1991 年版。

许钧:《改革开放以来中国翻译研究的发展之路》,《中国翻译》2018 年第 6 期。

张培基:《英汉翻译教程》,上海外语教育出版社 1983 年版。

中国对外翻译出版公司编:《外国翻译理论评介文集》,中国对外翻译出版公司 1983 年版。

翻译中的隐和显[①]

近年翻译研究开始探讨翻译之共性，翻译中的隐和显可能涉及共性。本文以英汉互译实例分析翻译中显化和隐化现象的发生，认为由语言、译者、社会文化等多种因素造成，并着重讨论了语言因素和译者因素。分析发现隐、显现象的发生和隐、显程度可能与语言的形式化程度和翻译方向相关。

一、翻译共性问题

译文是否忠实于原文，这可以说是检验翻译优劣的永恒的标准，也是翻译研究、翻译评论的一个主要话题。但语料库特别是双语语料库的出现，引发出人们对翻译研究的新的思考。例如，近十多年里国外学者致力探讨的翻译之共性问题，以及与之相关的译文语言特点问题。这是翻译研究中的一个新视角。语料库的发展为这一类翻译研究提供了更充分的资源和手段。

翻译的共性，即译文中呈现的有别于原文的一些典型的、跨语言的、有一定普遍性的特征。近年来涉及语料库与翻译的研究报告，有不少是围绕这一课题展开的，如以下值得注意的文献：

1) Baker(1993，1998)通过对“英语翻译语料库”(TEC)的考察，提出译文语言呈简化(simplification)特点；

① 系国家社科基金项目“基于大型双语对应语料库的翻译研究与翻译教学平台”(项目编号：05BYY013)成果。

2）Laviosa（1997，1998）考察译文与母语在词汇使用上的不同，发现译文比母语使用更多的高频词；这似乎可佐证 Baker 的观点，因高频词数量少，使用的多意味着词汇简化；

3）Øverås（1998）通过对英语和挪威语互译的考察，证明译文语言同母语相比，有显化（explicitation）倾向；

4）王克非（2003）基于对汉英/英汉对应语料库的考察，发现译本扩增现象，这与 Øverås（1998）的考察结果类似；

5）Kenny（2001）基于德语/英语文学素材平行语料库的考察，发现创造性新词翻译中呈现标准化/规范化（normalization）趋势；

6）Kenny（1998）通过对原文、译文的语义韵分析，发现同母语相比，译文语言有“净化”（sanitisation）现象；

7）但是译文也许不仅仅有“简化”、“显化”和“净化”等现象，我们认为，（a）翻译常常遇到较曲折的表达，从而可能更多地使用母语中较复杂的结构或句式；通过语料库考察某些结构的分布，我们发现汉语译文比汉语原文使用更多的“把字句”，尤其是文学译本中；（b）翻译过程中会不同程度地发生对原文的模仿，从而使译文变得复杂化、冗长化（柯飞 2003）；

8）陈瑞清（2004）从自建“大众科学英汉平行语料库”和台湾中研院平衡语料库原创汉语文本对部分汉语关联连词的使用情况作比较，发现汉译本有从意合转形合的潜在显化趋势；

9）秦洪武、柯飞（2004）通过个案考察“翻译语”（translationese），亦即既非原文又不完全是母语的、介乎原文和译文之间的“语际语”，并注意到非文学译本比文学译本在结构上更趋向于借鉴原文；

10）另外，Xiao & McEnery（2002）则通过深入的研究，发现在“体”标记的使用上，汉语译文比汉语原文多出约一倍。

11）其他还有 Ebeling（1998）比较英语和挪威语在存现句使用上的特点，Maia（1998）以双语对应语料库观察英语和葡萄牙语在人称主语使用频率上的差异等（参看王克非 2004：182-184）。

对以上涉及翻译共性问题的探讨，无论在国外或国内，还只是初步的，有待深入的，但却展现出广阔的研究前景，有助于我们加深对翻译和翻译过程的认识。例如下面要讨论的翻译的显化和隐化现象。

二、翻译中的显化现象

显化(explicitness / explicitation),又译外显化、明晰化、明朗化、明示等,指的是"目标文本以更明显的形式表述源文本的信息,是译者在翻译过程中增添解释性短语或添加连接词等来帮助译本的逻辑性和易解性"(Shuttleworth & Cowie 1997:55)。Blum-Kulka 最早对此进行系统的研究,她认为"译者对于原文进行解译的过程可能导致译语文本比原语文本冗长";这一冗长现象"可能是由于译语中提高了衔接上的外显程度造成的"(Blum-Kulka 1986:19)。

这一假说的提出,在西方翻译界引起研究兴趣。为检验显化假说,Øverås(1998)专门做了英语/挪威语双语语料库调查。她的调查涉及 40 个小说片段中的前 50 个句子,其中 20 本是挪威语作品及其英语译本,另 20 本是英语作品及其挪威语译本。她主要研究该假说所涉及的衔接外显程度是否有提高。她同时从英译挪、挪译英两个方向考察,并排除语言系统内因语法规则引发的显化转移,同时还细致地兼顾到与之相反的隐化现象。

她的发现是,英译挪文本中共有 347 处显化例证,平均每个文本 17.3 处;挪译英文本中有 248 处显化例证,平均每个文本 12.4 处。显见后者少于前者。这些显化更多的是体现在词汇上。如英译挪文本中的 347 处显化,其中 112 处体现在语法上,而词汇方面则有 235 处,占 2/3 强;挪译英文本中的有 82 处是语法上的,词汇上的显化有 166 处,也占 2/3。区别只是显化在英译挪文本中比在相反方向的挪译英文本中更为显著。

这一现象是否为翻译的普遍现象,还需多种语言的进一步论证。贺显斌(2003)就英译汉过程中的显化(明晰化)现象作了一项实证研究。他选取欧·亨利的短篇小说 *The Last Leaf* 及其汉译本进行显化现象的比较。他考察的结果是:英文小说全篇 134 句,译成汉语后明晰化程度提高的有 79 句,占 58.96%,也就是说,佐证了 Øverås(1998),认为在英译汉过程中有显化现象发生。不过,贺的考察还不够充分,其一是仅做了个案考察,篇幅也较小,其二是未考虑译者等因素。尽管如此,英汉语言之间的互译多少存在显化现象这一点应是可以明确的。

三、翻译中的显和隐

翻译中的显化现象是我们过去未曾注意的问题,其实也存在与之相反的隐化(implicitness)现象。英语和汉语分属不同语系,形式化程度相差很大,因此在不同的翻译方向上,显化或隐化的表现就不一样。我们不妨举例分析。

从英译汉来看,贺显斌(2003)证明了有较高程度的显化,主要是通过使用增词、改用具体词、转换人称、转换辞格等手段。但是鉴于汉语在连接词等衔接手段和指称形式上都不同于英语等印欧语言,所以应该还有一定的隐化现象发生。照顾到汉语表达习惯而做相应隐化处理的翻译通常比不做隐化的仿译(imitation)更为地道。

下面的两例英译汉(本文例句除特别注明外均取自北外通用汉英对应语料库),反映出汉语译者由于受原文影响而产生的仿译,并使译文扩增:

1)It was one of the few gestures of sentiment he was ever to make.

那是他在感情方面所作出的很少的几次表示中的一个例子。

此译若采取隐化策略,减少重复,避免长定语,则可译得更符合汉语的表达习惯:

他很少表露感情,这是难得的一次。

2)Can you tell me where is your cereal section?

您能告诉我你们的粮食科在哪里吗?

此译若采取隐化策略,减少不必要的人称代词等,则可译为地道的汉语:

请问粮食科在哪儿?

关于这一点,我们通过回译可以看得更清楚。王克非(2003)曾举贾平凹一篇散文(节选)的英译文及该英译“回译”成中文的例子。该例显示,因语言结构的需要,译文经显化而扩增,回译成中文时,篇幅上已比贾平凹原文多出

90字，增幅达57%。试分析该片段前头两句：

3）a 伯父家盖房，想以它垒山墙，但苦于它极不规则，没棱角儿，也没平面儿；（28字）

3）b *When* Uncle's family was building a house, *we* thought of using it to pile up *a side of* the house wall. *This proved to be impossible*, however, *since* the rock was of an extremely irregular *shape*, possessing *neither* sharp right angles *nor* any smooth, flat surfaces.

3）c 伯父家盖房子时，我们曾想到用它垒一面屋墙，但最后还是没能用上，因为这块岩石外形太不规则，既没有尖利的直角，又没有光滑的平面。（56字）

3）b 英译文的斜体部分是因英文表达的需要比较自然地"显化"而添加上去的词语，如连词when、since、neither...nor、主语we等，而且原文隐含的"未能用上该石头"之意也显化出来了：This proved to be impossible。3）c 则顺着英（译）文译成中文，即3）b中显化的斜体部分顺译/仿译为3）c下划线部分；再对照3）a原文，则可以看出，若回译的3）c隐化处理3）b斜体部分，便能基本回到地道的汉语原文。

又如向光（见"翻译工作坊"：http://sts.nthu.edu.tw/transws）批评林宗宪所译《毛泽东》（台北：左岸出版，2001）。原著为美国著名汉学家史景迁（J. Spence）1999年出版的*Mao Zedong*（New York：Viking Penguin）。向光批评林译为了"省事"，对西文著作中引用的中文未查找原文，自译引文，结果与毛泽东原文相差甚远。

请看史景迁书中引用的毛泽东《民众的大联合》中一段文字的原文：

4）a 洞庭闽水，更起高潮。天地为之昭苏，奸邪为之辟易。咳！我们知道了！我们觉醒了！天下者我们的天下。国家者我们的国家。社会者我们的社会。我们不说，谁说？我们不干，谁干？刻不容缓的民众大联合，我们应该积极进行！（收入《毛泽东早期文稿》，湖南出版社1990年版，第390页）

4）b 英译文（史）：

From Lake Dongting to the Min River, the tide rides ever higher. Heaven and earth are aroused by it, the wicked are put to flight by it. Ha! We know it! We are awakeded! The world is ours, the state is ours, society is ours. *If* we do not speak, who will speak? *If* we do not act, who will act? We must act energetically to carry out the great union of the popular masses, which will not brook a moment's delay!

4)c 中译文(林):

从洞庭湖到明湖,浪潮更汹涌。天地因而悲愤,邪恶者因而声势高涨。啊!我们知道了!我们惊醒了!世界是我们的,国家是我们的,社会是我们的。假如我们不说话,谁能为我们说话?假如我们不行动,谁能为我们行动?我们必须有活力地行动以实现广大群众大联合的理想,而那是刻不容缓的事!(林宗宪译,87—88页)

史景迁不愧为精通英、汉语和中国现代史的专家,其英译文颇显功夫,读来铿锵有力,与毛泽东原文不相伯仲。而林译4)c不仅多有错误(如首尾两句楷体部分),而且"使毛泽东原来力道十足的语言风味尽失"。如其中斜体部分,特别是两个假设条件句,因为有了"假如……"而力道顿失,韵味全无(试比较原文的隐含假设条件句)。

这又令人想到2005年4月,台湾地区的国民党主席连战在北京大学演讲时,以汉语翻译引用美国前总统罗纳德·里根的一段话:"(有些事情)如果我们不去做,谁去做?如果我们现在不做,什么时候做?"

这句引语带有明显的翻译腔,即对原文的仿译。若采用隐化策略加以改造的话,其译文应是类似上面毛泽东的那段话:"我们不做,谁做?现在不做,什么时候做?"显化出来的"如果"是没有必要的。

再看汉译英的例证。

5)"靠山吃山,靠水吃水,我老汉靠沙子,当然要吃沙!"

"*If* you live on a mountain, you live off the mountain; *if* you live by the water, you live off the water. I live on the sand, *and* I'll live off the sand."

6)"没有招待所有店,没店有生产队,有老乡窑洞。"

"*If* there's no guesthouse there'll be an inn; *if* there's no inn there'll be the cave home of a farmer in the production brigade."

7)国家这么大,这么穷,不努力发展生产,日子怎么过?

In a country *as* big and *as* poor *as ours*, *if* we don't try to increase production, how can we survive?

例5)—例7)是汉译英,因英文表达的需要,汉语原文的隐性条件句译成英语时都加上了if,成为显性条件句。如果按此显性英语条件句回译成汉语(或将类似的英文语句译成汉语),通常会仿译成为汉语的显性条件句,并增添其他连词和人称代词(如仿译英文斜体部分)。若知道做隐化处理,才有可能回到地道的汉语原文。

如下面的例句:

8)a With my present level(of French),I can not read French newspaper easily.

8)b 以我现在的(法语)水平,我还不能轻松地读法文报纸。

8)c 我的法语,看报很吃力。

9)a If you take this medicine,your illness will surely be cured.

9)b 你要是服用这个药,你的病肯定能治好。

9)c 这药吃了准好。

10)a You needn't care about the affairs in the home.

10)b 你不必担心家里的事。

10)c 家里的事,不用你管。

对于8)a,8)b是仿译,8)c做隐化处理,以汉语的主题句译之。对于9)a,9)b是仿译,9)c做隐化处理,以汉语隐性条件句译之,并省去人称代词。对于10)a,10)b是仿译,10)c以汉语的宾语前置主题句译之。由此可见,英译汉时做一定的隐化处理,译文会更地道,也比较简洁。仿译则将外语的表达法引入汉语,对于汉语来说,已经在形式上显化了,即本可以隐化表达的意思外在地显示出来了。这一类情况在英译汉中表现得非常明显和频繁。

除了上述有代表性的例句外,我们对双语对应语料库中80多万汉字的汉译英语料(汉语为原文)和近80万汉字的英译汉语料(汉语为译文)加以考察,发现以下表示时间的连词词组的用法在汉语原文和汉语译文中出现的频率大不相同:

在汉译英语料(汉语原文)中,在……时20处,在……时候99处,当……时6处,当……时候23处,共148处;

而在英译汉语料（汉语译文）中，在……时 279 处，在……时候 140 处，当……时 80 处，当……时候 18 处；共 527 处。

表示假设条件的连词用法在汉语原文和汉语译文中也相差很远：

“如果”句：汉语原文中仅见 44 句，汉语译文中多达 393 句。“要是”句，汉语原文语料中有 81 处，汉语译文语料中出现 139 处。

还有表示结果的连词“以致”，在汉语原文和译文中的使用差别很大：

“以致”句：上述汉译英语料中未见一句（0），英译汉语料中见到 20 句。

这些数据说明，与原文语言相比，译文语言确实有表达上的特点，是无形中受到的源语言影响，同时也说明翻译中采取隐化策略之必要。

此外，从上述分析（3.1—3.5）可以看出，隐化和显化与翻译方向有一定关系，至少在不同翻译方向上，隐化和显化程度是不同的。结合 Øverås（1998）的考察，我们不妨假设：由形式化程度较高的语言翻译成形式化程度较低的语言，如由挪威语翻译成英语，或由英语翻译成汉语，显化现象发生递减，而隐化现象发生递增。若是相反的翻译方向，则显化递增，隐化递减。这还有待于进一步的语料库验证。

四、广义上的翻译显化现象

作为一种翻译现象，显化（以及隐化）不应只是狭义地指语言衔接形式上的变化，还应包括意义上的显化转换，即在译文中增添了有助于译文读者理解的显化表达，或者说将原文隐含的信息显化于译文中，使意思更明确，逻辑更清楚。这也是翻译特有的现象。

许国璋论述翻译时，曾提出对哲学著作的翻译应采取“通译”“切译”或“阐译”“释译”方法（1991：248，262）。他力主译文必须通脱、醒豁，译出词的文化史含义。他特地翻译罗素的《西方哲学史》以其为“阐译”示范。他解释说：feudal 不译“封建”，译“拥据领地（之诸侯）”；anarchy 不译“无政府”（当时无中央政府），而译“诸侯纷争”；adventure 不译“冒险”，或译“猎奇于远方”，或译“探无涯之知”，视上下文而定，此而不济，则作“释译”以为助。例如 antiquity 不译"古代",译"希腊罗马"。又如 fame and beauty,在文艺复兴时期有特殊含义,今试译"享盛誉于邦国,创文艺之美";asceticism 译"绝欲弃俗,攻苦食淡之说教";prudential arguments 译"保身家保名誉之考虑"(1991:248)。

这些并不是 Øverås(1998)所讨论的衔接手段上的显化,而是意义上的显化,但这也是翻译中常见的情形,同意值得探讨。翻译家的责任不仅在于通过语言作翻译介绍,他还需要为自己的文化引进相应的概念系统,为读者更好地理解作品提供背景知识。我们再看两例许氏译文:

11) Gunpowder strengthened central government at the expense of feudal nobility.

a)火药用于争战,中央政府因之以强,拥据领地之公候因之而弱。

b)火药消灭了封建贵族而巩固了中央集权政治。(何、李译,p.589)

12) When Constantinople, the last survival of antiquity, was captured by the Turks, Greek refugees in Italy were welcomed by humanists. Vasco da Gama and Columbus enlarged the world, and Copernicus enlarged the heavens.

a)[十五世纪中]君士坦丁堡为土耳其所占。自希腊罗马之衰,古文化残存于世,仅君士坦丁堡一地。既陷,寓居于君士坦丁堡之希腊学人,相率流亡意大利,意大利倾慕希腊人文之学者,迎为上宾。达迦玛绕好望角抵印度,哥伦布西行发现新地,而世界为之扩大。哥白尼立日中心之说,而宇宙为之扩大。

b)当君士坦丁堡,这个古代最后的残余,被土耳其人攻陷后,逃往意大利的希腊难民曾受到人文学者的欢迎。瓦斯寇·达·伽马和哥伦布扩大了世界,而哥白尼扩大了天界。(何、李译,p.589)

对照原文,译文 a)在意思上充分显化,原文隐含的或在其文化上不言自明的内容,已为译者以加词、变通、阐释等方法在译文中显化出来,形成一种阐译,比直译(如例 11 和例 12 的译文 b))甚至比直接读原文更清晰、易懂。例如读例 11)b,读者不容易弄懂火药怎样消灭封建贵族而巩固中央集权,11)a 添加"用于争战",将原文隐含的因果关系之意显化,就明白易懂了。例 12)更是如此。相比于 b),a)的下划线部分添加了不少文化背景上的解释,如"最后的残余"解释为"古文化残存于世,仅君士坦丁堡一地",使人明白残余指文化之残存；达迦玛、哥伦布、哥白尼如何使世界扩大？a)将其背景显化在译文中："绕好望角抵印度"，"西行发现新地"，"立日中心之说"，读者于是明白。这种显化现象无疑与译者的翻译主张相关："翻译目的，在于便利不懂外文之读者，如不懂外文之读者读之不懂，翻译者不能说尽到责任。"(许国璋 1991:248)

五、小结

翻译中的隐和显，由多种因素造成，如 1)语言因素；隐、显现象的发生和隐、显程度可能与语言的形式化程度和翻译方向相关。例如，汉语同英语等印欧语言相比，其词汇、语法衔接上的显化度都比较低，汉译英时会比英译汉时更多地呈现形式上的"显化"，而英译汉时则呈现更多的模仿式的"显化"。2)译者因素；负责的译者在穿梭于两种语言之间进行协调时，总会尽量减少信息传输过程中的损耗和丢失，便于读者的理解和吸收。但另一方面，有些译者因其能力上的不足，在翻译中对原文亦步亦趋地仿译，也会导致译文过度"显化"。3)社会文化因素；翻译涉及的两种语言在社会和文化上的差距越大，可能越需要解释性的"显化"。4)文本因素；小说文本、科学文本、政论文本、新闻文本、应用文文本等在翻译中的显、隐程度可能有别，但本文未及论述。

(本文原载《外语教学与研究》2005 年第 4 期)

参考文献

Mona. Baker, "Corpus Linguistics and Translation Studies: Implication and Application", M. Baker et. al (eds.), *Text and Technology: In Honour of John Sinclair*, Amsterdam: John Benjamins, 1993, pp.233-250.

Mona Baker, *Routledge Encylopedia of Translation Studies*, London and New York: Routledge, 1998.

S.Blum-Kulka, "Shifts of Cohesion and Coherence in Translation", J. House & S. Blum-Kulka (eds.), *Interlingual and Intercultural Communication: Discourse and Cognition in*

Translation and Second Language Acquisition Studies, Tübingen: Narr, 1986.

J.Ebeling, "ContrastiveLinguistics, Translation, and Parallel Corpora", *Meta*, 1998, Vol. 43, No.4, pp.602-615.

D.Kenny, "Creatures of Habit? What Translators usually do with Words?" *Meta*, 1998, Vol.43, No.4.

D.Kenny, *Lexis and Creativity in Translation: A Corpus-based Study*, Manchester: St Jerome, 2001.

S.Laviosa, "How Comparable can 'Comparable Corpora' be?" *Target*, 1997, Vol.9, No. 2, pp.289-319.

S.Laviosa, "Core Patterns of Lexical Use in a Comparable Corpus of English Narrative Prose", *Meta*, 1998, Vol.43, No.4.

Belinda Maia, "Word Order and the First Person Singular in Portuguese and English", *Meta*, 1998, Vol.43, No.4.

Linn Øverås, "In Search of the Third Code: An Investigation of Norms in Literary Translation", *Meta*, 1998, Vol.43, No.4.

Mark Shuttleworth, & Moira Cowie, *Dictionary of Translation Studies*, Manchester: St.Jerome Publishing, 1997.

Z.Xiao, & T. McEnery, "A Corpus-based Approach to Tense and Aspect in English-Chinese Translation", Paper presented at *International Symposium on Contrastive and Translation Studies between Chinese and English*, Shanghai, 2002.

陈瑞清,《汉译文本的形合趋势:以语料库为本的翻译学研究》,《第九届口笔译教学研讨会论文集》,长荣大学翻译学系,2004 年。

罗素:《西方哲学史》,何兆武、李约瑟译,商务印书馆 1963/1980 年版。

贺显斌:《英汉翻译过程中的明晰化现象》,《解放军外国语学院学报》2003 年第 4 期。

柯飞:《汉语把字句特点、分布及英译研究》,《外语与外语教学》2003 年第 12 期。

秦洪武、王克非:《基于语料库的翻译语言分析——以"so...that"的汉语对应结构为例》,《现代外语》2004 年第 1 期。

王克非:《英汉/汉英语句对应的语料考察》,《外语教学与研究》2003 年第 6 期。

王克非:《双语对应语料库:研制与应用》,外语教学与研究出版社 2004 年版。

许国璋:《许国璋论语言》,外语教学与研究出版社 1991 年版。

近代翻译对汉语的影响

一、文化史背景下的近代翻译

中国近代从19世纪中叶开始的对西方科技文化的译介，到19世纪末对西方人文社会科学文化的译介，翻译达到高潮，并延续到五四时期，对整个社会各方面都产生了深远的影响。如小说翻译（一度在量上超过本族语的创作），不仅刺激了小说的创作，还引进了许多前所未有的新种类。翻译是在语言的平台上进行，大量的翻译必然带来对语言的冲击和改造。在近代日本，伴随翻译而来的是明治时期的“言文一致”运动；在中国，翻译对于汉语的发展和白话文的普及起到了推波助澜的作用。

清末翻译重意译，故对汉语语言的影响主要只是在词汇层面。五四前后的翻译开始注重直译，汉语受到的影响就不止词汇层面，而波及句法层面。至于先崇尚意译，后来提倡直译，则不是一二译者可以决定的，其后有深层的时代—文化背景。

清末重意译而轻直译，除了深重的传统文化影响和重己轻人之外，一是当时评翻译者多不懂外语，不核校原文，只看“译笔”，而译笔实际也就是文笔，自然为文人所重；换言之，时人看重译者的文字修养，而非翻译水平。二是意译容易为读者接受，而直译往往被看做“率尔操觚”、“诘屈聱牙”的代名词（参看陈平原1989:37）。也因为这个缘故，鲁迅兄弟当时（1909）翻译的《域外小说集》一、二册分别只卖二十本。不过鲁迅后来也承认其译文“句子生硬”，“不配再印”（鲁迅1920/1981:162）。周作人此期另外的译文也被《小说月报》退稿，称其译“行文生涩，读之如读古书，颇不通俗”（参看陈福康 1992:175）。

可是时代在变化，人们的观念在更新，表达思想观念的语言不可能一成不变。文言文虽有至尊地位，白话文视为鄙俗语言，但人们开始相信，从翻译得来的新字词和新语法，能较好地表达从西方输入的复杂思想，也能帮助改革汉语，于是直译开始占上风，导致欧化的语体白话文蔓延。当然这里面同样也有语言以外的时代—文化因素。

翻译方法上的这种转变也有一个过程。给一般民众看的书多用白话翻译，其他仍用文言文翻译。此外，一般文人长期用文言文写作，也有个习惯和喜好的问题，不是一下子就能转变过来。即使赞同白话文的梁启超，翻译《十五小豪杰》时也“原拟依《水浒》《红楼》等书体裁，纯用俗话，但翻译之时，甚为困难。参用文言，劳半功倍”（见罗新璋 1984:131）。又如鲁迅翻译《月界旅行》时：“初拟译以俗语，稍逸读者之思索，然纯用俗语，复嫌冗繁，因参用文言，以省篇页。”而以古文文笔翻译的林纾译作大为畅销。

晚清时，反对文言的人因白话简单易懂而推行之，提倡之，然而到了五四前后，光简单易懂已不行，人们感觉到白话干枯、贫乏，不能满足现代思想、复杂情感的表达。如何补救呢？傅斯年提出“欧化”：“就是直用西洋文的款式、方法、词法、句法、章法、词枝（figure of speech）……一切修辞学上的方法，造成一种超于现在的国语，欧化的国语，因而成就一种欧化国语的文学。”（参看胡适 1936:220）虽然这里面有“全盘西化”思想，但也反映了两点，一是白话文有缺陷，须借助西方语言补救，二是人们认为精密的思想要以精密的语言来表述，而当时的新思想主要来自西方，故表达这些思想的语言也应向西方语言学习。这也是直译开始大行其道的一个原因，而直译与欧化正相辅相成。

傅斯年在《怎样做白话文》中说：“我们在这里制造白话文，同时负了长进国语的责任，更负了思想改造语言、借语言改造思想的责任。”（同上，221）胡适说：“只有欧化的白话方才能够应付新时代的需要。欧化的白话文就是充分吸收西洋语言的细密的结构，使我们的文字能够传达复杂的思想、曲折的理论。”

又如颇具影响力的《小说月报》也鼓励欧化。茅盾：“创作家及翻译家该大胆把欧化文法使用”；郑振铎说：“中国的旧文体太陈旧而且成滥调了。有许多好的思想与情绪都为旧文体所拘，不能尽量地精微的达出。不唯文言文如此，就是语体文也是如此。所以为求文学艺术的精进起见，我极赞成语体的欧化。”

翻译西方作品自然容易欧化。大量的新名词、新概念进入汉语之后，大量欧化句法、文体现象也随之涌入，欧化成了补救白话的办法。当然也有反对的。如吴宓就认为“近年吾国人译西洋文学书籍、诗文、小说、戏曲等不少，然多用恶劣之白话及英语标点等，读之者殊觉茫然而生厌恶之心。盖彼多就英籍原文，一字一字度为中文，其句法字面，仍是英文。在通英文者读之，殊嫌其多此一举，徒灾枣梨。而在不通英文者观之，直如坐对原籍，甚或误解其意”。

鲁迅与瞿秋白关于翻译的讨论尤其有代表性（参看罗新璋 1984：265－287）：

> “文句仍然是直译……竭力想保存原书的口吻，大抵连语句的前后次序也不甚颠倒。”（鲁迅）
>
> “中国的文或话，法子实在太不精密了，作文的秘诀，是在避去熟字，删掉虚字，就是好文章，讲话的时候，也时时要词不达意，这就是话不够用。”（鲁迅）
>
> “我们的译书……首先要决定译给大众中怎样的读者。……即便为乙类读者（略能识字）而译的书，也应该时常加些新的字眼、新的语法在里面……必须这样，群众的言语才能后丰富起来。”（鲁迅）
>
> “翻译——除了能够介绍原本的内容给中国读者之外——还有一个很重要的作用：就是帮助我们创造出新的中国的现代言语。中国的言语（文字）是那么穷乏，甚至于日常用品都是无名氏的。……一切表现细腻的分别和复杂的关系的形容词、动词、前置词，几乎没有。宗法封建的中世纪的余孽，还紧紧地束缚着中国人的活的言语，这种情形之下，创造新的言语是非常重大的任务。……翻译，的确可以帮助我们造出许多新的字眼，新的句法，丰富的字汇和细腻的精密的正确的表现。”（瞿秋白）

因此，翻译时输入外语表达法到什么程度为宜？鲁迅是“逐字译”，“连语句的前后次序也不甚颠倒”，甚至以英语的词句法规范汉语的使用，造成费解的“硬译”。瞿秋白不同意鲁迅，认为输入外语新表达来丰富汉语虽然是必要的，但“所谓直译式的文章”是“五四式新文言”，它们“所容纳的外国字眼和外国文化并没有消化，而是囫囵吞枣的”。他因此提出，翻译“应用中国人口头上可以讲得出来的白话来写”，“遵照中国白话的文法公律”；即翻译要让普通大众看得懂。而欧化文最大的缺点是脱离大众，是知识分子人工化造成的（参看罗新璋 1984：280）。

可见，在近代中国社会文化背景下的翻译，一方面有不自觉的“人用亦用”，一方面有译者特意吸收外语的表现手法，以丰富汉语的表现力，两者结合，就形成了近代翻译对汉语的影响。

二、翻译对汉语有何影响？

翻译对一国文化包括语言有深远的影响，这在中外历史上都能找到许多例证，中国历时千年的佛经翻译对中国文化的巨大影响就是明证。但是近代以来翻译对汉语造成的影响应如何评估？关于这方面的研究，主要有王力（1943，1980）、北京师范学院中文系编著的《五四以来汉语书面语的变迁和发展》（1959）、Kubler（1985）、Masini（1993）、周光庆和刘玮（1996）、刁晏斌（1999）、Peyraube（2000）等。一般认为，在二十世纪早期的二三十年间，汉语在很大程度上受到西方语言影响，即发生欧化（虽然欧化不全是因为翻译）。王力先生是这派意见的代表，他在早年的《中国现代语法》（1943）书中就专辟一章论述“欧化的语法”，赞同者甚多。但另有一派意见以贝罗贝（A. Peyraube）为代表，怀疑汉语受到欧化（或西化），他认为同汉语受到的语言学意义上的影响相比，汉语更多的是受到社会文化性因素的影响。他从近代以前的汉语中寻找例证，认为持欧化论的学者所举之例证，实际上大多在中国同西方接触之前就已存在，故欧化的影响是很有限的。不过他也承认汉语书面语在欧化句法方面走得较远（Peyraube，2000）。

从近几十年汉语的情况看，西方语言的影响（很大程度上是通过翻译）还够不上欧化，但却不可低估。其影响主要是在词汇和语法两方面，其中在词汇上的争议略少，但也不是没有。例如关于现代汉语双音/复音词增多现象，贝罗贝(Peyraube,2000:5-6)认为与西化无关,汉语双音化早在东周时代就已出现。他统计出《论语》中1504个汉字里有1126个是单音节词(占74.9%),多音词为25.1%,到《孟子》中,2240个汉字里已有29%的多音词。佛经翻译之后,双/多音词更是大量增加。他还拿出马西尼(Masini 1993)书中的数字,说古代白话文学作品中已有不少双音词,《水浒传》:54.5%的多音词,《红楼梦》:50.7%的多音词,《儿女英雄传》和《骆驼祥子》中单、多音词的比例也类似《红楼梦》。

但我们也可以举出一些数字说明古代汉语中并无很多的双/多音词。马西尼承认他的统计只是抽样,而且数量不大(Masini 1993:121)。计算方法也可能不一样。比《论语》《孟子》晚数百上千年的韩愈、苏轼等人的名篇中,双/多音词其实大多不超过20%。《红楼梦》里的双/多音词似乎也不像马西尼的统计那么多。《红楼梦》第一回前两段约480个汉字,只有40个双/多音词(约合90个汉字),第十回第一段是20个多音词/167字,第二十回第一段是26个多音词/145字,第三十回第一段是19个多音词/176字,双/多音词的平均比例约是1∶3(其中双/多音词还包括了许多人名地名等专有名词)。而《骆驼祥子》里双/多音词较前为多,头两段中247个汉字里有48个双/多音词,约2∶3强,多于《红楼梦》等较早的书。王力说,即使没有翻译引进的外来语或译名,汉语也会走上多音化的道路,但有了前者,步子就快多了(1980:343)。这个论述是正确的。近代大量的文学翻译和社会科学等书刊的翻译,以及大量随之而创立或引入的新词(均为复音词),无疑使汉语中增添更多的复音词,它们的使用频率还相当高,使现代汉语语篇中的双/多音词可多达2/3以上。以著名的严复《天演论—译例言》为例:

“译事三难信达雅。求其信已大难矣。顾信矣不达。虽译犹不译也。”

这一段文言话语全是单音词,若以现代汉语表述,大致会是下面这样说:

“翻译工作有三项困难,就是忠实、通顺、典雅。做到忠实就已经很困难了,倘若照顾到忠实而不能做到通顺,那么虽然翻译了,也还是跟没有翻译差不多。”

这段现代白话译文中双/多音词有21个，合43个汉字，与这段文字60个汉字中的剩下17个单音汉字比，是2∶1以上。

此外在代词、连词、介词等方面，翻译带给汉语的影响也不小。由此可见，翻译对汉语的影响，大多不是“从无到有”，而是“由少变多”，“由窄变泛”，从而使汉语语言面貌为之改观。证之以句法也基本如此。

三、翻译对汉语句法的影响

翻译对汉语句法的影响涉及面很广，限于篇幅，我们选择性地谈其中几个方面。

1　被动式使用频率、范围扩大

被动式早在古代汉语中就出现了，但不多见，且一般是表示不幸或不愉快的事情、经历。受翻译西方语言影响，现代汉语中被动式也可表愉快的事情，即凡西文能用的，汉语随翻译跟而着用。例如，将 He was awarded Nobel Prize. 译为“他被授予诺贝尔奖”。（请比较：委员会授予他诺贝尔奖）

又如（参考刁晏斌1999）：

他被选为会长。（大家选他做会长）

昨天抓住的嫌疑犯，经警察局证明无罪，已被释放了。（……已经释放了）

同时，一种新式的赤外线高射炮也被使用。（……也已使用）

否则，我要被白天消失。（鲁迅语；我会要消失在白天里）

我从来没有这样被窘迫过。（柔石语；我从没有这样窘迫过）

英语文学作品中使用的被动句没有科技和新闻文献中多，而且因人而异。毛姆的《人性的枷锁》前40页据统计有115个被动句。奥斯汀的《傲慢与偏见》中被动句也很多，其书前30页中约有135个被动句，平均4.5句/页。这些英文作品翻译成汉语时，汉译文或多或少会受到原文影响，如台湾陈月菁的译本，我们统计其前30页约有被动式0.5句/页；但大陆的译本，如孙致礼译本，受原文影响就比较小，前30页译文中只有二三处使用了被动式。

汉语文学作品中,受西方语言影响较大的老舍的作品其被动句使用较多,如《骆驼祥子》全书221页,被类句(显性被动句)使用多达近100句,平均0.5句/页,虽然比英语作品还是少了许多(相差约8—9倍),却比未受西方语言影响的《红楼梦》的不到1句/10页多了不少。

此外,汉语作品中,被动式大多仍用于不愉快/不幸的事情,如《骆驼祥子》前六章约50页里,有近30处被动句,绝大多数都表述不太好的经历(如"被撤差的巡警"、"像被人抽着转的陀螺""被十来个兵追了去"、"铜纽也被揪下来"等),而汉语译文则不大受此限制。如《傲慢与偏见》的台湾陈月菁译本在第一句里就翻译出被动句:"容易被人联想到……",并无不好的意思。

2 句式复杂化,多样化

这表现在汉语句子的主谓关系较以前明显,即主语使用的频率高了;逻辑关系也更多地明示于语言表层,有别于传统隐含这种关系的意合方式,即多用"如果"、"因为"、"假如"、"当……时"、"作为"等。如:

[当]我再问他两句家常过日子的话[的时候],他就连眼圈儿都红了。

我们只是说着自己,每当我们不能再守沉默的时候。(周作人)

关于文学方面,这本说得很少。

做事恰到好处之好,可就两方面说:一方面就道德说,一方面就利害说。(冯友兰)

作为一个职业球员,我……

作为老师来说,应该抓紧教育,作为家长来说,也应该提醒和督促。

我们并不想对于逻辑中之层次论,有什么论列。(冯友兰)

与从前的汉语相比,使用的定语更长(参考刁晏斌1999),例如:

但我们不要忘记了其中的最明智的,最人情的,最永久地现代的那一卷书。——周作人;

懒懒地从衾褥狼藉的床上爬起来的我,——严既澄

我每看见一般有些天才而自愿著述终身的朋友在干着种种无聊的事情,我只好为著作界的损失一叹了。(陈西滢)

住客们沉没在鹏飞先生所叙述的奇特而又有悲剧性的那女人的追想中。——魏金枝

梁启超好用新文体、新词汇、新句式，有时不免生搬硬套，写出“上书于所最敬最爱之中国将来主人公留学生诸君阁下”这样的句子。五四后有些受到日本或欧式句法影响的人走得更远，写出“极狭隘极狭隘的个人生活的描写，极渺小极渺小的抒情文字的游戏”之类长定语怪句子。这些因距离汉语习惯太远，后来自然遭到淘汰。

徐志摩留学英美多年，二十年代初回国后曾任北京大学英文系主任，也是著名的诗人。在他的创作和译作中，翻译的痕迹尤为明显，长定语句子也很多，如：

我信生活绝不是我们大多数人仅仅从自身经验推得的那样暗惨。（徐志摩）

再参看他的译诗：

Juliet……As sweet repose and rest

Come to thy heart as that within my breast.

Romeo　O, wilt thou leave me so unsatisfied?

Juliet　What satisfaction canst thou have to-night?

Romeo　Th'exchange of thy love faithful vow for mine.

Juliet　I gave mine before thou didst request it

And yet I would it were to give again.

——William Shakespeare: *Romeo and Juliet*

朱：……我祝望一般甜蜜的安息与舒适降临到你的心胸如同我有我的。

罗：啊，难道你就这样丢下我不给我满足？

朱：哪一类的满足你想在今晚上向我要？

罗：你的相爱的忠贞的誓言来交换我的。

朱：我早已给你那时你还不曾向我要；

可是我也愿意我就重来给过一次。

由此可见翻译对徐志摩这位新文化时期著名文人的重大影响。

3　句序变得灵活多样

汉语中的因果、条件、假设和时间状语子句，通常是子句在前，主句在后，按时间顺序的原则支配，而英语等西方语言相对灵活。因翻译的影响，国人写作时也出现了类似英语的句序灵活的句子：

如果我能够，我要写下我的悔恨和悲哀，为子君，为我自己。（鲁迅）

你永远站在工人前面，忠实的，固执的。（巴金）

她哥哥笑一笑没有说，忠厚的。（柔石）

他今天不能参加我们的活动，因为家里有急事。

这事本来不会发生的，要是你听了我的劝告的话。

很懒的他立起来，看了她一眼，走过去帮忙。（老舍）

（比较：Fortunately，I caught the train.幸运地，我赶上了火车。）

特别是在引述语言的句子中，出现汉语原本没有的句序：

“It's the young man！I thought.”

“是那个年轻人！”我想。

“Have a little brandy，uncle.”Said my sister.

“喝点白兰地吧，叔叔。”我姐姐说。

文瑛必是爱他的，他想。（老舍）

“你休息一二天，去拜望亲戚本家一回，我们便可以走了。”母亲说。（鲁迅）

“Providence seems to have laid him here，”whispered she to her husband，“and to have brought us hither to find him...”

“好像上帝把他安排在这里的，”她低声对她丈夫说道，“并且带我们到这里发现了他……”

“王先生！”我对他叫着说：“请坐，请坐！喝茶，喝茶！”（鲁彦）

关于这种语言现象，鲁迅曾以调侃的语言写道：

子曰：“学而时习之，不亦乐乎？”

这太老式了，不好！

“学而时习之，”子曰：“不亦乐乎？”

这好！

“学而时习之，不亦乐乎？”子曰。

这更好。为什么好，欧化了。但子曰终于没有能欧化到曰子。

（鲁迅《玩笑只当它玩笑》）

没有翻译，外语本身也会对汉语产生影响，但有了翻译，其影响更大，更直接，受影响面更广（不懂外语的人跟着受影响），这一点大概不会有人反对的。

（本文原载《外语教学与研究》2002 年第 6 期。2001 年 1 月曾在台湾东吴大学和台湾师范大学以同题讲演，发表时有所修改）

参考文献

北京师范学院中文系汉语教研组编著：《五四以来汉语书面语言的变迁和发展》（中国语文丛书），商务印书馆 1959 年版。

陈福康：《中国译学理论史稿》，上海外语教育出版社 1992 年版。

陈平原：《20 世纪中国小说史》第一卷（1897—1916），北京大学出版社 1989 年版。

刁晏斌：《初期现代汉语语法研究》，洪叶文化事业有限公司 1999 年版。

胡适编选：《中国新文学大系——建设理论集》，良友图书公司 1936 年版。

刘正埮等编：《汉语外来词词典》，上海辞书出版社 1984 年版。

鲁迅：《域外小说集》，载《鲁迅全集》第 10 卷，人民文学出版社 1920/1981 年版。

罗新璋编：《翻译论集》，商务印书馆 1984 年版。

王力：《中国现代语法》，商务印书馆 1947 年版。

王力：《汉语史稿》（上、中、下），中华书局 1980 年版。

周光庆、刘玮：《汉语与中国新文化启蒙》，东大图书公司 1996 年版。

C.Kubler, *A Study of Europeanized Grammar in Modern Written Chinese*, Taipei: Student Book Co., Ltd., 1985.

F.Masini, "The Formation of Modern Chinese Lexicon and its Evolution toward a National Language: The Period from 1840 to 1898", *Journal of Chinese Linguistics*, Monograph Series No.6. Berkeley, 1993.（中译本：《现代汉语词汇的形成——十九世纪汉语外来词研究》，黄河清译，汉语大词典出版社 1997 年版）

A.Peyraube, "Westernization of Chinese Grammar in the 20th Century: Myth or Reality?", *Journal of Chinese Linguistics* 28/1, 2000, pp.1-25.

关于翻译共性的研究

语料库方法应用于翻译研究推动了关于翻译共性的研究。本文追述这一研究历程以及目前对此论说的质疑，指出以 Mona Baker 为代表的翻译共性研究在研究对象的界定和方法论方面存在一些问题，认为对翻译共性的研究不应仅仅局限于翻译过程本身，还应当从具体语言对、翻译方向、译者因素、文体类型等多个视角进行。

一、引言

20 世纪 90 年代以来，新型翻译语料库所拥有的大规模原文与译文文本语料与相关计算机分析技术结合所产生的数据为翻译研究提供了新视角，基于语料库的翻译研究方法应运而生，经过十多年的理论阐述与实证研究已经发展成为一种新的研究范式。其研究范围覆盖了从翻译过程到产品的各种翻译现象，特别是翻译语言普遍特征、翻译过程、翻译转换与规范、译者文体等方面。这些领域中以对翻译语言普遍特征的研究最为突出。翻译共性（translation universals），亦称翻译普遍性或翻译普遍特征①，Baker（1993：243）将其定义为"翻译文本而不是原话语中出现的典型语言特征，并且这些特征不是特定语言系统干扰的结果"，即指翻译语言作为一种客观存在的语言变

① 翻译共性指"译文中呈现的有别于原文的一些典型的、跨语言的、有一定普遍性的特征"（柯飞 2005）。

体，相对于目标语原创语言，在整体上表现出来的一些规律特征。这一定义有两重含义：第一，翻译共性是特定语言模式的概率性分布特征，主要在归纳的基础上获得；第二，翻译共性由翻译过程本身造成，与两种语言系统之间的差异无关。Baker 在前人研究成果（Vanderauwera 1985；Blum-Kulka 1986；Shlesinger 1991 等）的基础上，首先提出了基于语料库的翻译普遍特征（universal features of translation）的假设，包括六个方面：1）译文显化程度显著提高；2）消歧和简化；3）合乎语法性；4）避免重复；5）超额再现目标语语言特征；6）翻译过程往往会导致某些语言特征表现出特定的分布类型（Baker 1993：243-245）。随后，在此基础上的翻译共性研究不断深入、细化，逐步形成了一整套方法论。然而，其中一些个案研究的结果却与共性假设或多或少有些出入，由此引发了关于翻译共性存在与否的讨论。2001 年在丹麦哥本哈根举行的第三届 EST 大会和在芬兰萨翁林纳举行的关于翻译共性研究的大会上，与会者就这一话题进行了深入探讨（参见 Hansen *et al*.2004；Mauranen & Kujamäki 2004）。我们的问题是：应当如何对翻译共性进行界定？其表现形式和限度有多大？在对假设进行验证和阐述的过程中，Baker 的翻译普遍特征被归纳为简化（simplification）、显化（explicitation）和范化（normalization）三个方面①。因为基于语料库的翻译共性研究离不开对前人研究成果的传承，我们参照 Laviosa（2002）和 Olohan（2004）的做法，以 Baker（1993：233-250）的“Corpus Linguistics and Translation Studies：Implications and Applications”一文为界，将翻译共性研究划分为前语料库（pre-corpus）和基于语料库（corpus-based）两个时期加以评述。

二、前语料库时期的翻译共性研究

语料库用于翻译研究可以追溯到 20 世纪 80 年代（参见 Laviosa 2002：1，

① 对翻译普遍特征包含的具体内容目前尚未有完全统一的看法，但相关理论阐述与实证性研究主要集中于这三个方面。

21)，但当时文本采集的规模通常较小，并且多以手工统计为主。这里所谓“前语料库时期”就是指大规模机读翻译文本用于翻译研究之前，通过人工采集原文与译文文本，并对与翻译有关的语言现象进行人工对比、分析和统计的时期。这一时期的翻译共性研究主要表现为从词汇、句法和文体等角度关注简化、显化和范化三方面问题。

所谓简化，是指译者在目标语文本中对原语文本中的“语言/信息下意识地简单化”(Baker 1996:176)处理的倾向。语料库翻译研究途径正式提出之前对简化现象的探讨主要有 Blum-Kulka & Levenston(1983)、Vanderauwera(1985)、Baker(1992/2000)等，内容主要涉及对词汇、句法和文体的简化，又可分为由两种语言系统差异所造成的强制性简化，和由翻译过程本身、译者偏好、目标语语文规范等因素造成的非强制性简化两大类①。Blum-Kulka & Levenston(1983)所提出的五项策略②中，除两项外其他均属前者，与下文基于语料库的简化研究不同。Vanderauwera(1985)的研究可以说具备了语料库翻译共性研究的雏形，她所论及的简化手段大都属于非强制性简化的范畴，但在讨论中句法与文体之间的界限不甚清楚，总体上看只是翻译实践中译者遵循目标语语言使用规范的一些归化手法。

显化的概念最早由 Vinay & Darbelnet 作为一种文体翻译技巧提出，是指将原语中隐含的信息在目标语中加以明示，此类信息在原文本中可以根据语境或情境获得(1958/1995:342)。在语料库翻译方法提出之前，有关显化的研究主要有 Vinay & Darbelnet(1958/1995)、Nida(1964/2004)、Nida & Taber(1969)、Vanderauwera(1985)、Blum-Kulka(1986)、Klaudy(1998/2004)等。Vinay & Darbelnet 是从对比文体的角度提出这一概念的，他们将显化和隐化视为一组对立的文体翻译技巧，常与信息的获得与损失相联系。所涉及的显化包括词汇显化和信息显化两种，这两类显化表面上都是语境或情境要求的

---

① Kinga Klaudy 在讨论显化时，将其分为四类：强制性显化、非强制性显化、语用显化和翻译内在显化(参见 Baker 1998/2004:82-83)，其中非强制性显化的部分内容和翻译内在显化属于语料库翻译共性探讨的范围，此处借用 Klaudy 的说法。

② Laviosa 在其“Universals of translations”(Baker 1998/2004:288)一文中似乎将 Blum-Kulka & Levenston(1983)中的简化策略分为六类，原作中实际分为五类(Blum-Kulka & Levenston 1983:126-136)。

结果,但从本质上讲依然是语言系统差异造成的,属于强制性显化的范畴。Nida & Taber(1969:164-165)指出好的译文往往多少会比原文长,主要是因为在翻译过程中,译者会通过明示原文中的含蓄信息在适当限度内增加译文的冗余度。他主要是从语言文化差异和方便译文接受者理解原作的角度来探讨翻译中的新信息现象。Vanderauwera(1985)指出了译者所采用的各种显化技巧,这些技巧均不在语言系统差异影响之列,但与译者的个人文体偏好不无关系,这在一定程度上为后来用语料库研究译者的文体奠定了基础。Blum-Kulka(1986:19)从翻译中衔接与连贯的转换入手提出了显化假设(the explicitation hypothesis):翻译过程会使译文相对于原文更加冗长,其表现形式为衔接方式的显化程度提高。这一假设有两个特点:第一,将显化视为翻译过程内在的属性,摆脱了语言系统差异的影响,使显化研究具体化;第二,从句法的非强制性转换入手,将译者的文体偏好作为参数之一。Blum-Kulka 的论断为后来基于语料库的翻译共性研究提供了重要思路。Klaudy(1998/2004)将显化分成强制性显化、非强制性显化、语用显化和翻译内在显化四类,各类之间尽管存在一定程度的重合,却让我们认识到显化现象的多样性和多层次性,在此基础上能对翻译共性做出更加全面的认识。

范化是指"遵循、甚至夸大目标语中典型模式和做法的倾向"(Baker 1996:176-177)。Vanderauwera(1985)和 Toury(1995/2001)是前语料库时期范化研究的主要代表。Vanderauwera 发现译文语篇在标点、选词、文体、句子结构以及语篇构建方面的转换均趋向于目标语语言传统规范的特点(参见 Laviosa 2002:55)。Toury 从描写翻译研究的途径入手提出的标准化(standardization)法则既有语际转换基础上的对比,也包括目标语内翻译文本与原创文本的比较(参见 Paloposki 2001),这样的论断拓宽了翻译共性研究的视角,并且为进一步对翻译共性进行解释提供了多重角度。

相对于基于语料库的方法,前语料库时期的翻译共性研究除具有 Laviosa(2002:57-58)所提出的五个特点外,还表现出:1)每个研究都是从不同视角,如对比语言学、文体学或翻译研究的角度出发,在对个别概念的认识上存在一定的偏差;2)在关注焦点上,词汇、句法、文体等层面均有涉及,但缺乏统一的指导原则;3)对共性的研究主要以语际转换为基础,即相对原语而言译语的普遍特征。尽管如此,这些前期研究为基于语料库的翻译共性研究奠定了基础。

三、基于语料库的翻译共性研究

自 Baker(1993)提出基于语料库的翻译普遍特征研究以来,围绕这一主题的研究大量涌现,具代表性的主要有 Baker(1993,1995,1996)、Laviosa(1998a,b)、Kenny(1998,2001)、Øverås(1998)、Olohan & Baker(2000)、Mauranen(2002)、Mauranen & Kujamäki(2004)、Puurtinen(1998,2003a,b)、Tirkkonen-Condit(2002,2004)、柯飞(2003,2005)、Englund-Dimitrova(2003)、Frankenberg-Gacia(2004)等,内容主要是对简化、显化和范化等普遍特征在各语种大型双语语料库中的实证检验,既有证明也有质疑。Laviosa(2002:58-59)指出,Baker 关于简化的研究有三个特点:第一,翻译共性是翻译过程本身内在的特征;第二,共性研究所采纳的是翻译产品/目标语取向(product-/target-oriented)的视角和基于语料库的方法;第三,以类比语料库(comparable corpora)作为语料数据来源。这三个方面也是语料库翻译共性研究不同于前语料库时期相关研究的主要区别所在,Baker 的思想仍是这一研究途径方法论的基础。其中 Laviosa 对简化(1998b)以及核心词汇模式(1998a)的分析将共性研究完全局限在目标语语言环境内,树立了共性研究的单语类比语料库研究模式(monolingual comparable corpus-based model),尽管这一模式打破了传统上原语语篇的主宰地位和对等的观念,但在客观上也造成了排除原语文本的做法,缺少了对共性现象进行充分解释的一个维度(参见 Kenny 2005;Bernardini 2005)。Kenny(2005)还特别指出平行语料库的运用并不是要重新回到原语与译语文本二元对立的老问题上去,而是要探究如何在单语类比语料库研究范式的基础上,进一步通过平行语料库来完善翻译普遍现象研究的综合法。Øverås(1998)则以英语—挪威语平行语料库(ENPC)为基础,重新从句法角度在语篇衔接层面上考察显化,从而将前语料库时期的研究途径与基于语料库的方法结合在一起。Olohan & Baker 对非强

制性关系词 *that* 在原创英语与翻译英语中使用的研究虽都表明显化是语言转换中的一个普遍倾向（参见 Olohan 2004：93-97），但其采用的依然是单语类比语料库的研究模式，而且此类语言现象仅局限于英语，因此只是对翻译共性一个间接的证明。Mauranen、Puurtinen 和 Tirkkonen-Condit 等在翻译芬兰语语料库（Corpus of Translated Finnish）基础上对翻译芬兰语的研究结果不仅有对翻译共性的支持，同时也包括对现有翻译共性的质疑和挑战，为这一研究提出了一些新问题。柯飞以汉英/英汉平行语料库①为基础，分别从宏观和微观角度对显化进行了验证和探讨，并特别指出："作为一种翻译现象，显化（以及隐化）不应只是狭义地指语言衔接形式上的变化，还应包括意义上的显化转换，即在译文中添加了有助于译文读者理解的显化表达，或者说将原文隐含的信息显化于译文中，使意思更明确，逻辑更清楚"（2005：306）。Englund-Dimitrova（2003）通过有声思维法和书写过程的计算机记录等手段，对俄语—瑞典语翻译中转折连词在译文中显化与否进行了考察，各项数据表明：翻译中的显化与译者的翻译经验有关，职业译者对显化策略的使用往往要比学生译者多。这一研究从社会文化的视角指出，显化是俄—瑞翻译中职业译者所遵循的一种翻译规范。Frankenberg-Gacia（2004）以葡—英双向平行语料库（Compara）为基础，从译文与原文文本长度角度探讨了非强制性显化。该研究以定量分析的方法证明了翻译文本中词汇数量的整体增加表明译文往往比原文更为明晰，而且这并不受制于两种语言之间的差异。这些研究，特别是翻译芬兰语语料库和汉英/英汉平行语料库基础上的研究，将翻译共性延伸到了印欧语系以外的翻译研究中。

总的说来，基于语料库的共性研究呈现出四个特点：1）大多数研究都是以共时语料为研究对象，主要依靠计算机技术分析数据，如平均句子长度、类符/形符比率、词汇密度等手段对词汇多样性、信息负载度等方面进行考察；2）以对共性的验证和描写为主，解释较少；3）理论阐述与实证研究相结合；4）主要以单语类比语料库为基础，探究相对于目标语原创文本而言的翻译文本

---

① 该语料库由北京外国语大学中国外语教育研究中心研制，具体内容参见王克非等（2004）。

特征。这项研究总体上经历了一个由单语类比语料库范式向单、双语结合语料库(包括单语参照库和双语对应库)综合法发展的过程,研究内容由词汇向句法、语篇层次进行延伸,宏观与微观、理论阐述与实证性研究并举。

四、翻译共性研究中的问题

由上述可以发现,翻译共性研究目前依然处于对假设的验证阶段,学者们尚未就现有假设的共性(hypothesized universals)达成共识,对一些潜在共性(potential universals)的探索也在进行当中。那么翻译共性果然存在吗?若存在,是以何种形式存在?我们首先看一看对翻译共性的一些质疑,然后对产生问题的原因加以分析。

对翻译共性的质疑主要表现在三方面。

第一,对方法论的质疑。面对翻译共性研究中单语类比语料库(monolingual comparable corpus)的传统范式,Kenny 最先将平行语料库引入翻译共性研究中(1998,2001),并且提出如何在类比语料库研究发现的基础之上开展平行语料库研究,将后者作为前者的补充研究(2005:157),以弥补翻译现象研究中因忽略原语文本而造成的缺陷。针对 Olohan & Baker(2000)采用的类比语料库方法,Kenny 以一个德—英文学文本平行语料库(GEPCOLT)对其研究结果进行重新验证后指出:英语译者在 *say* 之后使用非强制性 *that* 的大多数情况并非为了去对应德语中的 *daβ*,乍看起来这属于语法上的显化,但还需要确认一下原语文本中是否使用了除 d 酒以外的其他连接词形式来明示从句的叙述性质,如果有的话,就很难断定英语译文中包含 *that* 的做法全都属于显化现象(2005:161)。由此可以看出,部分基于单语类比语料库研究范式的翻译共性研究结果在方法上有待于平行语料库研究的进一步验证和补充。Bernardini(2005:6)也指出,"正是翻译作为沟通媒介的本质,使得翻译分析中所使用的唯目标语取向的方法在方法论上值得怀疑",例如类比语料库设计中由于不平衡性所造成的可比性缺乏(lack of comparability)问题。可见,方法论上的缺陷是造成问题的根本原因之一。

第二，一些实证性个案研究的结果与共性假设相背离。Puurtinen（1998，2003a，b）以芬兰语类比语料库为基础，从句法角度将芬兰语翻译儿童文学中非限定性结构作为衡量可读性的标准之一，对翻译芬兰语的语言特征以及意识形态规范进行考察。她发现原创芬兰语作品中非限定性结构的出现频次低，而译自英语的翻译作品中，非限定性结构的使用频次明显高于当代原创芬兰语作品，由于非限定性结构的使用降低了译文的明晰度，增大了词汇密度和信息负载，而且大量的非限定性结构背离了芬兰语原创儿童文学的语言规范，这一发现显然与 Baker 等所提出的翻译文本的显化相矛盾。Laviosa 根据自己的研究（1998a，b）也指出，通过英语类比语料库所发现的简化证据在各个文本类型中的表现并不完全统一（2002：77），如翻译文本中平均句子长度在新闻和散文两类文本中呈现出相反的趋势，前者比原创新闻英语短，而后者明显长于原创散文。这样看来，文体类型不仅是简化研究中的一个变量，而且将平均句子长度作为简化的一个参数还有待于进一步验证。Kenny 以德—英文学文本平行语料库为基础对翻译中的范化和译者创造性进行考察后发现，在翻译中词汇范化现象的确存在，但原语文本中的创造性词汇在大多数情况下却没有发生范化（2001：187、210）。这说明对范化现象的研究还是不能完全脱离原语语篇的因素。Mauranen 对翻译和原创芬兰语学术及非小说文本的考察发现，多词语符串（multi-word strings）在翻译文本中的多样化程度高于其在原创文本中的程度，这说明在学术文本翻译中的范化特征并不明显，也说明这一普遍特征还会受到具体文体类型的局限（参见 Puurtinen 2003a）。Johansson（2004）针对 Jean-Claude Chevalier 提出的译文通常选择人称类主语（human subject）的倾向是简化或范化的表现这一观点，通过英语—挪威语平行语料库对英译挪中主语选择的调查发现：绝大多数情况下，译文会保留原文的主语形式，主语类型的改变往往由两种语言系统之间在结构或文体上的差异造成。以上这些个案研究的结果或多或少地表现出与现有共性假设的矛盾，暴露出存在的一些问题。

第三，印欧语系之外的共性研究对原有假设的挑战。印欧语系以外的翻译共性研究不仅有对已假设共性的支持，还包括对潜在共性的进一步探索，某些发现还对原有的假设提出了挑战。Tirkkonen-Condit（2002，2004）以芬兰语类比语料库为基础在探究翻译文本与原创文本之间是否存在系统的差异，以及是否由于翻译过程造成了翻译语言与原创语言的差异等问题时，提出了独特项假说（the unique items hypothesis）：目标语语言中的某些语言项/元素在源语中缺少语言对应项，相对于原创文本而言，此类语言项/元素在翻译文本中的频次低。也就是说，如果将目标语原创语言规范视为常态，那么翻译语言特征通常被认为是对常态的偏离（Tirkkonen-Condit 2002：209），即非标准化或非范化，这一点与“遵循、甚至夸大目标语中典型模式和做法”（Baker 1996：176-177）的范化相背离。柯飞（2003）以英汉/汉英平行语料库为基础对汉语中的特殊句式“把”字句在英汉转换中的分布特点进行考察发现：1）翻译汉语作品中的“把”字句要比原创汉语中的“把”字句频次高。2）文学类作品比非文学类作品中“把”字句的频次高。由于“把”字句适于表达复杂和细微的意思，因此“把”字句的频次说明了翻译文本中的显化现象。这一结果又与Tirkkonen-Condit 的独特项假说形成鲜明对比。柯飞（2005）进一步指出：翻译中的显与隐是共存的，翻译中的隐、显现象及其程度可能与语言的形式化程度和翻译方向相关，同时还会受到译者、社会文化和文本因素的影响。

产生以上质疑的原因主要有两方面：第一，研究对象的界定。Bernardini & Zanettin（2004）认为基于语料库的翻译共性研究在对共性概念的界定和所采用的方法论两方面存在问题。以 Baker 为代表的学者，将翻译共性的研究对象局限于翻译过程本身所造成的、翻译文本相对于目标语内原创文本而表现出的语言特征，仅以单语类比语料库方法论为模式，使得实证研究中语内类比和语际对比所造成的两大类翻译共性混杂在一起。第二，各个研究中对各种变量的关注与控制不尽一致。具体涉及语言对、翻译方向、译者因素、文体类型等多种因素，如译入文本与译出文本的差别、不同文体类型文本之间的差别都是影响研究结果的重要因素。

五、结语

基于语料库的翻译研究方法至少有两大特点：可观察性（observability）和

可重复性(replicability)。这一研究模式面对的是实实在在的语料,从假设出发,在各种语言中不断加以验证和置疑,周而复始,使得研究逐渐深入。如上所述,翻译共性研究中各种变量的介入,加上翻译共性假设本身在概念界定和方法论方面存在的问题,导致了个别实证性研究对翻译共性的质疑。随着越来越多的大型双语语料库在各语种中的建立,以及实证性研究的进一步深入,我们需要重新界定研究对象,发展方法论,在更加充分描写的基础上,从语言、认知和社会文化等视角建立一套系统的解释和预测机制,并将研究结果应用于(或验证于)翻译实践和翻译教学中。

(本文原载《外语教学与研究》2006 年第 5 期,作者王克非、黄立波)

参考文献

M.Baker,*In Other Words:A Coursebook on Translation*,Beijing:Foreign Language Teaching and Research Press,1992/2000.

M.Baker,"Corpus Linguistics and Translation Studies:Implications and Applications", M.Baker,G.Francis & E.Tognini-Bonelli(eds.),*Text and Technology:In Honour of John Sinclair*,Philadelphia & Amsterdam:John Benjamins,1993.

M.Baker,"Corpora inTranslation Studies:An Overview and some Suggestions for Future Research",*Target*,1995,Vol.7,No.2,pp.223-243.

M.Baker,"Corpus-basedTranslation Studies:The Challenges that Lie Ahead",H.Somers (ed.),*Terminology,LSP and Translation*,Amsterdam:John Benjamins,1996.

M.Baker,(ed.),*Routledge Encyclopedia of Translation Studies*,Shanghai:Shanghai Foreign Language Education Press,1998/2004.

S.Bernardini,"Reviving Old Ideas:Parallel and Comparable Analysis in Translation Studies-With an Example from Translation Stylistics",K.Aijmer & C.Alvstad(eds.),*New Tendencies in Translation Studies. Selected Papers from a Workshop Göteborg* 12 *December* 2003,Göteborg:Acta Universitatis Gothoburgensis,2005.

S.Bernardini & F.Zanettin,"When is a Universal not a Universal? Some Limits of Current Corpus-based Methodologies for the Investigation of Translation Universals",A.Mauranen & P.Kujamäki(eds.),2004.

S.Blum-Kulka, "Shifts of Cohesion and Coherence in Translation", J. House & S. Blum-Kulka(eds.), *Interlingual and Intercultural Communication.Discourse and Cognition in Translation and Second Language Acquisition Studies*, Tübingen: Gunter Narr Verlag, 1986.

S.Blum-Kulka & E.A.Levenston, "Universals of Lexical Simplification", C.Færch & G. Kasper(eds.), *Strategies in Interlanguage Communication*, London & New York: Longman, 1983.

B.Englund-Dimitrova, "Explicitation in Russian-Swedish Translation: Sociolinguistic and Pragmatic Aspects", B. Englund-Dimitrova & A. Pereswetoff-Morath (eds.), *Swedish Contributions to the Thirteenth International Congress of Slavists, Ljubljana, 15-21 August 2003*.Lund: Lund University, 2003.

A.Frankenberg-Gacia, "Are Translations Longer than Source Texts? A Corpus-based Study of Explicitation", 2004.

G.Hansen, K.Malmkjær & D.Gile(eds.), *Claims, Changes and Challenges in Translation Studies*, Amsterdam: John Benjamins, 2004.

S.Johansson, "Why Change Subject? On Changes in Subject Selection in Translation from English into Norwegian", *Target*, 2004, Vol.16, No.1, pp.29-52.

D.Kenny, "Creatures of Habit? What Translators Usually Do with Words", *Meta*, 1998, Vol.43, No.4, pp.515-523.

D.Kenny, *Lexis and Creativity in Translation: A Corpora-based Study*, Manchester: St.Jerome, 2001.

D.Kenny, "Parallel Corpora and Translation Studies: Old Questions, New Perspectives? Reporting *that* in Gepcolt: A case study", G.Barnbrook, P.Danielsson & M.Mahlberg(eds.), *Meaningful Texts: The Extraction of Semantic Information from Monolingual and Multilingual Corpora*, London & New York: Continuum, 2005.

K.Klaudy, "Explicitation", M.Baker(ed.), *Routledge Encyclopedia of Translation Studies*, Shanghai: Shanghai Foreign Language Education Press, 1998/2004.

S.Laviosa, "Core Patterns of Lexical Use in a Comparable Corpus of English Narrative Prose", *Meta*, 1998, Vol.43, No.2, pp.557-570.

S.Laviosa, "The English Comparable Corpus: A Resource and a Methodology", L.Bowker, M.Cronin, D.Kenny & J.Pearson(eds.), *Unity in Diversity? Current Trends in Translation Studies*, Manchester: St.Jerome, 1998.

S.Laviosa, *Corpus-based Translation Studies: Theory, Findings and Applications*, Amsterdam: Rodopi, 2002.

A.Mauranen, "Where's Cultural Adaptation. A corpus-based Study on Translation Strategies", 2002.

A.Mauranen & P.Kujamäki (eds.), *Translation Universals: Do They Exist?*, Amsterdam: John Benjamins, 2004.

E.A.Nida, *Toward a Science of Translating*, Shanghai: Shanghai Foreign Language Education Press, 1964/2004.

E.A.Nida, & C.Taber, *The Theory and Practice of Translation*, Leiden: E.J.Brill, 1969.

M.Olohan, *Introducing Corpora in Translation Studies*, London & New York: Routledge, 2004.

M.Olohan & M.Baker, "Reporting *that* in Translated English: Evidence for Subconscious Process of Explicitation", *Across Languages and Cultures*, 2000, No.1, pp.141-172.

L.Øverås, "In Search of the Third Code: An Investigation of Norms in Literary Translation", *Meta*, 1998, Vol.43, No.2, pp.571-588.

O.Paloposki, "Enriching Translations, Simplified Language? An Alternative Viewpoint to Lexical Amplification", *Target*, 2001, Vol.13, No.2, pp.265-288.

T.Syntax, Puurtinen, "Readability and Ideology in Children's Literature", *Meta*, 1998, Vol.43, No.4, pp.524-533.

T.Puurtinen, "Genre-specific Features of Translationese? Linguistic Differences between Translated and Non-translated Finnish Children's Literature", *Literary and Linguistic Computing*, 2003a, Vol.18, No.4, pp.389-406.

T. Puurtinen, "Nonfinite Constructions in Finnish Children's Literature: Features of Translationese Contradicting Translation Universals?", S. Granger, J. Lerot & S. Petch-Tyson (eds.), *Corpus-based Approaches to Contrastive Linguistics and Translation Studies*, Amsterdam: Rodopi, 2003.

M.Shlesinger, "Interpreter Latitude vs. Due Process: Simultaneous and Consecutive Interpretation in Multilingual trials", S.Tirkkonen-Condit (ed.), *Empirical Research in Translation and Intercultural Studies*, Tübingen: Gunter Narr Verlag, 1991.

S.Tirkkonen-Condit, "Translationese-A myth or an Empirical Fact? A Study into the Linguistic Identifiability of Translated Language", *Target*, 2002, Vol.14, No.2, pp.207-220.

S.Tirkkonen-Condit, "UniqueItems-Over-or Under-represented in Translated Language?", A.Mauranen & P.Kujamäki(eds.), 2004.

G.Toury, *Descriptive Translation Studies and Beyond*. Shanghai: Shanghai Foreign Language Education Press, 1995/2001.

R.Vanderauwera, *Dutch Novds Translated into English: The Transformation of a 'Minority' Literature*. Amsterdam: Rodopi, 1985.

J.P.Vinay & J.Darbelnet, *Comparative Stylistics of French and English-A Methodology for Translation*, (Translated and edited by J.C.Sager & M.J.Hamel), Amsterdam/Philadelphia: John Benjamins, 1958/1995.

柯飞:《汉语"把"字句特点、分布及英译》,《外语与外语教学》2003 年第 12 期。

柯飞:《翻译中的隐和显》,《外语教学与研究》2005 年第 4 期。

王克非等:《双语对应语料库:研制与应用》,外语教学与研究出版社 2004 年版。

阐译与显化

——许国璋翻译思想解析

许国璋先生（1915—1994）在语言、文学、文化、外语教育等领域都卓有建树。对于翻译，他是从语言和沟通的角度加以体认。他饶有兴致地比较了西方译家对中国文化的翻译，更多的是从学术著作的翻译来思考其中的问题和含义，从而提出其阐译观。本文即从阐译观及其解读来讨论翻译的显化问题。

许国璋的翻译论述并不多，主要见于《许国璋文集·文学与文化卷》（王克非、韩宝成编 2015c）中收录的几篇论文，但在其他论文里也有提及翻译，都不乏真知灼见。例如，“关于索绪尔的两本书”（许国璋 1983，又见王克非、韩宝成编 2015a，“从两本书看索绪尔的语言哲学”）一文，在条分缕析索绪尔的语言哲学思想时，专门以第 3.5 节讨论“索绪尔语言学中某些术语的翻译问题”，集中阐述了他对术语翻译的复杂性和重要性的认识。

更值得我们思考的是，他在上文末深刻地指出：“哲学著作的翻译家肩上负有完整介绍一种哲学体系的责任。他的责任超过翻译：他还必须要为自己的文化引进一种概念系统。因而，首先着眼的不宜是词而是它的定义，不必是符号施指而是符号受指，不必是约定俗成而是立言立解。”

从这段话可以看出他的阐译观之根本，那就是，负责任的译者要为本族文化引入新的思想、新的概念系统，因而不能只盯着词句，要注重内涵和定义，要注重立言立解。这自然是要经由阐译才能实现的。在他看来：“翻译目的，在于便利不懂外文之读者，如不懂外文之读者读之不懂，翻译者不能说尽到责任（303—304）。”［本文中未标具体出处的页码均出自王克非、韩宝成编 2015c］“我主张通译，切译，言之有文的翻译（317）。”他的翻译实践就是对他的阐译观最好的解释。例如，下面一段罗素《西方哲学史》的原文和译文。

The authority of science, which is recognized by most philosophers of the modern epoch, is a very different thing from the authority of the Church, since it is intellectual, not governmental. No penalties fall upon those who reject it; no prudential arguments influence those who accept it. It prevails solely by its intrinsic appeal to reason. It is, moreover, a piecemeal and partial authority; it does not, like the body of Catholic dogma, lay down a complete system, covering human morality, human hopes, and the past and future history of the universe.

科学的权威是近代大多数哲学家都承认的；由于它不是统治威信，而是理智上的威信，所以是一种和教会威信大不相同的东西。否认它的人并不遭到什么惩罚；承认它的人也决不为从现实利益出发的任何道理所左右。它在本质上求理性裁断，全凭这点制胜。并且，这是一种片段不全的威信；不像天主教的那套教义，设下一个完备的体系，概括人间道德，人类的希望，以及宇宙的过去和未来的历史。（罗素《西方哲学史》（下）马元德译，商务印书馆 1976 年版）

科学的权威，已为近世多数哲学家所承认。此一权威，殊不同于教会的权威。科学权威，理智的力量也；教会权威，统治的力量也。人于科学权威，可以拒绝，可以接受。拒绝，无须受惩罚；接受，无须出于保身家保名誉之考虑。科学所以有权威，唯一原因，是科学有内在的足以令人折服的力量。再者，科学的权威，明一理有一理之权威，明二理有二理之权威。科学的权威，止于已明之理；不若天主教义，乃包罗万象之体系，道德准则，人生理想，甚至世界之过去与未来，无一不在此体系之内。（许国璋译，307—308）

上面引文下划线处最容易看出其阐译之特点。前译是很贴近原文的，原文的每一个 it，译文大多以“它”或“这”对应之，而许译却不是，要将“it”的实指说明确，让读者易懂。比如下划线第一句，前译是紧随原文的，但意思不易读出，“它”字所指代要回看前面提到的科学权威，而“绝不为……所左右”这句也让人费解。许译将 it 所指明白地译为科学权威，并以人作为主语来看待科学权威及不同后果，prudential arguments 的含义也表述得更为清楚。下划线第二句的前译是很难读懂的，许译先是将所谓“它……全凭这点制胜”直截了当地译为"科学所以有权威,唯一原因……",然后将前译译不明白的"its intrinsic appeal to reason"晓畅地译成"科学有内在的足以令人折服的力量"。下划线的第三句虽然最短,却是最难移译的。什么是"piecemeal and partial authority"?前译告诉我们是"片段不全的威信"。但这能让读者明白吗?片段不全的威信是什么样的威信?许译阐释性地告诉我们:"科学的权威,明一理有一理之权威,明二理有二理之权威。科学的权威,止于已明之理。"原来,科学权威并不是所谓片段不全,而是对于每一业经探明的事物才具有权威的解释,不是事先就无所不知,如此而已。这是典型的许氏阐发式翻译,尽管语词超用许多,但意思非常明了,不晦涩,也不走形。

许国璋对此的解释是:"历史术语和哲学术语的翻译仅从字面上翻译是有困难的,必须同时考虑其文化内涵才比较完整(349)。"

由此,我们可以联系并思考翻译的显化问题。

所谓显化(或明晰化),是指"目标文本以更明显的形式表述源文本的信息,是译者在翻译过程中增添解释性短语或添加连接词等来帮助译本的逻辑性和易解性"(Shuttleworth & Cowie 1997:55),而翻译中的增添自然会导致译文比原文冗长,也有人解释说是"由于译语中提高了衔接上的明晰度造成的"(Blum-Kulka 1986:19)。学界对显化的关注主要在语言的表层。例如 Øverås(1998)专门做了英语/挪威语双语语料库调查,发现两个方向都有不同程度的词汇或语法的显化。不过,我们曾经(柯飞 2005:306)尝试性地论述了意义的显化,建议应将之纳入翻译研究的视野:"作为一种翻译现象,显化(以及隐化)不应只是狭义地指语言衔接形式上的变化,还应包括意义上的显化转换,即在译文中增添了有助于译文读者理解的显化表达,或者说将原文隐含的信息显化于译文中,使意思更明确,逻辑更清楚。这也是翻译特有的现象。"上面所举许国璋译文及其阐译思想,就是翻译中的意义显化的明证和理据。

不单是英译中,也不单是学术著作的翻译中会出现意义的显化,中译英以及文学作品里也有类似的例子。例如红楼梦里的一段。

(平儿在收拾衣物铺盖时)不承望枕套中抖出一绺青丝来。

To her surprise a long strand of hair fell out of the pillow-case.(杨宪益译)

To her surprise she felt something strange in the cover of Jia Lian's head-rest, and after groping inside it, fished out a black silky tress of woman's hair. (D. Hwakes 译)

杨译显然是贴近原文的英译,霍克斯却不然,他在英译文里添油加醋,如"she felt something strange…","after groping inside it","fished out","woman's hair"等,不仅是将意义显化了,甚至有为作者修改文章之意了。当然这点超出了我们说的意义显化的范畴,但中外翻译中仍不乏此类现象,也是值得讨论的。

比较而言,许国璋看来还是更欣赏霍克斯的翻译。他在"西方三位译家述评"(原"借鉴与拿来",载《外国语》1979 年 3 期)里曾这样点评:"霍氏译文……,我觉得最可重视之点,在于他注意到文化情境之移植,使西方读者不仅读到两个世纪以前的一部中国小说,而且看到中国社会的一个侧面,领略其中风光与人物。"他接着比较了霍跟另外一位译者的译文(327):

"形体倒也是灵物了! 只是没有实在的好处,须得镌上几个字,使人人见了便知你是件奇物……"

"Ha, I see you have magical properties! But nothing to recommend you. I shall have it cut a few words on you so that anybody seeing you will at once know that you are something special." (D. Hawkes 译)

"Your shape and substance are those of a spiritual object, but you lack real distinguishing merit. A few characters might be engraved on you so that everyone will know you for a unique thing." (Tsao and Kao 译)

许国璋对这两段译文的评价是,霍译"如果只是忠于作品——增一字不可,漏一字不许,必须字字扣紧——而忘了读者,那就会是完全另一种译法了"。他认为另一译文虽然确实做到字字扣紧了原文,但所说意思不清楚,行文也滞重。(327-328)他说:霍译里的"Ha, I see you have 是外加的;I shall have to cut 把原来的虚笔变成实话了;奇物译为 something special,也显得平淡,但是统篇读之,读者会觉得译文爽利、飘逸"……"读这段文字,读者会懂,还会被故事所吸引,轻快的散文节奏读起来完全不像翻译文字"。(328)类似的点评很多。在点赞霍克斯翻译的话语中,我们读到了许国璋主张的"翻译本身必须是艺术的创作"的观点,以及他赞成霍克斯忠于作者、读者、作品的翻译观。这些都与他的阐译观一脉相承。

我们在前文(柯飞 2005)提出过可能影响显化的因素,即语言因素、社会/文化因素、译者因素和文本因素等。上述译例部分说明了某个因素或某几个因素在翻译中起了显化的作用。这些还需要继续和深入的探讨。但是,许国璋先生早在 30 多年前即已认识到翻译的显化问题并提出阐译观,让我们感佩,也让我们感到需要更深入地研究翻译的显化问题,不仅仅是语言表层的形式显化,也包括底层的意义显化。

参考文献

柯飞:《翻译中的显和隐》,《外语教学与研究》2005 年第 4 期。

罗素著,何兆武、李约瑟译:《西方哲学史》,商务印书馆 1963/1980 年版。

王克非:《英汉/汉英语句对应的语料考察》,《外语教学与研究》2003 年第 6 期。

王克非、韩宝成编:《许国璋文集 · 语言卷》,外语教学与研究出版社 2015 年版。

王克非、韩宝成编:《许国璋文集 · 文学与文化卷》,外语教学与研究出版社 2015 年版。

许国璋:《关于索绪尔的两本书》,《外国语》1983 年第 1 期。

S.Blum－Kulka,"Shifts of Cohesion and Coherence in Translation",J. House & S. Blum－Kulka(eds.),*Interlingual and Intercultural Communication:Discourse and Cognition in Translation and Second Language Acquisition Studies*,Tübingen:Narr,1986.

Linn.Øverås,"In Search of the Third Code:An Investigation of Norms in Literary Translation",*Meta*,1998,Vol.43,No.4.

Mark Shuttleworth & Cowie Moira,*Dictionary of Translation Studies*,Manchester:St.Jerome Publishing,1997.

汉语文学翻译中人称代词的显化和变异

本文通过对汉语翻译文学语料库与汉语原创文学语料库的对比分析，探讨汉语翻译文学作品中人称代词使用的特征。本文发现：(1)汉语翻译文学中，各类人称代词的使用频率均高于原创文学；(2)第三人称代词“他”的复现率明显提高；(3)“他”在汉语翻译文学语料中的照应功能明显增强，出现了不同指“他”交替的偏离汉语语法常规的变异特征。人称代词语法显化和变异是汉语翻译文学的显著特征之一。这些特征可能反映了英语等形态比较丰富的语言对翻译汉语的干扰作用，体现了现代汉语翻译文学作品的陌生化操作规范。

一、人称代词与语料库翻译研究

现代汉语的代词除具备和名词相同的指别功能外，还具有照应功能，即与其他语言单位构成同指关系的功能。王力(1989)把代词归入“半虚词”，就是指代词的照应功能。人称代词的照应功能可按代词与名词性成分的关系分为同指和异指；按先行词与代词的位置关系分为前向照应和后向照应，也称为回指(anaphor)和前指(cataphor)(徐赳赳,2003)；按先行词与代词是否同在一个句子中分为句内照应和超句照应(董红源,2002:6-8)。代词可分三类：人称代词、指示代词和疑问代词，人称代词又分第一、二、三人称(即“三身代词”)，指示代词又分近指和远指。与英语及其他印欧语言相比，汉语代词的类型较少，使用频率较低(刘宓庆,1998:445-476;范仲英,1997:148-151)。汉语人称代词形式上没有主格宾格之分，代词所有格与英语的物主代词相比使用得更少。汉语常规的指代方式主要以“名词复现”和“零代词”为主，显性人称代词的使用频率一般较低。

据 Francis & Kučera（1982：547）和 Johansson & Hofland（1989：15，转引自 Leech 2001）对 BROWN 和 LOB 的统计，“想象型”语料比“信息型”语料明显更频繁地使用人称代词。胡显耀（2008）对汉语语料库的考察也说明汉语小说比其他文体更倾向于使用更多的人称代词。这说明多使用代词是英、汉语文学语料的共同特征之一，原因是以小说为主的文学语料通常以对话和叙述为主，而叙述通常以第三人称和第一人称为主。

在利用北京外国语大学“通用汉英对应语料库”①对翻译文学语料的人称代词考察中，我们发现，人称代词在汉语翻译文学语料中的使用频率、指代功能、照应方式等具有明显不同于汉语非翻译（即原创）语料的特征。总体而言，汉语翻译文学语料中人称代词的作用似乎更接近于英语等原语中的语法功能词或虚词，换言之，汉语翻译文学语料比原创文学语料更倾向于指代方式显化（explicitation），而不是遵循汉语常规，使用名词复现和零形代词的方式。此外，翻译汉语中人称代词的指代功能显著增强，照应方式上，出现了不同指的“他”同句和后向照应等一些汉语原创文本中少见的变异特征（deviation）。

二、翻译文学中人称代词的显化

根据各语料库的词性赋码标记，我们分别统计了主要人称代词在汉语原创文学语料和与之对应的英语翻译文学语料、英语原创文学语料和与之对应

① “通用汉英对应语料库”由北京外国语大学中国外语教育研究中心王克非主持建设。该语料库库容量达 3000 万字词。由翻译、百科、专科和对译语句等四个子库构成。其中翻译文本库容量为 2000 万字词，英译汉占 60%；汉译英占 40%，分别含文学和非文学语料。全部语料进行了句对齐和词性标注，可分类检索和考察词频、搭配等。文学语料中以小说为主。本文主要使用的语料为：A.汉语原创文学语料（73 万字）；B.与之对应的英语翻译文学语料（54 万词）；C.英语原创文学语料（60 万词）；D.与之对应的汉语翻译文学语料（104 万字）。

的汉语翻译文学语料（以下分别简称：汉语原创、英语翻译、英语原创和汉语翻译）中的使用频次，并标准化了各语料库每百万词中人称代词的数量。由于英语和汉语人称代词系统的差异，我们对统计数据进行了修正①。另外，为了全面了解两种语言的代词使用特征，我们将非人称代词“它”和“it”也列入了考察和比较范围。表1统计了上述四个子语料库中主要人称代词及其复数形式和所有格的频率。

表1　汉英文学（翻译）语料库主要人称代词词频比较（每百万词）

每百万词	原创汉语	翻译汉语	原创英语	翻译英语
我（I，me）	8 300	14 267	15 592	7 999
你（你们，you）	7 634	8 811	8 984	10 952
他（he，him）	11 726	17 328	19 149	15 950
她（she，her）	5 266	6 467	8 706	11 642
它（it）	531	2 058	14 600	8 035
我们（we）	1 716	2 787	2 644	3 007
他们（they，them）	2 781	4716	5 967	5 615
你的（your）	517	709	1 524	1 918
我的（my）	622	1 358	3 412	1 986
他的（his）	1 477	2 692	11 299	12 991
她的（her）	763	1 030	6 303	7 756
它的（its）	78	259	1421	724
合计	41 411	62 482	99 601	88 573

① 英语和汉语人称代词的形态不尽相同：汉语无主格宾格之分；英语 you 的单复数同形；英语的第三人称复数有 they、them 两种形式，而汉语有“他们、她们和它们”三种形式；英语的人称代词还有反身代词形式，而汉语以人称代词加“自己”来表示，等等。为了使两种语言的人称代词具有可比性，我们对统计各语料库的数据进行了修正，即“我”的英语对应频率应该是“I”及其宾格“me”之合；英语的 you 对应汉语“你”和“你们”；they/them 之合对应“他们、她们和它们”等。此外，由于汉语人称代词所有格是通过加“的”来实现的，因此我们从相应形式中扣除了人称代词加“的”的数量。

对表1数据进行分析，我们可以发现一些英汉语人称代词使用的系统差异，但更重要的是，汉语翻译文学与原创文学相比，人称代词使用中呈现的特殊性：

1　英汉语人称代词使用的系统差异

从表1中主要人称代词总频率来看，原创英语文学语料中人称代词总频率(99,601)是原创汉语文学语料(41,411)的2.4倍。图1列举了三个子语料库的主要人称代词的词频分布：最下面的曲线是原创汉语文学语料的人称代词频率，最上面是原创英语文学语料人称代词频率的变化曲线。可见，原创汉语全部人称代词频率均显著低于原创英语同类代词。

尽管已经有很多研究表明，英语的人称代词使用频率高于汉语，但语料库的量化研究使我们能够更精确地发现汉语比英语少用人称代词的具体程度和在不同形式间的分布。除总词频高低外，较明显的差别还有：

a.英语"it"的词频是汉语"它"的27.5倍。这是由于it在英语中除充当代词外，还有作为先行词、虚义词和强调词等功能(连淑能1993:81-82)。

b.英语第三人称"he/him"及其所有格"his"的使用频率与汉语相比有明显差别。其中"he/him"为"他"的1.6倍；"his"为"他的"的7.6倍。这一方面说明汉语文学语料通常较少使用人称代词所有格，另一方面可能是由于his在英语中可同时兼任形容词性和名词性所有格。

c.原创英语文学语料第一人称代词(I及其宾格me)总使用频率明显高于汉语"我"。

d.原创英语文学语料第三人称"he/him"的词频高于其他英语人称代词，是"she/her"的2倍；而汉语"他"虽略多与"她"但无明显差别。

2　汉语翻译文学与原创文学人称代词使用频率差异

图1中间实线为翻译汉语人称代词频率曲线。可看到，除了由于汉语语法规则的限制，"它"和"他的"远低于英语的"it"和"his"的频率之外，汉语翻译文学语料中人称代词的分布规律与原创汉语相近，但翻译汉语全部人称代词的使用频率皆高于原创汉语。较显著的差异是：a.第一人称单数"我"，翻译汉语是原创汉语的1.7倍；b.第三人称单数"他"，翻译汉语是原创汉语的1.5倍。

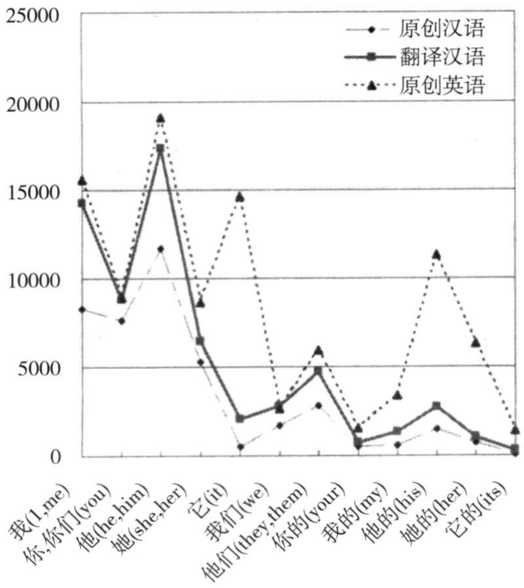

图 1　翻译汉语与原创英汉语人称代词频率比较

不少翻译教材和论文在谈到代词翻译的时候提出,英语倾向于更频繁地使用代词,而汉语更频繁地使用原词复现和“零形回指”(即省略代词或名词)的方式,因而在翻译中应少用代词多用原词复现等方式(如冯庆华 1997)。但从对翻译文学语料中人称代词的实际使用的统计分析来看,汉语翻译文学中人称代词的实际使用频率远远高出原创文学,除 it 和所有格 his/her 外,汉语翻译文学中的人称代词频率非常接近于英语。我们把汉语翻译文学中人称代词的这一特征称为人称代词的“语法显化”(grammatical explicitation)。

三、人称代词的变异:以“他”为例

人称代词回指研究表明第三人称代词“他”在汉语中具有特殊的作用。罗选民(2001:221)认为:“(人称指称)在汉语中最常见的是使用第三人称代词单复数形式”;王灿龙(2000:228)也提出:“在现代汉语系统中,人称代词

‘他’是使用频率最高的照应语之一（‘他’实际上也指‘她’‘他们’‘她们’）。”（以上转引自赵宏、邵志洪，2002；封宗颖、邵志洪，2004）。徐赳赳（2003：106-137）对“他”的格分布、语序列和延续性进行了统计研究。他认为照应语之间的语序列通常是名词最先出现接着以人称代词、零形式或名词复现的方式进行回指（即前向照应），而代词和零形式在前，名词后出现的前指（即后向照应）情况在汉语中虽然存在但非常少；他还提出汉语照应语延续性强弱依次是零形式、代词和名词（同上：111-114）。延续性实际上是同指的照应词（代词、名词和零形式）之间的距离①。照应词的使用受人物、情节、时间、连词和结构等的制约（同上：130-137）。本文以下具体分析“他”在翻译和原创文学语料中的使用特征：其一，“他”的复现率，即“他”和其他“他”之间的距离。其二，多“他”同时出现于一个句子的频率及特征，包括：（1）“他”的指代能力；（2）多“他”同句；（3）不同指“他”交替使用等。

1.“他”的复现率

本文所谓的“复现率”指“他”与其他“他”之间相隔的距离。这个概念是受回指理论的“延续性”影响产生的（徐赳赳，2003）。所谓延续性实际上就是同指的照应词（代词、名词和零形式）之间的距离。篇章语言学是通过“回数法”来计算同指词之间小句的数量。这种方法适用于小规模的篇章分析，但对于上百万词的语料库而言，人工回数小句是不现实的。因此，本文用复现率的概念来计算代词和名词的“延续性”，具体方法是：[复现率=语料库的句子数÷“他”的实际频率]。复现率的意义是衡量语料库中“他”与“他”之间平均相隔多少个句子，也就是各个“他”之间的平均距离。复现率的值越大，代词之间相隔的距离越远。为了比较翻译文学语料中人名和“他”的复现率，我们分别计算了各语料库中“他”和人名的复现率，见表2②：

---

① 具体方法是采用“回数法”数出指同代词或名词（token）之间的小句数量（value），再用该值除以代词或名词的数量得到平均每隔n个小句出现的代词或名词数（徐赳赳，2003：111-114）。

② 本表中的句数和频次皆为语料库的实际统计数。其中“他”不含“他的”和“他自己”；“he/him”为“he”和“him”频次之和，不含“his”。

表 2 “他”与人名的复现率

	原创汉语	翻译汉语	原创英语	翻译英语
句数	30 070	39 963	41 159	36 107
他(he/him)	6 582	13 092	12 719	13 577
复现率	4. 57	3. 05	3. 24	2. 66
人名	19 671	12 212	—	—
复现率	1. 53	3. 27	—	—

我们可以看到,汉语原创文学语料中的“他”的复现率为 4. 57,其含义为:平均每隔 4. 57 个句子会出现一个“他”。汉语翻译文学中“他”的复现率为 3. 05,即约每隔 3 个句子出现一次。显然,原创汉语中“他”的平均距离明显大于翻译汉语。而另一方面,一般认为汉语倾向于使用“名词复现”的指代方式,为了证实这个看法,我们也统计了汉语语料库中人名的复现率。结果发现:汉语翻译文学中人名的平均距离(3. 27)明显高于汉语原创文学(1. 53)。简言之,语料统计表明:汉语翻译文学中“他”更为密集,人名则更为稀疏。

由于“通用汉英平行语料库”由英汉双向的原创和翻译语料构成,故我们也以同样的方法计算了英语语料中的“he/him”的复现率。可以看到,翻译英语中“he/him”也比原创英语更为密集。这是否能在一定程度上说明“显化”是翻译汉语和翻译英语的共同特征,还有待进一步考察。应当指出的是,上述计算方法只能非常粗略地比较“他”或人名在语料库中的平均距离,而未考虑原创汉语和翻译汉语的句子长度。对于具体篇章中的“他”更适合用延续性来考察其回指特征。

2. 多“他”同句

同一句子中出现多个他的现象在现代汉语中并不少见,但一般而言,汉语更倾向于用“零形回指”或名词复现的方式来进行照应。先来看多“他”同句的频率,我们用 Xaira 检索编码器(query builder)对汉语原创文学和翻译文学语料中 2~6 个“他”在同一句子中共现的频率进行了统计:

表 3　多“他”同句的频率

	原创汉语		翻译汉语	
	原始频率	每百万词	原始频率	每百万词
总频率	7 666	13 658	15 447	20 445
2“他”同句	1 708	3 043	4 202	5 562
3“他”同句	377	672	1 128	1 493
4“他”同句	87	155	311	412
5“他”同句	26	46	93	123
6“他”同句	10	18	29	38

由上表可见，汉语翻译文学语料中同一个句子中多个“他”连用的现象比汉语原创文学高很多。2—6“他”同句的情况，翻译汉语几乎都是原创汉语的2倍多。因此，相对来说，同一句子中多个“他”并用的现象在翻译文学语料中是较常见的现象（如例（1）），而汉语通常采用人名与“他”交替使用的方式（如例（2））。而例（3）这样同一句子中出现多个音译人名的情况，在翻译文学语料中出现的情况很少，该句读起来非常吃力，人名音译加重了读者的阅读负担。

例（1）那顶帽子使他很是为难，他刚想往上衣口袋里塞的时候就被前面的人夺了过去，那动作既轻巧又自然，不由得这位笨拙的年轻人心里不感激。“他能体谅人，”他想，“他准会帮俺帮到底的。”（《马丁·伊登》）

例（2）但他没有走远，他只是在一个别人不注意的地方躲起来，他要跟着红艳去找王新——他断定红艳一定要找王新的。

例（3）波里娜·盖奥尔吉耶芙娜虽然没有向奥列格说明刘季柯夫叫他和杜尔根尼奇去的是什么地方，但是杜尔根尼奇立刻猜到，这是通往游击队的道路。（《青年近卫军》）

3. 不同指多“他”同句

值得注意的是，如果一段篇章中有多个人物交替出现，汉语通常都会以人名来指代，一般不会在同一句子中同时使用多个不同指的“他”。然而，我们对翻译文学语料中多“他”同句的索引和分析中发现，翻译文学语料中存在不少不同指“他”在同一句话中出现的例句：

例(4)他$_1$背上的孩子会不会突然掉下来，他$_2$腰上的孩子会不会因为他$_3$父亲的动作打扰了他$_4$的美梦而大声啼哭？(《本性》)[他$_{123}$同指父亲，他$_4$指小孩，两个不同指“他”交替]

例(5)他$_1$作为军事审判官决定的事，只有作为文职特派的他$_2$才能改变。(《九三年》)[他$_1$他$_2$各为两人，两个不同指“他”交替]

例(6)像这样被拖上街以前，别的孩子就不止一次大声喊他$_1$，讥笑他$_2$父亲，讥笑他$_3$老是当众宣扬他$_4$的宗教信仰。(《美国的悲剧》)[他$_1$他$_2$指儿子，他$_3$他$_4$指父亲]

例(7)他$_1$特别指给他$_2$看一个胖子，这人脸上流露出天真和善的神情，懒洋洋地倚在他$_3$身边一个女伴的肩上，用充满父爱的眼神深情地注视着他$_4$的女伴——一个纯朴的年轻姑娘。(《娜娜》[他$_1$他$_2$和他$_{34}$分别指三人，三个不同指“他”交替]

例(8)他$_1$又一次挥动左手，击中了那个炮手，炮手向他$_2$扑过来，抓住了他$_3$的上衣，扯下了他$_4$的袖子，他$_5$往他$_6$的耳朵后面狠狠揍了两拳，接着在他$_7$把他$_8$推开的时候，又用右手把他$_9$击倒在地。(《海明威短篇小说选》)[共出现9个“他”，他$_{1\text{-}4}$同指一人，他$_5$到他$_9$很难分清所指。]

我们在汉语非翻译语料库中未发现上述这种同一句子中多个不同指的“他”交替使用的情况。从汉语的角度来看，这种不同指“他”混用容易造成语义含混，让读者分不清“他”的所指。我们认为，这种现象可能有三个方面的原因：一是原文如此，英语等语言的句法结构层次清楚，因此，出现在主句和从句中的 he/him/his 很容易从句法形式上得到区分，故不同指的 he/him/his 同句也不会造成歧义。二是由于翻译文学语料中人名音译复杂冗长的客观情况，译者在译文中无法采用人名复现的方式来明确代词所指。三是在使用“他”还是使用零形回指两种选择中，多数译者选择了“他”的复现，这体现了翻译显化的基本取向，因为“他”的复现至少相对于零形回指来说更为明确一些。然而，译者没想到的是不同指的“他”交替使用反而造成了译文的含混和歧义。因此，我们认为，人称代词“他”的不同指同句是一种变异的翻译操作。

四、讨论和小结

综上所述，翻译文学语料中人称代词，尤其是第三人称代词“他”的使用频率显著高于原创文学语料。与英语原创小说相比，英语翻译文学语料除了 it 和人称代词的所有格频率较低外，其他人称代词的频率都呈现出与英语小说一致的高频率。人称代词在文学翻译语料中的复现率显著区别于原创文学语料和汉语总体，“他”之间的距离相隔更短。“他”在文学翻译语料中的照应功能显著增强，明显不同于原创文学语料更多使用“零形回指”的趋势。人称代词的增多和不同指的“他”交叉使用做法客观上产生了变异的效果。

人称代词显化的原因可能跟以英语为主的外国文学（主要是小说）的性质有关：一是人称代词所指代的人物的姓名译为汉语一般采取音译的方式。在汉语读者看来，外国人名显得冗长怪异。翻译中若让这些冗长和怪异的姓名不断“原词复现”显然是自找麻烦，有碍小说的可读性。第二，对英语等欧洲语言来说，人称代词，尤其是第三人称代词的语篇照应功能很强，人称照应是语篇衔接的重要手段。从欧洲语言翻译入汉语，第三人称“他”明显多于其他人称，可能也反映了这一特征。因为第三人称代词除了具有指别的功能外，还有第一、二人称代词所不具备的照应功能。

但为什么翻译文学语料中没有出现更多的“零形回指”而是选择了反复使用第三人称代词呢？这种“他他”不已的现象是出于怎样的操作规范？对译文又造成了什么影响呢？本文认为，汉语翻译文学中人称代词的差异性特征反映了现代汉语翻译文学（小说）显化的操作规范，即外译汉的小说翻译者在汉语的意合特征与欧洲语言的形合特征二者之间的实际选择是倾向于语法显化或“形合”。语法显化的总体目标是通过语法关系的明确化，降低文本阅读难度，增强翻译文本可接受性，但从汉语翻译文学的实际结果来看，显化的结果未必一定能降低翻译文本的阅读难度，有时反而出现了对汉语语法规范的偏离和变异。

（本文原载《中国外语》2010 年第 4 期。作者为王克非、胡显耀）

参考文献

W.N.Francis & H.Kučera, *Frequency Analysis of English Usage: Lexicon and Grammar*, Boston: Houghton Mifflin, 1982.

G. Kennedy, *An Introduction to Corpus Linguistics*, London and New York: Longman, 1998.

G.Leech, P.Rayson & A.Wilson, *Word Frequencies in Written and Spoken English based on the British National Corpus*, Harlow & London: Pearson Education, 2001.

G. Toury, *Descriptive Translation Studies and Beyond*, Amsterdam/Philadelphia: John Benjamins Publishing Company, 1995.

董红源:《汉语代词"他"的句内照应规则研究》,硕士学位论文,北京大学 2002 年。

范仲英:《实用翻译教程》,外语教学与研究出版社 1997 年版。

封宗颖、邵志洪:《英第三人称代词深层回指对比与翻译》,《外语学刊》2004 年第 5 期。

冯庆华:《实用翻译教程》,上海外语教育出版社 1997 年版。

胡显耀:《基于语料库的汉语翻译小说词语特征研究》,《外语教学与研究》2007 年第 3 期。

连淑能:《英汉对比研究》,高等教育出版社 1993/2002 年版。

刘宓庆:《文体与翻译》,中国对外翻译出版公司 1998 年版。

王力:《中国现代语法》,商务印书馆 1989 年版。

徐赳赳:《现代汉语篇章回指研究》,中国社会科学出版社 2003 年版。

赵宏、邵志洪:《英汉第三人称代词语篇照应功能对比研究》,《外语教学与研究》2002 年第 3 期。

关于翻译批评的思考

——兼谈《文学翻译批评研究》

大凡一件事有人开始从事,就有人开始批评。有文学创作发生,于是有文学批评;有翻译活动发生,翻译批评随之而来。汉末开始佛经翻译,三国时期支谦就提出翻译要“因循本,不加文饰”,东晋人道安提出“五失本三不易”等翻译主张。在近代西学翻译活动中,围绕严复的翻译而出现的评论就更多了。还有鲁迅与瞿秋白关于翻译的通信,近人茅盾、王宗炎等对译品的分析,以及近年在《读书》《中国翻译》《外语教学与研究》等刊物上关于翻译的种种讨论,都是在进行翻译批评,同时也是对翻译批评本身的探讨。翻译批评反映了人们进一步认识翻译和提高翻译水平的努力,它的作用逐渐受到重视。贺麟在谈及几十年前中国翻译界“芜滥沉寂”时认为,缺乏好的翻译批评是造成那种境况的原因之一。王佐良在《新时期的翻译观》(见《翻译:思考与试笔》,外语教学与研究出版社 1989 年版)文中将翻译研究分为三大类,即翻译理论探讨、译文品评、译文研究,其中译文品评即是翻译批评的内容。

但是以往对于翻译批评本身的认识和探讨却不够,对于如何恰当地准确地进行翻译批评,或者说,对翻译批评应用的方法和范围,还未开展充分的研究。南京大学的年轻教授许钧以其论文集《文学翻译批评研究》,“在探索合理、科学、公允地平价文学翻译的丛本途径与方法”上,走出了很有意义的一步。此书 1992 年由译林出版社出版,书中有关文学翻译批评的种种讨论,一方面拓深了我们的认识,另一方面促进了我们对翻译批评的思考。

一个文学批评家,他可以潜心于理论和作品的研究,不一定要从事文学创作。而一个翻译批评者,恐怕就需要理论和翻译实践兼得。许钧就是这样的两面兼得的批评者。他有二十年的口笔译实践，有500万字以上的译作，足可作为翻译批评的本钱。对于翻译问题，他多年来一直注意理论上的探讨，打下了翻译批评的理论基础。这样，他对翻译批评的论述就是有意义的，值得思索的。

全书共13篇。前4篇是对文学翻译批评的基本问题的理论探讨。后9篇则是结合具体译品（尤其是最后5篇结合名著《追忆似水年华》的翻译），凭借前述翻译批评方法开展翻译批评，论之有据，言之有物。

作者正确地表明自己不是要构建一门文学翻译批评学科理论体系（我对是否有这一学科和理论体系深为怀疑），不故弄玄虚，而是做实在的翻译批评研究。书中对于翻译批评的本质和方法，翻译作品的风格处理、文学翻译批评等问题的论述，以及作者自己译品的分析，都体现出实在的翻译批评研究。

什么是文学翻译批评？这可以从它所处的关系去理解；它以文学翻译作品为对象，而借助于翻译理论的指导。许钧认为“文学翻译批评不同于文学批评，但两者之间又存在着一定的共性”（194页）。他由两者的异同去认识文学翻译批评的本质。依据文学批评家叶维廉的观点，文学作品的产生有五个因素：1）作者；2）作者所观、感的世界（物象、人、事件）；3）作品；4）承受作品的读者；5）语言（包括文化历史因素）。借鉴这个分析，许钧推论一个文学译作的产生有五方面因素：

一是译者，他是翻译活动的主体；二是译者对作者所观、所感的世界的观、感；三是译作；四是承受译著的读者；五是语言（同样包括文化历史因素）。从上面五个相关的方面进行比较，我们可以发现翻译与创造（作）的根本区别在于第二个方面，那就是作者是通过文化，历史和语言等因素去观察、感受世界，作品中体现了他对世界的选择和认识（作品的思想内容），对世界所持有的观点（作品的思想倾向）；同时，作者还要用文字将他对世界的观，感的体验与经历表达出来……而读者也无形地制约着作者……文学翻译作品的五个方面中，译者所面对的是语言化了的、作者所观、所感的世界……同时，面对的读者变了，采刚的语言符号体系也改变了。因此，从大的方面讲，原作与译作之间的可比较因素主要集中在以下几个方面：1. 译者在具体作品中所观、所感的世界与作者意欲表现的世界是否吻合(包括思想内容、思想倾向、思维程式)？2. 译者所使用的翻译方法和手段与作者的具体创作方法和技巧(包括艺术安排、技巧、语言手段)是否统一？3. 译作对读者的意图、目的与效果与原作者对读者的意图、目的与效果是否一致(包括对读者审美的期待及读者的反应)？(第 44—45 页)

从文学翻译与文聿创作的关系、译作与原作的关系考察文学翻译批评问题,富有启发意义,道理讲得也更清楚。我们可以简明地顺着信、达、雅标准展开翻译批评,但上面这段论述有助于我们明了具体从哪些方面入手翻译批评,比如上述三个主要的可比较因素(不过我个人对某些说法——如翻译方法和手段与创作方法和技巧的一致、译作和原作的读者的意图等——持保留态度)。把翻译批评仅仅集中于译作本身——这是我们常能见到的——还不够,还只是单层次的,如果能兼及多方面因素及其关系,翻译批评才可能更具说服力,并解释译风、译德、译效等问题。

有一点需要补充解释的是,文学翻译批评同文学批评还是有很大差别的。文学艺术以其塑造的文学形象反映主、客观世界,表现出作者的情感和认识(即对世界所观、所感),是社会意识形态范畴。文学批评就是批评者以其关于文学的本质、特征、社会作用等的认识,对作者、作品(包括思想内容和艺术手法等)以及文学思潮、社会效果等进行探讨,这是本体的、第一性的批评。翻译基本上是两种(或多种)语言转换的一种艺术或技能,思想、形象、风格、手法等等均是原著的,翻译批评则主要是就语言转换后的译品与原作在思想、形象、风格、手法诸方面的差距大小以及造成差距的原因加以探讨,这种批评是非本体的,第二性的。

因此,翻译批评的指归在研究译品、褒优斥劣、探讨译法、提高翻译质量,这与文学批评也是不一样的。

许钧对于文学翻译批评的原则、层次和方法等也有深入的思考。他指出译文原文对照式的评论或凭印象评说的弊病,对批评的原则提出了四条意见。论及批评层面和角度时,他提出应注意动态地看待译作语言符号系统、注重内容的比较、选取译作与原作间的比较重点和承认译作的限度四方面问题。书中又归纳了六种基本的批评方法,即 1)逻辑验证的方法;2)定量定性分析的方法;3)语义分析的方法;4)抽样分析的方法;5)不同翻译版本的比较和6)佳译赏析的方法。这自然比对照式的和凭印象式的评说方法进了一大步。

谈到翻译批评的层面和方法,我们不妨再考虑一下翻译批评的侧重。

英国翻译理论研究者纽马克(Peter Newmark)在《翻译教科书》(A Textbook of Translation)(1988)中辟有专章讨论翻译批评。纽马克认为翻译批评应注意五个方面:1)分析原文,即分析作者的意图和语言特点,据此可在译文中采用相应文体和译法。2)分析译文,重点是分析译者对原作的理解,译法如何,但也应注意影响译者的翻译的其他因素。3)比较原文和译文,以语言比较为主,抽取有代表意义的部分比较。4)评价译文质量。5)关于译本在目的语文化氛围中的价值。

不过我们注意到,3)、4)两方面也可以并入到第2)方面,而5)基本上是翻译文化史上的问题。因此,简洁地说,翻译批评主要侧重1)、2)方面,而前者涉及的是理解,后者涉及的主要是表达。转了一圈,翻译批评又回到了翻译的两个主要问题即理解和表达上。翻译的要害(理解——包括对原作思想、文化、语言等表达——在准确理解的基础上运用好译文语言)就是翻译批评的侧重,至于对译本的评价、对译者的工作态度和水平的评价,都包含于其中。

能否再现原作风格一直是翻译的难题,也是翻译批评关注的重点。这方面最有名的例子是关于荷马史诗的译文,阿诺德所提出的批评。阿诺德认为“在节奏上荷马是轻快的;在文字风格上荷马是清晰的;在意义上荷马总是单纯的;在作法上荷马是庄严的”,可是考珀、蒲柏的译文在风格的处理上都是失败的。英国另一批评家杨(Edward Young,1683~1765)认为“庄严壮丽是(荷马)英雄诗歌的高贵本质所不可缺的”,蒲柏及其以前的译者均未能保持住这个风格,因而影响了阿喀琉斯英勇形象的再现(参看伍蠡甫编《西言文论选》499页)。可以说,译作成功与否同原作风格的再现有很大关系。许钧以傅雷为例对风格所做的评析是有说服力的。一部作品的风格有两方面因素,一是作者和作品中表现的思想、气质等,二是作品的语言、体裁以及社会文化影响等,而在翻译中再现原作风格时,又不免受到详者的思想认识、气质和语言习惯等因素影响,所以风格的再现虽然重要,却难以完整无损。翻译艺术大师傅雷的译品为人称道，也不免在风格上有失，许钧举的几例能说明问题。如傅雷喜用“倘若”一词，有时与作品中人物身份、教育水平不符，就是译者遣词造句习惯影响到原文语言风格再现。又如在翻译梅里美、巴尔扎克、莫罗阿等人作品时，由于傅译语言风格，各具风格的三位法国作家在译文中却走到相似的风格上来了。

可见，文学翻译有个“度”的问题。这个“度”，一是说明翻译有限度，有局限性，批评家不可苛责。二是说明翻译还是有可度量的标准；不及这个度，可能是硬译死译；太过，犹不及，有滥译之嫌。许钧论“文学翻译再创造的度”也是值得读读的文章。

许钧还是一位细心的译者。他参与巨著《追忆似水年华》的翻译，积累了不少批评的素材，书中后五篇论文就是讨论自己这一翻译实践中对句式的处理、风格的再现，以及整体的评价。这也反映出作者勇于剖析自己的探索精神，文中不乏给人启发的译例。不过有些译法，我们有不同意见，借此提出一例以就教于作者。

在112—113页上，有段法文的直译是“在古教堂附近，几乎与古教堂一样古老、可敬，长满青苔的鸨母站在声名狼藉的（妓）院门前……”。作者认为以教堂的古老、可敬、长满青苔来形容鸨母不妥，且形象模糊，难以引起读者共鸣。于是做一番变通，以教堂的古老比鸨母的人老，以古教堂门面长满青苔喻鸨母脸皮厚，而“令人肃然起敬”，则是一种反讽。修订译文为：“在古教堂附近，鸨母老脸皮厚，却又令人肃然起敬，可与古教堂长满青苔的门面相比，只见她站在声名狼藉的（妓）院门前……”。可是后译似乎还不及前译。句子不大通顺，“鸨母……，只见她……”这之间连接不起来。“老腔皮厚”与“像教堂一样古老”差别很大，贬义过显，后面又跟着“肃然起敬”、“可与……相比”，意义衔接不好，反倒形象模糊，句子也拖沓，所以还不如稍有些欧化的直译。直译若作修改，可试改为“在古教堂附近，一个像这座布满青苔的、古老肃穆的教堂似的鸨母，正站在……”

另外，书中有些文字错误以后应避免。如有几处将李健吾误写成李键吾，曹禺误写成曹寓（也许这是按拼音法进行电脑排版造成的）。人名的书写宜慎重。

无论原作、译作，都离不开语言这个载体，思想、情感、形象都是通过语言呈现的，因此，在翻译和翻译批评研究中，第一位的重点是语言。但是，言可表意，却不可尽意，文可载道，却不能尽道。用本族语表达所思所感尚且如此，经过翻译而以另种语言表达就更有局限了，这是一个有哲学意味的话题，贺麟说："意属形而上，言属形而下，前者为一，后者为多。二者颇似哲学中谈论的体与用、道与器的关系"（张岂之等编《译名论集》贺麟序）。就是说，同一意思可有多种传达。这是翻译之所以成立的哲学基础。同时，不同的传达对于意思总有微妙的差异，这又是翻译的困难与技巧所在。

罗素（B.Russell）在《人类的知识》中说，知识有社会的，也有个人的。同理，语言基本上是社会性的，但也是有个性化的。我们把语言放到世界范围看，可知语言中还有民族文化的历史的沉淀。

金岳霖对此的思索是：语词中意念上的意义越清楚，情感上的寄托越少；意念上的意义越不清楚，情感上的寄托越容易丰富。前者是"意"，相当于社会性的，后者是"味"，相当于个性的、民族性的。"意"因为是社会性的，在翻译中易找对应语词。"味"因为是个性的、民族性的，富于情感力量与色彩，在翻译中不易找到对应者。至于"意境"，即作者主观情感与一定客观事物交融而得的境界，常常具有特定性，"味"更足，尤难译。

因此，对于不同作品，翻译时可有不同的考虑，不同的取舍，不同的要求，翻译批评也应充分认识到这一点。

纽马克注意到这个问题，他提出一切翻译在某种程度上说可以是科学的、技巧的、艺术的、情趣的问题（A Textbook of Translation，p.189）。这四个特点，决定了在进行译文分析批评时的四个视角。这看来是有意义的。对于理论性的、叙述性的科学著作，我们多用前两个视角，对于文学作品，后两个视角更为主要。

最后应当提出的一点是，翻译批评还应有翻译文化史的意识。翻译毕竟是跨文化的沟通与交流。歌德就特别指出应从世界各民族文化及其交流的大背景中考察翻译及其方法。他认为有三种翻译：1）以了解外界为目的的翻译；2）试图吸收世界文化精神的翻译；3）注重译文与原文一致的翻译（参看许钧《文学翻译与世界文学——歌德对翻译的思考及论述》），《中国翻译》1991

年第4期)。从翻译文化史看,起到重大的文化作用的译本,不一定是翻译精品。翻译常常是一种再创造,尽管有时掺杂一些误解、删改、发挥种种不准确现象,但就总体来看,它依然能够创生出很有意义的效果。

(本文原载《外语教学与研究》1994年第3期)

译学工具书的分类与研编

本节综合考察了中外十多种翻译工具书，从翻译研究的角度对翻译工具书作了基本的分类，提出可区分翻译实务类、翻译研究类和翻译史类三大类翻译工具书。作者认为宜借助翻译研究的成果，特别是国外成功的翻译史与翻译研究类词典，研、译结合，编纂出新型多卷本《翻译大百科全书》（含译学译史卷、翻译书目卷、翻译鉴赏卷、翻译参考卷、翻译人物卷、译名卷等）。

一、绪言

20 世纪是翻译学科大发展的世纪。据初步统计，近 50 年我国出版有关翻译的书籍多达七百余种，有关翻译的论文则在一万篇左右。但其中工具类书籍以及相关论文，截至 20 世纪 90 年代前，寥寥无几；而此后十几年却有多部翻译工具书相继编纂出版，显示这方面工作开始受到重视。其实也正是翻译实践的增长和翻译理论的深入，使人们需要将积累下来的大量翻译知识、资料、论述等系统地加以整理，方便学习者和研究者查取，也利于对该学科开展进一步的探讨。本文首先从翻译研究的角度区分翻译工具书的种类，并就我们已有的以及国际上主要的翻译词典，讨论翻译工具书的研制和编纂。

二、翻译工具书的种类

翻译应区分翻译实务和翻译研究；前者是应用型的，后者是理论性的。翻译工具书因此也应区分是为实务类还是为研究类翻译服务的。

我们还曾论述(1997a)关于翻译的研究可大致分为三类,即翻译技巧研究,翻译理论研究和翻译(文化)史研究。相应地,翻译工具书除了上述为实务类和为研究类服务之外,还有一种可用做翻译文化史研究。以下是我们试对翻译工具书所作的三类六种之区分。

1. 人、地、事件、机构等专名词典

这一类工具书为翻译工作者在实际翻译中常常会遇到的各种人物、地名、事件、机构、组织、商标等提供查寻之便利,商务印书馆、新华出版社、外研社等都出版过这类词典(如《外国地名译名手册》《英语姓名译名手册》等),是翻译工具书中较早被编辑出版的。

2. 翻译参考书

这类工具书约在 20 世纪 80 年代后期才出现。根据参考性又可分语句类和百科类,即为翻译工作者提供可资参考的翻译例句和有关翻译的各种知识。

最早的翻译参考书(语句和百科兼有)大概是曹焰、张奎武主编的《英汉百科翻译大词典》(人民日报出版社,1992)。全书约 1000 万字,分上、下两册;译例丰富,多达 15 万条。该书的百科性体现在所收的 13 种附录,即地名译名表、人名译名表、世界著名公司译名、重要英文报刊译名、各国政党译名、各国通讯社译名、国际事件及条约译名、重要国际组织译名、常见商标译名、希腊罗马神话重要人物译名、圣经人物译名、英美社会文化背景专有名词及缩略语表。

属于语句类参考工具书的还有:刘重德主编《英汉翻译例句词典》,湖南文艺出版社 1999 年版;1169 页,收例句 5 万多条。日本中村保男编《英和翻译表现词典》(及续编),日本研究社,1999/2002,940 页,翻译例句 4 万多条。这些都是既便于学习又便于教学的很实用的参考书。

百科类翻译参考书主要有林煌天主编《中国翻译词典》(湖北教育出版社 1997 年版,245 万字)。该词典共分 10 个领域:翻译理论、翻译技巧与翻译术语、翻译人物、翻译史话、译事知识、翻译与文化交流、翻译论著、翻译社团、翻译出版机构、百家论翻译,计 3700 余条。其主要部分是“综合条目”和“百家论翻译”,后者收有中外 200 多译家对翻译的论述。其附录也有价值,计有

“中国翻译大事记”、“外国翻译大事记”、“中国文学作品书名汉英对照目录”、“外国文学作品书名外汉对照目录”、“中国当代翻译论文索引”、“世界著名电影片名英汉对照索引”、“联合国及有关国际组织、职务和职称、国际文献与条约译名录”。

以上两种应属于为实务类翻译服务的工具书。

3. 翻译家词典

顾名思义,这种工具书收录著名的或有一定成就的翻译家的业绩。国内出版的有林辉等编的《中国翻译家辞典》(中国对外翻译出版公司1988年版),约收1100余人。还有林煌天、贺冲寅主编的《中国科技翻译家词典》(上海翻译出版公司1991年版)。这种词典对我们了解翻译界人物、书目、史实等都非常有用,虽然在所收人物词条上总不免有遗珠之憾。如《中国翻译家辞典》就漏收近现代史上著名的翻译家吴趼人、吴梼、戢翼翚、徐念慈、陈鸿璧、陈嘏、陆志韦等,而同时却收录了一些不必收入的人名。1999年马珂、孙承唐等在该书基础上续编《中国当代翻译工作者词典》(陕西教育出版社),对十年前的《中国翻译家辞典》作了保留和增补。增补的大多是中青年翻译工作者,跟时代更为贴近。但该书的一个缺点是,编者似缺乏审定,有急就之感,译者条目大多为译者自己撰写,在格式、篇幅和风格上差别很大,而且有些条目含个人评价色彩(例如说某人是“全世界有史以来唯一的……”),影响了辞书的客观性和中立性。

4. 翻译书目

这类工具书与其说是供译者使用,不如说是供研究者使用的。它大概是最早出现的翻译工具书。如阿英编《晚清小说目录》,日本国会图书馆编《明治、大正、昭和翻译文学目录》(1959),谭汝谦编《中国译日本书综合目录》和《日本译中国书综合目录》(1980)两大本,以及日本学者樽本照雄历时十多年辛苦编录的《新编清末民初小说目录》(1997)等。这些书目为翻译史、文化史、文学史、社会史等方面的学者提供了极为有益的参考,它们的史料价值我们已讨论过(王克非1997b,2001),此处不赘。

以上两种属于翻译史类的工具书。

5. 翻译研究类词典/百科

这类词典是近十年随着翻译研究升温而兴起的一类工具书,重在收集和解释有关翻译的学术研究和术语等问题。如 Sin-wai Chan & D.Polard(eds.), *An Encyclopeadia of Translation: Chinese-English, English-Chinese*(《中英、英中翻译百科全书》,香港中文大学出版社,1995);M.Shuttleworth and M.Cowie, *Dictionary of Translation Studies*(《翻译研究词典》,St.Jerome,1997),该词典收词条420多条,每条均有详细的解释,对了解译学术语来源、含义、理论归属等都很有帮助;还有 Mona Baker(ed.), *Routledge Encyclopedia of Translation Studies*(《翻译研究百科全书》,Routledge,1998),我们曾做过简要介绍(王克非,2000);以及孙迎春编《译学大词典》(中国世界语出版社,1999)等。近年英国伦敦大学学院(UCL)Theo Hermans 教授正组织翻译研究领域的学者编写规模更大的《国际翻译研究百科全书》(*An International Encyclopedia of Translation Studies*),详情见下节。

6. 翻译研究书目、文摘

这也是因翻译研究成果积累所需而编辑的一类工具书,便于研究者查找有关文献资料。如 Sinwai Chan(陈善伟)编 *A Topical Bibliography of Translation and Interpretation*(《翻译与传译主题分类书目》,香港中文大学出版社,1995)。此书特点是,中外研究论著兼收,将全部约1万条书目细分为169个主题,并附有作者检索,便于使用者翻检。但这样的书目若干年后就需要新编。近年来,英国曼彻斯特大学科技学院 Sara Laviosa 主持编辑的 *Translation Studies Abstracts*(《翻译研究文摘》,St.Jerome 出版社),以期刊形式出版,能及时反映国际译学界最新研究成果。同类工具书还有新出版的罗选民主编《中华翻译文摘》(清华大学出版社2002年版),以及即将出版的朱纯深、王克非等编《中文翻译研究论文题录与文摘》(1995—1999,英汉双语),后者在筛选、提要以及分类、检索上均有独特之处,英汉双语形式编排,利于中文翻译研究成果为世界所了解。

以上两种属于翻译研究类工具书。

三、工具书的研编

以上既讨论种类,也点评了国内外十多种翻译词典或百科全书。从总的情况看，目前的翻译工具书，以实务类的编纂得比较好，翻译史类的中等，即强于人物部分（仅限于中国翻译家），而弱于书目部分，翻译研究类则显得较弱，还难以同国际上几部翻译研究类词典相比。

关于翻译工具书的研编，我们还是分别探讨。

以实务类工具书即上述一、二种来说，有四点需要注意。一是这类工具书应该在出版后 5—10 年间重新编辑或修订，以适应翻译实务上的需要。因为新的人名、地名和事物名称以及翻译上所需各种知识是不断涌现的。二是香港、台湾在较长时间里与内地（大陆）隔离，语言表达上特别是译名上，有许多不同之处。例如人名，原美国总统 Bush，内地（大陆）通译布什，香港译为布殊，台湾译为布希；原美国国防部长 Lamsfield，大陆通译拉姆斯菲尔德，台湾译为伦斯斐；伊拉克被推翻的总统，大陆译为萨达姆—侯赛因，台湾译为海珊，让大陆人完全不知所称为何人。其他人名、地名、机构名称等也有诸多迥异之处，对实际交往造成一些不便，这些都应该在这类工具书上予以适当的解决。三是供学习参考用的翻译例句词典似还可在体例、编排上更进一步。从曹焰、张奎武（1991）和刘重德（1999）看，两本词典都按英文词语的顺序排列，以常用词语为主体，兼收各学科基本术语，“突出翻译的多样性和灵活性”。这是做得比较成功的。拿常用词例句来说，在刘（1999）中，有的词条仅一二例句，而 answer，join 等配有几十个例句，go，make，do，get，give 等更是有一二百例句之多。至于翻译的多样性和灵活性，刘（1999）在序言里举例谈到，最普通的 and 的翻译也不仅限于“和”、“与”“同”之类，曹、张（1991）在 and 词条下所举例句也证明了这一点。如：

He accepted the job, no *and* about it.他接受了这项工作，没有附加条件。

I guess I lost faith, *and* I was wrong.我想我失去了信心，然而我错了。

Instead of putting it off and hastening along, she yielded herself up to the pull, *and* stood passively still.她并没有把棘树用手摘开，往前快快走去，却就着棘树这一拉的劲儿，索性就老老实实地站住了。

我们看到，这三处 and 在汉译文里均为活译，虽然二、三句的翻译略有点小问题。另外，这两本例句词典都是英译汉，目前还没有看到汉译英的例句词典，而这方面显然也是非常需要的。

第四点就是，编写翻译参考书，在语句方面必须依靠大型双语语料库，才便于获得更多的对译材料（参看王克非 2002）。

关于第二类工具书的研编，应当在两方面上下工夫。其一，如上所述，中国翻译家的词条有待增补，国外翻译家词条更是需要从零做起。其实国际上尚未出版这类翻译家词典，我们需要仔细收集材料，从几大语种分别入手，才能编纂出适当的翻译家词典，同时也是为世界翻译史的研究做出一份重要的贡献。其二，翻译书目是我们对翻译史的总结，是对翻译文化史进行深入研究必不可少的，否则我们无从了解翻译与文化发生作用及其影响的真实面貌。以中国翻译书目而言，文学方面做得稍好，但也只是在小说这部分。科学文献的翻译情况有黎难秋的《中国科学文献翻译史稿》（1993）作了基本探讨，具体书目等后续工作还有待艰苦的努力。近代以来社会科学文献的翻译情况就只能说不甚了了，因为我们至今还没有编出相关的书目和文献资料。

至于第三类工具书的研编，如上所述，是相对薄弱的。孙迎春《译学大词典》（1999）在这方面起了个头。该词典第一、二部分，即“名词、术语、理论概念”和“翻译的方法与技巧”，名副其实，属翻译研究类，应当说做得还不错；第五部分“学术著作选介”也可视为此类。但第四部分“译学名人”所列并非“译学”上的名人，而多半是翻译上的名人，与翻译家词典类同；其第三部分“译文赏析”和第六部分“著名译作选介”、第七部分“英汉、汉英翻译实例”均不属于译学范畴。所以主编邀请翻译理论家奈达为词典题写书名时，奈达题写的是 Aspects of Translation，即“翻译面面观”，倒是恰如其分。不过以孙迎春（2002）对编纂译学工具书的孜孜探求，人们相信他会取得更可观的成就。

反观国际上在研究类翻译工具书的编写方面确实有我们可借鉴的地方。Mark Shuttleworth & Moira Cowie（1997）合编的《翻译研究辞典》（*Dictionary of Translation Studies*），对 420 多个译学术语做了较为详尽的定义和解释，包括对其源出和不同观点中含义都做了说明，是对这一学科及其术语规范化的贡献。Mona Baker（1998）的《翻译研究百科全书》则侧重理论和历史两个方面，全书相当于 112 篇论文，很有参考价值。我们（2000）已做过评介。特别值得一提的是 Theo Hermans 等七人主编的《国际翻译研究百科全书》（*An International Encyclopedia of Translation Studies*）。这是一项巨大的工程。主编者约请了世界上几十位译学专家撰写条目。全书分三卷，共五大部分，45 章，415 节；这 415 节其实就是 415 篇独立的论文。我们不妨先由其章节窥其全貌，为我所参考。

一、翻译的人类学基础、文化语境与形式（11 节）
二、现代世界中翻译的出现（4 节）
三、翻译是学术研究问题（17 节）
四、从语言学和语篇方面研究翻译：语言学基础（8 节）
五、语言学翻译研究的领域、概念和方法（17 节）
六、语言学翻译研究中语言与风格的问题（23 节）
七、语言学翻译研究中的语篇类型（13 节）
八、语言学翻译研究：翻译分析、翻译比较和翻译批评（6 节）
九、机器翻译或机助翻译（3 节）
十、口译与口译研究（2 节）
十一、翻译与文化研究的基本概念和研究方法（3 节）
十二、文学与文化翻译研究中的问题：1）文体（7 节）
十三、文学与文化翻译研究中的问题：2）语篇的宏观/微观结构（6 节）
十四、文学与文化翻译研究中的问题：3）诗歌（3 节）
十五、文学与文化翻译研究中的问题：4）散文（3 节）
十六、文学与文化翻译研究中的问题：5）多媒介翻译（6 节）
十七、不同文化间的翻译：1）条件、背景与影响（15 节）
十八、不同文化间的翻译：2）古代世界（11 节）
十九、不同文化间的翻译：3）中古时期、近东地区（11 节）
二十、不同文化间的翻译：4）中世纪、东南亚（6 节）
二十一、不同文化间的翻译：5）中世纪、欧洲（15 节）
二十二、不同文化间的翻译：6）欧洲文艺复兴（17 节）
二十三、现代不同文化间的翻译：1）世界文学的时代（6 节）
二十四、现代不同文化间的翻译：2）社会文化背景（5 节）
二十五、现代不同文化间的翻译：3）历史和地区的动力（13 节）
二十六、现代不同文化间的翻译：4）革新与背离（9 节）

二十七、现代不同文化间的翻译:5)现代世界的全球化现象(6节)

二十八、德语地区的翻译与文化史(18节)

二十九、英国、爱尔兰的翻译与文化史(14节)

三十、法国的翻译与文化史(7节)

三十一、意大利的翻译与文化史(7节)

三十二、伊比利亚半岛的翻译与文化史(7节)

三十三、欧洲其他国家和地区的翻译与文化史(19节)

三十四、北非与近东国家和地区的翻译与文化史(6节)

三十五、撒哈拉以南(中北非)国家和地区的翻译与文化史(4节)

三十六、亚、澳、太平洋地区的翻译与文化史(8节)

三十七、南北美洲国家和地区的翻译与文化史(8节)

三十八、因翻译而传布于世界的文本:1)圣经(13节)

三十九、因翻译而传布于世界的文本:2)荷马(8节)

四十、因翻译而传布于世界的文本:3)莎士比亚(10节)

四十一、因翻译而传布于世界的文本:4)其他有世界读者的作品(10节)

四十二、因翻译而传布于世界的文本:5)翻译选本和系列(4节)

四十三、口笔译者:1)职业译员(12节)

四十四、口笔译者:2)培训/课程和工作环境(12节)

四十五、索引(2节)

这部正在编写中的百科全书,如编者所言,是对翻译研究的不同种类和不同分支的全面评述,它涉及所有翻译现象,包括语内、语际和符际之间的翻译转换,也包括翻译而引起的社会、物质、语言、思想和文化等方面的变异,即从历时、共时和系统的方面综合考察翻译现象,并记录迄今为止最重要的翻译研究成果。简单地讲,第一部分1—10章,包含翻译的基本问题和对这些问题的不同争论,第二部分11—16章,从语言、文学、文化的角度分析翻译问题,第三部分17—27章,从纵向和横向历时地考察不同文化间的翻译交往,第四部分28—42章,则将翻译置于更广泛的跨文化背景中加以考察,实即翻译文化史研究,最后第五部分的两章是关于口笔译者的,属于应用翻译研究。

值得注意的是，这部翻译百科全书特别关注翻译与文化史的联系，45 章中就有 26 章的大半篇幅专门讨论翻译文化史。它以基于文化史的翻译研究，从宏观和微观两方面，考察翻译现象及其与语言、思想、物质生活之间的相互关联，认为正是这些语言、思想、物质生活的需要使翻译活动得以产生，后者反过来又促进了前者的发展。如此开展的翻译研究主要从文化、历史的层面上进行人文科学的比较，以期对文化传统以及对文化的交流与接受有更充分的理解。

由上述看来，在翻译研究类工具书方面，我们宜充分借鉴国际上的成果。但国外译界对中国情况，包括汉语与外语之间的翻译，缺乏了解甚至有差误。我们应当研究与编译结合，编纂出多卷本的《翻译大百科全书》，它包括译学译史卷、翻译书目卷、翻译鉴赏卷、翻译参考卷、翻译人物卷、译名卷（分中外），推动我国的翻译研究和翻译事业。至于翻译研究书目和文摘，则需每年连续出版，如 Sara Laviosa 所编 *Translation Studies Abstracts* 一样。

无论对哪一类翻译工具书的研编，网络和双语平行语料库都是新兴的和非常必要的工具，这一点我们另文探讨。

（本文原载《中国翻译》2003 年第 4 期）

参考文献

Mona Baker(ed.), *Routledge Encyclopedia of Translation Studies*, London & New York: Routledge, 1998.

Sinwai Chan (ed.), *A Topical Bibliography of Translation and Interpretation, Chinese-English, English-Chinese*, Hong Kong: The Chinese University Press, 1995.

Sinwai Chan and D. Polard (eds.), *An Encyclopedia of Translation: Chinese-English, English-Chinese*, Hong Kong: The Chinese University Press, 1995.

Theo Hermans, *An International Encyclopedia of Translation Studies*. Berlin: Walter de Gruyter. 2010.

M. Shuttleworth & M. Cowie. *Dictionary of Translation Studies*, St. Jerome Publishers, 1997.

曹焰、张奎武主编:《英汉百科翻译大词典》,人民日报出版社 1992 年版。

台湾国立国会图书馆编:《明治、大正、昭和翻译文学目录》,风间书房 1959 年版。

黎难秋:《中国科学文献翻译史稿》,中国科学技术大学出版社 1993 年版。

林煌天主编:《中国翻译词典》,湖北教育出版社 1997 年版。

林煌天、贺冲寅主编:《中国科技翻译家词典》,上海翻译出版公司 1991 年版。

林辉主编:《中国翻译家辞典》,中国对外翻译出版公司 1988 年版。

刘重德主编:《英汉翻译例句词典》,湖南文艺出版社 1999 年版。

罗新璋编:《翻译论集》,商务印书馆 1984 年版。

罗选民主编:《中华翻译文摘》,清华大学出版社 2002 年版。

马珂、孙承唐主编:《中国当代翻译工作者词典》,陕西教育出版社 2001 年版。

孙迎春主编:《译学大词典》,中国世界语出版社 1999 年版。

孙迎春:《论译学词典的描写性》,《外语与外语教学》2002 年第 9 期。

谭汝谦编:《中国译日本书综合目录》,香港中文大学出版社 1980 年版。

王克非:《论翻译研究之分类》,《中国翻译》1997 年第 1 期。

王克非:《翻译文化史论》,上海外语教育出版社 1997 年版。

王克非:《翻译研究百科全书》点评,《外语教学与研究》2000 年 1 期。

王克非:《论翻译文化研究的基础工作》,《外国语言文学研究》2001 年第 1 期。

王克非:《基于语料库的多重语言翻译研究》,张后尘编:《来自首届中国外语教授沙龙的报告》,商务印书馆 2002 年版。

[日]中村保男编:《英和翻译表现词典》(及续编),日本研究社 1999/2002 年版。

[日]樽本照雄编:《新编清末民初小说目录》,清末小说研究会 1997 年版。

翻译测试中的理论与实践问题

本文首先从理论上探讨翻译测试的分类及性质，分析翻译测试的构念，然后通过比较国内外翻译测试在侧重与方式上的异同，重点讨论翻译测试设计实施过程中的考试方式、试题编制、评分方式等环节，认为翻译测试的设计应明确测试的构念，即“何为翻译能力”，并根据不同的测试目的，选择直接或间接的考试方式，选取待译文本，确定其难度和文本特征以及适合的评分方式。

翻译测试是一项具有理论意义和应用价值的研究课题。设计合理的测试可以更好地对受试翻译水平进行认证，有助于学校或社会团体选拔优秀翻译人才，也有利于教师更客观有效地评估学生的翻译能力，并在此基础上调整教学目标、教学内容和教学方法。

Holmes（1972/1988）将翻译研究分为纯翻译学和应用翻译学两部分。前者包括理论翻译学和描述翻译学，后者包括翻译批评、译员培训和翻译辅助研究。翻译测试涉及翻译批评和译员培训，属于应用翻译学研究。但是正如 Hatim & Mason（1997：197）所说，人们对翻译测试的关注较少，相关研究也缺乏，是应用翻译学的一个薄弱环节。从我国情况看，可以说，翻译测试的研究与当前翻译学科的蓬勃发展以及译员培训的现实需求不相适应。翻译测试有哪些类型、哪些课题？如何设计实施？这些都是值得我们关注的问题。测试研究在其他领域已经较为成熟（Bachman 1990），然而语言测试的研究成果很少被应用到翻译测试领域（Campbell & Hale 2003）。因此，本文拟借鉴语言测试领域的相关理论和概念，探讨翻译测试设计与实施中的问题。

一、翻译测试的分类及性质

Bachman(1990:71)指出根据内容测试可以分为水平测试、成绩测试以及潜能测试。水平测试考察受试者是否达到了某一水平,与教学内容及学生以往的学习没有直接的联系。成绩测试主要出现在翻译培训课程的教学中,同课程要求、教学大纲、教学内容密切相关,包括完成某一阶段学习后进行的期中测试、期末测试等。潜能测试用来预示受试者进行相关学习的潜力和天赋,往往通过考察受试者模仿、记忆等方面的能力来判断他们是否有潜力完成课程。

在翻译测试领域,Campbell & Hale(2003:208)认为当前西方翻译测试主要有两类:资格认证以及教学。Li(2006:81)持类似观点,认为翻译测试主要有两个目的:资格准入以及用于教学。对照 Bachman 的观点,前者大致相当于水平测试,后者相当于成绩测试。

翻译水平测试并不基于某一特定的教学大纲。根据国内外翻译测试的具体情况,我们认为它还可以细分为两种。第一种:考生在通过考试之后会获得一项证书,分资格证书与能力证书。前者主要是对受试者进行资格认证,如我国国家人事部的翻译专业资格考试就属于这一类,后者只是对考生的翻译能力进行鉴定,通过该考试并不意味着考生获得了相应的岗位资格认证,如教育部的全国外语翻译证书考试、英国语言学会的翻译测试。第二种:翻译专业研究生入学考试、各类翻译竞赛测试等,也属于水平测试范畴,考生在通过之后并不会获得资格或能力证书,其主要目的是筛选人才。

翻译成绩测试主要出现在译员培训课程的教学过程中,这类测试与教学大纲密切相关,简单来说“所测即所教”,即 Campbell 所说的教学测试。

一般来说,如 Hatim & Mason(1997:199)所言,翻译水平测试的性质是“终结性评估”(summative assessment),成绩测试则属于“形成性评估”(formative assessment)。不过也不必一概而论,成绩测试是形成性评估,而在课程结束时也可作为终结性评估。

二、翻译测试的构念:翻译能力

翻译测试的目的是评估考生的翻译能力,因此,明确“翻译能力”的定义,即测试的构念(construct)问题,是设计翻译测试的首要任务(Bachman & Palmer 1996)。目前较为主流的观点认为翻译能力包含多项分能力。例如Bell(1991:41)认为翻译能力包括语法能力(语言层面的句法、词汇知识)、社会语言学能力、语篇能力(语篇类型知识、衔接与连贯)和策略能力。Neubert(2000:6)主张翻译能力包括语言能力、语篇能力、学科知识能力、文化能力、转换能力。Campbell(1998)主要构建了从母语译入外语的翻译能力模式,包括文本能力、监控能力、性情三项能力。

对于“翻译能力”,较早也较为系统的论述主要是Cao(1996)以及PACTE(2000)。根据Bachman的交际语言能力理论模型,Cao(1996)提出翻译能力包括语言能力、知识能力以及策略能力。其中语言能力包括组织能力与语用能力。组织能力由语法能力与语篇能力组成。语用能力由以言行事能力与社会语言能力组成。PACTE早期提出的翻译能力模式包括语言能力、语言外能力、工具能力、心理生理能力、转换能力和策略能力六项,以转换能力为中心(PACTE 2000)。后期对该模式进行了修订:(1)放弃转换能力。实证研究表明转换能力是其他能力的综合,很难独立析取出来;(2)将策略能力提升至中心位置;(3)将心理生理能力修正为统摄各能力的心理生理机制;(4)将原来属于语言外能力、工具职业能力的翻译知识(如对翻译过程、翻译市场的认识)析取出来,成为一个独立的次能力(PACTE 2003)。

翻译能力的上述定义只是理论构念,看不见摸不着,对于翻译测试的具体实施而言,需要使理论构念可操作化(operationalization)(Bachman 1990:46-48)。下面比较国内外翻译水平测试,从测试内容、评分方法等方面来考察不同考试对“翻译能力”构念的具体定义及对设计翻译测试的启示。

三、翻译测试的实施

1. 国外翻译水平测试

(1)澳大利亚国家口笔译认证局(National Accreditation Authority for Translators and Interpreters,简称 NAATI)考试。以汉语和英语笔译(专业级)考试为例,分英译汉和汉译英两个方向分别测试。考试要求从 3 篇文章中选择两篇翻译,文章题材包括文化、科技、医疗、商务等,长度为 250 字左右。翻译占 90 分,加上 10 分职业道德准则试题,总分 100 分。

(2)美国翻译者协会(American Translator Association,简称 ATA)的考试。涉及英汉语的目前仅有英译汉方向。考试时间为 3 小时,要求考生翻译三篇长度为 225—275 字左右的文章,其中一篇为通用题材,为必选题。另外两篇中,其中一篇从涉及科学、技术、医药的题材中选,另一篇从法律、商务、金融的题材中选。

(3)英国语言学会(Institute of Linguists,简称 IOL)翻译证书考试(Diploma in Translation)。分三部分,第一部分为通用性题材翻译。第二、第三部分均为半专业性题材翻译,考生从所给的六种题材(技术、商务、文学、科学、社会科学和法律)中任选两种完成翻译。

(4)加拿大口笔译暨术语工作者委员会(Canadian Translators,Terminologists and Interpreters Council,简称 CTTIC)的考试。考生须翻译两篇文章,每篇 175—185 字左右。一篇是通用性题材,为必选题。另外再从两篇中选一篇翻译,其中一篇为科技或医药题材,另一篇偏文学。

2. 国内翻译水平测试

国内大型翻译水平测试主要是人事部主办的全国翻译专业资格(水平)考试和教育部主办的全国外语翻译证书考试。全国英语四六级考试以及英语专业八级考试也有翻译部分,但考试本身并不主要针对翻译,因此,本文不讨论,对前两项考试的讨论也只涉及笔译部分。

全国翻译专业资格(水平)考试(CATTI)分笔译综合能力和笔译实务两

块。以三级为例,笔译综合能力主要考词汇和语法、阅读理解和完形填空。笔译实务包括汉译英一篇(300—400字)、英译汉一篇(500—650字)。前者实际上是以语言技能为主,后者以翻译技能为主,按照Campbell & Hale(2003:208)的观点,这样的测试实际上是语言能力测试与翻译测试的混合体,笔译综合能力部分的题目也适合其他语言测试,非翻译测试所特有。

教育部的外语翻译证书考试主要是翻译实务,并不考察语言综合能力。考试分为两部分,第一部分英译汉,要求考生将两篇250词左右的英语文章译成汉语。第二部分汉译英,要求考生将两篇各250字左右的汉语文章译成英语。

3. 国内外翻译测试比较

从现有文献中难以直接获知各翻译测试对"翻译能力"这一理论构念的认识与定位,因此,只能从具体的测试内容等方面,即构念的操作性定义来推断。根据这一方法,我们发现国外翻译水平测试所测能力大致可以概括为三项:语言能力、文本功能能力、学科知识能力。

语言能力:注重源语理解,考察是否存在漏译、误译现象;注重译语表达,对语言形式评分较细,包括微观方面的拼写、标点、词汇、时态等,以及宏观方面的衔接、篇章组织、语域等。Angelelli(2009:23)认为与理论构念相比,西方现有翻译测试中体现出来的翻译能力应用构念内涵相对较为狭窄,尤其偏重语言能力。

文本功能能力:国外翻译水平测试一般比较注重考试的真实性特点,例如IOL考试向考生明确说明原文的来源及写作背景,有助于译者根据翻译的情境选择合适的翻译策略。

学科知识能力:考生需翻译的文章为两篇(NATTI、CTTIC)至三篇不等(ATA、IOL),有一个共同特征,即原文按题材分为两大模块:第一模块为必选题,原文以通用题材为主,第二模块中涉及半专业题材,常见领域包括科技、医药、法律、金融、社会文化等,考生可从中选择,考生需具备一定的学科专业知识,但往往并不要求具备该领域的专家知识。

在这三项能力上,国内的翻译水平考试与之相同的特点是比较注重语言能力,注重原文的理解、译语的表达。而对译者的文化、文本功能能力及学科知识要求则有所差异。

在学科知识要求方面，翻译专业资格考试大纲中列出的考试基本要求是（以二级为例）：（1）能够正确应用翻译策略和技巧，熟练进行双语互译；（2）译文忠实原文，无错译、漏译；（3）译文表达流畅，用词恰当；（4）译文无语法错误；（5）英译汉速度每小时500—600个单词；汉译英速度每小时301—400个汉字。大纲没有明确说明原文的体裁及文体。

教育部的翻译证书考试大纲明确规定不同级别翻译任务的体裁及难度："通过二级笔译证书考试的考生能够翻译较高难度的各类文本；能够胜任机关、企事业单位的科技、法律、商务、经贸等方面材料的翻译以及各类国际会议一般性文件的翻译。通过三级笔译证书考试的考生能够翻译一般难度的文本；能够胜任机关、企事业单位的一般性文本和商务类材料的翻译。"但这些要求在实际试题中体现得不清楚。

在文本功能方面，国内翻译水平考试中均不向考生说明译文的功能与目标读者。而在真实的翻译任务中，译者应根据译文的功能、读者群选择合适的翻译策略。翻译是一项交际活动，语言形式的语际转换总是在一定的交际情境中发生，译文总是为一定的目标读者服务，具有一定的功能。如果不提供这样一个情境，对译者的翻译以及评卷者的评分都将带来很大困难。翻译测试设计如何反映考试的"真实性"（authenticity）特征值得我们思考。

另外，国外翻译水平测试的一个显著特点是单向翻译，同一试卷中一般不会出现译入与译出两个方向的试题。国内翻译水平测试大多要求考生完成英译汉与汉译英两个方向的试题。这可能与国内翻译需求有关，尽管当前国际上对于L1-L2（即从母语到外语）的翻译日趋重视，但总体而言仍以译入母语为主流，而中国的情况是对汉译英、汉译外的需求旺盛，因此考试中常常要求考生具备双向翻译的能力。

由上述比较，我们认为国内的翻译测试大有可改进之处。一是测试构念上的研究，即究竟考察什么样的能力；二是测试方式上的考量，是否应考察学科和文本功能方面的知识；三是测试的实施问题。

4. 翻译测试设计实施中的问题

测试的设计与实施是一个复杂的过程，涉及诸多环节。Bachman & Palmer（1996：87）将测试分为三个阶段：设计、操作、实施。每一个阶段涵盖不同的任务。根据翻译测试的特点，我们重点分析讨论测试方式与题型、试题编制、评分方式三个环节。

（1）测试方式与题型

首先，设计翻译测试应注意水平测试与成绩测试的区别。水平测试主要采用直接测试的方法，即要求考生直接运用所测技能完成翻译任务，也就是说，以行为测试为主。翻译教学测试则强调结合间接测试，在要求考生完成翻译任务的同时，采用其他方式评估考生翻译能力，这样有助于教师了解学生的翻译能力习得过程，并进行诊断。

翻译教学中评估学习者翻译能力主要有两种方式："从产品入手（即目的语文本、其质量、是否达到了特定目的），或者从过程角度考察（即决策过程的效度）"（Schäffner & Adab 2000：xiii）。前者是成品视角，后者是过程视角。翻译水平测试的重点往往是"成品"，而翻译成绩测试中"过程"与"成品"都很重要。体现在题型设计上，翻译成绩测试除了翻译实务以外，还有以下几种题型。简答题。具体操作形式包括：译文鉴赏，要求学生对所给译文进行评判；给出原文及翻译述要，要求学生对翻译时应考虑的问题进行分析。选择题。给出原文及几篇译文，根据翻译述要（translation brief）选择合适的译文；根据上下文，选择段落中特定词组或句子的最恰当译文。注释说明。学生翻译一段或几段文章，要求在给出译文的同时，对其中某些翻译问题说明翻译的思维过程，具体例子参见 Colina（2003：147）。值得注意的是，这种方法虽然在翻译教学测试中受到欢迎，但在翻译水平测试中很少出现（据我们掌握的资料，唯一例外的是英国语言学会的考试，考生可以通过"译者说明"（translator's note）对翻译过程中的问题作出解释，但是一般不鼓励考生这样做，而且不计入总分）。这也从另一方面说明翻译水平测试主要关注的是考生的翻译成品，并不是其翻译过程。

其次，应注意综合测试与分离式测试的区别。所谓综合测试，主要指测试项目主要注重综合的"交流效果"而非单个具体的词汇或语法项目，例如外语写作测试和语篇翻译。而分离式测试中往往“一道题目一次只牵涉一个考点”(邹申,2005:30),如选择题中对不同词汇的测试。国内外翻译水平测试的具体形式主要为综合测试,即以语篇翻译为主。成绩测试则有所不同,可根据具体教学内容设计句子翻译,侧重某一具体考点。罗选民等(2008:77)根据 Neubert 提出的翻译能力五个成分,提出“测试翻译能力的关键,是要把‘翻译能力’分解成可以评估的因素,或在命题时设法使翻译能力通过翻译实际操作体现出来”。例如对文化能力的测量:原文为“You are just a doubting Thomas. You won't believe what I tell you.”,学生在翻译时需要了解 doubting Thomas 源于圣经故事,Thomas 是耶稣的门徒,生性多疑,因此可将原文翻译为:你这个人真是个多疑的托马斯,我说什么你都不信。对语篇能力的测量:On my introduction into the Presidency,译为“值此就任总统之际”就比“在我就任总统时”体现出来的译者语篇能力就更强一些。这样的翻译任务与语篇翻译不同,属于针对各分项能力的句子或句段翻译,具备分离项目测试的特征,有助于教师了解学生对教学内容的具体掌握情况,测试开发者可根据测试目的的不同选择合适的考试方法与题型。

(2)试题编写

此处重点讨论直接测试题,尤其是语篇测试题的编写。对于水平测试来说,不同的测试等级所用的原文在题材、难度上要求不一,因此选择什么样题材的原文以及如何确定原文的翻译难度是一个值得我们考虑的问题。

首先,应在明确翻译测试构念的基础上,选择合适的题材。例如,根据 PACTE 的模式,翻译能力包括“学科知识能力”这一分项能力,则在此构念基础上开发的翻译测试要注意通过原文题材的多样化来体现对考生这一能力的考察。

其次,确定原文难度。目前主要有两种做法。设定参数,选择不同翻译难度的原文。Reiss(转引自 Hale & Campbell 2002:16)提出以下几个参数:题材、语域、语言功能、读者对象、原文的时空及文化特征。例如在“题材”这一参数上,原文从易到难可分为四级:通用题材且文化特征不明显、通用题材且具备明显源语文化特征、专业题材且文化特征不明显、专业题材且具备明显源语文化特征。该方法的主要问题是主观性较大,原文翻译难度的分级从本质上来说主要依靠测试开发者的主观判断。

文本特征法。通过寻找具体的文本特征来确定翻译难度。Jensen(2009)提出可根据以下几个特征来确定原文的复杂程度:可读性、词频、原文中习语、借代及隐喻等的数量。与“参数法”相比,通过具体文本特征来衡量原文的难度大大提高了判断的客观性。在口译界,Liu & Chiu(2009)选择了以下文本特征:可读性程度、信息密度以及新概念密度,来区分用于交传考试的三篇原文难度,尽管实证结果发现这些特征对原文难度的区分尚未达到显著性意义,但研究表明信息密度以及原文句子长度是相对有效的区分特征。迄今为止,笔译界对原文翻译难度较为系统的实证研究是 Campbell(2000a,b),主要针对英语和阿拉伯语以及西班牙语组合,通过分析考生译文的差异,以及对考生翻译过程中选择网络的分析来估计原文的翻译难度差异。Hale & Campbell(2002)重点考察了原文中的专有名词、复杂名词短语、被动句以及隐喻等方面的文本特征,通过比较不同考生的译文,来判断哪些文本特征的翻译难度较大。

关于原文难度的研究对指导翻译测试实施具有重要意义,然而目前针对英汉语笔译尚无相关实证研究,值得我们下一步去探讨。

(3)评分方式

翻译测试的题型中,一些间接测试题如选择题、配对题、判断题属于客观性测试,一般只有一个答案,评分时几乎不受主观因素影响。而直接测试,如语篇翻译,则属主观性测试,需要阅卷人作出主观判断,这就涉及评分方式问题。

国内翻译测试主要采取两种评分方式(穆雷 2006:467):一种是阅卷者根据总体印象给分;一种是根据经验对错误扣分。相比之下,国外大型翻译水平测试大多实施错误扣分法,并已经形成了较为明确的操作规范。例如美国 ATA 考试的做法是将错误按严重程度不同分为五级,从最轻微到最严重的错误依序扣 1 分、2 分、4 分、8 分、16 分,如果总扣分达到 18 分及以上就不能通过。加拿大 CTTIC 考试评分时看两方面:翻译(是否表达了原文的意思);语言(表达是否符合译语语法等规范)。主要采用错误扣分法,

“翻译”部分严重错误（如完全错误表达原文意思）扣 10 分，次要错误（如某一词语的误译、漏译）扣 5 分；“语言”部分严重错误（如整体组织不通顺）扣 10 分，次要错误中重复、句型结构不地道扣 5 分、拼写标点大小写错误扣 3 分。

错误评分法的优点在于它对错误的分类较细，根据扣分类别，能较为直观地看出考生较为欠缺的是哪方面能力。这一点对于翻译教学尤其有用，因此有学者提倡将之运用于平时的翻译教学测试中，以此提高测试的“反拨”效应（Koby & Baer 2005）。该评分法的缺点是预设了一个完美译文的存在，实际上译文有着多种多样的形式，并不存在一个绝对正确的答案（Hatim & Mason 1997：199），而且容易受到译文长度影响，文本越长，越容易被扣分，因此在具体操作中需要设定基准长度。另外对于评分者而言，判断错误的性质易受主观因素影响（赖慈芸 2008：87）。

总体而言，印象法过于主观，错误评分法评分较细，但对阅卷者要求较高。从实际操作来看，有学者认为以筛选为目的的大型翻译测试可能更适合分析评分法（同上）。所谓分析法，是基于将所测能力视作是由多项能力组成的观点。在翻译界，虽然各研究者关于翻译能力到底包含哪些成分各有不同看法，但基本的出发点是一致的，都将翻译能力视为各分项能力的集合，可以说翻译能力的多成分模式是当前的主流观点（Colina 2003：132）。根据 Cao（1996）提出的翻译能力模式，Colina（2003）提出在翻译测试时应对不同能力分项打分，如语言能力总分 30 分、知识结构总分 20 分、策略能力总分 50 分，每项可以分不同的等级，如知识结构能力细分为三档：20 分、10 分、5 分，各档均有详细的描述，使评分者能对照描述要求给分。

分析评分法的优点在于：第一，能体现考生翻译能力的具体情况，如源语理解得分多少，语篇能力得分多少；第二，和总体印象法相比，分析法更能清晰地指导评分者的评分过程（Bachman & Palmer，1996：211）。但是它要求对翻译能力的成分作出较为清晰的定义才能据此进行分项评分，如果能力成分过多，分析评分法的步骤就会相当复杂，因为有多少种能力成分，就会有多少个分数。现实操作中评分者可能会先给出一个总分，然后按各分项要求将总分拆开，分配到各分项目上（Campbell & Hale，2003：217）。总体而言，实施分析评分法的前提是对“翻译能力”的构成有较为清晰的认识，并要考虑操作的可行性，分项不可过多。

四、结语

随着翻译专业的发展，翻译测试的开发、设计以及相关研究日益受到关注。限于篇幅，本文主要讨论了测试设计中的几个基础性问题如题型设置、试题编制及评分方式，认为翻译测试的设计首先应明确测试的构念，即“何为翻译能力”，并根据不同的测试目的选择直接或间接考试方式。至于原文的选择、评分方式的确定等问题还有待进一步的实证研究。

（本文原载《外国语》2010年第6期，作者为王克非、杨志红）

参考文献

C.Angelelli,“Using a Rubric to Assess Translation Ability:Define the Construct”,C.Angelelli & H.Jacobson(eds.),*Testing and Assessment in Translation and Interpreting Studies*, Amsterdam:John Benjamins,2009,pp.13-48.

L.F.Bachman,*Fundamental Considerations in Language Testing*,Oxford:OUP,1990.

L.F.Bachman & A.S.Palmer,*Language Testing in Practice*,Oxford:OUP,1996.

R.Bell,*Translation and Translating Theory and Practice*,London:Longman,1991.

S.Campbell,*Translation into the Second Language*,New York:Longman,1998.

S.Campbell,“Critical Structures in the Evaluation of Translation from Arabic into English as a Second Language”,*The Translator*,2000,Vol.6,No.2,pp.211-229.

S.Campbell,“Choice Network Analysis in Translation Research”,M.Olohan(ed.),*Intercultural Faultlines:Research Models in Translation Studies* Ⅰ,*Textual and Cognitive Aspects*, Manchester:St.Jerome,2000,pp.29-42.

S.Campbell & S.Hale,“Translation and Interpreting Assessment in the Context of Educational Measurement”,G.Anderman & M.Rogers(eds.),*Translation Today:Trends and Perspectives*,Multilingual Matters Ltd.,2003,pp.205-224.

D.A Cao,"Model of Translation Proficiency",*Target*,1996,Vol.8,No.2,pp.325-340.

S.Colina,*Translation Teaching:from Research to the Classroom:A Handbook for Teachers*,McGraw-Hill Higher Education,2003.

S.Hale & S.Campbell,"The Interaction between Text Difficulty and Translation Accuracy",*Babel*,2002,Vol.48,No.1,pp.14-33.

B.Hatim & I.Mason,*The Translator as Communicator*,London:Routledge,1990.

J.Holmes,"The Name and Nature of Translation Studies",J.Holmes translated,*Papers on Literary Translation and Translation Studies*,Amsterdam:Rodopi,1972/1988,pp.67-80.

K.T.H.Jensen,"Indicators ofText Complexity",S.Gopferich *et al.*(eds.),*Behind the Mind:Methods,Models and Results in Translation Process Research*,Copenhagen:Samfundslitteratur Press,2009,pp.61-80.

G.Koby & B.Baer,"From Professional Certification to the Translator Training Classroom:Adapting the ATA Error Marking Scale",*Translation Watch Quarterly*,2005,No.1,pp.33-45.

Defeng Li,"Making Translation Testing More Teaching-oriented:A Case Study of Translation Testing in China",*Meta*,2006,Vol.51,No.1,pp.72-88.

M.Liu & Y.Chiu,"Assessing Source Material Difficulty for Consecutive Interpreting:Quantifiable Measures and Holistic Judgment",*Interpreting*,2009,Vol.11,No.2,pp.244-266.

A.Neubert,"Competence in Language,in Languages and in Translation",C.Schäffner & B.Adab(eds.),*Developing Translation Competence*,Amsterdam & Philadelphia:John Benjamins,2000,pp.3-18.

PACTE,"Acquiring Translation Competence:Hypotheses and Methodological Problems of a Research Project",A.Beeby,D.Ensinger & M.Presas(eds.),*Investigating Translation:Selected Papers from the 4th International Congress on Translation,Barcelona*,1998,Amsterdam & Philadelphia:John Benjamins,2000,pp.99-106.

PACTE,"Building a Translation Competence Model",F.Alves(ed.),*Triangulating Translation:Perspectives in Process Oriented Research*,Amsterdam & Philadelphia:John Benjamins,2003,pp.43-68.

C.Schäffner & B.Adab(eds.),*Developing Translation Competence*,Amsterdam & Philadelphia:John Benjamins,2000.

赖慈芸:《四种翻译评量工具的比较》,《翻译论丛》2008 年第 1 期。

罗选民、黄勤、张健:《大学翻译教学测试改革与翻译能力的培养》,《外语教学》2008 年第 1 期。

穆雷:《翻译测试及其评分问题》,《外语教学与研究》2006 年第 6 期。

邹申:《语言测试》,上海外语教育出版社 2005 年版。

后　记

整理这本文集，就是回首自己走过的求学治学之路。路的这头站着留恋地看着工作多年的办公室的我，路的那头是遥远的三十四年前满怀憧憬和激情踏入北外校园的年轻的我。曾经很可能以测绘队绘图员或地质部门资料员为职业，因为许国璋先生不拘一格的录取，我成为他的弟子，成为北外的一员，穿山越水走到今天。这是我经常以至永远感恩于先生的地方。

犹记三十年前，为了北外五十周年校庆，许先生想将过去写下的文字加以收集和整理。他将此事郑重地交付给我。我欣然领受，于是数次钻进学校的图书馆、资料室以及北京图书馆，在短短两周内，搜集了先生所发表的各种论述七十多万字。整理出目录和分类后，我送到许先生家中。先生一生忙于授业解惑，编写出国人尽知的"许国璋《英语》"，未曾想到原来自己已撰写发表了七十多万字，自然喜出望外。其中一部分就编成了1991年外研社出版的《许国璋论语言》。岁月匆匆，三十年倏然而过，当时给先生编辑文集的情景历历如在眼前，如今学校也命我挑选整理自己部分论述编写一部文选。

转眼进入2020年。文库工作组的刘博然同志耐心的敦促我，也等候我。未料寒假遇到大疫，举国抗击，举世关切，我自然也日日惦记武汉地区。由于疫情而滞留南方，倒是难得有了充裕的时间来编写文稿。春节后开始行动。构想和筛选花费了一段时间，扫描转写旧稿更费时日（感谢王斌、刘鼎甲二位协助），整理、校对和修订亦小心翼翼，断续竟耗费五个月时光，才向久仰的人民出版社递交了文稿。

望着书稿，心里生出几许与许先生同样的欣喜。感谢学校组稿，自己部分著述得以结集成册。感谢人民出版社编辑,收稿即迅速仔细编辑完毕。感谢我服务的中国外语与教育研究中心,许多研究成果在这个可敬的团队里完成。最后感谢夫人、儿子和诸多亲人,他们的爱和鼓励,是我踽踽前行的永恒的力量。

王克非于北外东院寓所

2020 年 7 月

统　　筹:张振明　孙兴民
责任编辑:张双子
封面设计:徐　晖
版式设计:王　婷

图书在版编目(CIP)数据

语言与文化之间/王克非 著. —北京:人民出版社,2021.9
(新时代北外文库/王定华,杨丹主编)
ISBN 978－7－01－023682－7

Ⅰ.①语…　Ⅱ.①王…　Ⅲ.①文化语言学-研究　Ⅳ.①H0-05

中国版本图书馆 CIP 数据核字(2021)第 168523 号

语言与文化之间

YUYAN YU WENHUA ZHIJIAN

王克非　著

人民出版社 出版发行
(100706　北京市东城区隆福寺街 99 号)

北京新华印刷有限公司印刷　新华书店经销

2021 年 9 月第 1 版　2021 年 9 月北京第 1 次印刷
开本:710 毫米×1000 毫米 1/16　印张:25　插页:1 页
字数:390 千字

ISBN 978－7－01－023682－7　定价:106.00 元

邮购地址 100706　北京市东城区隆福寺街 99 号
人民东方图书销售中心　电话 (010)65250042　65289539